Exam Ref 70-485: Advanced Windows Store App Development Using C#

Roberto Brunetti
Vanni Boncinelli

Published with the authorization of Microsoft Corporation by:

O'Reilly Media, Inc.
1005 Gravenstein Highway North
Sebastopol, California 95472

ISBN: 978-0-7356-7686-2

1 2 3 4 5 6 7 8 9 QG 8 7 6 5 4 3

Printed and bound in the United States of America.

Microsoft Press books are available through booksellers and distributors worldwide. If you need support related to this book, email Microsoft Press Book Support at *mspinput@microsoft.com*. Please tell us what you think of this book at *http://www.microsoft.com/learning/booksurvey*.

Acquisitions Editor: Jeff Riley

Developmental Editor: Kim Lindros

Production Editor: Kristen Brown

Editorial Production: Box Twelve Communications

Technical Reviewer: Luca Regnicoli

Copyeditor: Nancy Sixsmith

Indexer: Angie Martin

Cover Design: Twist Creative • Seattle

Cover Composition: Ellie Volckhausen

Illustrator: Rebecca Demarest

This book is dedicated to my parents.

— Roberto Brunetti

This book is dedicated to my family.

— Vanni Boncinelli

Contents at a glance

	Introduction	*xv*
CHAPTER 1	Develop Windows Store apps	1
CHAPTER 2	Discover and interact with devices	57
CHAPTER 3	Program user interaction	131
CHAPTER 4	Enhance the user interface	193
CHAPTER 5	Manage data and security	275
CHAPTER 6	Prepare for a solution deployment	335
	Index	*415*
	About the authors	*443*

Contents

Introduction **xv**

Microsoft certifications *xv*

Acknowledgments *xv*

Errata & book support *xvi*

We want to hear from you *xvi*

Stay in touch *xvi*

Chapter 1 Develop Windows Store apps **1**

Objective 1.1: Create background tasks 1

Creating a background task 2

Declaring background task usage 5

Enumerating registered tasks 7

Using deferrals with tasks 7

Objective summary 8

Objective review 8

Objective 1.2: Consume background tasks 9

Understanding task triggers and conditions 9

Progressing through and completing background tasks 11

Understanding task constraints 14

Cancelling a task 15

Updating a background task 18

Debugging tasks 19

Understanding task usage 21

Transferring data in the background 22

Keeping communication channels open 28

Objective review 37

Objective 1.3: Create and consume WinMD components. 38
Understanding the Windows Runtime and WinMD 38
Consuming a native WinMD library 40
Creating a WinMD library 46
Objective summary 50
Objective review 50
Chapter summary 51
Answers. 52

Chapter 2 Discover and interact with devices 57

Objective 2.1: Capture media with the camera and microphone. 57
Using *CameraCaptureUI* to capture pictures or video 58
Using *MediaCapture* to capture pictures, video, or audio 68
Objective summary 79
Objective review 80
Objective 2.2: Get data from sensors 80
Understanding sensors and location data in the Windows Runtime 81
Accessing sensors from a Windows Store app 81
Determining the user's location 99
Objective summary 108
Objective review 108
Objective 2.3: Enumerate and discover device capabilities. 109
Enumerating devices 110
Using the *DeviceWatcher* class to be notified of changes to the device collection 117
Enumerating Plug and Play (PnP) devices 122
Objective summary 124
Objective review 124
Chapter summary 125
Answers. 126

Chapter 3 Program user interaction 131

Objective 3.1: Implement printing by using contracts and charms 131

Registering a Windows Store app for the Print contract 132

Handling *PrintTask* events 137

Adding the user interface 138

Creating a custom print template 140

Understanding the print task options 142

Paginating and previewing the document 144

Choosing options to display in the preview window 148

Reacting to print option changes 149

Adding custom print options 152

Implementing in-app printing 153

Objective summary 154

Objective review 154

Objective 3.2: Implement Play To by using contracts and charms 155

Introducing the Play To contract 156

Testing sample code using Windows Media Player on a different machine 159

Implementing a Play To source application 161

Registering your app as a Play To receiver 167

Objective summary 174

Objective review 175

Objective 3.3: Notify users by using Windows Push Notification Service (WNS) 176

Requesting and creating a notification channel 176

Sending a notification to the client 178

Objective summary 186

Objective review 187

Chapter summary 187

Answers. 188

Chapter 4 Enhance the user interface 193

Objective 4.1: Design for and implement UI responsiveness 193
- Understanding .NET asynchronous patterns 194
- Writing methods using *async* techniques 202
- Implementing asynchronous methods 204
- Waiting for an event in an asynchronous way 207
- Implementing asynchronous calls 208
- Cancelling asynchronous operations 209
- Cancelling an operation in asynchronous calls 210
- Tracking operation progress 211
- Tracking progress in asynchronous operations 212
- Synchronizing multiple asynchronous calls 215
- Waiting for multiple asynchronous calls executed in parallel 217
- Choosing the right *SynchronizationContext* in libraries 218
- Objective summary 220
- Objective review 220

Objective 4.2: Create animations and transitions 221
- Creating and customizing storyboarded animations 222
- Exploring dependent animations vs. independent animations 225
- Creating key-frame animations 228
- Using interpolations and easing functions in animations 229
- Using discrete animations 232
- Applying animations from the animation library 233
- Objective summary 238
- Objective review 238

Objective 4.3: Create custom controls. 239
- Adding a custom control to your Windows Store app 239
- Creating your own dependency properties for a custom control 243
- Reacting to changes in the visual state of the custom control 246
- Objective summary 251
- Objective review 251

Objective 4.4: Design Windows Store apps for globalization and localization 252

Planning for globalization 252

Localizing your app 256

Localizing your manifest 265

Using the Multilingual App Toolkit 265

Objective summary 267

Objective review 267

Chapter summary 268

Answers. 269

Chapter 5 Manage data and security 275

Objective 5.1: Design and implement data caching. 275

Understanding application and user data 275

Caching application data 276

Understanding Microsoft rules for using roaming profiles with Windows Store apps 286

Caching user data 287

Objective summary 290

Objective review 290

Objective 5.2: Save and retrieve files from the file system 291

Using file pickers to save and retrieve files 291

Accessing files and data programmatically 298

Working with folders, files, and streams 300

Setting file extensions and associations 301

Compressing files to save space 304

Objective summary 305

Objective review 306

Objective 5.3: Secure app data 306

Introducing the *Windows.Security.Cryptography* namespaces 307

Using hash algorithms 308

Generating random numbers and data 311

Encrypting messages with MAC algorithms 313

Using digital signatures 316

Enrolling and requesting certificates 319
Protecting your data with the *DataProtectionProvider* class 325
Objective summary 328
Objective review 329

Chapter summary 329

Answers. 330

Chapter 6 Prepare for a solution deployment 335

Objective 6.1: Design and implement trial functionality in an app 335
Choosing the right business model for your app 336
Exploring the licensing state of your app 338
Using custom license information 344
Purchasing an app 345
Handling errors 349
Setting up in-app purchases 350
Retrieving and validating the receipts for your purchases 356
Objective summary 358
Objective review 358

Objective 6.2: Design for error handling 359
Handling exceptions in the .NET Framework 359
Catching errors and exceptions at the application level 361
Handling device capability errors 364
Handling asynchronous errors 368
Objective summary 373
Objective review 374

Objective 6.3: Design and implement a test strategy. 374
Understanding functional testing vs. unit testing 375
Implementing a test project for a Windows Store app 378
Objective summary 387
Objective review 387

Objective 6.4: Design a diagnostics and monitoring strategy 388

Profiling a Windows Store app and collecting performance counters 388

Tracing and logging events for Windows Store apps 398

Using Windows Store reports to improve the quality of your app 402

Objective summary 405

Objective review 406

Chapter summary 407

Answers..408

Index *415*

What do you think of this book? We want to hear from you!

Microsoft is interested in hearing your feedback so we can continually improve our books and learning resources for you. To participate in a brief online survey, please visit:

www.microsoft.com/learning/booksurvey/

Introduction

The Microsoft 70-485 certification exam tests your knowledge of Windows Store application development using C#. Readers are assumed to be Windows Store app developers with deep knowledge of the Windows Runtime architecture, the application life cycle managed by the system (including suspend, termination, resume, and launch), the Visual Studio 2012 project structure, the application manifest, app deployment, and Windows Store requirements. The reader must have also a strong background in XAML and C#.

This book covers every exam objective, but it does not cover every exam question. Only the Microsoft exam team has access to the exam questions themselves, and Microsoft regularly adds new questions to the exam, making it impossible to cover specific questions. You should consider this book a supplement to your relevant real-world experience and other study materials. If you encounter a topic in this book that you do not feel completely comfortable with, use the links you'll find in text to find more information and take the time to research and study the topic. Great information is available on MSDN, TechNet, and in blogs and forums.

Microsoft certifications

Microsoft certifications distinguish you by proving your command of a broad set of skills and experience with current Microsoft products and technologies. The exams and corresponding certifications are developed to validate your mastery of critical competencies as you design and develop, or implement and support, solutions with Microsoft products and technologies both on-premise and in the cloud. Certification brings a variety of benefits to the individual and to employers and organizations.

> ***MORE INFO*** **All Microsoft certifications**
>
> **For information about Microsoft certifications, including a full list of available certifications, go to *http://www.microsoft.com/learning/en/us/certification/cert-default.aspx.***

Acknowledgments

I'd like to thank Vanni for his side-by-side work. He has shared with me all the intricacies of writing a book with this level of detail.

— Roberto Brunetti

I'd like to thank Roberto for teaching me everything I know today about software development, and Marika for her support and infinite patience during the writing of this book.

— *Vanni Boncinelli*

Roberto and Vanni want to thank all the people who made this book possible. In particular, we thank Kim Lindros, for her exceptional support throughout the editing process of this book; Jeff Riley, for giving us this opportunity; and Russell Jones, for introducing our team to Jeff.

Special thanks to Wouter de Kort for providing some of the content in Chapter 4.

Errata & book support

We've made every effort to ensure the accuracy of this book and its companion content. Any errors that have been reported since this book was published are listed on our Microsoft Press site at oreilly.com:

http://aka.ms/ER70-485/errata

If you find an error that is not already listed, you can report it to us through the same page.

If you need additional support, email Microsoft Press Book Support at *mspinput@microsoft.com.*

Please note that product support for Microsoft software is not offered through the addresses above.

We want to hear from you

At Microsoft Press, your satisfaction is our top priority, and your feedback our most valuable asset. Please tell us what you think of this book at:

http://www.microsoft.com/learning/booksurvey

The survey is short, and we read every one of your comments and ideas. Thanks in advance for your input!

Stay in touch

Let's keep the conversation going! We're on Twitter: *http://twitter.com/MicrosoftPress.*

CHAPTER 1

Develop Windows Store apps

In this chapter, you learn how to create background tasks and implement the appropriate interfaces for a Windows Store app. You also find out how to consume them using timing and system triggers, request lock screen access, and create download and upload operations using the *BackgroundTransfer* class. The last part of the chapter is dedicated to creating and consuming WinMD components.

Objectives in this chapter:

- Objective 1.1: Create background tasks
- Objective 1.2: Consume background tasks
- Objective 1.3: Create and consume WinMD components

Objective 1.1: Create background tasks

Windows 8 changes the way applications run. Windows Store application life-cycle management of the Windows Runtime (WinRT) is different from previous versions of Windows: only one application (or two in snapped view) can run in the foreground at a time. The system can suspend or even terminate other apps from the Windows Runtime. This behavior forces the developer to use different techniques to implement some form of background work, such as to download a file or perform tile updates.

This section covers how to implement a background task using the provided classes and interfaces, and how to code a simple task.

This objective covers how to:

- Create a background task
- Use the *Windows.ApplicationModel.Background* classes
- Implement the *IBackgroundTask* interface

Creating a background task

In Windows Store apps, when users work on an app in the foreground, background apps cannot interact directly with them. In fact, due to the architecture of Microsoft Windows 8 and because of the application life-cycle management of Windows Store apps, only the foreground app has the focus and is in the running state; the user can choose two applications in the foreground using the snapped view. All the other background apps can be suspended and even terminated by the Windows Runtime. A suspended app cannot execute code, consume CPU cycles or network resources, or perform disk activity such as reading or writing files.

You can define a background task that runs in the background, however, even in a separate process from the owner app, and you can define background actions. When these actions need to alert users about their outcomes, they can use a toast. A background task can execute code even when the corresponding app is suspended, but it runs in an environment that is restricted and resource-managed. Moreover, background tasks receive only a limited amount of system resources.

You should use a background task to execute small pieces of code that require no user interaction. You can also use a background task to communicate with other apps via instant messaging, email, or Voice over IP (VoIP). Avoid using a background task to execute complex business logic or calculations because the amount of system resources available to background apps is limited. Complex background workloads consume battery power as well, reducing the overall efficiency and responsiveness of the system.

To create a background task, you have to define a class and register it with the operating system. To do this, create a Windows Metadata (WinMD) project and then create a class in it. A *background task* is a public and not-inheritable class that implements the *IBackgroundTask* interface defined by the Windows Runtime and is registered by using a *BackgroundTaskBuilder* class instance.

> ***MORE INFO*** **WINMD**
>
> **WinMD is covered in the section titled "Objective 1.3: Create and consume WinMD components" later in this chapter.**

The *IBackgroundTask* imposes the implementation of a single self-explaining method: *Run*. Listing 1-1 shows the implementation of this interface in a sample class.

LISTING 1-1 Class skeleton for *IBackground* task interface implementation

```
using System;
using System.Collections.Generic;
using System.Linq;
using System.Text;
using System.Threading.Tasks;
using Windows.ApplicationModel.Background;

namespace BikeGPS
{
```

```
    public sealed class BikePositionUpdateBackgroundTask : IBackgroundTask
    {
        public void Run(IBackgroundTaskInstance taskInstance)
        {
            // Update the GPS coordinates
        }
    }
}
```

You have to assign the event that will fire the task. When the event occurs, the operating system calls the defined *Run* method. You can associate the event, called a *trigger*, via the *SystemTrigger* or the *MaintenanceTrigger* class.

The code is straightforward. Using an instance of the *BackgroundTaskBuilder* class, associate the name of the task and its entry point by using the syntax *namespace.class*. The *entry point* represents the background task class, as shown in the following code:

Sample of C# code

```
var taskName = "bikePositionUpdate";
var builder = new BackgroundTaskBuilder();
builder.Name = taskName;
builder.TaskEntryPoint = "BikeGPS.BikePositionUpdateBackgroundTask";
```

You must also create the trigger to let the system know when to start the background task:

```
builder.SetTrigger(new SystemTrigger(SystemTriggerType.TimeZoneChange, false));
```

The *SystemTrigger* class accepts two parameters in its constructor. The first parameter of the trigger is the type of system event associated with the background task; the second, called *oneShot*, tells the Windows Runtime to start the task only once or every time the event occurs.

The complete enumeration, which is defined by the *SystemTriggerType* enum, is shown in Listing 1-2.

LISTING 1-2 Types of system triggers

```
// Summary:
// Specifies the system events that can be used to trigger a background task.
[Version(100794368)]
public enum SystemTriggerType
{
// Summary:
//     Not a valid trigger type.
    Invalid = 0,
    //
    // Summary:
    //     The background task is triggered when a new SMS message is received by an
    //     installed mobile broadband device.
    SmsReceived = 1,
    //
    // Summary:
    //     The background task is triggered when the user becomes present. An app must
    //     be placed on the lock screen before it can successfully register background
    //     tasks using this trigger type.
```

```
    UserPresent = 2,
    //
    // Summary:
    //     The background task is triggered when the user becomes absent. An app must
    //     be placed on the lock screen before it can successfully register background
    //     tasks using this trigger type.
    UserAway = 3,
    //
    // Summary:
    //     The background task is triggered when a network change occurs, such as a
    //     change in cost or connectivity.
    NetworkStateChange = 4,
    //
    // Summary:
    //     The background task is triggered when a control channel is reset. An app must
    //     be placed on the lock screen before it can successfully register background
    //     tasks using this trigger type.
    ControlChannelReset = 5,
    //
    // Summary:
    //     The background task is triggered when the Internet becomes available.
    InternetAvailable = 6,
    //
    // Summary:
    //     The background task is triggered when the session is connected. An app must
    //     be placed on the lock screen before it can successfully register background
    //     tasks using this trigger type.
    SessionConnected = 7,
    //
    // Summary:
    //     The background task is triggered when the system has finished updating an
    //     app.
    ServicingComplete = 8,
    //
    // Summary:
    //     The background task is triggered when a tile is added to the lock screen.
    LockScreenApplicationAdded = 9,
    //
    // Summary:
    //     The background task is triggered when a tile is removed from the lock screen.
    LockScreenApplicationRemoved = 10,
    //
    // Summary:
    //     The background task is triggered when the time zone changes on the device
    //     (for example, when the system adjusts the clock for daylight saving time).
    TimeZoneChange = 11,
    //
    // Summary:
    //     The background task is triggered when the Microsoft account connected to
    //     the account changes.
    OnlineIdConnectedStateChange = 12,
}
```

You can also add conditions that are verified by the system before starting the background task. The *BackgroundTaskBuilder* class exposes the *AddCondition* method to add a single condition, as shown in the following code sample. You can call it multiple times to add different conditions.

```
builder.AddCondition(new SystemCondition(SystemConditionType.InternetAvailable));
```

The last line of code needed is the registration of the defined task:

```
BackgroundTaskRegistration taskRegistration = builder.Register();
```

Declaring background task usage

An application that registers a background task needs to declare the feature in the application manifest as an extension, as well as the events that will trigger the task. If you forget these steps, the registration will fail. There is no <Extensions> section in the application manifest of the Microsoft Visual Studio standard template by default, so you need to insert it as a child of the *Application* tag.

Listing 1-3 shows the application manifest for the sample task implemented by the previous code (see Listing 1-2). The <Extensions> section is highlighted in bold.

LISTING 1-3 Application manifest

```
<?xml version="1.0" encoding="utf-8"?>
<Package xmlns="http://schemas.microsoft.com/appx/2010/manifest">

  <Identity Name="e00b2bde-0697-4e6b-876b-1d611365485f"
            Publisher="CN=Roberto"
            Version="1.0.0.0" />

  <Properties>
    <DisplayName>BikeApp</DisplayName>
    <PublisherDisplayName>Roberto</PublisherDisplayName>
    <Logo>Assets\StoreLogo.png</Logo>
  </Properties>

  <Prerequisites>
    <OSMinVersion>6.2.1</OSMinVersion>
    <OSMaxVersionTested>6.2.1</OSMaxVersionTested>
  </Prerequisites>

  <Resources>
    <Resource Language="x-generate"/>
  </Resources>

  <Applications>
    <Application Id="App"
        Executable="$targetnametoken$.exe"
        EntryPoint="BikeApp.App">
      <VisualElements
          DisplayName="BikeApp"
          Logo="Assets\Logo.png"
          SmallLogo="Assets\SmallLogo.png"
          Description="BikeApp"
```

```
            ForegroundText="light"
            BackgroundColor="#464646">
          <DefaultTile ShowName="allLogos" />
          <SplashScreen Image="Assets\SplashScreen.png" />
        </VisualElements>
        <Extensions>
          <Extension Category="windows.backgroundTasks"
             EntryPoint="BikeGPS.BikePositionUpdateBackgroundTask">
            <BackgroundTasks>
              <Task Type="systemEvent" />
            </BackgroundTasks>
          </Extension>
        </Extensions>
      </Application>
    </Applications>
    <Capabilities>
      <Capability Name="internetClient" />
    </Capabilities>
</Package>
```

You have to add as many task elements as needed by the application. For example, if the application uses a system event and a push notification event, you must add the following XML node to the *BackgroundTasks* element:

```
<BackgroundTasks>
   <Task Type="systemEvent" />
   <Task Type="pushNotification" />
</BackgroundTasks>
```

You can also use the Visual Studio App Manifest Designer to add (or remove) a background task declaration. Figure 1-1 shows the same declaration in the designer.

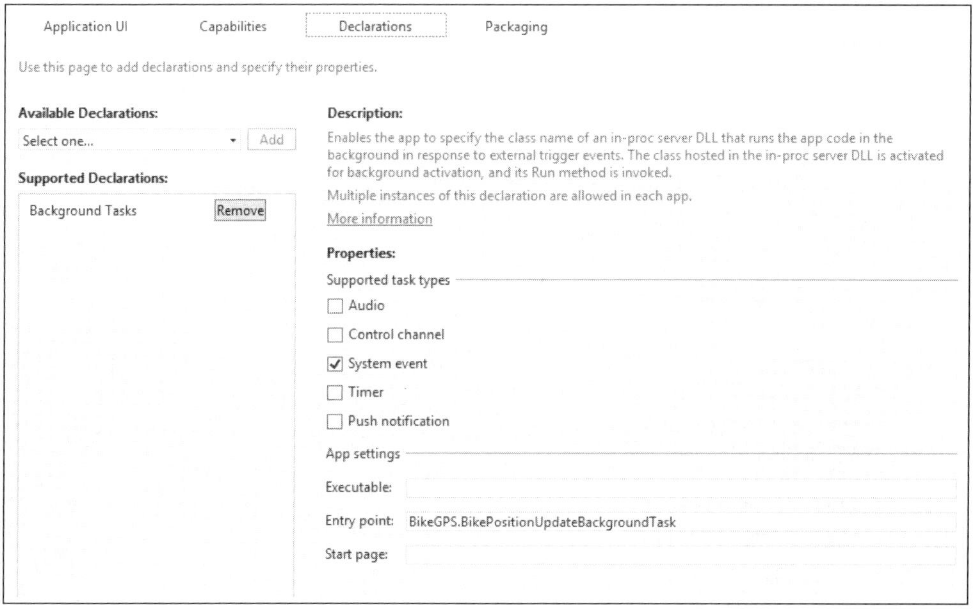

FIGURE 1-1 Background task declaration in the Visual Studio App Manifest Designer

Enumerating registered tasks

Be sure to register the task you implement just once in your application. If you forget to check the presence of the task, you risk registering and executing the same task many times.

To see whether a task is registered, you can iterate all the registered tasks using the *BackgroundTaskRegistration* class and checking for the *Value* property that exposes the *Name* property, as follows:

Sample of C# code

```
var taskName = "bikePositionUpdate";
var taskRegistered = false;
foreach (var task in BackgroundTaskRegistration.AllTasks)
{
   if (task.Value.Name == taskName)
   {
      taskRegistered = true;
      break;
   }
}
if (!taskRegistered)
   // Register the task
```

Using deferrals with tasks

If the code for the *Run* method is asynchronous, the background task needs to use a deferral (the same techniques of the suspend method) using the *GetDeferral* method, as shown in the following code:

```
public async void Run(IBackgroundTaskInstance taskInstance)
{
    BackgroundTaskDeferral _deferral = taskInstance.GetDeferral();

    //
    // Start one (or more) async
    // Use the await keyword
    //
    await UpdateGPSCoordinatesAsync();

    _deferral.Complete();
}
```

After requesting the deferral, use the *async/await* pattern to perform the asynchronous work and, at the end, call the *Complete* method on the deferral. Be sure to perform all the work after requesting the deferral and before calling the *Complete* method. Otherwise, the system thinks that your job is already done and can shut down the main thread.

Thought experiment

Implementing background tasks

In this thought experiment, apply what you've learned about this objective. You can find answers to these questions in the "Answers" section at the end of this chapter.

Your application needs to perform some lengthy cleaning operations on temporary data. To avoid wasting system resources during application use, you want to perform these operations in the background. You implement the code in a background thread, but notice that your application sometimes does not clean all the data when the user switches to another application.

1. **Why does the application not clean the data all the time?**
2. **How can you solve this problem?**

Objective summary

- A background task can execute lightweight action invoked by the associated event.
- A task needs to be registered using WinRT classes and defined in the application manifest.
- There are many system events you can use to trigger a background task.
- You have to register a task just once.
- You can enumerate tasks that are already registered.

Objective review

Answer the following questions to test your knowledge of the information in this objective. You can find the answers to these questions and explanations of why each answer choice is correct or incorrect in the "Answers" section at the end of this chapter.

1. How can an application fire a background task to respond to a network state modification?
   - **A.** By using a time trigger that polls the network state every minute, and checks for changes to this value
   - **B.** By using a *SystemTrigger* for the *InternetAvailable* event and checking to see whether the network is present or not
   - **C.** By using a *SystemTrigger* for the *NetworkStateChange* event and using *false* as the second constructor parameter (called *oneShot)*
   - **D.** By using a *SystemTrigger* for the *NetworkStateChange* event and using *true* as the second constructor parameter

2. Which steps do you need to perform to enable a background task? (Choose all that apply.)
   - **A.** Register the task in the Package.appxmanifest file.
   - **B.** Use the *BackgroundTaskBuilder to create the task.*
   - **C.** Set the trigger that will fire the task code.
   - **D.** Use a toast to show information to the user.
3. Is it possible to schedule a background task just once?
   - **A.** Yes, using a specific task.
   - **B.** No, only system tasks can run once.
   - **C.** Yes, using a parameter at trigger level.
   - **D.** No, only a time-triggered task can run once at certain time.

Objective 1.2: Consume background tasks

The Windows Runtime exposes many ways to interact with the system in a background task and many ways to activate a task. System triggers, time triggers, and conditions can modify the way a task is started and consumed. Moreover, a task can keep a communication channel open to send data to or receive data from remote endpoints. An application might need to download or upload a large resource even if the user is not using it. The application can also request lock screen permission from the user to enhance other background capabilities.

This objective covers how to:

- Use timing and system triggers
- Keep communication channels open
- Request lock screen access
- Use the *BackgroundTransfer* class to finish downloads

Understanding task triggers and conditions

Many types of background tasks are available. They respond to different kinds of *triggers for any kind of application,* which can be the following:

- ***MaintenanceTrigger*** Raised when it is time to execute system maintenance tasks
- ***SystemEventTrigger*** Raised when a specific system event occurs

A maintenance trigger is represented by the *MaintenanceTrigger* class. This class implements the *IBackgroundTrigger* interface, as do other triggers available in the Windows Runtime library. The interface in this version of the Windows Runtime declares nothing, but will be implemented in future versions of the library. To create a new instance of a trigger, you can use the following code:

```
MaintenanceTrigger taskTrigger = new MaintenanceTrigger(60, true);
```

The first parameter is the *freshnessTime* expressed in minutes, and the second parameter, called *oneShot*, is a Boolean indicating whether the trigger should be fired only one time or every *freshnessTime* occurrence.

Whenever a system event occurs, you can check a set of conditions to determine whether your background task should execute. When a trigger is fired, the background task does not run until all its conditions are met, which means the code for the *Run* method is not executed if a condition is not met.

All the conditions are enumerated in the *SystemConditionType* enum:

- ***InternetAvailable*** An Internet connection must be available.
- ***InternetNotAvailable*** An Internet connection must be unavailable.
- ***SessionConnected*** The session must be connected.
- ***SessionDisconnected*** The session must be disconnected.
- ***UserNotPresent*** The user must be away.
- ***UserPresent*** The user must be present.

The maintenance trigger can schedule a background task as frequently as every 15 minutes if the device is plugged in to an AC power source. It is not fired if the device is running on batteries.

System triggers and maintenance triggers run for every application that registers them (and declares them in the application manifest). In addition, an application that leverages the lock screen–capable feature of the Windows Runtime can also register background tasks for other events.

An application can be placed on the lock screen to show important information to the user: The user can choose the application he or she wants on the lock screen (up to seven in the first release of Windows 8).

You can use the following triggers to run code for an app on the lock screen:

- ***PushNotificationTrigger*** Raised when a notification arrives on the Windows Push Notifications Service channel.
- ***TimeTrigger*** Raised at scheduled intervals. The app can schedule a task to run as frequently as every 15 minutes.
- ***ControlChannelTrigger*** Raised when there are incoming messages on the control channel for apps that keep connections alive.

It is important to note that the user must place the application on the lock screen before the application can use triggers. The application can ask the user to access the lock screen by calling the *RequestAccessAsync* method. The system presents a dialog box to the user, asking for her or his permission to use the lock screen.

The following triggers are usable only by lock screen–capable applications:

- ***ControlChannelReset*** The control channel is reset.
- ***SessionConnected*** The session is connected.
- ***UserAway*** The user must be away.
- ***UserPresent*** The user must be present.

In addition, when a lock screen–capable application is placed on the lock screen or removed from it, the following system events are triggered:

- ***LockScreenApplicationAdded*** The application is added to the lock screen.
- ***LockScreenApplicationRemoved*** The application is removed from the lock.

A time-triggered task can be scheduled to run either once or periodically; this kind of task is useful to update the application tile or badge with some kind of information. For example, a weather app updates the temperature to show the most recent one in the application tile, whereas a finance application refreshes the quote for the preferred stock.

The code to define a time trigger is similar to the code for a maintenance trigger:

```
TimeTrigger taskTrigger = new TimeTrigger(60, true);
```

The first parameter *(freshnessTime)* is expressed in minutes, and the second parameter (*oneShot*) indicates whether the trigger will fire only once or at every *freshnessTime* occurrence.

The Windows Runtime has an internal timer that runs tasks every 15 minutes. If the *freshnessTime* is set to 15 minutes and *oneShot* is set to *false*, the task will run every 15 minutes, starting between the time the task is registered and the 15 minutes ahead. If the *freshnessTime* is set to 15 minutes and *oneShot* is set to *true*, the task will run 15 minutes from the registration time.

EXAM TIP

You cannot set the *freshnessTime* to a value less than 15 minutes. An exception occurs if you try to do this.

Time trigger supports all the conditions in the *SystemConditionType* enum presented earlier in this section.

Progressing through and completing background tasks

If an application needs to know the result of the task execution, it can provide a callback for the *OnCompleted* event. The callback receives the instance of the *BackgroundTaskRegistration* used to register the task and the corresponding event arguments.

The following code creates a task and registers an event handler for the completion event:

```
var builder = new BackgroundTaskBuilder();

builder.Name = taskName;
builder.TaskEntryPoint = "BikeGPS.BikePositionUpdateBackgroundTask";
builder.SetTrigger(new SystemTrigger(SystemTriggerType.TimeZoneChange, false));

builder.AddCondition(new SystemCondition(SystemConditionType.InternetAvailable));

BackgroundTaskRegistration taskRegistration = builder.Register();

taskRegistration.Completed += taskRegistration_Completed;
```

A simple event handler, receiving the *BackgroundTaskRegistration* as the sender, can show something to the user as in the following code, or it can update the application tile with some information:

```
void taskRegistration_Completed(BackgroundTaskRegistration sender,
    BackgroundTaskCompletedEventArgs args)
{
    if (sender.Name == "BikeGPS.BikePositionUpdateBackgroundTask")
    {
        var dialog = new MessageDialog("Task BikePositionUpdateBackgroundTask
            completed.");
        dialog.ShowAsync();
    }
}
```

EXAM TIP

A background task can be executed when the application is suspended or even terminated. The *OnCompleted* event callback will be fired when the application is resumed from the operating system or the user launches it again. If the application is in the foreground, the event callback is fired immediately.

A well-written application needs to check errors in the task execution. Because the task is already completed, you need to see whether the result is available or whether something went wrong. To do that, the code can call the *CheckResult* method of the received *BackgroundTaskCompletedEventArgs*. This method throws the exception that occurred during task execution, if any; otherwise, it simply returns a void.

Listing 1-4 shows the correct way to handle an exception inside a single task.

LISTING 1-4 Completed event with exception handling

```
void taskRegistration_Completed(BackgroundTaskRegistration sender,
    BackgroundTaskCompletedEventArgs args)
{
    if (sender.Name == "BikeGPS.BikePositionUpdateBackgroundTask")
    {
        try
```

```
        {
            args.CheckResult();
            var dialog = new MessageDialog(
               "Task BikePositionUpdateBackgroundTask completed successfully");
            dialog.ShowAsync();
        }
        catch (Exception ex)
        {
            var dialog = new MessageDialog(
                "Task BikePositionUpdateBackgroundTask Errors " + ex.Message);
            dialog.ShowAsync();
        }
    }
}
```

Right after the check for the task name, exposed by the *Name* property of the *BackgroundTaskRegistration* received in the event handler parameter, use a *try/catch* block to intercept the exception fired by the *CheckResult* method, if any. In the sample presented in Listing 1-4, we simply create a dialog box to show the correct completion or the exception thrown by the background task execution.

Another useful event a background task exposes is the *OnProgress* event that, as the name implies, can track the progress of an activity. The event handler can update the user interface that is displayed when the application is resumed, or update the tile or the badge with the progress (such as the percent completed) of the job.

The code in Listing 1-5 is an example of a progress event handler that updates application titles manually:

LISTING 1-5 Sample progress event handler that updates the application tile

```
void taskRegistration_Progress(BackgroundTaskRegistration sender,
    BackgroundTaskProgressEventArgs args)
{
    string tileXmlString = "<tile>"
        + "<visual>"
        + "<binding template='TileWideText03'>"
        + "<text id='1'>" + args.Progress.ToString() + "</text>"
        + "</binding>"
        + "<binding template='TileSquareText04'>"
        + "<text id='1'>" + args.Progress.ToString() + "</text>"
        + "</binding>"
        + "</visual>"
        + "</tile>";

    var tileXml = new Windows.Data.Xml.Dom.XmlDocument();
    tileXml.LoadXml(tileXmlString);

    var tile = new Windows.UI.Notifications.TileNotification(tileXml);

    Windows.UI.Notifications.TileUpdateManager.CreateTileUpdaterForApplication()
        .Update(tile);
}
```

The code in Listing 1-5 builds the XML document using the provided template and creates a *TileNotification* with a single value representing the process percentage. Then the code uses the *CreateTileUpdaterForApplication* method of the *TileUpdateManager* class to update the live tile.

The progress value can be assigned in the *Run* method using the *Progress* property of the *IBackgroundTaskInstance* instance that represents the task. This instance is received directly as the parameter of the *Run* method.

The following code shows a simple example of progress assignment:

```
public sealed class BikePositionUpdateBackgroundTask : IBackgroundTask
{
    public void Run(IBackgroundTaskInstance taskInstance)
    {
        // Update the GPS coordinates

        // First operation
        taskInstance.Progress = 10;

        // Second operation
        taskInstance.Progress = 20;

        /// ....
    }
}
```

Understanding task constraints

As stated, background tasks have to be lightweight so they can provide the best user experience with foreground apps and battery life. The runtime enforces this behavior by applying resource constraints to the task:

- **CPU for application not on the lock screen** The CPU is limited to 1 second. A task can run every 2 hours at a minimum. For application on the lock screen, the system will execute a task for 2 seconds with a 15-minute maximum interval.
- **Network access** When running on batteries, tasks have network usage limits calculated based on the amount of energy used by the network card. This number can be very different from device to device based on their hardware. For example, with a throughput of 10 megabits per second (Mbps), an app on the lock screen can consume about 450 megabytes (MB) per day, whereas an app that is not on the lock screen can consume about 75 MB per day.

> ***MORE INFO*** **TASK CONSTRAINTS**
>
> **Refer to the MSDN documentation at *http://msdn.microsoft.com/en-us/library/windows/apps/xaml/hh977056.aspx* for updated information on background task resource constraints.**

To prevent resource quotas from interfering with real-time communication apps, tasks using *ControlChannelTrigger* and *PushNotificationTrigger* receive a guaranteed resource quota (CPU/network) for every running task. The resource quotas and network data usage constraints remain constant for these background tasks rather than varying according to the power usage of the network interface.

Because the system handles constraints automatically, your app does not have to request resource quotas for *ControlChannelTrigger* and *PushNotificationTrigger* background tasks. The Windows Runtime treats these tasks as "critical" background tasks.

If a task exceeds these quotas, it is suspended by the runtime. You can check for suspension by inspecting the *SuspendedCount* property of the task instance in the *Run* method, choosing to stop or abort the task if the counter is too high. The following code illustrates how to check for suspension:

```
public sealed class BikePositionUpdateBackgroundTask : IBackgroundTask
{
    public void Run(IBackgroundTaskInstance taskInstance)
    {
        // Update the GPS coordinates
        if (taskInstance.SuspendedCount > 5)
            return;
    }
}
```

Cancelling a task

When a task is executing, it cannot be stopped unless the task recognizes a cancellation request. A task can also report cancellation to the application using the persistent storage.

The *Run* method has to check for cancellation requests. The easiest way is to declare a Boolean variable in the class and set it to *true* if the system has cancelled the task. This variable will be set to *true* in the *OnCanceled* event handler and checked during the execution of the *Run* method to exit it.

Listing 1-6 shows the simplest complete class to check for cancellation.

LISTING 1-6 Task cancellation check

```
public sealed class BikePositionUpdateBackgroundTask : IBackgroundTask
{
    volatile bool _cancelRequested = false;

    public void Run(IBackgroundTaskInstance taskInstance)
    {
        taskInstance.Canceled += new BackgroundTaskCanceledEventHandler(OnCanceled);

        // Update the GPS coordinates

        // First operation
        taskInstance.Progress = 10;
```

```
            if (_cancelRequested == true)
                return;

            // Second operation
            taskInstance.Progress = 20;

            /// ....
        }

        private void OnCanceled(IBackgroundTaskInstance sender,
            BackgroundTaskCancellationReason reason)
        {
            // you can use sender.Task.Name to identity the task

            _cancelRequested = true;
        }
    }
```

In the *Run* method, the first line of code sets the event handler for the *Canceled* event to the *OnCanceled* method. Then it does its job setting the progress and testing the value of the variable to stop working (return or break, in case of a loop). The *OnCanceled* method sets the *_cancelRequested* variable to *true.* To recap, the system will call the *Canceled* event handler (*OnCanceled)* during a cancellation. The code sets the variable tested in the *Run* method to stop working on the task.

If the task wants to communicate some data to the application, it can use local persistent storage as a place to store some data the application can interpret. For example, the *Run* method can save the status in a *LocalSettings* key to let the application know if the task has been successfully completed or cancelled. The application can then check this information in the *Completed* event for the task.

Listing 1-7 shows the revised *Run* method.

LISTING 1-7 Task cancellation using local settings to communicate information to the app

```
public void Run(IBackgroundTaskInstance taskInstance)
{
    taskInstance.Canceled += new BackgroundTaskCanceledEventHandler(OnCanceled);

    // Update the GPS coordinates

    // First operation
    taskInstance.Progress = 10;

    if (_cancelRequested == true)
    {
        ApplicationData.Current.LocalSettings.Values["status"] = "canceled";
        return;
    }

    // Second operation
    taskInstance.Progress = 20;
```

```
    /// ....
    ///
    ApplicationData.Current.LocalSettings.Values["status"] = "completed";
}
```

Before "stopping" the code in the *Run* method, the code sets the *status* value in the *LocalSettings*; that is, the persistent storage dedicated to the application, to *canceled.* If the task completes its work, the value will be *completed.*

The code in Listing 1-8 inspects the *LocalSettings* value to determine the task outcome. This is a revised version of the *taskRegistration_Completed* event handler used in a previous sample.

LISTING 1-8 Task completed event handler with task outcome check

```
void taskRegistration_Completed(BackgroundTaskRegistration sender,
    BackgroundTaskCompletedEventArgs args)
{
    if (sender.Name == "BikeGPS.BikePositionUpdateBackgroundTask")
    {
        try
        {
            args.CheckResult();

            var status = ApplicationData.Current.LocalSettings.Values["status"];
            MessageDialog dialog;

            if(status == "canceled")
                dialog = new MessageDialog(
                    "Task BikePositionUpdateBackgroundTask canceled");
            else
                dialog = new MessageDialog(
                    "Task BikePositionUpdateBackgroundTask completed");
                dialog.ShowAsync();
        }
        catch (Exception ex)
        {
            var dialog = new MessageDialog(
            "Task BikePositionUpdateBackgroundTask Errors " + ex.Message);
                dialog.ShowAsync();
        }
    }
}
```

The registered background task persists in the local system and is independent from the application version.

Updating a background task

Tasks "survive" application updates. If a newer version of the application needs to update a task or modify its behavior, it can register the background task with the *ServicingComplete* trigger; this way the app is notified when the application is updated and unregisters tasks that are no longer valid.

Listing 1-9 shows a task that unregisters the previous version and registers the new one.

LISTING 1-9 Using the *ServicingComplete* task to update a previous version of a task

```
using System;
using System.Collections.Generic;
using System.Linq;
using System.Text;
using System.Threading.Tasks;
using Windows.ApplicationModel.Background;
using Windows.Storage;

namespace BikeGPS
{
    public sealed class ServicingCompleteTask : IBackgroundTask
    {

        public void Run(IBackgroundTaskInstance taskInstance)
        {
            // Look for Task v1
            var task = FindTask("BikeGPS.BikePositionUpdateBackgroundTask");

            if (task != null)
            {
                task.Unregister(true);
            }

            var builder = new BackgroundTaskBuilder();

            builder.Name = task.Name;
            builder.TaskEntryPoint = "BikeGPS.BikePositionUpdateBackgroundTask";
            builder.SetTrigger(new SystemTrigger(SystemTriggerType.TimeZoneChange,
                false));

            builder.AddCondition(new
                SystemCondition(SystemConditionType.InternetAvailable));

            BackgroundTaskRegistration taskRegistration = builder.Register();

        }
```

```
        public static BackgroundTaskRegistration FindTask(string taskName)
        {
            foreach (var task in BackgroundTaskRegistration.AllTasks)
            {
                if (task.Value.Name == taskName)
                {
                    return (BackgroundTaskRegistration)(task.Value);
                }
            }

            return null;
        }
    }
}
```

The parameter of the *Unregister* method set to *true* forces task cancellation, if implemented, for the background task. The *FindTask* method is simply a helper you can use throughout the code to find a task by name in the list of already registered tasks and return it to the caller.

The last thing to do is use a *ServicingComplete* task in the application code to register this "system" task as other tasks using the *ServicingComplete* system trigger type:

```
SystemTrigger servicingCompleteTrigger =
      new SystemTrigger(SystemTriggerType.ServicingComplete, false);
```

Debugging tasks

Debugging a background task can be a challenging job if you try to use a manual tracing method.

A timer or a maintenance-triggered task can be executed in the next 15 minutes based on the internal interval, so debugging manually is not so effective. To ease this job, the Visual Studio background task integrated debugger simplifies the task activation.

Make sure that the Windows Store application references the background task project and the latter is configured as WinMD File. In addition, the project has to declare the background task in the application manifest. Figure 1-2 shows the complete solution with the BikeBackgroundTask project referenced by the main application, and the project property showing the output type set to Windows Runtime Component (also referred to as the WinMD library or file).

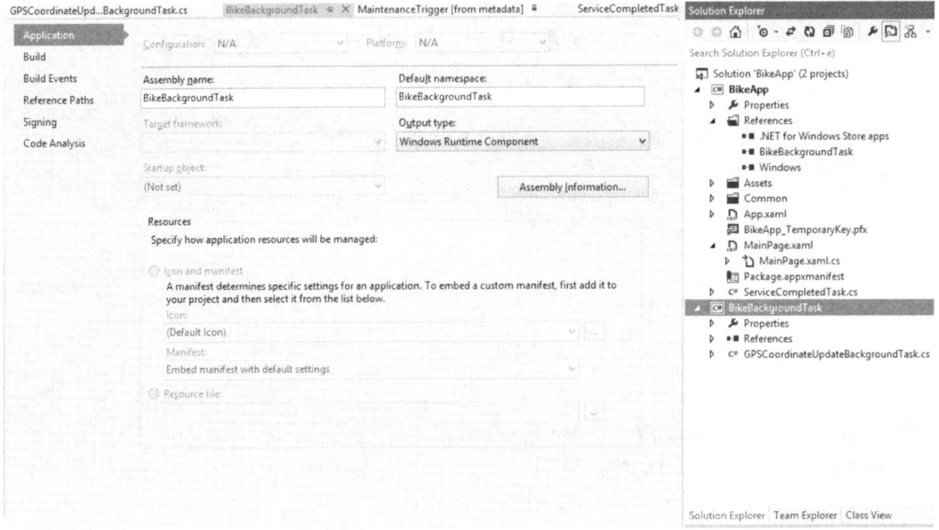

FIGURE 1-2 Solution structure and output type for a background task

Place a breakpoint in the *Run* method or use the *Debug* class to write some values in the output window. Start the project at least one time to register the task in the system and then use the Debug Location toolbar in Visual Studio to activate the background task. The toolbar can show only registered tasks waiting for the trigger. The toolbar can be activated using the View command on the Toolbars menu.

Figure 1-3 shows the background registration code and the Debug Location toolbar.

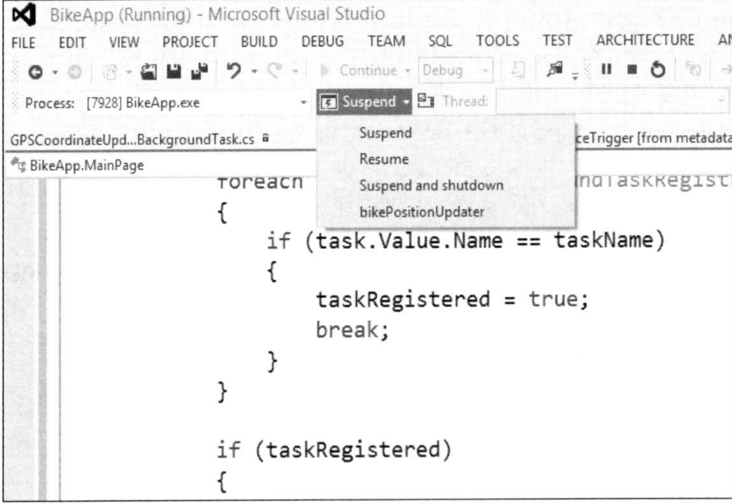

FIGURE 1-3 Visual Studio "hidden" Debug Location toolbar to start tasks

Figure 1-4 shows the debugger inside the Run method.

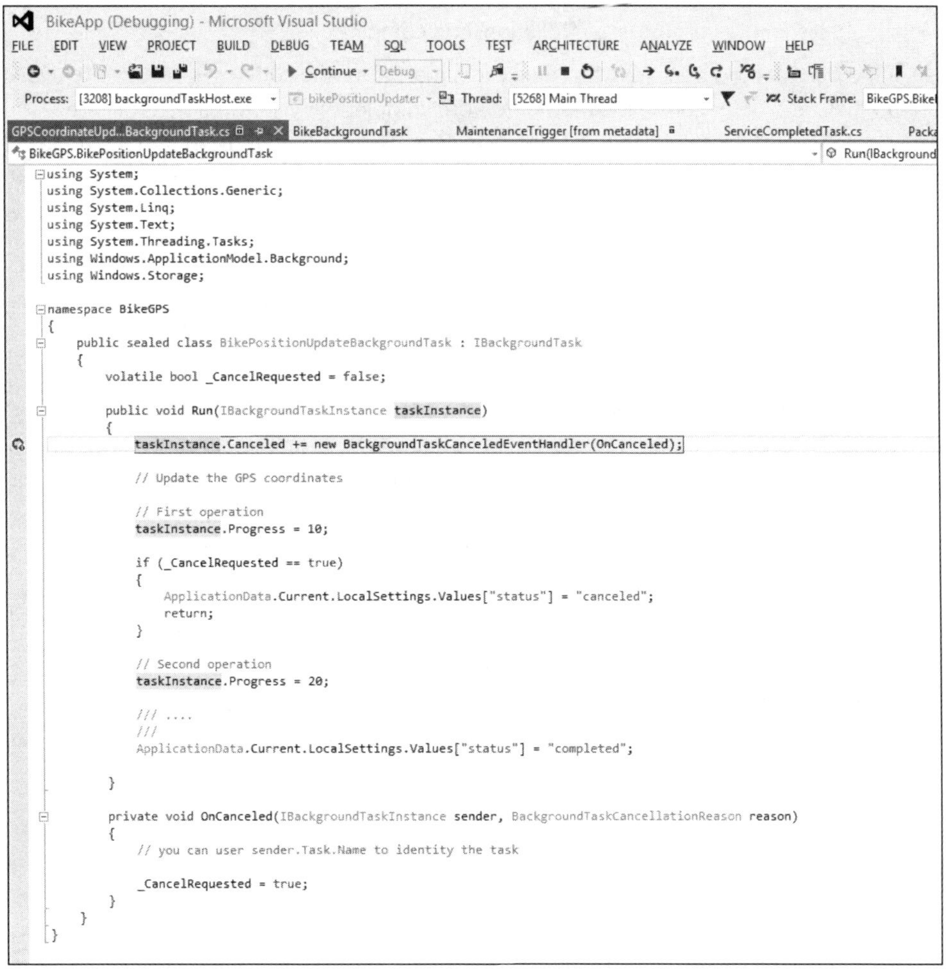
BikeApp (Debugging) - Microsoft Visual Studio
FILE EDIT VIEW PROJECT BUILD DEBUG TEAM SQL TOOLS TEST ARCHITECTURE ANALYZE WINDOW HELP
Continue
Debug
Process: [3208] backgroundTaskHost.exe
bikePositionUpdater
Thread: [5268] Main Thread
Stack Frame: BikeGPS.Bike
GPSCoordinateUpd...BackgroundTask.cs
BikeBackgroundTask
MaintenanceTrigger [from metadata]
ServiceCompletedTask.cs
BikeGPS.BikePositionUpdateBackgroundTask
Run(IBackground
using System;
using System.Collections.Generic;
using System.Linq;
using System.Text;
using System.Threading.Tasks;
using Windows.ApplicationModel.Background;
using Windows.Storage;
namespace BikeGPS
{
public sealed class BikePositionUpdateBackgroundTask : IBackgroundTask
{
volatile bool _CancelRequested = false;
public void Run(IBackgroundTaskInstance taskInstance)
{
taskInstance.Canceled += new BackgroundTaskCanceledEventHandler(OnCanceled);
// Update the GPS coordinates
// First operation
taskInstance.Progress = 10;
if (_CancelRequested == true)
{
ApplicationData.Current.LocalSettings.Values["status"] = "canceled";
return;
}
// Second operation
taskInstance.Progress = 20;
/// ....
///
ApplicationData.Current.LocalSettings.Values["status"] = "completed";
}
private void OnCanceled(IBackgroundTaskInstance sender, BackgroundTaskCancellationReason reason)
{
// you can user sender.Task.Name to identity the task
_CancelRequested = true;
}
}
}

FIGURE 1-4 Debugging tasks activated directly from Visual Studio

Understanding task usage

Every application has to pass the verification process during application submission to the Windows Store. Be sure to double-check the code for background tasks using the following points as guidance:

- Do not exceed the CPU and network quotas in your background tasks. Tasks have to be lightweight to save battery power and provide a better user experience for the application in the foreground.

- The application should get the list of registered background tasks, register for progress and completion handlers, and handle these events in the correct manner. The classes should also report progress, cancellation, and completion.
- If the *Run* method uses asynchronous code, make sure the code uses deferrals to avoid premature termination of the method before completion. Without a deferral, the Windows Runtime thinks that your code has finished its work and can terminate the thread. Request a deferral, use the *async/await* pattern to complete the asynchronous call, and close the deferral after the *await* keyword.
- Declare each background task and every trigger associated with it in the application manifest. Otherwise, the app cannot register the task at runtime.
- Use the *ServicingComplete* trigger to prepare your application for updating.
- If you use the lock screen–capable feature, remember that only seven apps can be placed on the lock screen, and the user can choose the application she wants on it at any time. Furthermore, only one app can have a wide tile. The application can provide a good user experience by requesting lock screen access using the *RequestAccessAsync* method. Be sure the application can work without permission to use the lock screen because the user can deny access to it or remove the permission later.
- Use tiles and badges to provide visual clues to the user and use the notification mechanism in the task to notify third parties. Do not use any other UI elements in the run method.
- Use persistent storage as *ApplicationData* to share data between the background task and the application. Never rely on user interaction in the task.
- Write background tasks that are short-lived.

Transferring data in the background

Some applications need to download or upload a resource from the web. Because of the application life-cycle management of the Windows Runtime, if you begin to download a file and then the user switches to another application, the first app can be suspended; the file cannot be downloaded during suspension because the system gives no thread and no I/O slot to a suspended app. If the user switches back to the application again, the download operation can continue but will take more time to be completed. Moreover, if the system needs resources, it can terminate the application. The download is then terminated together with the app.

The *BackgroundTransfer* namespace provides classes to avoid these problems. It can be used to enhance the application with file upload and download features that run in the background during suspension. It supports HTTP and HTTPS for download and upload operations, and File Transfer Protocol (FTP) for download-only operations. This class is aimed at large file uploads and downloads.

The process started by this class runs separately from the Windows Store app and can be used to work with resources such as files, music, large images, and videos. During the operation, if the runtime chooses to put the application in the suspended state, the capability provided by the Background Transfer APIs continues to work in the background.

> ***NOTE*** **BACKGROUND TRANSFER API**
>
> **Background Transfer APIs work for small resources (a few kilobytes), but Microsoft suggests using the traditional *HttpClient* class for these kind of files.**

The process to create a file download operation involves the *BackgroundDownloader* class: The settings and initialization parameters provide different ways to customize and start the download operation. The same applies for upload operations using the *BackgroundUploader* class. You can call multiple download/upload operations using these classes from the same application because the Windows Runtime handles each operation individually.

During the operation, the application can receive events to update the UI (if the application is still in the foreground), and you can provide a way to stop, pause, resume, or cancel the operation. You can also read the data during the transfer operation.

These operations support credentials, cookies, and the use of HTTP headers, so you can use them to download files from a secured location or provide a custom header to a custom server-side HTTP handler.

The operations are managed by the Windows Runtime, promoting smart usage of power and bandwidth. They are also independent from sudden network status changes because they intelligently leverage connectivity and carry data-plan status information provided by the *Connectivity* namespace.

The application can provide a cost-based policy for each operation using the *BackgroundTranferCostPolicy*. For example, you can provide a cost policy to pause the task automatically when the machine is using a metered network and resume it if the user comes back to an "open" connection. The application has to do nothing to manage these situations; it is sufficient to provide the policy to the background operation.

To enable a transfer operation in background, first enable the network in the Package.appxmanifest file using one of the provided options in the App Manifest Designer. You must use one of the following capabilities:

- **Internet (Client)** The app has outbound access to the Internet and networks in public areas, such as coffee shops, airports, and parks.
- **Internet (Client & Server)** The app can receive inbound requests and make outbound requests in public areas.
- **Private Networks** The app can receive inbound requests and make outbound requests in trusted places, such as at home and work.

Figure 1-5 shows the designer with the application capabilities needed for background data transferring.

FIGURE 1-5 Capabilities for background transferring

Then you can start writing code to download a file in the local storage folder. The code excerpt in Listing 1-10 starts downloading the session1.wmv file in the Videos Library folder.

LISTING 1-10 Code to activate a background transfer

```
private async void Download_Click(object sender, RoutedEventArgs e)
{
    try
    {
        var fileName = "session1.wmv";

        Uri source = new Uri("http://videos.devleap.com/" + fileName);

        var targetFile = await KnownFolders.VideosLibrary.CreateFileAsync(fileName,
            CreationCollisionOption.GenerateUniqueName);

        var downloader = new BackgroundDownloader();

        var downloadOperation = downloader.CreateDownload(source, targetFile);

        await downloadOperation.StartAsync();

        LogOperation(String.Format("Current Download {0} to {1}, {2}",
           source.AbsoluteUri, targetFile.Name, downloadOperation.Guid));
```

```
    }
    catch (Exception ex)
    {
        LogOperation("Download Error", ex);
    }
}
```

The first line of code sets a local variable representing the file name to download and uses it to create the URI for the source file. Then the *CreateFileAsync* method creates a file in the user's Videos library represented by the *KnownFolders.VideosLibrary* storage folder using the *async/await* pattern.

The *BackgroundDownloader* class exposes a *CreateDownload* method to begin the download operation: It returns a *DownloadOperation* class representing the current operation. The *BackgroundDownloader* class exposes the *StartAsync* method to start the operation.

The main properties of this class are:

- ***Guid*** Represents the autogenerated unique id for the download operation you can use in the code to create a log for every download operation
- ***RequestedUri* (read-only)** Represents the URI from which to download the file
- ***ResultFile*** Returns the *IStorageFile* object provided by the caller when creating the download operation

The *BackgroundDownloader* class also exposes the *Pause* and the *Resume* method as well as the *CostPolicy* property to use during the background operation.

To track the progress of the download operation, you can use the provided *StartAsync* method, transforming the result in a *Task* and passing the progress callback using an instance of the *System.Progress<T>* class. Listing 1-11 shows the revised sample.

LISTING 1-11 Activating a background transfer and providing progress information

```
private async void Download_Click(object sender, RoutedEventArgs e)
{
    try
    {
        var fileName = "session1.wmv";

        Uri source = new Uri("http://video.devleap.com/" + fileName);

        var targetFile = await KnownFolders.VideosLibrary.CreateFileAsync(fileName,
            CreationCollisionOption.GenerateUniqueName);

        var downloader = new BackgroundDownloader();

        var downloadOperation = downloader.CreateDownload(source, targetFile);

        Progress<DownloadOperation> progressCallback = new
            Progress<DownloadOperation>(DownloadProgress);
```

```
        await downloadOperation.StartAsync().AsTask(progressCallback);

        LogOperation(String.Format("Current Download {0} to {1}, {2}",
            source.AbsoluteUri, targetFile.Name, downloadOperation.Guid));

    }
    catch (Exception ex)
    {
        LogOperation("Download Error", ex);
    }
}

private void DownloadProgress(DownloadOperation downloadOperation)
{
    LogOperation(String.Format("Downloading {0} to {1}, {2}",
        downloadOperation.RequestedUri, downloadOperation.Progress ,
        downloadOperation.Guid)
}
```

In the preceding code, right after the creation of the download operation, the *StartAsync* method returns the *IAsyncOperationWithProgress<DownloadOperation, DownloadOperation>* interface that is transformed in a *Task* using the *AsTask* method; this method receives the *Progress<T>* instance that represents the callback.

This way, the callback can receive the *DownloadOperation* class and can use the *Guid*, *RequestedUri*, or *ResultFile* properties to track the progress or to log them (or display them if the application is in the foreground) as appropriate for the application.

The *BackgroundDownloader* tracks and manages all the current download operations; you can enumerate them using the *GetCurrentDownloadAsync* method.

Because the system can terminate the application, it is important to reattach the progress and completion event handler during the next launch operation performed by the user. Use the following code as a reference in the application launch:

```
IReadOnlyList<DownloadOperation> downloads = await
BackgroundDownloader.GetCurrentDownloadsAsync();

if (downloads.Count > 0)
{
    List<Task> tasks = new List<Task>();

    foreach (DownloadOperation download in downloads)
    {
        Progress<DownloadOperation> progressCallback = new
            Progress<DownloadOperation>(DownloadProgress);

        await download.AttachAsync().AsTask(progressCallback);
    }
}
```

This method iterates through all the current download operations and reattaches the progress callback to each of them using the *AttachAsync* method. The method returns an asynchronous operation that can be used to monitor progress and completion of the attached download. Calling this method enables an app to reattach download operations that were started in a previous app instance.

Finally, you should address the time-outs enforced by the system. When establishing a new connection for a transfer, the connection request is aborted if it is not established within five minutes. After establishing a connection, an HTTP request message that has not received a response within two minutes is aborted.

The same concepts apply to resource upload. The *BackgroundUploader* class works in a similar way as the *BackgroundDownloader* class. It is designed for long-term operations on resources such as files, images, music, and videos. As mentioned for download operations, small resources can be uploaded using the traditional *HttpClient* class.

You can use *CreateUploadAsync* to create an asynchronous operation that, on completion, returns an *UploadOperation*. There are three overloads for this method. The "BackgroundUploader class" page in the MSDN official documentation provides these descriptions:

- ***CreateUploadAsync(Uri, IIterable(BackgroundTransferContentPart))*** Returns an asynchronous operation that, on completion, returns an *UploadOperation* with the specified URI and one or more *BackgroundTransferContentPart* objects
- ***CreateUploadAsync(Uri, IIterable(BackgroundTransferContentPart), String)*** Returns an asynchronous operation that, on completion, returns an *UploadOperation* with the specified URI, one or more *BackgroundTransferContentPart* objects, and the multipart subtype
- ***CreateUploadAsync(Uri, IIterable(BackgroundTransferContentPart), String, String)*** Returns an asynchronous operation that, on completion, returns an *UploadOperation* with the specified URI, multipart subtype, one or more *BackgroundTransferContentPart* objects, and the delimiter boundary value used to separate each part

Alternatively, you can use the more specific *CreateUploadFromStreamAsync* that returns an asynchronous operation that, on completion, returns the *UploadOperation* with the specified URI and the source stream. This is the method definition:

```
public IAsyncOperation<UploadOperation> CreateUploadFromStreamAsync(
  Uri uri,
  IInputStream sourceStream
)
```

As for the downloader classes, this class exposes the *ProxyCredential* property to provide authentication to the proxy and *ServerCredential* to authenticate the operation with the target server. You can use the *SetRequestHeader* method to specify HTTP header key/value pairs.

Keeping communication channels open

For applications that need to work in the background, such as VoIP, instant messaging, and email, the new Windows Store application model provides an always-connected experience for the end user. In practice, an application that depends on a long-running network connection to a remote server can still work even when the Windows Runtime suspends the application. As you learned, a background task enables the application to perform some kind of work in the background when the application is suspended.

Keeping a communication channel open is required for an application that sends data to or receives data from a remote endpoint. It is also required for long-running server processes to receive and process any incoming requests from the outside.

Typically, this kind of application sits behind a proxy, a firewall, or a Network Address Translation (NAT) device. This hardware component preserves the connection if the endpoints continue to exchange data: if there is no traffic for some time (it can be few seconds or minutes) these devices close the connection.

To ensure that the connection is not lost and remains open between server and client endpoints, the application can be configured to use some kind of keep-alive connection (that is, a message is sent on the network at periodic intervals) so that the connection lifetime is prolonged.

These messages can be easily sent in previous versions of Windows because the application stays in the Running state until the user decides to close (or terminate) it. In this scenario, keep-alive messages can be sent without any problems. The new Windows 8 application life-cycle management, on the contrary, does not guarantee that packets are delivered to a suspended app. Moreover, incoming network connections can be dropped and no new traffic is sent to a suspended app; these behaviors have an impact on the network devices that cut the connection between apps because they become "idle" from a network perspective.

To be always connected, a Windows Store app needs to be a lock screen–capable application. Only applications that use one or more background tasks can be lock screen apps.

An app on the lock screen can do the following:

- Run code when a time trigger occurs.
- Run code when a new user session is started.
- Receive a raw push notification from Windows Push Notification Service and run code when a notification is received.
- Maintain a persistent transport connection in the background to remote services or endpoints, and run code when a new packet is received or a keep-alive packet needs to be sent using a network trigger.

Remember that a user can have a maximum of seven lock screen apps at any given time. A user can also add or remove an app from the lock screen at any time.

Windows Push Notification Service (WNS) is a cloud service hosted by Microsoft for Windows 8. Windows Store apps can use WNS to receive notifications that can run code, update a live tile, or raise an on-screen notification. To use WNS, the local computer must be connected to the Internet so that the WNS service can communicate with it. A Windows Store app in the foreground can use WNS to update live tiles, raise notifications to the user, or update badges. Apps do not need to be on the lock screen to use WNS. You should consider using WNS in your app if it must run code in response to a push notification.

MORE INFO **WINDOWS PUSH NOTIFICATION SERVICE (WNS)**

For a complete discussion of WNS, see Chapter 3, "Program user interaction."

The *ControlChannelTrigger* class in the *System.Net.Sockets* namespace implements the trigger for applications that must maintain a persistent connection to a remote endpoint: Use this feature if the application cannot use WNS. For example, an email application that uses some POP3 servers cannot be modified to use a push notification because the server does not implement WNS and does not send messages to POP3 clients.

The *ControlChannelTrigger* can be used by instances of one of the following classes: *MessageWebSocket, StreamWebSocket, StreamSocket, HttpClient, HttpClientHandler,* and related classes in the *System.Net.Http* namespace in .NET Framework 4.5. The *IXMLHTTPRequest2,* an extension of the classic *XMLHttpRequest,* can also be used to activate a *ControlChannelTrigger.*

The main benefits of using a network trigger are compatibility with existing client/server protocols and the guarantee of message delivery. The drawbacks are a little more complex in respect to WNS, and the maximum number of triggers an app can use is five in the current version of the Windows Runtime.

EXAM TIP

An application written in JavaScript cannot use a *ControlChannelTrigger* if it uses other background tasks.

An application that uses a network trigger needs to request the lock screen permission. This feature supports two different resources for a trigger:

- **Hardware slot** The application can use background notification even when the device is in low-power mode or standby (connected to a plug).
- **Software slot** The application cannot use network notification when not in low-power mode or standby (connected to a plug).

This resource capability provides a way for your app to be triggered by an incoming notification even if the device is in low-power mode. By default, a software slot is selected if the developer does not specify an option. A software slot enables your app to be triggered when the system is not in connected standby. This is the default on most computers.

There are two trigger types:

- **Push notification network trigger** Enables a Windows Store app to process incoming network packets on an already established TCP socket, even if the application is suspended. This socket, which represents the control channel that exists between the application and a remote endpoint, is created by the application to trigger a background task when a network packet is received by the application. In practice, the control channel is a persistent TCP/IP connection maintained alive by the Windows Runtime even if the application is sent in the background and suspended.
- **Keep-alive network trigger** Enables a suspended application to send keep-alive packets to a remote service or endpoint. To avoid connection cutting, the keep-alive packets tell the network device that a connection is still in use.

Before using a network trigger, the application has to be a lock screen app. You need to declare application capability and then call the appropriate method to ask the user for permission to place the application on the lock screen.

> ***NOTE*** **LOCK SCREEN REMOVAL**
>
> **You also have to handle a situation in which the user removes the application from the lock screen.**

To register an application for the lock screen, ensure that the application has a *WideLogo* definition in the application manifest on the *DefaultTile* element:

```
<DefaultTile ShowName="allLogos" WideLogo="Assets\wideLogo.png" />
```

Add a *LockScreen* element that represents the application icon on the lock screen inside the *VisualElements* node in the application manifest:

```
<LockScreen Notification="badge" BadgeLogo="Assets\badgeLogo.png" />
```

You can use the App Manifest Designer, shown in Figure 1-6, to set these properties. The Wide Logo and the Badge Logo reference the relative images, and the Lock Screen Notifications element is set to Badge.

FIGURE 1-6 Badge and wide logo definition

Declare the extensions to use a background task, and define the executable file that contains the task and the name of the class implementing the entry point for the task. The task has to be a *controlChannel* background task type. For this kind of task, the executable file is the application. Apps using the *ControlChannelTrigger* rely on in-process activation for background task. The following code declares the background task:

Sample of XML code

```
<Extensions>
  <Extension Category="windows.backgroundTasks"
      Executable="$targetnametoken$.exe"
      EntryPoint="ControlChannelTriggerTask.ReceiveTask">
    <BackgroundTasks>
      <Task Type="controlChannel" />
    </BackgroundTasks>
  </Extension>
</Extensions>
```

The dynamic-link library (DLL) or the executable file that implements the task for keep-alive or push notifications must be linked as a WinRT component (WinMD library). You can also use the App Manifest Designer to set these extensions in an easier way, as shown in Figure 1-7.

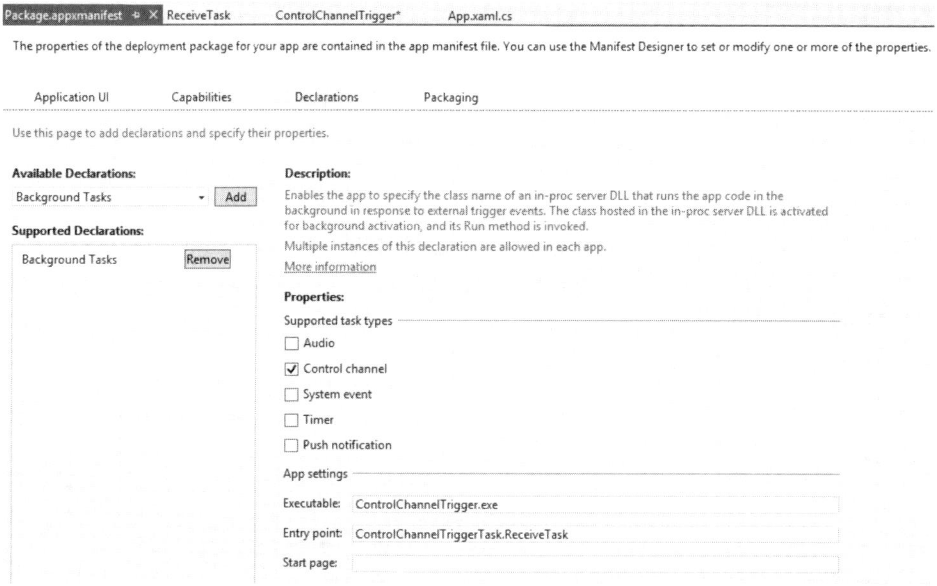

FIGURE 1-7 Background tasks app settings

The next step is to ask the user for permission to become a lock screen application using the *RequestAccessAsync* method of the *BackgroundExecutionManager* class of the *Windows.ApplicationModel.Background* namespace. See Listing 1-12. The call to this method presents a dialog box to the user to approve the request.

> ***NOTE*** **PERMISSION FOR LOCK SCREEN APP**
>
> **The consent dialog box prompts the user just one time. If the user denies permission for the lock screen, you cannot prompt the user again. The user can decide later to bring the application on the lock screen from the system permission dialog box, but the application has no possibility to ask for the permission again.**

LISTING 1-12 Requesting use of the lock screen

```
private Boolean lockScreenPermitted = false;

private async void LockScreenEnabling_Click(object sender, RoutedEventArgs e)
{

    BackgroundAccessStatus status = await
        BackgroundExecutionManager.RequestAccessAsync();

    switch (status)
    {
        case BackgroundAccessStatus.AllowedWithAlwaysOnRealTimeConnectivity:
            //
            // The user chose "allow" in the dialog box. The app is added
            // to the lock screen,
            // can set up background tasks, and, if it has the capability,
            // can use the real-time connectivity (RTC) broker. This means that
            // the app can function while the device is in the connected standby state.
            //
            lockScreenPermitted = true;
            break;
    case BackgroundAccessStatus.AllowedMayUseActiveRealTimeConnectivity:
            //
            // The user chose "allow" in the dialog box. The app is added to the lock screen
            // and can set up background tasks, but it cannot use the real-time connectivity
            // (RTC) broker. This means that the app might not function while the device
            // is in connected standby.Note that apps that do not specify RTC in their
            // manifest will always demonstrate this behavior.
            //
            lockScreenPermitted = true;
            break;
    case BackgroundAccessStatus.Denied:
            //
            // App should switch to polling mode (example: poll for email based
            // on time triggers)
            //
            break;
    }
    return;
}
```

The *BackgroundAccessStatus* enumeration lets you know the user's choice. See the comments in Listing 1-12 that explain the various states.

After your app is added to the lock screen, it should be visible in the Personalize section of the PC settings. Remember to handle the removal of the application's lock screen permission by the user: The user can deny the permission to use the lock screen at any time, so you must ensure that the app is always functional.

When the application is ready for the lock screen, you have to do the following:

1. Create a control channel.
2. Open a connection.
3. Associate the connection with the control channel.
4. Connect the socket to the endpoint server.
5. Establish a transport connection to your remote endpoint server.

You have to create the channel to be associated with the connection so the connection is kept open until you close the control channel.

After a successful connection to the server, synchronize the transport created by your app with the lower layers of the operating system by using a specific API, as shown in Listing 1-13.

LISTING 1-13 Control channel creation and connection opening

```
private Windows.Networking.Sockets.ControlChannelTrigger channel;

private void CreateControlChannel_Click(object sender, RoutedEventArgs e)
{
    ControlChannelTriggerStatus status;

    //
    // 1: Create the instance.
    //

    this.channel = new Windows.Networking.Sockets.ControlChannelTrigger(
        "ch01", // Channel ID to identify a control channel.
        20,     // Server-side keep-alive in minutes.
        ControlChannelTriggerResourceType.RequestHardwareSlot); //Request hardware slot.

    //
    // Create the trigger.
    //
    BackgroundTaskBuilder controlChannelBuilder = new BackgroundTaskBuilder();
    controlChannelBuilder.Name = "ReceivePacketTaskChannelOne";
    controlChannelBuilder.TaskEntryPoint = "ControlChannellTriggerTask.ReceiveTask";
    controlChannelBuilder.SetTrigger(channel.PushNotificationTrigger);
    controlChannelBuilder.Register();

    //
    // Step 2: Open a socket connection (omitted for brevity).
    //
```

```
    //
    // Step 3: Bind the transport object to the notification channel object.
    //
    channel.UsingTransport(sock);

    // Step 4: Connect the socket (omitted for brevity).
    //  Connect or Open

       //
       // Step 5: Synchronize with the lower layer
       //
       status = channel.WaitForPushEnabled();
}
```

Despite its name, the *WaitForPushEnabled* method is not related in any way to WNS. This API enables the hardware or software slot to be registered with all the underlying layers of the stack that will handle an incoming data packet, including the network device driver.

There are several types of keep-alive intervals that can relate to network apps:

- **TCP keep-alive** Defined by the TCP protocol
- **Server keep-alive** Used by *ControlChannelTrigger*
- **Network keep-alive** Used by *ControlChannelTrigger*

The keep-alive option for TCP lets an application send packets from the client to the server endpoint automatically to keep the connection open even when the connection is not used by the application itself. This way, the connection is not cut from the underlying systems.

The application can use the *KeepAlive* property of the *StreamSocketControl* class to enable or disable this feature on a *StreamSocket*. The default is disabled.

Other socket-related classes that do not expose the *KeepAlive* property (for example, *MessageWebSocket*, *StreamSocketListener*, and *StreamWebSocket)* have the keep-alive options disabled by default. Also, the *HttpClient* class and the *IXMLHTTPRequest2* interface do not have an option to enable TCP keep-alive.

When using the *ControlChannelTrigger* class, take into consideration these two types of keep-alive intervals.

- **Server keep-alive interval** Represents how often the application is woken up by the system during suspension. The interval is expressed in minutes in the *ServerKeepAliveIntervalInMinutes* property of the *ControlChannelTrigger* class. You can provide the value as a class constructor parameter called server keep-alive because the application sets its value based on the server time-out for cutting an idle connection. For example, if you know the server has a keep-alive of 20 minutes, you can set this property to 18 minutes to avoid the server cutting the connection.
- **Network keep-alive interval** Represents the value, in minutes, that the lower level TCP stack uses to maintain a connection open. In practice, this value is used by the network intermediaries (proxy, gateway, NAT and so on) to maintain an idle connection open. The application cannot set this value because it is determined automatically by lower-level network components of the TCP stack.

The last thing to do is to implement the background task and perform some operations, such as updating a tile or sending a toast when something arrives from the network. The following code implements the *Run* method imposed by the interface:

```
public sealed class ReceiveTask : IBackgroundTask
{
    public void Run(Windows.AppModel.Background.IBackgroundTaskInstance taskInstance)
    {
        var channelEventArgs =
            (IControlChannelTriggerEventDetails)taskInstance.TriggerDetails;
        var channel = channelEventArgs.ControlChannelTrigger;

        string channelId = channel.ControlChannelTriggerId;

        // Send Toast - Update Tile...

        channel.FlushTransport();
    }
}
```

The *TriggerDetails* property provides the information needed to access the raw notification and exposes the *ControlChannelTriggerId* of the *ControlChannelTrigger* class the app can use to identify the various instances of the channel. The *FlushTransport* method is required as the application sends data.

Remember that an application can receive background task triggers when the application is also in the foreground. You can provide some visual clues to the user in the current page if the application is up and running.

Thought experiment

Transferring data

In this thought experiment, apply what you've learned about this objective. You can find answers to these questions in the "Answers" section at the end of this chapter.

Your application needs to upload photos to a remote storage location in the cloud. Because photos can be greater than 10 MB, you implement a background task that performs this operation. The process works fine, but you discover a slowdown in the process with respect to the same code executed in an application thread (up to 10 times).

1. **What is the cause of the slowdown?**
2. **How can you solve the problem?**

Objective summary

- An application can use system and maintenance triggers to start a background task without needing to register the application in the lock screen.
- A lock screen application can use many other triggers, such as *TimeTrigger* and *ControlChannelTrigger*.
- Background tasks can provide progress indicators to the calling application using events and can support cancellation requests.
- If an app needs to upload or download resources, you can use the *BackgroundTransfer* classes to start the operation and let the system manage its completion.
- Background tasks have resource constraints imposed by the system. Use them for short and lightweight operations. Remember also that scheduled triggers are fired by the internal clock at regular interval.
- Applications that need to receive information from the network or send information to a remote endpoint can leverage the network triggers to avoid connection closing by intermediate devices.

Objective review

Answer the following questions to test your knowledge of the information in this objective. You can find the answers to these questions and explanations of why each answer choice is correct or incorrect in the "Answers" section at the end of this chapter.

1. What is the lowest frequency an app can schedule a maintenance trigger?
   - **A.** 2 hours
   - **B.** 15 minutes every hour
   - **C.** 7 minutes if the app is in the lock screen
   - **D.** None; there is no frequency for maintenance triggers
2. How many conditions must be met for a background task to start?
   - **A.** All the set conditions
   - **B.** Only one
   - **C.** At least 50 percent of the total conditions
   - **D.** All the set conditions if the app is running on DC power
3. How can a task be cancelled or aborted?
   - **A.** Abort the corresponding thread.
   - **B.** Implement the *OnCanceled* event.
   - **C.** Catch a *ThreadAbortedException*.
   - **D.** A background task cannot be aborted.

4. An application that needs to download a file can use which of the following? (Choose all that apply.)
   A. *BackgroundTask* class
   B. *HttpClient* class if the file is very small
   C. *BackgroundTransfer* class
   D. *BackgroundDownloader* class
   E. *BackgroundUploader* class

Objective 1.3: Create and consume WinMD components

The Windows Runtime exposes a simple way to create components that can be used by all the supported languages without any complex data marshaling. A WinMD library, called Windows Runtime Component, is a component written in one of the WinRT languages (C#, VB, C++, except JavaScript) that can be used by any supported languages.

This objective covers how to:

- Create a WinMD component in C#
- Consume a WinMD component
- Handle WinMD reference types
- Reference a WinMD component

NOTE **REFERENCE**

The content in this section is from *Build Windows 8 Apps with Microsoft Visual C# and Visual Basic Step by Step*, written by Paolo Pialorsi, Roberto Brunetti, and Luca Regnicoli (Microsoft Press, 2013).

Understanding the Windows Runtime and WinMD

Since its earliest version, Windows has provided developers with libraries and APIs to interact with the operating system. Before the release of Windows 8, those APIs and libraries were often complex and challenging to use, however. Moreover, while working in .NET Framework using C# or VB.NET, you often had to rely on COM Interop, and Win32 interoperability via Platform Invoke (P/Invoke) to directly leverage the operating system. For example, the following code sample imports a native Win32 DLL and declares the function *capCreateCaptureWindows* to be able to call it from a .NET code:

Sample of C# code

```
[DllImport("avicap32.dll", EntryPoint="capCreateCaptureWindow")]
static extern int capCreateCaptureWindow(
  string lpszWindowName, int dwStyle,
  int X, int Y, int nWidth, int nHeight,
  int hwndParent, int nID);

[DllImport("avicap32.dll")]
static extern bool capGetDriverDescription(
  int wDriverIndex,
  [MarshalAs(UnmanagedType.LPTStr)] ref string lpszName,
  int cbName,
  [MarshalAs(UnmanagedType.LPTStr)] ref string lpszVer,
  int cbVer);
```

Microsoft acknowledged the complexity of the previously existing scenario and invested in Windows 8 and the Windows Runtime to simplify the interaction with the native operating system. In fact, the Windows Runtime is a set of new APIs that were reimagined from the developer perspective to make it easier to call to the underlying APIs without the complexity of P/Invoke and Interop. Moreover, the Windows Runtime is built so that it supports the Windows 8 application development with many of the available programming languages/environments, such as HTML5/Windows Library for JavaScript (WinJS), common language runtime (CLR), and C++.

The following code illustrates how the syntax is clearer and easier to write, which makes it easier to read and maintain in the future, when leveraging the Windows Runtime. In this example, *Photo* is a Extensible Application Markup Language (XAML) image control:

Sample of C# code

```
using Windows.Media.Capture;

var camera = new CameraCaptureUI();
camera.PhotoSettings.CroppedAspectRatio = new Size(4, 3);

var file = await camera.CaptureFileAsync(CameraCaptureUIMode.Photo);

if (file != null)
{
    var bitmap = new BitmapImage() ;
    bitmap.SetSource(await file.OpenAsync(FileAccessMode.Read));
    Photo.Source = bitmap;
}
```

If you prefer to write code using WinJS and HTML5, the code will be similar to the C# version, as follows:

Sample of JavaScript code

```
var camera = new capture.CameraCaptureUI();

camera.captureFileAsync(capture.CameraCaptureUIMode.photo)
    .then(function (file) {
        if (file != null) {
            media.shareFile = file;
        }
    });
```

The Windows Runtime is a set of APIs built upon the Windows 8 operating system (see Figure 1-8) that provides direct access to all the main primitives, devices, and capabilities for any language available for developing Windows 8 apps. The Windows Runtime is available only for building Windows 8 apps. Its main goal is to unify the development experience of building a Windows 8 app, regardless of which programming language you choose.

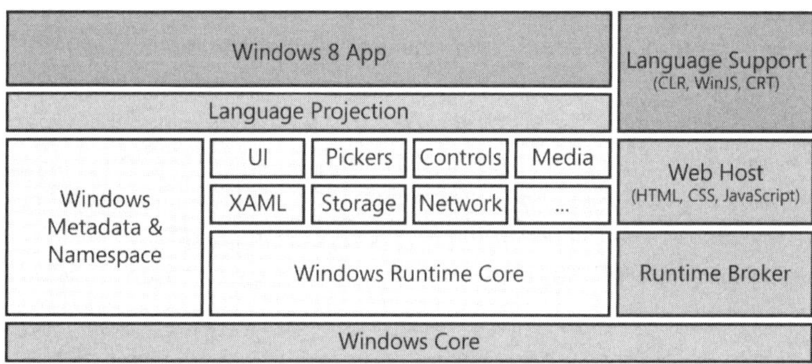

FIGURE 1-8 The Windows Runtime architecture

The Windows Runtime sits on top of the WinRT core engine, which is a set of C++ libraries that bridges the Windows Runtime with the underlying operating system. On top of the WinRT core is a set of specific libraries and types that interact with the various tools and devices available in any Windows 8 app. For example, there is a library that works with the network and another that reads and writes from storage (local or remote). There is a set of pickers to pick up items (such as files and pictures), there are several classes to leverage media services, and so on. All these types and libraries are defined in a structured set of namespaces and are described by a set of metadata called Windows Metadata (WinMD). All metadata information is based on a new file format, which is built upon the common language interface (CLI) metadata definition language (ECMA-335).

Consuming a native WinMD library

The WinRT core engine is written in C++ and internally leverages a proprietary set of data types. For example, the *HSTRING* data type represents a text value in the Windows Runtime. In addition, there are numeric types such as *INT32* and *UINT64*, enumerable collections represented by *IVector<T> interface*, enums, structures, runtime classes, and many more.

To be able to consume all this sets of data types from any supported programming language, the Windows Runtime provides a projection layer that shuttles types and data between the Windows Runtime and the target language. For example, the WinRT *HSTRING* type is translated into a *System.String* of .NET for a CLR app or to a *Platform::String* for a C++ app.

Next to this layered architecture is a Runtime Broker that acts as a bridge between the operating system and the host executing Windows 8 apps, whether they are CLR, HTML5/WinJS, or C++ apps.

Using the Windows Runtime from a CLR Windows 8 app

To better understand the architecture and philosophy behind the Windows Runtime, the example in Listing 1-14 consumes the Windows Runtime from a CLR Windows 8 app. You can test the use of the native WinMD library by creating a new project in Visual Studio 2012 and use the XAML code for the main page.

LISTING 1-14 Main page with a button control

```
<Page x:Class="WinRTFromCS.MainPage"
    xmlns="http://schemas.microsoft.com/winfx/2006/xaml/presentation"
    xmlns:x="http://schemas.microsoft.com/winfx/2006/xaml"
    xmlns:local="using:WinRTFromCS"
    xmlns:d="http://schemas.microsoft.com/expression/blend/2008"
    xmlns:mc="http://schemas.openxmlformats.org/markup-compatibility/2006"
    mc:Ignorable="d">
        <Grid Background="{StaticResource ApplicationPageBackgroundThemeBrush}">
            <StackPanel>
                <Button Click="UseCamera_Click" Content="Use Camera" />
            </StackPanel>
        </Grid>
    </Page>
```

In the event handler for the *UserCamera_Click* event, use the following code:

```
private async void UseCamera_Click(object sender, RoutedEventArgs e)
{
    var camera = new Windows.Media.Capture.CameraCaptureUI();
    var photo = await camera.CaptureFileAsync(
            Windows.Media.Capture.CameraCaptureUIMode.Photo);
}
```

Notice the *async* keyword and the two lines of code inside the event handler that instantiate an object of type *CameraCaptureUI* and invoke its *CaptureFileAsync* method.

You debug this simple code by inserting a breakpoint in the first line of code (the one starting with *var camera =*). As shown in in Figure 1-9, when the breakpoint is reached, the call stack window reveals that the app is called by external code, which is native code.

Call Stack
Name
WinRTFromCS.exe!WinRTFromCS.MainPage.ChooseFiles_Click(object sender, Windows.UI.Xaml.RoutedEventArgs e) Line 40
[External Code]

FIGURE 1-9 Call stack showing external code

If you try to step into the code of the *CameraCaptureUI* type constructor, you see that it is not possible in managed code because the type is defined in the Windows Runtime, which is unmanaged.

Using the Windows Runtime from a C++ Windows 8 app

In the example in this section, you use the WinRT Camera APIs to capture an image from a C++ Windows 8 app. First, you need to create a fresh app, using C++ this time. Assuming that you are using the same XAML code as in Listing 1-14, the event handler for the *UseCamera_Click* event instantiates the same classes and calls the same methods you saw in C# using a C++ syntax (and the C++ compiler). See Listing 1-15.

LISTING 1-15 Using the CameraCaptureUI class from C++

```
void WinRTFromCPP::MainPage::UseCamera_Click(
    Platform::Object^ sender, Windows::UI::Xaml::RoutedEventArgs^ e) {
        auto camera = ref new Windows::Media::Capture::CameraCaptureUI();
        camera->CaptureFileAsync(Windows::Media::Capture::CameraCaptureUIMode::Photo);
}
```

If you debug this code as in the previous section, the outcome is very different because you can step into the native code of the *CameraCaptureUI* constructor, as well as into the code of the *CaptureFileAsync* method.

The names of the types, as well as the names of the methods and enums, are almost the same in C# and in C++. Nevertheless, each individual language has its own syntax, code casing, and style. Through this procedure, you have gained hands-on experience with the real nature of the Windows Runtime: a multilanguage API that adapts its syntax and style to the host language and maintains a common set of behavior capabilities under the covers. What you have just seen is the result of the language projection layer defined in the architecture of the Windows Runtime.

To take this sample one step further, you can create the same example you did in C# and C++ using HTML5/WinJS. You can see that the code casing adapts to the JavaScript syntax.

The language projection of the Windows Runtime is based on a set of new metadata files: WinMD. By default, those files are stored under the path <*OS Root Path*>\System32\WinMetadata, where <*OS Root Path*> should be replaced with the Windows 8 root installation folder (normally C:\Windows). Here's a list of the default contents of the WinMD folder:

- Windows.ApplicationModel.winmd
- Windows.Data.winmd
- Windows.Devices.winmd
- Windows.Foundation.winmd
- Windows.Globalization.winmd
- Windows.Graphics.winmd
- Windows.Management.winmd

- Windows.Media.winmd
- Windows.Networking.winmd
- Windows.Security.winmd
- Windows.Storage.winmd
- Windows.System.winmd
- Windows.UI.winmd
- Windows.UI.Xaml.winmd
- Windows.Web.winmd

Note that the folder includes a Windows.Media.winmd file that contains the definition of the *CameraCaptureUI* type used in Listing 1-15.

You can inspect any WinMD file using the Intermediate Language Disassembler (IL-DASM) tool available in the Microsoft .NET software development kit (SDK), which ships with Microsoft Visual Studio 2012 and that you can also download as part of the Microsoft .NET Framework SDK. For example, Figure 1-10 shows the ILDASM tool displaying the content outline of the Windows.Media.winmd file, which contains the definition of the *CameraCaptureUI* type from Listing 1-15.

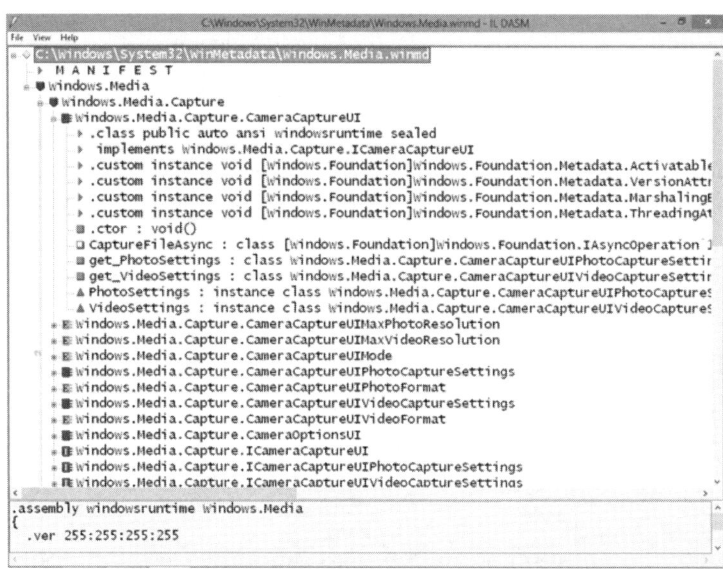

FIGURE 1-10 ILDASM displaying the outline of the Windows.Media.winmd file

The MANIFEST file listed at the top of the window defines the name, version, signature, and dependencies of the current WinMD file. Moreover, there is a hierarchy of namespaces grouping various types. Each single type defines a class from the Windows Runtime perspective. In Figure 1-10, you can clearly identify the *CaptureFileAsync* method you used in the previous example. By double-clicking the method in the outline, you can see its definition, which is not the source code of the method but instead the metadata mapping it to the native library that will be leveraged under the cover. In the following code excerpt, you can see the metadata definition of the *CaptureFileAsync* method defined for the *CameraCaptureUI* type:

```
method public hidebysig newslot virtual final
        instance class [Windows.Foundation]Windows.Foundation.IAsyncOperation`1<class
[Windows.Storage]Windows.Storage.StorageFile>
        CaptureFileAsync([in] valuetype Windows.Media.Capture.CameraCaptureUIMode mode)
runtime managed {
  .override Windows.Media.Capture.ICameraCaptureUI::CaptureFileAsync
} // end of method CameraCaptureUI::CaptureFileAsync
```

The language projection infrastructure translates this neutral definition into the proper format for the target language.

Whenever a language needs to access a WinRT type, it inspects its definition through the corresponding WinMD file and uses the *IInspectable* interface, which is implemented by any single WinRT type. The *IInspectable* interface is an evolution of the already well-known *IUnknown* interface declared many years ago in the COM world.

First, there is a type declaration inside the registry of the operating system. All the WinRT types are registered under the path HKEY_LOCAL_MACHINE\SOFTWARE\Microsoft\WindowsRuntime\ActivatableClassId.

For example, the *CameraCaptureUI* type is defined under the following path:

```
HKEY_LOCAL_MACHINE\SOFTWARE\Microsoft\WindowsRuntime\ActivatableClassId\
    Windows.Media.Capture.CameraCaptureUI
```

The registry key contains some pertinent information, including the activation type (in process or out of process), as well as the full path of the native DLL file containing the implementation of the target type.

The type implements the *IInspectable* interface, which provides the following three methods:

- ***GetIids*** Gets the interfaces that are implemented by the current WinRT class
- ***GetRuntimeClassName*** Gets the fully qualified name of the current WinRT object
- ***GetTrustLevel*** Gets the trust level of the current WinRT object

By querying the *IInspectable* interface, the language projection infrastructure of the Windows Runtime translates the type from its original declaration into the target language that will consume the type.

As illustrated in Figure 1-11, the projection occurs at compile time for a C++ app consuming the Windows Runtime and it produces native code that does not need any more access to the metadata. In the case of a CLR app (C#/VB), it happens during compilation into IL code, as well as at runtime through a runtime callable wrapper. The cost of communication between CLR and the WinRT metadata is not so different from the cost of talking with the CLR metadata in general, however. Finally, in the case of an HTML5/WinJS app, it occurs at runtime through the Chakra engine.

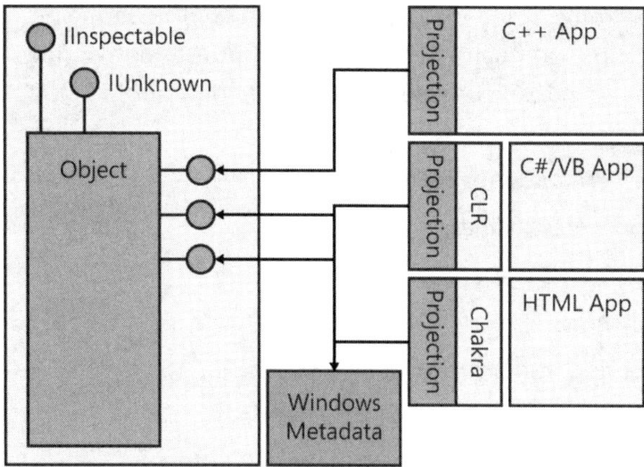

FIGURE 1-11 Projection schema

The overall architecture of the Windows Runtime is also versioning-compliant. In fact, every WinRT type is capable of supporting a future version of the operating system and/or of the WinRT engine by simply extending the available interfaces implemented and providing the information about the new extensions through the *IInspectable* interface.

To support the architecture of the Windows Runtime and the language projection infrastructure, every Windows 8 app—regardless of the programming language used to write it—runs in a standard code execution profile that is based on a limited set of capabilities. To accomplish this goal, the Windows Runtime product team defined the minimum set of APIs needed to implement a Windows 8 app. For example, the Windows 8 app profile has been deprived of the entire set of console APIs, which are not needed in a Windows 8 app. The same happened to ASP.NET, for example; the list of .NET types removed is quite long. Moreover, the Windows Runtime product team decided to remove all the old-style, complex, and/or dangerous APIs and instead provide developers with a safer and easier working environment. As an example, to access XML nodes from a classic .NET application, you have a rich set of APIs to choose from, such as the XML Document Object Model (DOM), Simple API for XML, LINQ to XML in .NET, and so on. The set also depends on which programming language you are using. In contrast, in a Windows 8 app written in CLR (C#/VB) you have only the LINQ to XML support; the XML DOM has been removed.

Furthermore, considering a Windows 8 app is an application that can execute on multiple devices (desktop PCs, tablets, ARM-based devices, and Windows Phone 8 mobile phones), all APIs specific to a particular operating system or hardware platform have been removed.

The final result is a set of APIs that are clear, simple, well-designed, and portable across multiple devices. From a .NET developer perspective, the Windows 8 app profile is a .NET 4.5 profile with a limited set of types and capabilities, which is the minimum set useful for implementing a real Windows 8 app.

Consider this: The standard .NET 4.5 profile includes more than 120 assemblies, containing more than 400 namespaces that group more than 14,000 types. In contrast, the Windows 8 app profile includes about 15 assemblies and 70 namespaces that group only about 1,000 types.

The main goals in this profile design were to do the following:

- Avoid duplication of types and/or functionalities.
- Remove APIs not applicable to Windows 8 apps.
- Remove badly designed or legacy APIs.
- Make it easy to port existing .NET applications to Windows 8 apps.
- Keep .NET developers comfortable with the Windows 8 app profile.

For example, the Windows Communication Foundation (WCF) APIs exist, but you can use WCF only to consume services, therefore leveraging a reduced set of communication bindings. You cannot use WCF in a Windows 8 app to host a service—for security reasons and for portability reasons.

Creating a WinMD library

The previous sections contained some information about the WinRT architecture and the WinMD infrastructure, which enables the language projection of the Windows Runtime to make a set of APIs available to multiple programming languages. In this section, you will learn how to create a library of APIs of your own, making that library available to all other Windows 8 apps through the same projection environment used by the Windows Runtime.

Internally, the WinRT types in your component can use any .NET Framework functionality that's allowed in a Windows 8 app. Externally, however, your types must adhere to a simple and strict set of requirements:

- The fields, parameters, and return values of all the public types and members in your component must be WinRT types.
- Public structures cannot have any members other than public fields, and those fields must be value types or strings.
- Public classes must be *sealed* (*NotInheritable* in Visual Basic). If your programming model requires polymorphism, you can create a public interface and implement that interface on the classes that must be polymorphic. The only exceptions are XAML controls.
- All public types must have a root namespace that matches the assembly name, and the assembly name must not begin with "Windows."

To verify this behavior, you need to create a new WinMD file.

To create a WinMD library, create a new project choosing the Windows Runtime Component–provided template. The project outputs not only a DLL but also a WinMD file for sharing the library with any Windows 8 app written with any language.

You must also rename the Class1.cs file in SampleUtility.cs and rename the contained class. Then add this method to the class and the corresponding *using* statement for the *System.Text.RegularExpressions* namespace.

Sample of C# code

```
public Boolean IsMailAddress(String email)
{
    Regex regexMail = new Regex(@"\b[A-Z0-9._%+-]+@[A-Z0-9.-]+\.[A-Z]{2,4}\b");
        return(regexMail.IsMatch(email));
}
```

Build the project and check the output directory. You will find the classic bin/debug (or Release) subfolder containing a .winmd file for the project you create. You can open it with ILDASM to verify its content.

Add a new project to the same solution using the Blank App (XAML) template from the Visual C++ group to create a new C++ Windows Store application.

Add a reference to the WinMD library in the Project section of the Add Reference dialog box, and then add the following XAML code in the *Grid* control:

Sample of XAML code

```
<StackPanel>
    <Button Click="ConsumeWinMD_Click" Content="Consume WinMD Library" />
</StackPanel>
```

Create the event handler for the click event in the code-behind file using the following code:

Sample of C++ code

```
void WinMDCPPConsumer::MainPage::ConsumeWinMD_Click(Platform::Object^ sender,
    Windows::UI::Xaml::RoutedEventArgs^ e) {
        auto utility = ref new WinMDCSLibrary::SampleUtility();
        bool result = utility->IsMailAddress("paolo@devleap.com");
}
```

Build the solution and place a breakpoint in the *IsMailAddress* method of the WinMD library and then start the C++ project in debug mode. You might need to select Mixed (Managed and Native) in the debugging properties of the consumer project, as shown in Figure 1-12.

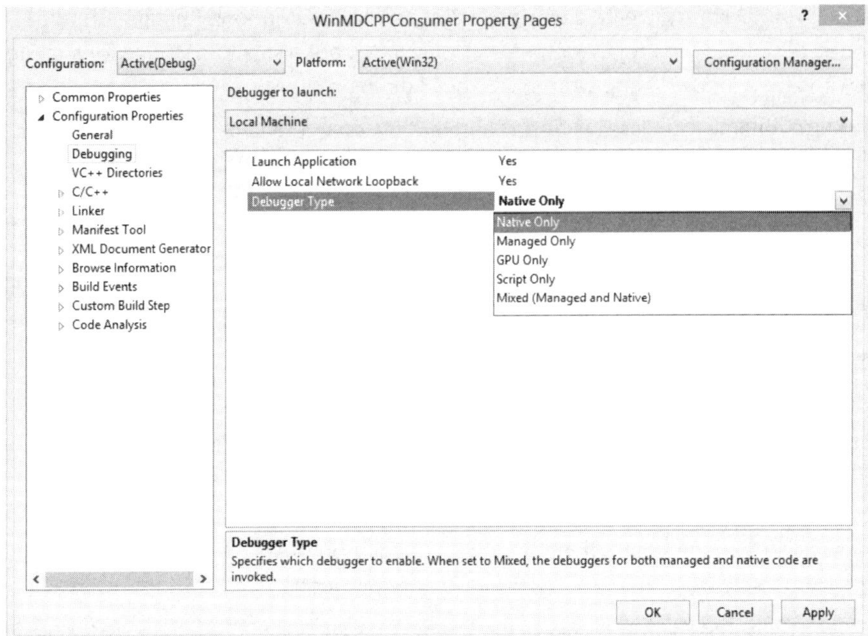

FIGURE 1-12 Debugger settings to debug mixed code

As you can verify, the debugger can step into the WinMD library from a C++ Windows Store application.

You can also verify compatibility with HTML/WinJS project creating a new project based on the Windows Store templates for JavaScript (Blank App).

Reference the WinMD library as you did in the C++ section and add an HTML button that will call the code using JavaScript:

Sample of HTML code

```
<body>
    <p><button id="consumeWinMDLibrary">Consume WinMD Library</button></p>
</body>
```

Open the Default.js file, which is in the js folder of the project, and place the following event handler inside the file, just before the *app.start()* method invocation:

Sample of JavaScript code

```
function consumeWinMD(eventInfo) {
    var utility = new WinMDCSLibrary.SampleUtility();
    var result = utility.isMailAddress("paolo@devleap.com");
}
```

Notice that the case of the *IsMailAddress* method, defined in C#, has been translated into *isMailAddress* in JavaScript thanks to the language projection infrastructure provided by the Windows Runtime.

Insert the following lines of code into the function associated with the *app.onactivated* event, just before the end of the *if* statement:

```
// Retrieve the button and register the event handler.
var consumeWinMDLibrary = document.getElementById("consumeWinMDLibrary");
consumeWinMDLibrary.addEventListener("click", consumeWinMD, false);
```

Listing 1-16 shows how the complete code of the Default.js file should look after you make the edits.

LISTING 1-16 Complete code for the Default.js file

```
// For an introduction to the Blank template, see the following documentation:
// http://go.microsoft.com/fwlink/?LinkId=232509
(function () {
    "use strict";

    WinJS.Binding.optimizeBindingReferences = true;

    var app = WinJS.Application;
    var activation = Windows.ApplicationModel.Activation;

    app.onactivated = function (args) {
        if (args.detail.kind === activation.ActivationKind.launch) {
            if (args.detail.previousExecutionState !==
                activation.ApplicationExecutionState.terminated) {
                // TODO: This application has been newly launched. Initialize
                // your application here.
            } else {
                // TODO: This application has been reactivated from suspension.
                // Restore application state here.
            }
            args.setPromise(WinJS.UI.processAll());

            // Retrieve the button and register our event handler.
            var consumeWinMDLibrary = document.getElementById("consumeWinMDLibrary");
            consumeWinMDLibrary.addEventListener("click", consumeWinMD, false);
        }
    };

    app.oncheckpoint = function (args) {
        // TODO: This application is about to be suspended. Save any state
        // that needs to persist across suspensions here. You might use the
        // WinJS.Application.sessionState object, which is automatically
        // saved and restored across suspension. If you need to complete an
        // asynchronous operation before your application is suspended, call
        // args.setPromise().
    };

    function consumeWinMD(eventInfo) {
        var utility = new WinMDCSLibrary.SampleUtility();
        var result = utility.isMailAddress("paolo@devleap.com");
    }

    app.start();
})();
```

Place a breakpoint in the *IsMailAddress* method or method call, and start debugging, configuring Mixed (Managed and Native) for the consumer project and verify that you can step into the WinMD library.

Thought experiment

Using libraries

In this thought experiment, apply what you've learned about this objective. You can find answers to these questions in the "Answers" section at the end of this chapter.

In one of your applications, you created classes that leverage some WinRT features, such as a webcam, pickers, and other device-related features. You decide to create a library to enable other applications to use this reusable functionality.

1. **Should you create a C# library or a WinMD library, and why?**
2. **What are at least three requirements for creating a WinMD library?**

Objective summary

- Visual Studio provides a template for building a WinMD library for all supported languages.
- Language projection enables you to use the syntax of the application language to use a WinMD library.
- The field, parameters, and return type of all the public type of a WinMD library must be WinRT types.

Objective review

Answer the following questions to test your knowledge of the information in this objective. You can find the answers to these questions and explanations of why each answer choice is correct or incorrect in the "Answers" section at the end of this chapter.

1. What do public classes of a WinMD library have to be?
   - **A.** Sealed
   - **B.** Marked as *abstract*
   - **C.** Implementing the correct interface
   - **D.** None of the above

2. Portable classes in a WinMD library can use which of the following?
   - **A.** All the .NET 4.5 Framework classes
   - **B.** Only a subset of the C++ classes
   - **C.** Only WinRT classes
   - **D.** Only classes written in C++
3. What is a possible call path?
   - **A.** A WinJS application can instantiate a C++ WinMD class.
   - **B.** A C++ application can instantiate a C# WinMD class.
   - **C.** A C# application can instantiate a WinJS WinMD.
   - **D.** All of the above.

Chapter summary

- Background tasks can run when the application is not in the foreground.
- Background tasks can be triggered by system, maintenance, time, network, and user events.
- A task can be executed based on multiple conditions.
- Lengthy download and upload operations can be done by using transfer classes.
- The Windows Runtime enables applications written in different languages to share functionality.

Answers

This section contains the solutions to the thought experiments and the answers to lesson review questions in this chapter.

Objective 1.1: Thought experiment

1. When not used by the user, your application is put in a suspended state by the Windows Runtime and, if the system needs resources, it, can be terminated. This is the most common problem that might explain why the app sometimes does not clean all data. The application cannot rely on background threads to perform operations because the application can be terminated if not in the foreground.
2. To solve the problem, you need to implement a background task using the provided classes and register the task during application launch. Because the operations are lengthy, it is important to use a deferral. Do not forget to define the declaration in the application manifest.

Objective 1.1: Review

1. **Correct answer:** C
   - **A. Incorrect:** You cannot schedule a time trigger every minute. The minimum frequency is 15 minutes. Moreover, polling is not a good technique when an event-based technique is available.
   - **B. Incorrect:** The *InternetAvailable* event fires when an Internet connection becomes available. It does not tell the application about changes in the network state.
   - **C. Correct:** *NetworkStateChange* is the correct event. The *false* value for the *oneShot* parameter enables the application to be informed every time the state of the network changes.
   - **D. Incorrect:** *NetworkStateChange* is the correct event, but the value of *true* for the *oneShot* parameter fires the event just one time.
2. **Correct answers:** A, B, C
   - **A. Correct:** The task has to be declared in the application manifest.
   - **B. Correct:** The task can be created by the *BackgroundTaskBuilder* class.
   - **C. Correct:** A trigger must be set to inform the system on the events that will fire the task.
   - **D. Incorrect:** There is no need to use a toast to enable a background task. You can use it, but this is optional.

3. **Correct answer:** C
   - **A. Incorrect:** There is no specific task in the Windows Runtime library to fire a task just once.
   - **B. Incorrect:** Every task can be scheduled to run just once.
   - **C. Correct:** Many triggers offer a second parameter in the constructor to enable this feature.
   - **D. Incorrect:** You can create different tasks to be run once. For example, a task based on network changes can run just once.

Objective 1.2: Thought experiment

1. A background task has network and CPU quotas. Tasks have to be lightweight and short-lived, and they cannot be scheduled to run continuously. You have to rely on the specific class of the *BackgroundTransfer* namespace to upload and download files in the background.
2. To solve the problem, you need to use the *BackgroundUploader* class and declare the use of the network in the application manifest.

Objective 1.2: Review

1. **Correct answer:** B
   - **A. Incorrect:** You can schedule a task to run every 15 minutes.
   - **B. Correct:** Fifteen minutes is the internal clock frequency. You cannot schedule a task to run at a lower interval.
   - **C. Incorrect:** You can schedule a task to run every 15 minutes.
   - **D. Incorrect:** You can schedule a task to run every 15 minutes.
2. **Correct answer:** A
   - **A. Correct:** All assigned conditions need to be met to start a task.
   - **B. Incorrect:** All assigned conditions must return *true*.
   - **C. Incorrect:** All assigner conditions need to be met to start a task.
   - **D. Incorrect:** There is no difference of condition evaluation if the device in on AC or DC power.

3. **Correct answers:** B

   A. **Incorrect:** The application has no reference to background task threads.

   B. **Correct:** You need to implement the *OnCanceled* event that represents the cancellation request from the system.

   C. **Incorrect:** There is no request to abort the thread during the cancellation request.

   D. **Incorrect:** The system can make a cancellation request.

4. **Correct answers:** B, D

   A. **Incorrect:** This class has no methods to download files.

   B. **Correct:** To download small resources, the *HttpClient* is the preferred class.

   C. **Incorrect:** The *BackgroundTransfer* is a namespace.

   D. **Correct:** The *BackgroundDownloader* is the class to request a lengthy download operation.

   E. **Incorrect:** The *BackgroundUploader* class cannot download files.

Objective 1.3: Thought experiment

1. Although you can choose a traditional C# library that is suited for reuse by other C# applications, a traditional library cannot be reused by applications written in other languages. If you create a WinMD library, you can reuse the exposed features in applications written in other languages. Moreover, you can give the library functionalities that work in the background using background tasks.

2. To create a WinMD library, you have to follow some simple requirements:

   A. The fields, parameters, and return values of all the public types and members in your component must be WinRT types.

   B. Public structures cannot have any members other than public fields, and those fields must be value types or strings.

   C. Public classes must be sealed. If your programming model requires polymorphism, you can create a public interface and implement that interface on the classes that must be polymorphic. The only exceptions are XAML controls.

   D. All public types must have a root namespace that matches the assembly name, and the assembly name must not begin with "Windows."

Objective 1.3: Review

1. **Correct answer:** A
   - **A. Correct:** A class must be sealed.
   - **B. Incorrect:** There is no need to mark the class as abstract.
   - **C. Incorrect:** There is no interface required.
   - **D. Incorrect:** Answer choice A is correct.
2. **Correct answer:** C
   - **A. Incorrect:** You do not have access to all the .NET 4.5 classes because they simply are not available for a Windows Store app.
   - **B. Incorrect:** You cannot access C++ classes directly.
   - **C. Correct:** You can access WinRT classes.
   - **D. Incorrect:** WinMD library can be written in C# and Visual Basic, not only in C++.
3. **Correct answers:** A, B, D
   - **A. Correct:** A WinJS app can access C++ classes because they are wrapped in a WinMD library.
   - **B. Correct:** A C++ app can access C# classes because they are wrapped in a WinMD library.
   - **C. Incorrect:** A WinMD library cannot be written in JavaScript.
   - **D. Correct:** Answer choice C is incorrect.

CHAPTER 2

Discover and interact with devices

In this chapter, you learn how to capture media and audio using the provided standard user interface (UI) and from code. You also learn how to get data from sensors such as global positioning system (GPS), and how to discover device capabilities.

Objectives in this chapter:

- Objective 2.1: Capture media with the camera and microphone
- Objective 2.2: Get data from sensors
- Objective 2.3: Enumerate and discover device capabilities

Objective 2.1: Capture media with the camera and microphone

The Windows Runtime (WinRT) provides simple application programming interfaces (APIs) to interact with a device's camera and microphone from .NET, C++, or JavaScript code. As with other WinRT APIs, you do not need references to class libraries. Microsoft Visual Studio 2012 automatically adds the .NET for Windows Store app reference when you create a new Windows Store app project.

This objective covers how to:

- Use *CameraCaptureUI* to capture pictures or video
- Use *MediaCapture* to capture pictures, video, or audio
- Configure camera settings
- Set media formats
- Handle media capture events

Using *CameraCaptureUI* to capture pictures or video

This section is dedicated to the most simple and effective way to use the WinRT Webcam APIs to capture a photo or video. You need just a few lines of code to configure some settings and you can let the system manage all the details. In the next section, you will learn how to access the webcam at a lower level.

There are two ways in which your applications can interact with a camera:

- **By code** Leverages the WinRT APIs to gain complete control over the entire flow of operations.
- **By using the provided user interface** Lets the runtime use the standard camera control and manages many of the capturing details.

In other words, if you need complete control over the capturing operation, want to manage the stream directly, want to perform some operations during the recording, or simply want to create a custom user interface (UI), you need some lines of codes that interact with the *MediaCapture* APIs. On the contrary, if you just want to take a picture or a video from the webcam, you can use the provided *CameraCaptureUI* API and let the system manage all the details.

Using a standard UI from your application is important. The user will see the common UI that every Windows Store application uses for capturing photos and video. Remember that the WinRT APIs can be used by any Windows Store app written in any language; the *CameraCaptureUI* class provides a consistent UI for all of them.

Add the Extensible Application Markup Language (XAML) shown in Listing 2-1 to your MainPage.xaml page as a reference to create a *Button* control that fires the code to show the camera standard UI and an *Image* control to show the captured photo.

LISTING 2-1 MainPage.xaml with a *Button* and an *Image* control

```
<Page x:Class="Camera.MainPage"
    xmlns="http://schemas.microsoft.com/winfx/2006/xaml/presentation"
    xmlns:x="http://schemas.microsoft.com/winfx/2006/xaml"
    xmlns:local="using:Camera"
    xmlns:d="http://schemas.microsoft.com/expression/blend/2008"
    xmlns:mc="http://schemas.openxmlformats.org/markup-compatibility/2006"
    mc:Ignorable="d">
    <Grid Background="{StaticResource ApplicationPageBackgroundThemeBrush}">
        <StackPanel Orientation="Horizontal">
            <Button Click="CapturePhoto_Click" Content="Capture Photo"/>
            <Image x:Name="takenImage" Height="900" />
         </StackPanel>
    </Grid>
</Page>
```

The page contains a *Button* control that lets the system call the *CapturePhoto_Click* method in Listing 2-2. In addition, an *Image* control named *takenImage* contains the captured stream if the user decides to take a photo from the standard camera UI.

LISTING 2-2 Code to show the camera UI

```
using System;
using System.Collections.Generic;
using System.IO;
using System.Linq;
using Windows.Foundation;
using Windows.Foundation.Collections;
using Windows.Media.Capture;
using Windows.Storage;
using Windows.UI.Popups;
using Windows.UI.Xaml;
using Windows.UI.Xaml.Controls;
using Windows.UI.Xaml.Controls.Primitives;
using Windows.UI.Xaml.Data;
using Windows.UI.Xaml.Input;
using Windows.UI.Xaml.Media;
using Windows.UI.Xaml.Media.Imaging;
using Windows.UI.Xaml.Navigation;

// The Blank Page item template is documented at
// http://go.microsoft.com/fwlink/?LinkId=234238

namespace Camera
{
    /// <summary>
    /// An empty page that can be used on its own or navigated to within a Frame.
    /// </summary>
    public sealed partial class MainPage : Page
    {
        public MainPage()
        {
            this.InitializeComponent();
        }

        /// <summary>
        /// Invoked when this page is about to be displayed in a Frame.
        /// </summary>
        /// <param name="e">Event data that describes how this page was reached.
        /// The Parameter property is typically used to configure the page.</param>

        protected override void OnNavigatedTo(NavigationEventArgs e)
        {
        }

        private async void CapturePhoto_Click(object sender, RoutedEventArgs e)
        {
            var camera = new CameraCaptureUI();
            var img = await camera.CaptureFileAsync(CameraCaptureUIMode.Photo);
            if (img != null)
            {
                var stream = await img.OpenAsync(FileAccessMode.Read);
                var bitmap = new BitmapImage();
                bitmap.SetSource(stream);
                takenImage.Source = bitmap;
            }
```

```
            else
            {
                var dialog = new MessageDialog("The user has not taken a photo");
                dialog.ShowAsync();
            }
        }
    }
}
```

The first line of code in the *CapturePhoto_Click* event handler creates an instance of the *CameraCaptureUI* class. This class is responsible for managing the UI for capturing photos and videos in the Windows Runtime.

The second line waits for the completion of the *CaptureFileAsync* method, which captures the stream asynchronously. This method prevents blocking the UI thread when the user is in front of the camera UI. The method accepts the *CameraCaptureUIMode* parameter, which can assume the value of *Photo*, *Video*, or *PhotoOrVideo*.

NOTE **WEBCAM**

In the scenario presented in this section, the webcam will be activated to take a photo.

The *CaptureFileAsync* method returns an instance of the *StorageFile* WinRT class representing the stream taken from the camera as a file.

MORE INFO **ACCESSING FILES AND STREAMS**

You can learn more about accessing files and streams in Chapter 5, "Manage data and security."

The stream, represented by the file, can be opened using the *OpenAsync* method that returns an instance of *IRandomAccessStream* interface. Every class that implements this interface can be used to set the source for a *BitmapImage* object.

Finally, the instance of the bitmap can be assigned to the *Source* property of the XAML *Image* control in Listing 2-1.

If you run the application at this point and click the Capture Photo button, the webcam screen occupies the entire screen, but you cannot take a photo. The result is shown in Figure 2-1.

FIGURE 2-1 *CameraCaptureUI* used without capability declaration

The message that displays informs you that the application needs the user's permission to use the webcam. The reason is simple: you cannot use the Webcam API without declaring the Webcam capability in the application manifest. If you do not have a camera attached to your PC, the application will first ask you to connect the device. This message is part of the standard UI and is displayed in the user's language.

You need to define the use of the webcam in the application manifest by using the Visual Studio App Manifest Designer, shown in Figure 2-2. Note that Visual Studio 2012 automatically adds the Internet (Client) capability.

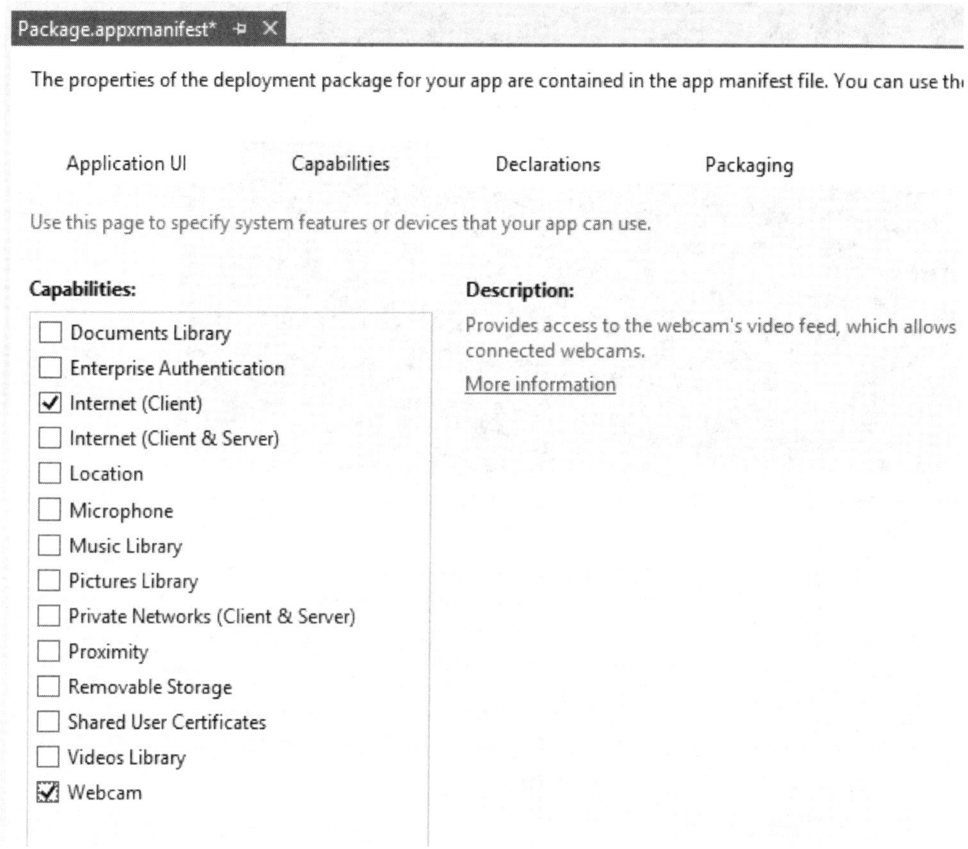

Package.appxmanifest* ⊕ ✕

The properties of the deployment package for your app are contained in the app manifest file. You can use th

Application UI Capabilities Declarations Packaging

Use this page to specify system features or devices that your app can use.

Capabilities:

- [ ] Documents Library
- [ ] Enterprise Authentication
- [x] Internet (Client)
- [ ] Internet (Client & Server)
- [ ] Location
- [ ] Microphone
- [ ] Music Library
- [ ] Pictures Library
- [ ] Private Networks (Client & Server)
- [ ] Proximity
- [ ] Removable Storage
- [ ] Shared User Certificates
- [ ] Videos Library
- [x] Webcam

Description:

Provides access to the webcam's video feed, which allows connected webcams.

More information

FIGURE 2-2 Selecting the Webcam capability in the Visual Studio App Manifest Designer

You can also add capabilities in the Package.appxmanifest XML file, as shown in Listing 2-3.

LISTING 2-3 Package.appxmanifest XML file

```
<?xml version="1.0" encoding="utf-8"?>
<Package xmlns="http://schemas.microsoft.com/appx/2010/manifest">
  <Identity Name="70e52984-9c4f-4cb1-acbb-c5b1d9f17618" Publisher="CN=Roberto"
      Version="1.0.0.0" />
  <Properties>
    <DisplayName>Camera</DisplayName>
    <PublisherDisplayName>Roberto</PublisherDisplayName>
    <Logo>Assets\StoreLogo.png</Logo>
  </Properties>
  <Prerequisites>
    <OSMinVersion>6.2.1</OSMinVersion>
    <OSMaxVersionTested>6.2.1</OSMaxVersionTested>
  </Prerequisites>
  <Resources>
    <Resource Language="x-generate" />
  </Resources>
```

```
  <Applications>
    <Application Id="App" Executable="$targetnametoken$.exe" EntryPoint="Camera.App">
      <VisualElements DisplayName="Camera" Logo="Assets\Logo.png"
          SmallLogo="Assets\SmallLogo.png" Description="Camera" ForegroundText="light"
          BackgroundColor="#464646">
        <DefaultTile ShowName="allLogos" />
        <SplashScreen Image="Assets\SplashScreen.png" />
      </VisualElements>
    </Application>
  </Applications>
  <Capabilities>
    <Capability Name="internetClient" />
    <DeviceCapability Name="webcam" />
  </Capabilities>
</Package>
```

The file declares the Webcam device capability in the <DeviceCapability> node of the <Capabilities> section node. Although Visual Studio 2012 automatically adds the InternetClient capability, you can remove it if the app will not use the Internet, as is the case with this sample app.

If you run the application now, the Windows Runtime presents a dialog box requesting the user's permission to use the webcam, as shown in Figure 2-3. The user can select only Allow or Block, and cannot use other buttons. This is one of the standard UIs and message dialog boxes of the Windows Runtime.

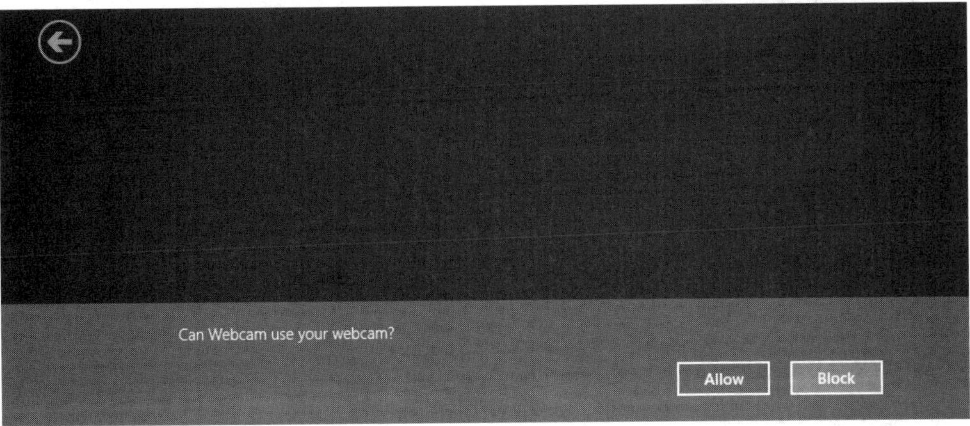

FIGURE 2-3 The standard UI for requesting user permission

To recap, the application needs to declare its capabilities in the application manifest, but the user has to provide permission to the application explicitly for each capability.

If the user blocks the webcam, the corresponding feature cannot be used. In the sample application, the webcam shows a black screen in which the user cannot do anything but click the Back button to return to the application. The system retains the user's choice forever. However, users can remove a specific permission at any time for any application or restore a permission at any time.

You can deny the permission using the *Block* button. The webcam UI will close and the value returned to the code will be *null*. The code presented in Listing 2-1 can handle this situation, displaying a message dialog box that informs the user that no photo has been taken.

As stated, the system remembers the user's choice. If the user tries to open the camera again, the message in Figure 2-1 displays again because the application has no permission to use the device.

To restore a permission, open the application's settings in the Windows 8 charms bar. (Move the mouse to the lower-right corner to open the charms bar and select Settings.) A panel appears on the right of the screen with some settings in the lower section, such as the network joined by the system, the volume level, the language, and a button to turn off/sleep/restart the system.

In the upper section of the panel, you can see the application's name, current user, version, and the permissions for the webcam (shown in Figure 2-4).

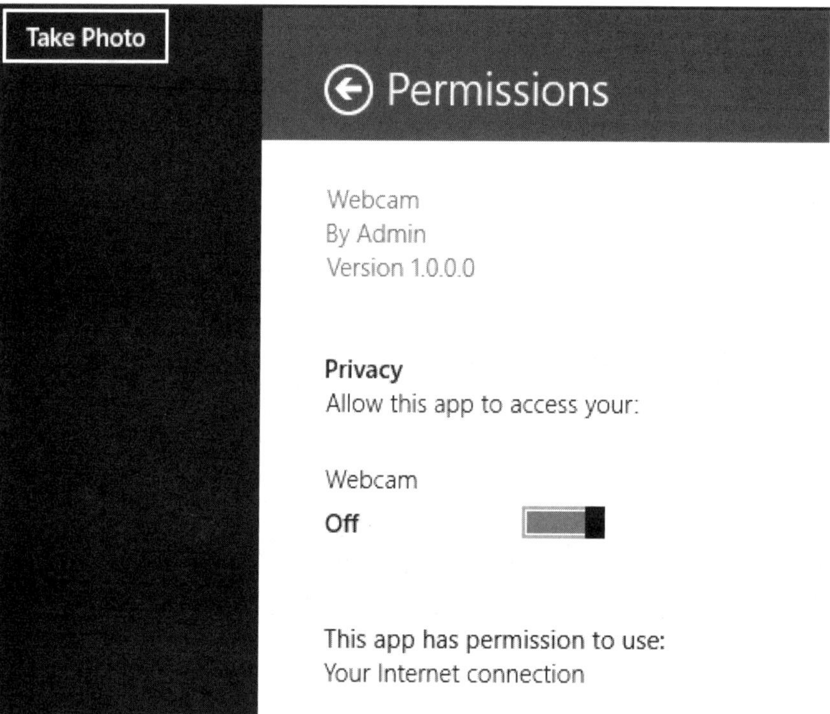

FIGURE 2-4 Settings for the application

The lower section of the pane presents the capabilities requested in the application manifest. Switching the slider to On immediately gives the application permission to use the webcam. The application presents the lens image, as shown in Figure 2-5.

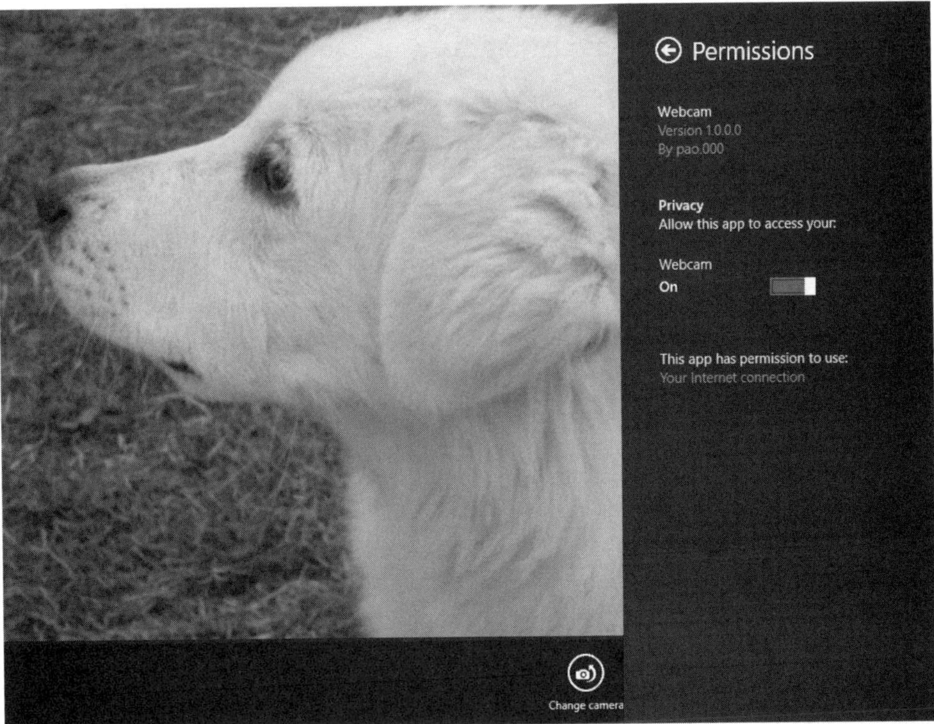

FIGURE 2-5 Standard UI for an enabled webcam

You can remove the permission at any time; if you move the slider to the Off position, the image will be blanked.

The standard UI enables you to choose some settings using the provided buttons. To take a photo, just tap the screen on a tablet or touch screen–enabled PC, or use the left mouse button directly on the image. The camera enables you to crop the photo on the fly and if you accept the shot, the image is returned to the code as an *IRandomAccessStream* interface.

The code in Listing 2-1 tests the result; if not *null*, the image is provided as the source for the *Image* control.

The *CameraCaptureUI* enables you to define some initial settings to be used to take pictures. For example, the following code sets the *AllowCropping* to *true* to enable the user to crop the image on the fly, sets the image format to *Jpeg*, and sets the maximum resolution:

```
camera.PhotoSettings.AllowCropping = true;
camera.PhotoSettings.Format = CameraCaptureUIPhotoFormat.Jpeg;
camera.PhotoSettings.MaxResolution = CameraCaptureUIMaxPhotoResolution.HighestAvailable;
```

The enumeration for the *CameraCaptureUIPhotoFormat* can be *Jpeg*, *JpegXR*, or *Png*. The values of the *CameraCaptureUIMaxPhotoResolution* enumeration and their descriptions are shown in Listing 2-4.

LISTING 2-4 *CameraCaptureUIMaxPhotoResolution* enumeration

```
#region Assembly Windows.winmd, v255.255.255.255
// C:\Program Files (x86)\Windows
// Kits\8.0\References\CommonConfiguration\Neutral\Windows.winmd
#endregion

using System;
using Windows.Foundation.Metadata;

namespace Windows.Media.Capture
{
    // Summary:
    //     Determines the highest resolution the user can select for capturing photos.
    [Version(100794368)]
    public enum CameraCaptureUIMaxPhotoResolution
    {
        // Summary:
        //     The user can select any resolution.
        HighestAvailable = 0,
        //
        // Summary:
        //     The user can select resolutions up to 320 X 240, or a similar 16:9
        //     resolution.
        VerySmallQvga = 1,
        //
        // Summary:
        //     The user can select resolutions up to 320 X 240, or a similar 16:9
        //     resolution.
        SmallVga = 2,
        //
        // Summary:
        //     The user can select resolutions up to 1024 X 768, or a similar 16:9
        //     resolution.
        MediumXga = 3,
        //
        // Summary:
        //     The user can select resolutions up to 1920 X 1080, or a similar 4:3
        //     resolution.
        Large3M = 4,
        //
        // Summary:
        //     The user can select resolutions up to 5MP.
        VeryLarge5M = 5,
    }
}
```

After a photo has been taken, you can examine the *CroppedAspectRatio* and the *CroppedSizeInPixels* properties of the *PhotoSettings* properties of the *CameraCaptureUI* instance. They tell you the aspect ratio of the cropping area used by the user and the relative size.

To record a video using the standard UI, set the parameter of the *CaptureFileAsync* method of the *CameraCaptureUI* to *CameraCaptureUIMode.Video,* as shown in the following code:

```
var camera = new CameraCaptureUI();
var img = await camera.CaptureFileAsync(CameraCaptureUIMode.Video);
```

You can also set the value of the parameter to *CameraCaptureUIMode* or *PhotoOrVideo* to enable the user to choose between the two.

The video mode can be configured using the *VideoSettings* property of the *CameraCaptureUI* class, as follows:

```
var camera = new CameraCaptureUI();

camera.VideoSettings.AllowTrimming = true;
camera.VideoSettings.Format = CameraCaptureUIVideoFormat.Mp4;
camera.VideoSettings.MaxDurationInSeconds = 30;
camera.VideoSettings.MaxResolution = CameraCaptureUIMaxVideoResolution.HighDefinition;
```

The *CameraCaptureUIVideoFormat* property can be set to *Mp4* or *Wmv*, and the *MaxResolution* property can be set to a different video quality. Video resolutions are explained by the corresponding enum definition:

```
using System;
using Windows.Foundation.Metadata;

namespace Windows.Media.Capture
{
    // Summary:
    //     Determines the highest resolution the user can select for capturing video.
    [Version(100794368)]
    public enum CameraCaptureUIMaxVideoResolution
    {
        // Summary:
        //     The user can select any resolution.
        HighestAvailable = 0,
        //
        // Summary:
        //     The user can select resolutions up to low definition resolutions.
        LowDefinition = 1,
        //
        // Summary:
        //     The user can select resolutions up to standard definition resolutions.
        StandardDefinition = 2,
        //
        // Summary:
        //     The user can select resolutions up to high definition resolutions.
        HighDefinition = 3,
    }
}
```

If you also want to record the audio, you need to select the *Microphone* capability in the application manifest.

If you forget to catch the exception in your code and the webcam does not function or the driver is not correctly installed, you will receive the exception shown in Figure 2-6.

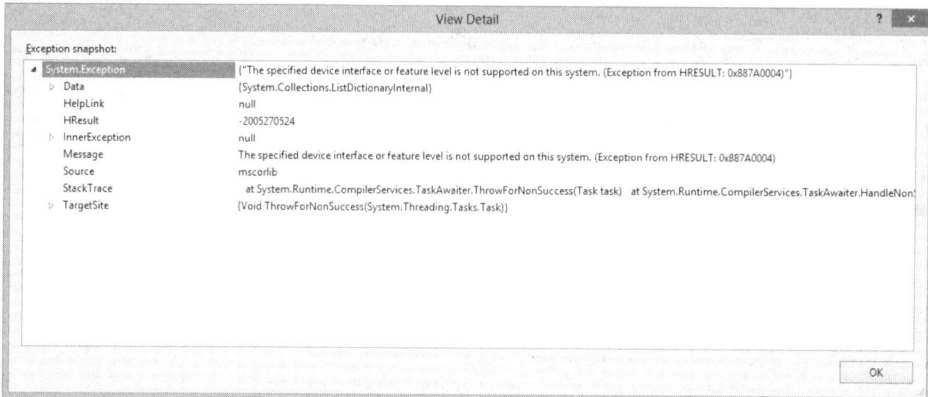

FIGURE 2-6 Exception properties for a malfunctioning device

Using *MediaCapture* to capture pictures, video, or audio

As mentioned at the beginning of this section, sometimes you might want more control over the flow of the capture operation. Perhaps you want to perform some sort of operation directly on the data stream or during the recording phase, or you simply want to create a custom UI rather than using the standard interface.

In this case, you can leverage the *MediaCapture* APIs (exposed by the same *Windows.Media.Capture* namespace of its companion class, *CameraCaptureUI*) to achieve more fine-grained control over the entire process of audio and video recording.

Listing 2-5 shows sample code that takes advantage of the *MediaCapture* class to display the webcam feed on the screen. Before using the sample code presented in this section, you need to add a few declarations to your application manifest. Because the sample code needs to access both the camera and the microphone, if present, the two capabilities you must declare are the Webcam and the Microphone capabilities in the Package.appxmanifest file of your app. Because the sample code saves the recorded video in the user's Videos library, you also need to declare the corresponding Videos Library capability as well. In the listing, note the *_mediaCapture* variable definition at the page level and its use in the various methods presented.

LISTING 2-5 Using the *MediaCapture* class to display a video stream from the webcam

```
private MediaCapture _mediaCapture;

private async void StartDevice_Click(object sender, RoutedEventArgs e)
{
```

```
    try
    {
        this._mediaCapture = new MediaCapture();

        this._mediaCapture.RecordLimitationExceeded +=
            MediaCapture_RecordLimitationExceeded;
        this._mediaCapture.Failed += MediaCapture_Failed;

        await this._mediaCapture.InitializeAsync();

    }
    catch (UnauthorizedAccessException ex)
    {
        ErrorMessageTextBlock.Text = "This app needs your permission to use the webcam";
    }
    catch (Exception ex)
    {
        ErrorMessageTextBlock.Text = "Unable to initialize the webcam";
    }
}

private async void MediaCapture_Failed(MediaCapture sender,
    MediaCaptureFailedEventArgs errorEventArgs)
{
    await Dispatcher.RunAsync(Windows.UI.Core.CoreDispatcherPriority.Normal, () =>
    {
        ErrorMessageTextBlock.Text = "Media capture failed!";
    });
}

private async void MediaCapture_RecordLimitationExceeded(MediaCapture sender)
{
    await this._mediaCapture.StopRecordAsync();

    await Dispatcher.RunAsync(Windows.UI.Core.CoreDispatcherPriority.Normal, () =>
    {
        ErrorMessageTextBlock.Text = "Record limitation exceeded!";
    });
}
```

After the *MediaCapture* class has been instantiated in the *StartDevice_Click* method, the code subscribes the two events exposed by the *MediaCapture* class: the *Failed* event, which is raised when an error occurs during media capture; and the *RecordLimitationExceeded* event, which is raised when the record limit is exceeded. (In Windows 8, the current record limit is three hours.)

EXAM TIP

When the *RecordLimitationExceeded* event is raised, the app is expected to finalize the file being recorded by calling the *StopRecordingAsync* method. If the file is not finalized, the capture engine will stop sending samples to the file.

The code then calls the *StartAsync* method of the *MediaCapture* class to initialize the capture device. The first time the app is executed, the *InitializeAsync* displays a consent prompt to get the user's permission to access the camera or the microphone. (For this reason, the *InitializeAsync* method should be called from the main UI thread of your app.)

After the device has been initialized, you can use the following code to start the camera stream:

```
private async void StartPreview_Click(object sender, RoutedEventArgs e)
{
    if (this._mediaCapture != null)
    {
        try
        {
            PreviewElement.Source = this._mediaCapture;
            await this._mediaCapture.StartPreviewAsync();
        }
        catch (Exception ex)
        {
            // exception handling
        }
    }
}
```

In the *StartPreview_Click* button click's event handler, the code sets the *Source* property of the *CaptureElement* XAML control to point to the current *MediaCapture* object and then starts the video preview by calling the *StartPreviewAsync* method of the *MediaCapture* instance. (The *MediaCapture* class also exposes a *StartPreviewToCustomSinkAsync* method, in two different versions, to send the preview to a custom media sink.) At this point, your app can display the stream from the camera on the screen, as shown in Figure 2-7.

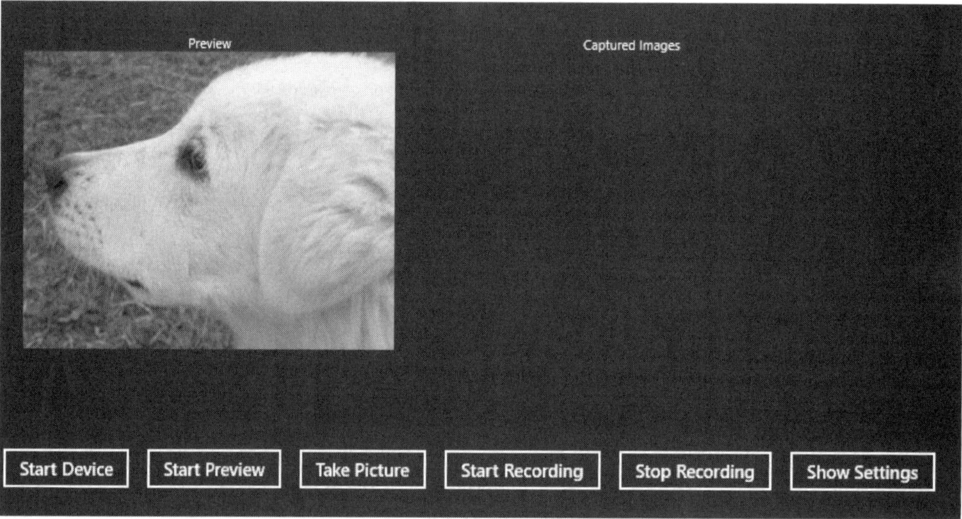

FIGURE 2-7 The camera preview

Another thing worth noticing is the ability to add video and audio effects to your stream by calling the *AddEffectAsync* method, as illustrated in the following revised version of the *StartPreview_Click* method (changes are in bold):

```
private async void StartPreview_Click(object sender, RoutedEventArgs e)
{
    if (this._mediaCapture != null)
    {
        try
        {
            await this._mediaCapture.AddEffectAsync(MediaStreamType.VideoPreview,
                VideoEffects.VideoStabilization, null);

            PreviewElement.Source = this._mediaCapture;

            await this._mediaCapture.StartPreviewAsync();
        }
        catch (Exception ex)
        {
            // handle exception
        }
    }
}
```

The *AddEffectAsync* method is used in this sample to apply a video stabilization effect to a video preview stream. This method accepts three parameters. The first parameter is an instance of the *MediaStreamType* enum that specifies on what kind of stream you want the filter to be applied: photo, audio, video preview, or video recording. The second parameter is a string representing the effect Id; that is, the Id of the runtime class that contains the internal calculations for applying the audio or video effect. Finally, the third parameter is represented by a dictionary implementing the *IPropertySet* interface (an empty interface at the time of this writing) and containing configuration parameters for the effect.

In the example, to retrieve the Id of the video stabilization effect, the code leverages the *VideoStabilization* property of the *VideoEffects* class, which returns a string with the corresponding Id. When you are done with the effect, you can invoke the *ClearEffectsAsync* method, which removes all audio and video effects from a certain stream.

> ***MORE INFO*** **CUSTOM EFFECTS**
>
> **To browse an example of a custom video effect applied to a video stream, download the Windows 8 SDK official sample at *http://code.msdn.microsoft.com/windowsapps/Media-Capture-Sample-adf87622*.**

The next step is to add the option to take a picture from the webcam stream. Listing 2-6 shows one of several options available for your app.

LISTING 2-6 Using the *MediaCapture* class to take a picture from the webcam stream

```
private async void TakePhoto_Click(object sender, RoutedEventArgs e)
{
    if (this._mediaCapture != null)
    {
        try
        {
            ImageEncodingProperties encodingProperties =
                ImageEncodingProperties.CreateJpeg();

            WriteableBitmap bitmap =
                new WriteableBitmap((int)ImageElement.Width, (int)ImageElement.Height);

            using (var imageStream = new InMemoryRandomAccessStream())
            {
                await this._mediaCapture.CapturePhotoToStreamAsync(
                    encodingProperties, imageStream);

                await imageStream.FlushAsync();
                imageStream.Seek(0);
                bitmap.SetSource(imageStream);

                await Dispatcher.RunAsync(Windows.UI.Core.CoreDispatcherPriority.Normal,
                   () =>
                {
                    ImageElement.Source = bitmap;
                });
            }
        }
        catch (Exception ex)
        {
            // handle exception
        }
    }
}
```

This code takes advantage of the *CapturePhotoToStreamAsync* method of the *MediaCapture* class to asynchronously capture a photo as a stream of data (which is then displayed on the screen through the corresponding *Image* control). However, the *MediaCapture* class exposes also a *CapturePhotoToStorageFileAsync* method, which enables you to save the picture as a storage file. (See Chapter 5, "Manage data and security," for further details on storage files and user libraries.) Figure 2-8 shows the UI with the new captured photo.

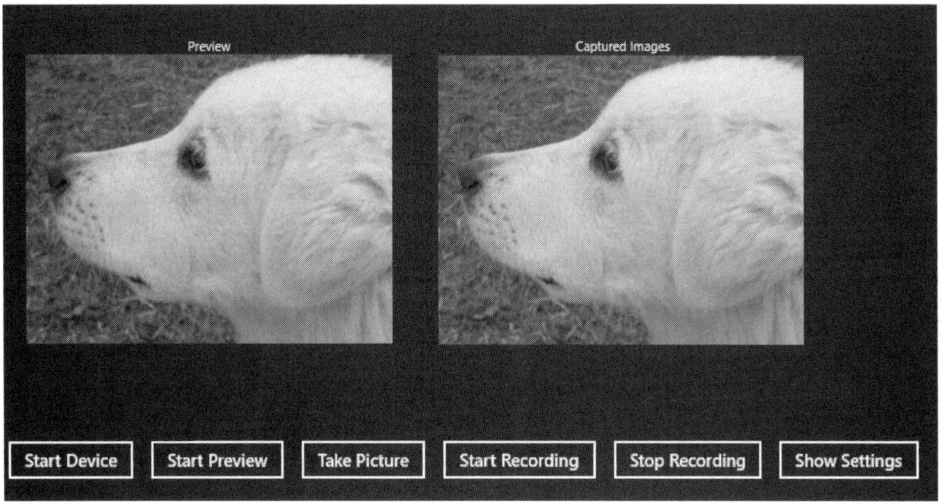

FIGURE 2-8 The captured photo

The *MediaCapture* class also exposes an overloaded version of the *InitializeAsync* method, which takes an object of type *MediaCaptureInitializationSettings*. As its name suggests, *MediaCaptureInitializationSettings* contains some initialization settings for the media capture device. You can choose, for example, among audio capture, video capture, or combined audio and video capture (through the *StreamingCaptureMode* property); or the stream source to use for the photo capture (through the *PhotoCaptureSource* property).

Listing 2-7 shows a revised version of the *StartDevice_Click* method presented in Listing 2-5 (changes are in bold) that takes advantage of the overloaded version of the *InitializeAsync* method.

LISTING 2-7 Initializing the media capture device

```
private async void StartDevice_Click(object sender, RoutedEventArgs e)
{
    try
    {
        this._mediaCapture = new MediaCapture();

        this._mediaCapture.RecordLimitationExceeded +=
            MediaCapture_RecordLimitationExceeded;
        this._mediaCapture.Failed += MediaCapture_Failed;

        var settings = new MediaCaptureInitializationSettings();
        settings.StreamingCaptureMode = StreamingCaptureMode.AudioAndVideo;
        settings.PhotoCaptureSource = PhotoCaptureSource.VideoPreview;

        await this._mediaCapture.InitializeAsync(settings);

    }
    catch (UnauthorizedAccessException ex)
    {
```

```
        ErrorMessageTextBlock.Text = "This app needs your permission to use the webcam";
    }
    catch (Exception ex)
    {
        ErrorMessageTextBlock.Text = "Unable to initialize the webcam";
    }
}
```

The *VideoDeviceId* and *AudioDeviceId* properties, exposed by the *MediaCaptureInitializationSettings* class, enable you to specify the device unique identification number of the video camera and the microphone, respectively, that you want to use. Listing 2-8 shows an example of their usage (changes to the code are shown in bold). You will learn details about finding and enumerating devices in Objective 2.3 of this chapter.

LISTING 2-8 Deciding which camera to use for video capturing

```
private async void StartDevice_Click(object sender, RoutedEventArgs e)
{
    try
    {
        this._mediaCapture = new MediaCapture();

        this._mediaCapture.RecordLimitationExceeded +=
            MediaCapture_RecordLimitationExceeded;
        this._mediaCapture.Failed += MediaCapture_Failed;

        var settings = new MediaCaptureInitializationSettings();
        settings.StreamingCaptureMode = StreamingCaptureMode.AudioAndVideo;
        settings.PhotoCaptureSource = PhotoCaptureSource.VideoPreview;

        var devices = await
            Windows.Devices.Enumeration.DeviceInformation.FindAllAsync(
                Windows.Devices.Enumeration.DeviceClass.VideoCapture);

        if (devices.Count > 0)
        {
            settings.VideoDeviceId = devices[0].Id;
            await this._mediaCapture.InitializeAsync(settings);
        }
        else
            ErrorMessageTextBlock.Text = "No device connected";
    }
    catch (UnauthorizedAccessException ex)
    {
        ErrorMessageTextBlock.Text =
            "This app needs your permission to use the webcam";
    }
    catch (Exception ex)
    {
        ErrorMessageTextBlock.Text = "Unable to initialize the webcam";
    }
}
```

Listing 2-9 shows how to record a video from the webcam and save it in the user's Videos library (hence, the need to add the corresponding capability in the Package.appxmanifest of your app).

LISTING 2-9 Recording a video in the user's Videos library

```
private async void StartRecordingVideo_Click(object sender, RoutedEventArgs e)
{
    if (this._mediaCapture != null )
    {
        try
        {
            var videoStorage = Windows.Storage.KnownFolders.VideosLibrary;
            var file = await videoStorage.CreateFileAsync(
                "samplevideo.mp4",
                Windows.Storage.CreationCollisionOption.GenerateUniqueName);

            var recordProfile = MediaEncodingProfile.CreateMp4(
                Windows.Media.MediaProperties.VideoEncodingQuality.Auto);

            await this._mediaCapture.StartRecordToStorageFileAsync(recordProfile, file);

            await Dispatcher.RunAsync(Windows.UI.Core.CoreDispatcherPriority.Normal, ()
                =>
            {
                PreviewTextBlock.Text = "Now recording...";
            });
        }
        catch (Exception ex)
        {
            // handle exception
        }
    }
}
```

The proposed code leverages the *StartRecordToStorageFileAsync* method of the *MediaCapture* class to start recording the video in a storage file. This method accepts a *MediaEncodingProfile* object as its first parameter, which describes the encoding profile for an audio or video file. The encoding profile includes the description of the audio and video encoding formats, and a description of the media container. (The *MediaCapture* class also exposes a *StartRecordToStreamAsync* to start recording to a random-access stream; and a *StartRecordToCustomSinkAsync* method, in two different versions, to start recording to a custom media sink.)

EXAM TIP

In the *StartRecordingVideo_Click* method, the code uses the *MediaEncodingProfile.CreateMp4* method to create an encoding profile for a MP4 video. However, the *MediaEncodingProfile* class also exposes methods to create encoding profiles for different audio and video files. These profiles include the Advanced Audio Codec (AAC) audio profile (corresponding to the M4a format), MP3 audio profile, as well as the Windows Media Audio (WMA) and Windows Media Video (WMV) profiles.

During the recording, you can adjust some basic camera settings by taking advantage of the *CameraOptionsUI* class, which exposes only a single method, *Show*, to display a flyout panel containing options for the capture of photos, audio recordings, and videos. The method accepts, as its only parameter, the *MediaCapture* object that the options refer to. The following C# code excerpt shows how to use it:

```
private void ShowSettings_Click(object sender, RoutedEventArgs e)
{
    try
    {
        if (this._mediaCapture != null)
        {
            CameraOptionsUI.Show(this._mediaCapture);
        }
    }
    catch (Exception ex)
    {
        // handle exception
    }
}
```

The camera settings flyout is shown in Figure 2-9.

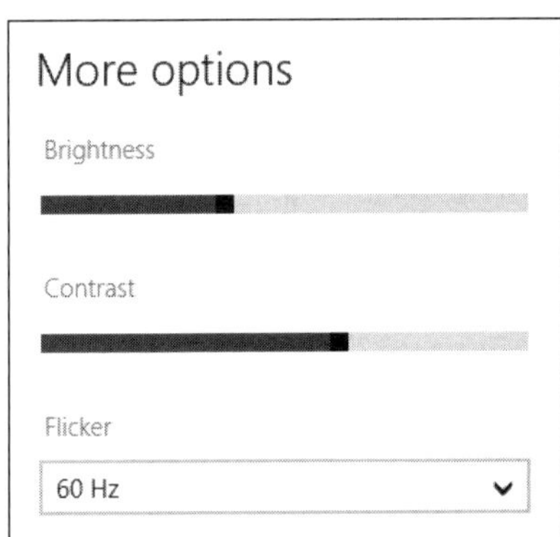

FIGURE 2-9 Camera settings flyout

Finally, to stop the video recording, call the *StopRecordAsync* method of the *MediaCapture* class, as shown in the following code snippet:

```
private async void StopRecordingVideo_Click(object sender, RoutedEventArgs e)
{
    if (this._mediaCapture != null)
    {
        await this._mediaCapture.StopRecordAsync();

        await Dispatcher.RunAsync(Windows.UI.Core.CoreDispatcherPriority.Normal, () =>
        {
            PreviewTextBlock.Text = "Video saved";
        });
    }
}
```

The complete XAML code for the page presented in Figure 2-8 is shown in Listing 2-10.

LISTING 2-10 Complete XAML definition of the MainPage.xaml file used for this sample

```
<Page
    x:Class="MediaCaptureSample.MainPage"
    xmlns="http://schemas.microsoft.com/winfx/2006/xaml/presentation"
    xmlns:x="http://schemas.microsoft.com/winfx/2006/xaml"
    xmlns:local="using:MediaCaptureSample"
    xmlns:d="http://schemas.microsoft.com/expression/blend/2008"
    xmlns:mc="http://schemas.openxmlformats.org/markup-compatibility/2006"
    mc:Ignorable="d">

    <Grid Background="{StaticResource ApplicationPageBackgroundThemeBrush}">
        <StackPanel Orientation="Horizontal" Margin="0,10,0,0">
            <Button Click="StartDevice_Click" Margin="0,0,10,0">Start Device</Button>
            <Button Click="StartPreview_Click" Margin="0,0,10,0">Start Preview</Button>
            <Button Click="TakePhoto_Click" Margin="0,0,10,0">Take Photo</Button>
            <Button Click="StartRecordingVideo_Click" Margin="0,0,10,0">
                Start Recording
            </Button>
            <Button Click="StopRecordingVideo_Click" Margin="0,0,10,0">
                Stop Recording
            </Button>
            <Button Click="ShowSettings_Click" Margin="0,0,10,0">
                Show Settings
            </Button>
            <TextBlock x:Name="ErrorMessageTextBlock" Width="600" Height="Auto"
                TextWrapping="Wrap" Margin="0, 10" />
        </StackPanel>
        <StackPanel Orientation="Horizontal" Margin="0,10,0,0">
            <StackPanel Margin="20">
                <TextBlock x:Name="PreviewTextBlock"
                           HorizontalAlignment="Center"
                           VerticalAlignment="Center"
                           TextAlignment="Center"
                           Text="Preview" />
                <Canvas Width="320" Height="240" Background="Gray">
                    <CaptureElement x:Name="PreviewElement" Width="320" Height="240" />
                </Canvas>
            </StackPanel>
            <StackPanel Margin="20">
```

```
                <TextBlock  HorizontalAlignment="Center"  VerticalAlignment="Center"
                    TextAlignment="Center"  Text="Captured Images" />
                <Canvas Width="320" Height ="240" >
                    <Image x:Name="ImageElement"  Width="320"   Height="240"/>
                </Canvas>
            </StackPanel>
        </StackPanel>
    </Grid>
</Page>
```

So far, you have seen how to capture a video and take some pictures from a camera. The audio was recorded as part of the stream coming from the camera. The usage of the *MediaCapture* class to capture audio coming from another source, typically a microphone, follows the same pattern of video and photo capturing, as shown in Listing 2-11.

LISTING 2-11 Capturing audio from the microphone

```
private MediaCapture _mediaCapture;

private async void StartDevice_Click(object sender, RoutedEventArgs e)
{
    try
    {
        this._mediaCapture = new MediaCapture();

        this._mediaCapture.RecordLimitationExceeded +=
            MediaCapture_RecordLimitationExceeded;
        this._mediaCapture.Failed += MediaCapture_Failed;

        MediaCaptureInitializationSettings settings =
           new MediaCaptureInitializationSettings();
        settings.StreamingCaptureMode = StreamingCaptureMode.Audio;

        var microphones = await
            Windows.Devices.Enumeration.DeviceInformation.FindAllAsync(
                Windows.Devices.Enumeration.DeviceClass.AudioCapture);

        if (microphones.Count > 0)
        {
            settings.AudioDeviceId = microphones[0].Id;
            await this._mediaCapture.InitializeAsync(settings);
        }
        else
            // No device connected
    }
    catch (UnauthorizedAccessException ex)
    {
        // handle exception
    }
    catch (Exception ex)
    {
        // handle exception
    }
}
```

```
private async void StartRecordingAudio_Click(object sender, RoutedEventArgs e)
{
    if (this._mediaCapture != null )
    {
        try
        {
            var audioStorage = Windows.Storage.KnownFolders.MusicLibrary;
            var file = await audioStorage.CreateFileAsync("sampleaudio.mp3",
               Windows.Storage.CreationCollisionOption.GenerateUniqueName);

            var recordProfile = MediaEncodingProfile
                .CreateMp3(AudioEncodingQuality.High);

            await this._mediaCapture.StartRecordToStorageFileAsync(recordProfile, file);
        }
        catch (Exception ex)
        {
            // handle exception
        }
    }
}
```

Thought experiment

Capturing pictures for a travel application

In this thought experiment, apply what you've learned about this objective. You can find answers to these questions in the "Answers" section at the end of this chapter.

You are creating a travel application that enables the user to capture pictures when visiting interesting places. The user can add audio comments to the photos and tag the photos with text to find them more easily.

What strategy would you follow to manage the camera, shoot a photo, tag it with some text, and add audio comments?

Objective summary

- The *CameraCaptureUI* class provides a standard UI to capture pictures and/or video from a webcam.
- The *CameraCaptureUI* class enables you to define the format for the media and camera settings using the provided properties.
- Use the *MediaCapture* class, instead of the *CameraCaptureUI*, whenever you want complete control over the entire process of audio and video capturing, including customization of the UI.

- Start device initialization by calling the *StartAsync* method of *MediaCapture*, or use the overloaded version of this method if you want to supply the media capture device with one or more initialization settings.
- You can use the *CameraOptionsUI.Show* method to display some basic audio and video options in a flyout or create your own custom controls.

Objective review

Answer the following questions to test your knowledge of the information in this objective. You can find the answers to these questions and explanations of why each answer choice is correct or incorrect in the "Answers" section at the end of this chapter.

1. How can an application set the media format for capturing a video using the standard UI?
   - **A.** You cannot set the media format using the standard UI.
   - **B.** Use the *VideoSettings* properties of the *CameraCaptureUI* instance.
   - **C.** Use the *VideoSettings.MaxResolution* property of the *CameraCaptureUI* class.
   - **D.** Use *CameraCaptureUIMode* as a parameter of the *CaptureFileAsync* method of the *CameraCaptureUI* instance.
2. When is the *RecordLimitationExceeded* event raised?
   - **A.** When an error occurs during media capture
   - **B.** When the app does not have permission to access the capture device
   - **C.** When the user stops recording an audio or video stream
   - **D.** When the record limit is exceeded
3. Which class contains initialization settings for the *MediaCapture* object that can be passed as a parameter to the *MediaCapture.InitializeAsync* method?
   - **A.** *MediaCaptureInitializationSettings* class
   - **B.** *CameraCaptureUIPhotoFormat* class
   - **C.** *CameraCaptureUIVideoCaptureSettings* class
   - **D.** *CameraOptionsUI* class

Objective 2.2: Get data from sensors

Modern devices expose an incredible number of sensors, from web and GPS receiver to accelerometer and near field communication (NFC). In the past, interacting with these devices was challenging because you had to manage the various drivers by code or by using external libraries. Windows Runtime aims to unify the programming model for all devices.

This objective covers how to:

- Determine the availability of a sensor (*Windows.devices.sensors*)
- Add sensor requests to the app manifest
- Handle sensor events
- Get sensor properties
- Determine location via GPS

Understanding sensors and location data in the Windows Runtime

All the APIs discussed throughout this section are built on top of the Windows Sensor and Location platform, which greatly simplifies the integration and use of different sensors, such as accelerometers, inclinometers, light sensors, GPS sensors, and so on.

From a developer's point of view, the platform provides two namespaces for Windows Store apps: *Windows.Devices.Sensors*, which includes support for a variety of motion, device-orientation, and light sensors; and the *Windows.Devices.Geolocation* namespace, which is capable of retrieving the computer's location using a location provider.

MORE INFO **WINDOWS SENSOR LOCATION PLATFORM**

For details on the platform, visit *http://msdn.microsoft.com/en-us/library/windows/hardware/gg463473.aspx*.

Accessing sensors from a Windows Store app

The *Windows.Devices.Sensors* namespace provides classes, methods, and types to access the various sensors that can be integrated in a device with Windows 8 onboard, such as accelerometer, gyrometer, compass, orientation, inclinometer, and light sensor. Each of these sensors can be accessed through simple APIs that follow similar patterns, with few variations.

First, you need to obtain a reference to the class that wraps the specific sensor you want to use by invoking the *GetDefault* static method of the sensor class. Then you can follow two strategies to retrieve the data from the sensor: polling the device at regular intervals or subscribing the *ReadingChanged* event to be notified of any update in the sensor's readings. You will see all the details of these steps in the following sections.

Responding to user movements with the accelerometer sensor

The accelerometer sensor measures the acceleration transmitted to a device along the three axes (X, Y, and Z); that is, the relationship between the speed variation and the time interval considered (expressed through the G-force acceleration). Figure 2-10 illustrates the axis orientation in a tablet and in a notebook.

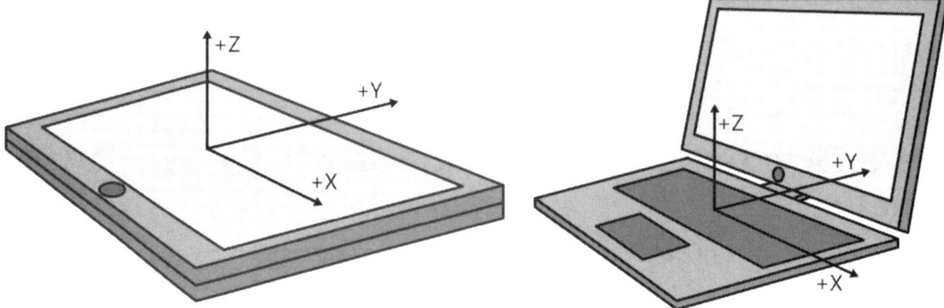

FIGURE 2-10 The position of the X, Y, and Z axes for a tablet (left) and for a notebook (right) Source: Adapted from the MSDN article, "Motion and device orientation for simple apps (Windows Store apps)," at *http://msdn.microsoft.com/en-us/library/windows/apps/jj155767.aspx*

To leverage the accelerometer from a Windows Store app, the first thing to do is to get a reference to an *Accelerometer* object by calling the *GetDefault* static method of the *Accelerometer* class, as follows:

```
Accelerometer accelerometer = Accelerometer.GetDefault();
if (accelerometer == null)
{
   // No accelerometer found

}
```

EXAM TIP

The *GetDefault* method returns a value only if an accelerometer is detected. A *null* value means the requested sensor is not available in the system, so it is important to check for the returning value before going any further.

The simple UI that presents accelerometer data can be similar to the one presented in the following XAML code excerpt:

```
<Page
    x:Class="AccelerometerSensorSample.MainPage"
    xmlns="http://schemas.microsoft.com/winfx/2006/xaml/presentation"
    xmlns:x="http://schemas.microsoft.com/winfx/2006/xaml"
    xmlns:local="using:AccelerometerSensorSample"
    xmlns:d="http://schemas.microsoft.com/expression/blend/2008"
    xmlns:mc="http://schemas.openxmlformats.org/markup-compatibility/2006"
    mc:Ignorable="d">
```

```
    <Grid Background="{StaticResource ApplicationPageBackgroundThemeBrush}">
        <TextBlock x:Name=" AccelerometerTextBlock" Width="Auto" Height="Auto"
            Margin="20" FontSize="22" />
    </Grid>
</Page>
```

Listing 2-12 shows an example of the code-behind of the page that will be analyzed shortly.

LISTING 2-12 Initializing the accelerometer sensor

```
public sealed partial class MainPage : Page
{
    public MainPage()
    {
        this.InitializeComponent();
        this.InitializeAccelerometer();
    }

    private Accelerometer _accelerometer;
    private void InitializeAccelerometer()
    {
        this._accelerometer = Accelerometer.GetDefault();

        if (_accelerometer == null)
        {
            AccelerometerTextBlock.Text = "No accelerometer found.";
            return;
        }

        uint minReportInterval = _accelerometer.MinimumReportInterval;
        var desiredReportInterval = minReportInterval > 16 ? minReportInterval : 16;
        this._accelerometer.ReportInterval = desiredReportInterval;
    }
```

The *ReportInterval* property indicates the time interval (expressed in milliseconds) between two readings. The report interval must be set to a non-zero value before registering an event handler or calling the *GetCurrentReading* method, to inform the sensors (through their drivers) to allocate the resources needed to satisfy the application's requirements.

To improve battery efficiency, this property should explicitly be set to its default value by setting the property to zero as soon as the app no longer needs the sensor. By setting this property to zero, you are telling the sensor to use its default report interval. The next code excerpt illustrates this point (the same principle applies to all the sensors discussed in this section):

```
protected override void OnNavigatingFrom(NavigatingCancelEventArgs e)
{
    if (this._accelerometer != null)
        this._accelerometer.ReportInterval = 0;

    base.OnNavigatingFrom(e);
}
```

Before setting the report interval, you should check whether the sensor can keep up with the requested interval by calling the *MinimumReportInterval* property. If you set a value that is lower than the minimum supported interval, the code will either trigger an exception or get unexpected results. The code shown in Listing 2-12 checks whether the minimum supported interval is lower than 16 milliseconds and, in this case, sets 16 milliseconds as the desired report interval to avoid too many readings (hence saving battery power).

However, consider that even if you set a valid report interval or you set it back to its default value (by setting the property to zero), the sensor might still use a different report interval, based on its internal logic.

***NOTE* SENSOR CHANGE SENSITIVITY**

The Sensor platform automatically adjusts the sensitivity of the accelerometer sensor based on the current report interval. As the interval increases, the force that must be applied to the device to trigger a new reading must increase as well. The following table, repurposed from the official MSDN documentation, specifies the change sensitivity values for given intervals.

Current report interval (in milliseconds)	Change sensitivity (in G-force)
1 to 16	0.01
17 to 32	0.02
33 or greater	0.05

After initializing the sensor, there are three different ways to read the sensor's data: implement event-driven readings, define a polling strategy, or wait for a shake. The first two patterns are commonly used by all the sensors discussed in this section, whereas the last one is specifically supported only by the accelerometer sensor.

The first pattern leverages the *ReadingChanged* event, which is raised every time the accelerometer reports a new sensor reading. The code in Listing 2-13 shows an example of its usage (changes to Listing 2-12 are shown in bold).

LISTING 2-13 Leveraging the event-driven reading pattern through the *ReadingChanged* event

```
private Accelerometer _accelerometer;

private void InitializeAccelerometer()
{
    this._accelerometer = Accelerometer.GetDefault();

    if (_accelerometer == null)
    {
        AccelerometerTextBlock.Text = "No accelerometer found.";
        return;
    }
```

```
    uint minReportInterval = _accelerometer.MinimumReportInterval;
    var desiredReportInterval = minReportInterval > 16 ? minReportInterval : 16;
    this._accelerometer.ReportInterval = desiredReportInterval;

    this._accelerometer.ReadingChanged += Accelerometer_ReadingChanged;
}

private async void Accelerometer_ReadingChanged(Accelerometer sender,
    AccelerometerReadingChangedEventArgs args)
{
    if (args.Reading != null)
    {
        await Dispatcher.RunAsync(Windows.UI.Core.CoreDispatcherPriority.Normal, () =>
        {
            AccelerometerTextBlock.Text = String.Format(
                "X: {0,5:0.00} - Y: {1,5:0.00} - Z: {2,5:0.00} - Timestamp: {3}",
                args.Reading.AccelerationX,
                args.Reading.AccelerationY,
                args.Reading.AccelerationZ,
                args.Reading.Timestamp);
        });
    }
}
```

In the *ReadingChanged* event handler, you can inspect the *Reading* property (of type *AccelerationReading*) exposed by the *AccelerometerReadingChangedEventArgs* instance and received as a parameter to retrieve the values that represent the G-force acceleration along the three axes. The values are stored in the *AccelerationX*, *AccelerationY*, and *AccelerationZ* properties. The fourth property of the *AccelerationReading* class is *Timestamp*, which, as its name suggests, indicates the time at which the sensor reported the reading.

The second method to retrieve the data coming from the sensor is to poll the sensor device at regular intervals. Before polling the sensor, the application must set a desired value for the *ReportInterval* property. Listing 2-14 shows how to poll the sensor to retrieve the current reading (changes to Listing 2-12 are in bold).

LISTING 2-14 Polling the sensor at regular interval for the current reading

```
private Accelerometer _accelerometer;
private DispatcherTimer _timer;

private void InitializeAccelerometer()
{
    this._accelerometer = Accelerometer.GetDefault();

    if (_accelerometer == null)
    {
        AccelerometerTextBlock.Text = "No accelerometer found.";
        return;
    }

    uint minReportInterval = _accelerometer.MinimumReportInterval;
    var desiredReportInterval = minReportInterval > 16 ? minReportInterval : 16;
    this._accelerometer.ReportInterval = desiredReportInterval;
```

```
        this._timer = new DispatcherTimer();
        this._timer.Tick += PollAccelerometerSensorReadings;
        this._timer.Interval = new TimeSpan(0, 0, 0, 0, (Int32)desiredReportInterval);
        this._timer.Start();
    }

    private async void PollAccelerometerSensorReadings(object sender, object e)
    {
        if (this._accelerometer != null)
        {
            var readings = this._accelerometer.GetCurrentReading();

            await Dispatcher.RunAsync(Windows.UI.Core.CoreDispatcherPriority.Normal, () =>
            {
                AccelerometerTextBlock.Text = String.Format(
                    "X: {0,5:0.00} - Y: {1,5:0.00} - Z: {2,5:0.00} - Timestamp: {3}",
                    readings.AccelerationX,
                    readings.AccelerationY,
                    readings.AccelerationZ,
                    readings.Timestamp);
            });
        }
    }
```

The third method of detecting the user's movements through the accelerometer sensor relies on a different event. Besides the already explained *ReadingChanged* event, the *Accelerometer* class exposes a *Shaken* event that is raised by the system when the user shakes the device. When subscribing to the *Shaken* event, you do not get detailed readings of the acceleration along the three axes, nor any other indication about the G-force impressed by the user to the device. In this case, it is up to the system to determine whether a fast shake motion has occurred by analyzing the sequence of acceleration changes. Notice that unlike the other two methods, setting a report interval prior to registering for the *Shaken* event is not required. The code in Listing 2-15 shows a revised sample of the *InitializeSensor* method used in Listing 2-12 (changes are in bold).

LISTING 2-15 Leveraging the *Shaken* event to detect movements

```
private Accelerometer _accelerometer;

private void InitializeAccelerometer()
{
    this._accelerometer = Accelerometer.GetDefault();

    if (_accelerometer == null)
    {
        AccelerometerTextBlock.Text = "No accelerometer found.";
        return;
    }

    this._accelerometer.Shaken += Accelerometer_Shaken;
}

private Int32 _numberOfShakens = 0;
```

```
private async void Accelerometer_Shaken(Accelerometer sender,
    AccelerometerShakenEventArgs args)
{
    await Dispatcher.RunAsync(Windows.UI.Core.CoreDispatcherPriority.Normal, () =>
    {
        this._numberOfShakens++;
        ShakenCounterTextBlock.Text =
        String.Format("Number of shakens: {0}", this._numberOfShakens);
    });
}
```

If you want to test the accelerometer on your device, you can use the following XAML code as a reference for MainPage.xaml:

```
<Page
    x:Class="AccelerometerSensorSample.MainPage"
    xmlns="http://schemas.microsoft.com/winfx/2006/xaml/presentation"
    xmlns:x="http://schemas.microsoft.com/winfx/2006/xaml"
    xmlns:local="using:AccelerometerSensorSample"
    xmlns:d="http://schemas.microsoft.com/expression/blend/2008"
    xmlns:mc="http://schemas.openxmlformats.org/markup-compatibility/2006"
    mc:Ignorable="d">

    <Grid Background="{StaticResource ApplicationPageBackgroundThemeBrush}">
        <TextBlock x:Name="ShakenCounterTextBlock"
            Text="Number of shakens: 0" Width="Auto" Height="Auto"
            Margin="20" FontSize="22" />
    </Grid>
</Page>
```

Measuring angular velocity with the gyrometer

The gyrometer sensor measures the angular velocity along the three axes. Its usage is very similar to the accelerometer sensor. First, you get a reference to a *Gyrometer* object by calling the *GetDefault* static method of the *Gyrometer* class. Then you can subscribe to the *ReadingChanged* event to be notified about any change in the current angular velocity or poll the sensor at regular intervals through the *GetCurrentReading* method.

You can use the following XAML code as a reference for MainPage.xaml:

```
<Page
    x:Class="GyrometerSensorSample.MainPage"
    xmlns="http://schemas.microsoft.com/winfx/2006/xaml/presentation"
    xmlns:x="http://schemas.microsoft.com/winfx/2006/xaml"
    xmlns:local="using:GyrometerSensorSample"
    xmlns:d="http://schemas.microsoft.com/expression/blend/2008"
    xmlns:mc="http://schemas.openxmlformats.org/markup-compatibility/2006"
    mc:Ignorable="d">

    <Grid Background="{StaticResource ApplicationPageBackgroundThemeBrush}">
        <TextBlock x:Name="GyrometerTextBlock" Width="Auto" Height="Auto"
            Margin="20" FontSize="20" />
    </Grid>
</Page>
```

Listing 2-16 uses the *ReadingChanged* event handler to display the current reading values.

LISTING 2-16 Getting data from the gyrometer sensor by subscribing to the *ReadingChanged* event

```
public MainPage()
{
    this.InitializeComponent();
    this.InitializeGyrometer();
}

private Gyrometer _gyro;

private void InitializeGyrometer()
{
    this._gyro = Gyrometer.GetDefault();

    if (this._gyro == null)
    {
        GyrometerTextBlock.Text = "No gyrometer found";
        return;
    }

    uint minReportInterval = _gyro.MinimumReportInterval;
    var desiredReportInterval = minReportInterval > 16 ? minReportInterval : 16;
    this._gyro.ReportInterval = desiredReportInterval;

    this._gyro.ReadingChanged += Gyro_ReadingChanged;
}

private async void Gyro_ReadingChanged(Gyrometer sender,
    GyrometerReadingChangedEventArgs args)
{
    if (args.Reading != null)
    {
        await Dispatcher.RunAsync(Windows.UI.Core.CoreDispatcherPriority.Normal, () =>
        {
            GyrometerTextBlock.Text = String.Format(
                "X: {0,5:0.00} - Y: {1,5:0.00} - Z: {2,5:0.00} - Timestamp: {3}",
                args.Reading.AngularVelocityX,
                args.Reading.AngularVelocityY,
                args.Reading.AngularVelocityZ,
                args.Reading.Timestamp);
        });
    }
}

protected override void OnNavigatingFrom(NavigatingCancelEventArgs e)
{
    if (this._gyro != null)
        this._gyro.ReportInterval = 0;

    base.OnNavigatingFrom(e);
}
```

NOTE **SENSOR CHANGE SENSITIVITY**

The Sensor platform automatically sets the change sensitivity for the gyrometer sensor based on the current report interval. The following table, repurposed from the official MSDN documentation, specifies the change sensitivity values for given intervals.

Current report interval (in milliseconds)	Change sensitivity (degrees per second)
1 to 16	0.1
17 to 32	0.5
33 or greater	1.0

Alternatively, you can interrogate the sensor at regular intervals, as shown in Listing 2-17, which is similar to Listing 2-16. However, the code in Listing 2-17 uses a polling strategy (changes in bold).

LISTING 2-17 Polling the gyrometer sensor at regular intervals

```
private Gyrometer _gyro;
private DispatcherTimer _timer;

private void InitializeGyrometer()
{
    this._gyro = Gyrometer.GetDefault();

    if (this._gyro == null)
    {
        GyrometerTextBlock.Text = "No gyrometer found";
        return;
    }

    uint minReportInterval = _gyro.MinimumReportInterval;
    var desiredReportInterval = minReportInterval > 16 ? minReportInterval : 16;

    this._gyro.ReportInterval = desiredReportInterval;

    this._timer = new DispatcherTimer();
    this._timer.Tick += PollGyrometerSensorReadings;
    this._timer.Interval = new TimeSpan(0, 0, 0, 0, (Int32)desiredReportInterval);
    this._timer.Start();
}

private async void PollGyrometerSensorReadings(object sender, object e)
{
    if (this._gyro != null)
    {
        var readings = this._gyro.GetCurrentReading();

        await Dispatcher.RunAsync(Windows.UI.Core.CoreDispatcherPriority.Normal, () =>
        {
```

```
            GyrometerTextBlock.Text = String.Format(
                "X: {0,5:0.00} - Y: {1,5:0.00} - Z: {2,5:0.00} - Timestamp: {3}",
                readings.AngularVelocityX,
                readings.AngularVelocityY,
                readings.AngularVelocityZ,
                readings.Timestamp);
        });
    }
}
```

Retrieving compass data

The compass sensor indicates the heading in degrees relative to magnetic north and, depending on the implementation of the sensors, geographic (or true) north.

Use the following XAML code as a reference for your MainPage.xaml to test the compass sensor on your device:

```
<Page
    x:Class="CompassSensorSample.MainPage"
    xmlns="http://schemas.microsoft.com/winfx/2006/xaml/presentation"
    xmlns:x="http://schemas.microsoft.com/winfx/2006/xaml"
    xmlns:local="using:CompassSensorSample"
    xmlns:d="http://schemas.microsoft.com/expression/blend/2008"
    xmlns:mc="http://schemas.openxmlformats.org/markup-compatibility/2006"
    mc:Ignorable="d">

    <Grid Background="{StaticResource ApplicationPageBackgroundThemeBrush}">
        <StackPanel>
            <TextBlock x:Name="CompassTextBlock" Width="Auto" Height="Auto"
                Margin="20" FontSize="20" />
            <TextBlock x:Name="TrueNorthTextBlock" Width="Auto" Height="Auto"
                Margin="20" FontSize="20" />
        </StackPanel>
    </Grid>
</Page>
```

As for the other sensors, the first thing to do is to obtain a reference to the default compass through the *GetDefault* static method of the *Compass* class. Then you need to set the *ReportInterval* property to let the system know how many resources need to be allocated.

After the sensor has been initialized, you have the usual two ways to collect data from the sensor: adopting an event-based strategy or defining a polling technique to get data from the sensor at some interval.

Listing 2-18 shows an example of the first strategy for retrieving the values (in degrees) of the *HeadingMagneticNorth* and *HeadingTrueNorth* properties of the *CompassReading* class.

LISTING 2-18 Retrieving the direction from the compass sensor by subscribing to the *ReadingChanged* event

```
public MainPage()
{
    this.InitializeComponent();
    this.InitializeCompass();
}

private Compass _compass;

private void InitializeCompass()
{
    this._compass = Compass.GetDefault();

    if (this._compass == null)
    {
        CompassTextBlock.Text = "No compass found";
        return;
    }

    uint minReportInterval = this._compass.MinimumReportInterval;
    var desiredReportInterval = minReportInterval > 16 ? minReportInterval : 16;
    this._compass.ReportInterval = desiredReportInterval;

    this._compass.ReadingChanged += Compass_ReadingChanged;
}

private async void Compass_ReadingChanged(Compass sender,
    CompassReadingChangedEventArgs args)
{
    if (args.Reading != null)
    {
        await Dispatcher.RunAsync(Windows.UI.Core.CoreDispatcherPriority.Normal, () =>
        {
            CompassTextBlock.Text = String.Format("Magnetic North: {0,5:0.00} degrees.",
                args.Reading.HeadingMagneticNorth);

            if (args.Reading.HeadingTrueNorth != null)
                TrueNorthTextBlock.Text = String.Format(
                    "True North: {0,5:0.00} degrees.", args.Reading.HeadingTrueNorth);
            else
                TrueNorthTextBlock.Text =
                    String.Format("True North: no data available");
        });
    }
}
```

EXAM TIP

Because not all of the sensors implement the capability to detect geographic (or true) north, it is important to check the corresponding *HeadingTrueNorth* property before using it.

NOTE SENSOR CHANGE SENSITIVITY

The Sensor platform automatically sets the change sensitivity for the compass sensor based on the current report interval. The following table, taken from the official MSDN documentation, specifies the change sensitivity values for given intervals.

Current report interval (in milliseconds)	Change sensitivity (in degrees)
1 to 16	0.01
17 to 32	0.5
33 or greater	2

Combining different data using the orientation sensor

The orientation sensor combines data coming from three different sensors to determine the orientation of the device: the accelerometer, the gyrometer, and the compass. The orientation sensor includes two different APIs. The first API is represented by the *SimpleOrientationSensor* class, which uses the orientation sensor to detect the current quadrant orientation of the device. As its name suggests, the *SimpleOrientationSensor* provides an easy and intuitive way to determine the orientation of a device without the need to analyze complex data.

The detected orientation can assume one of the following values, expressed by the *SimpleOrientation* enum:

- ***NotRotated*** The device is not rotated. This corresponds to portrait-up orientation.
- ***Rotated90DegreesCounterclockwise*** The device is rotated 90 degrees counterclockwise. This corresponds to landscape-left orientation.
- ***Rotated180DegreesCounterclockwise*** The device is rotated 180 degrees counterclockwise. This corresponds to portrait-down orientation.
- ***Rotated270DegreesCounterclockwise*** The device is rotated 270 degrees counterclockwise. This corresponds to landscape-right orientation.
- ***Faceup*** The device is positioned face-up (the display is visible to the user).
- ***Facedown*** The device is positioned facedown (the display is hidden from the user).

Using the *SimpleOrientationSensor* class follows the same patterns of the other sensors discussed in this section, with few differences.

The following code snippet shows the XAML definition of the MainPage.xaml that you can use as a reference to test the *SimpleOrientationSensor*:

```
<Page
    x:Class="SimpleOrientationSensorSample.MainPage"
    xmlns="http://schemas.microsoft.com/winfx/2006/xaml/presentation"
    xmlns:x="http://schemas.microsoft.com/winfx/2006/xaml"
    xmlns:local="using:SimpleOrientationSensorSample"
```

```
    xmlns:d="http://schemas.microsoft.com/expression/blend/2008"
    xmlns:mc="http://schemas.openxmlformats.org/markup-compatibility/2006"
    mc:Ignorable="d">

    <Grid Background="{StaticResource ApplicationPageBackgroundThemeBrush}">
        <TextBlock x:Name="SimpleOrientationSensorTextBlock" Width="Auto" Height="Auto"
            Margin="20" FontSize="22" />
    </Grid>
</Page>
```

The code in Listing 2-19 displays the current orientation by leveraging the *SimpleOrientationSensor* class.

LISTING 2-19 Determining the device orientation through the *SimpleOrientationSensor* class

```
public MainPage()
{
    this.InitializeComponent();
    this.InitializeSimpleOrientationSensor();
}

private  SimpleOrientationSensor _simpleOrientationSensor;

private void InitializeSimpleOrientationSensor()
{
    this._simpleOrientationSensor = SimpleOrientationSensor.GetDefault();

    if (this._simpleOrientationSensor == null)
    {
        SimpleOrientationSensorTextBlock.Text = "No orientation sensor found";
        return;
    }

    this._simpleOrientationSensor.OrientationChanged +=
        SimpleOrientationSensor_OrientationChanged;
}

private async void SimpleOrientationSensor_OrientationChanged(
    SimpleOrientationSensor sender,
    SimpleOrientationSensorOrientationChangedEventArgs args)
{
    await Dispatcher.RunAsync(Windows.UI.Core.CoreDispatcherPriority.Normal, () =>
    {
        switch (args.Orientation)
        {
            case SimpleOrientation.Facedown:
                SimpleOrientationSensorTextBlock.Text =
                    String.Format("Current orientation: Face-Down");
                break;
            case SimpleOrientation.Faceup:
                SimpleOrientationSensorTextBlock.Text =
                    String.Format("Current orientation: Face-Up");
                break;
```

```
            case SimpleOrientation.NotRotated:
                SimpleOrientationSensorTextBlock.Text =
                    String.Format("Current orientation: Portrait-Up");
                break;
            case SimpleOrientation.Rotated180DegreesCounterclockwise:
                SimpleOrientationSensorTextBlock.Text =
                    String.Format("Current orientation: Portrait-Down");
                break;
            case SimpleOrientation.Rotated270DegreesCounterclockwise:
                SimpleOrientationSensorTextBlock.Text =
                    String.Format("Current orientation: Landscape-Right");
                break;
            case SimpleOrientation.Rotated90DegreesCounterclockwise:
                SimpleOrientationSensorTextBlock.Text =
                    String.Format("Current orientation: Landscape-Left");
                break;
        }
    });
}
```

The API hides most of the internal mechanisms used to determine the current orientation by combining complex data from three different sensors. Compared with the other sensors discussed in this section, the main difference is that in the case of the *SimpleOrientationSensor* class, you do not have to set the report interval before subscribing to the *OrientationChanged* event. The *OrientationChanged* event replaces the *ReadingChanged* event commonly used by the other sensors, and it is raised whenever the user rotates the devices in a different position. Alternatively, you can leverage the polling strategy to interrogate the sensor at regular intervals.

The second API at your disposal is represented by the *OrientationSensor* class, which enables more fine-grained control over the data collected by the orientation sensor. The *OrientationSensor* is generally used for games and other apps that need to calculate the camera view based on screen orientation, such as those dealing with augmented reality. Listing 2-20 shows how to use an event-based strategy with the *OrientationSensor* class.

LISTING 2-20 Retrieving data from the *OrientationSensor* by leveraging the *ReadingChanged* event

```
private OrientationSensor _orientationSensor;

private void InitializeOrientationSensor()
{
    this._orientationSensor = OrientationSensor.GetDefault();

    if (this._orientationSensor == null)
    {
        // no sensor available
        // notify user
    }
```

```
    uint minReportInterval = this._orientationSensor.MinimumReportInterval;
    var desiredReportInterval = minReportInterval > 16 ? minReportInterval : 16;
    this._orientationSensor.ReportInterval = desiredReportInterval;

    this._orientationSensor.ReadingChanged +=
        OrientationSensor_OrientationChanged;
}

private void OrientationSensor_OrientationChanged(OrientationSensor sender,
    OrientationSensorReadingChangedEventArgs args)
{
    SensorRotationMatrix rotationMatrix = args.Reading.RotationMatrix;
    SensorQuaternion quaternion = args.Reading.Quaternion;

    // adjust the view displayed on screen based on rotation and orientation
}
```

In Listing 2-20, the pattern of the *OrientationSensor* is identical to the one followed by the other sensors discussed in this section, including the name of the event raised when a new reading is available and the need to set the *ReportInterval* property before subscribing to the event. The *Reading* property (of type *OrientationSensorReading*) exposed by the *OrientationSensorReadingChangedEventArgs* received as a parameter by the event handler encapsulates two properties: *RotationMatrix* and *Quaternion*. Rotation matrices and quaternions are used for describing mathematically the rotation of the device in the space. These mathematical objects can be used to adjust the scene rendered on the screen according to the device's movements.

> ***NOTE*** **ADVANCED MATHEMATICS**
>
> **Illustrating the mathematical nature and usage of matrices and quaternions in game development and computer graphics are beyond the scope of this book.**

Getting data from the inclinometer sensor

An inclinometer sensor can determine the rotation angles of a device around the three axes. The rotation around the vertical axis (Y) is also known as "roll" (or "gamma"), whereas the term "pitch" (or "beta") indicates the rotation around the lateral axis (X). The term "yaw" (or "alpha") indicates the rotation around the longitudinal axis (Z). Figure 2-11 shows the orientation of the three axes in a device running on Windows 8.

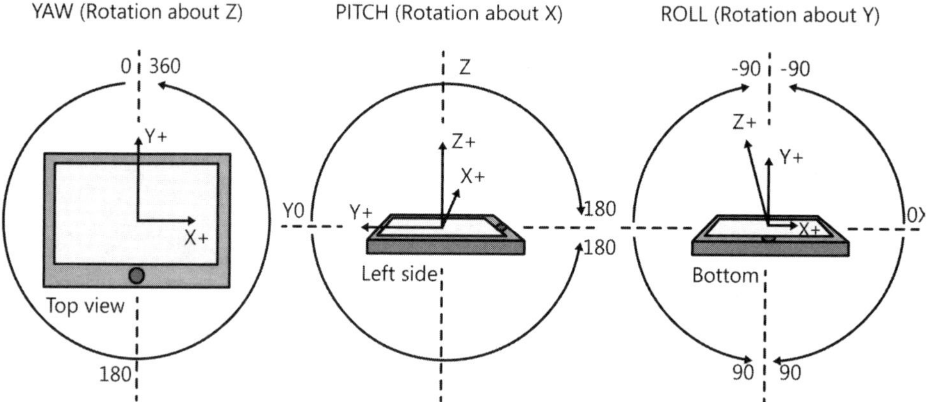

FIGURE 2-11 Yaw, pitch, and roll rotations on a tablet device
Source: Adapted from the MSDN article "Motion and device orientation for simple apps (Windows Store apps)," at *http://msdn.microsoft.com/en-us/library/windows/apps/jj155767.aspx*

Listing 2-21 shows an example of usage of the *Inclinometer* class that leverages the polling strategy to retrieve data from the sensor at regular intervals and displays the corresponding values of the *PitchDegrees*, *YawDegrees*, and *RollDegrees* properties.

LISTING 2-21 Polling the inclinometer to retrieve data about the inclination around the three axes

```
public MainPage()
{
    this.InitializeComponent();
    this.InitializeInclinometer();
}

private Inclinometer _inclinometer;
private DispatcherTimer _timer;

private void InitializeInclinometer()
{
    this._inclinometer = Inclinometer.GetDefault();

    if (this._inclinometer == null)
    {
        InclinometerTextBlock.Text = "No inclinometer found";
        return;
    }

    uint minReportInterval = this._inclinometer.MinimumReportInterval;
    var desiredReportInterval = minReportInterval > 16 ? minReportInterval : 16;

    this._timer = new DispatcherTimer();
    this._timer.Tick += PollInclinometerSensorReadings;
    this._timer.Interval = new TimeSpan(0, 0, 0, 0, (Int32)desiredReportInterval);
    this._timer.Start();
}
```

```
private async void PollInclinometerSensorReadings(object sender, object e)
{
    if (this._inclinometer != null)
    {
        var readings = this._inclinometer.GetCurrentReading();
        await Dispatcher.RunAsync(Windows.UI.Core.CoreDispatcherPriority.Normal, () =>
        {
            InclinometerTextBlock.Text = String.Format("Pitch (X) rotation: {0,5:0.00} -
                Yaw (Y) rotation: {1,5:0.00} - Roll (Z) rotation: {2,5:0.00}",
                readings.PitchDegrees,
                readings.YawDegrees,
                readings.RollDegrees);
        });
    }
}
```

NOTE **SENSOR CHANGE SENSITIVITY**

The Sensor platform automatically sets the change sensitivity for the inclinometer sensor based on the current report interval. The following table, repurposed from the official MSDN documentation, specifies the change sensitivity values for given intervals.

Current report interval (in milliseconds)	Change sensitivity (in degrees)
1 to 16	0.01
17 to 32	0.5
33 or greater	2

To test the inclinometer on your device, you can use the following XAML code as a reference for your MainPage.xaml:

```
<Page
    x:Class="InclinometerSensorSample.MainPage"
    xmlns="http://schemas.microsoft.com/winfx/2006/xaml/presentation"
    xmlns:x="http://schemas.microsoft.com/winfx/2006/xaml"
    xmlns:local="using:InclinometerSensorSample"
    xmlns:d="http://schemas.microsoft.com/expression/blend/2008"
    xmlns:mc="http://schemas.openxmlformats.org/markup-compatibility/2006"
    mc:Ignorable="d">

    <Grid Background="{StaticResource ApplicationPageBackgroundThemeBrush}">
        <TextBlock x:Name="InclinometerTextBlock" Width="Auto" Height="Auto"
            Margin="20" FontSize="22" />
    </Grid>
</Page>
```

Using the light sensor

A Windows Store app can use the light sensor to detect and respond to changes in ambient lighting. Changing the contrast between the background and the font used to render the content, for example, improves the readability of the content. If you want to measure ambient light through the light sensor of your device, you can use the following XAML code as a reference for your MainPage.xaml:

```
<Page
    x:Class="LightSensorSample.MainPage"
    xmlns="http://schemas.microsoft.com/winfx/2006/xaml/presentation"
    xmlns:x="http://schemas.microsoft.com/winfx/2006/xaml"
    xmlns:local="using:LightSensorSample"
    xmlns:d="http://schemas.microsoft.com/expression/blend/2008"
    xmlns:mc="http://schemas.openxmlformats.org/markup-compatibility/2006"
    mc:Ignorable="d">

    <Grid Background="{StaticResource ApplicationPageBackgroundThemeBrush}">
        <TextBlock x:Name="LightSensorTextBlock" Width="Auto" Height="Auto"
            Margin="20" FontSize="22" />
    </Grid>
</Page>
```

The measurement of ambient lighting is expressed in lux and can be accessed through the *IlluminanceLux* property of the *LightSensorReading* class, as shown in Listing 2-22.

> ***NOTE*** **LUX AND LUMEN**
>
> **A "lux" is a unit of measure of the intensity (as perceived by the human eye) of light that hits or passes through a surface. Lux is equal to one lumen per square meter. A lumen represents the intensity of visible light emitted by a source.**

LISTING 2-22 Determining the intensity of the ambient light through the light sensor

```
public MainPage()
{
    this.InitializeComponent();
    this.InitializeLightSensor();
}

private LightSensor _lightSensor;

private void InitializeLightSensor()
{
    this._lightSensor = LightSensor.GetDefault();

    if (this._lightSensor == null)
    {
        LightSensorTextBlock.Text = "No light sensor found";
        return;
    }
```

```
    uint minReportInterval = this._lightSensor.MinimumReportInterval;
    var desiredReportInterval = minReportInterval > 16 ? minReportInterval : 16;
    this._lightSensor.ReportInterval = desiredReportInterval;

    this._lightSensor.ReadingChanged += LightSensor_ReadingChanged;
}

private async void LightSensor_ReadingChanged(LightSensor sender,
    LightSensorReadingChangedEventArgs args)
{
    await Dispatcher.RunAsync(Windows.UI.Core.CoreDispatcherPriority.Normal, () =>
    {
        LightSensorTextBlock.Text = String.Format(
            "Illuminance in lux : {0}", args.Reading.IlluminanceInLux);
    });
}
```

NOTE **SENSOR CHANGE SENSITIVITY**

The Sensor platform automatically sets the change sensitivity for ambient light sensors based on the current report interval. The following table, repurposed from the official MSDN documentation, specifies the change sensitivity values for given intervals.

Current report interval (in milliseconds)	Change sensitivity (percentage)
1 to 16	1%
17 to 32	1%
33 or greater	5%

Determining the user's location

The Windows Runtime can determine the user's location in two ways. The first way is to get the information from the Windows Location Provider, which uses Wi-Fi triangulation and IP address data to determine the user's location. The second and more precise way to determine the user's location is to leverage a GPS sensor, if present.

NOTE **LOCATION PROVIDER**

A location provider is a hardware device or software that generates geographic data to determine the location of a computer or device.

It is up to the Location API to determine the most accurate location sensor for a given scenario. When the Windows Location Provider and GPS both exist on the same system and are providing data, the Location API will use the sensor with the most accurate data. In most cases, the GPS will be more accurate, and its data will be passed to the application. From a developer's viewpoint, however, the internal mechanisms used by the system to determine the user's location are completely transparent. Just use the same Location API and enable the system to determine the right strategy to retrieve the data from all the available sources.

If you are developing Windows Store apps on a traditional desktop PC, you should not expect to get accurate data about your location. Determining location through Wi-Fi triangulation can give you only coarse-grained results. According to the official MSDN documentation, locations calculated from Wi-Fi data are accurate to within 350 meters in urban areas. If no Wi-Fi networks are available, the Windows Location Provider uses IP address resolution to get approximate location with an accuracy of 50 kilometers.

To test your app with more accurate data, you can use the Windows 8 Simulator. The simulator enables you to set geographic data such as longitude, latitude, altitude, and accuracy, which will be used as a simulated location to test your app's behavior. Figure 2-12 shows the Set Location dialog box in the Windows 8 Simulator.

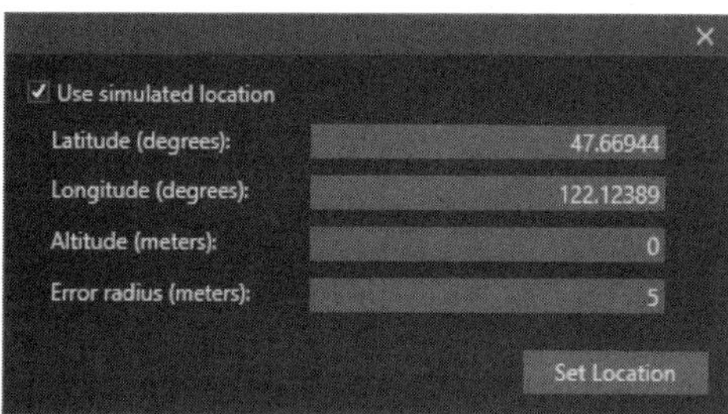

FIGURE 2-12 The Windows 8 Simulator showing the dialog box to use a simulated location

In Windows 8, location providers and GPS sensors are considered "sensitive devices" because they provide information that's potentially harmful to the user's privacy. For this reason, before you access the Location API programmatically, you have to add the corresponding Location capability in the Package.appxmanifest file of your app, as shown in Figure 2-13.

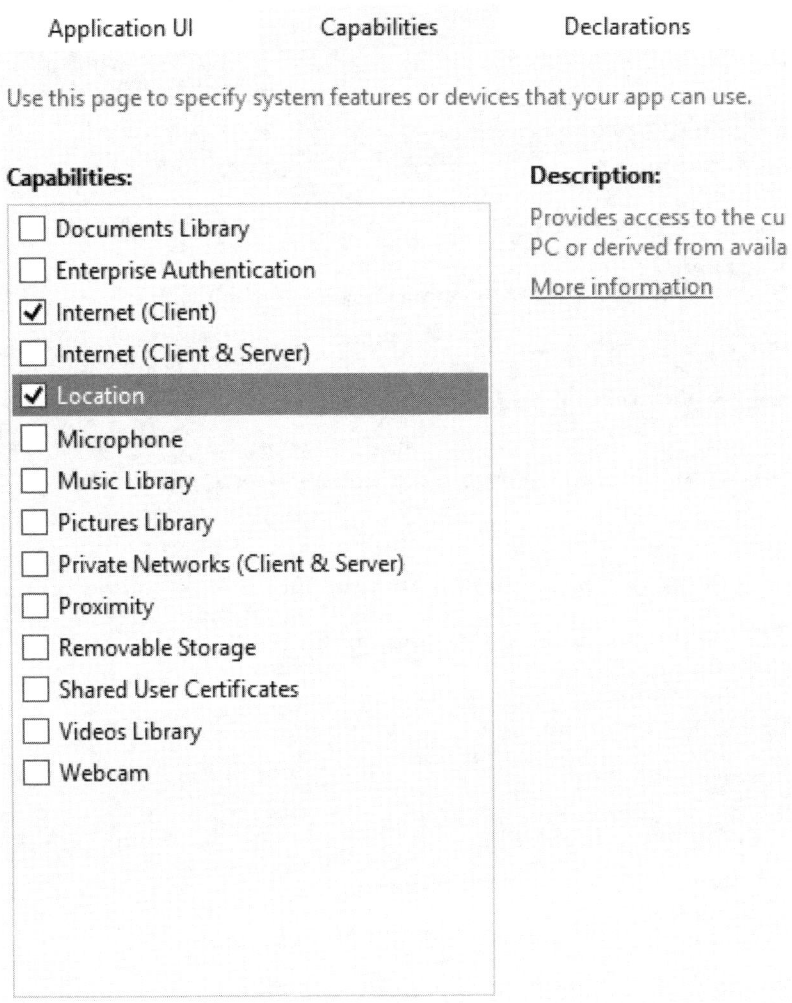

Application UI   Capabilities   Declarations

Use this page to specify system features or devices that your app can use.

Capabilities:

- [ ] Documents Library
- [ ] Enterprise Authentication
- [x] Internet (Client)
- [ ] Internet (Client & Server)
- [x] Location
- [ ] Microphone
- [ ] Music Library
- [ ] Pictures Library
- [ ] Private Networks (Client & Server)
- [ ] Proximity
- [ ] Removable Storage
- [ ] Shared User Certificates
- [ ] Videos Library
- [ ] Webcam

Description:

Provides access to the cu
PC or derived from availa

More information

FIGURE 2-13 The App Manifest Designer with the Location capability enabled

The first time your app needs to access the user's location, a dialog box appears asking for the user's permission to use the Location API. If a user denies permission to access the GPS sensor, make sure that your app can deal with this scenario gracefully.

MORE INFO **PERMISSIONS**

In Chapter 6, Objective 6.2, "Handling device capability errors," provides details about user permissions for device access.

Retrieving geographic data

The *Windows.Devices.Geolocation* namespace contains all the classes, types, and methods that your app needs to access the computer's geographic location. The class responsible for retrieving data about the user's current location is the *Geolocator* class. Listing 2-23 shows how to use this class to determine the current position.

LISTING 2-23 Retrieving the user's current location

```
private Geolocator _geoLocator;
protected override void OnNavigatedTo(NavigationEventArgs e)
{
    this._geoLocator = new Geolocator();

    this._geoLocator.StatusChanged += GeoLocator_StatusChanged;
}

private async void GetLocation_Click(object sender, RoutedEventArgs e)
{
    try
    {
        this._geoLocator.DesiredAccuracy = PositionAccuracy.High;

        var position = await this._geoLocator.GetGeopositionAsync();
        this.DisplayPosition(position);
    }
    catch (Exception)
    {
        // handle exception
    }
}

private async void DisplayPosition(Geoposition position)
{
    await Dispatcher.RunAsync(Windows.UI.Core.CoreDispatcherPriority.Normal, () =>
    {
        LongitudeTextBlock.Text = String.Format("Longitude: {0}",
            position.Coordinate.Longitude);
        LatitudeTextBlock.Text = String.Format("Latitude: {0}",
            position.Coordinate.Latitude);
        HeadingTextBlock.Text = String.Format("Heading: {0} degrees",
            position.Coordinate.Heading == null ? 0 : position.Coordinate.Heading);
        SpeedTextBlock.Text = String.Format("Speed: {0} m/s",
            position.Coordinate.Speed == null ? 0 : position.Coordinate.Speed);
        AltitudeTextBlock.Text = String.Format("Altitude: {0} meters",
            position.Coordinate.Altitude == null ? 0 : position.Coordinate.Altitude);
        AccuracyTextBlock.Text = String.Format("Accuracy: {0} meters",
            position.Coordinate.Accuracy);
        TimestampTextBlock.Text = String.Format("Timestamp: {0:H:mm:ss.FF}",
            position.Coordinate.Timestamp);

        TrackPositionPanel.Visibility = Windows.UI.Xaml.Visibility.Visible;
    });
}
```

```
private async void GeoLocator_StatusChanged(Geolocator sender,
    StatusChangedEventArgs args)
{
    await Dispatcher.RunAsync(Windows.UI.Core.CoreDispatcherPriority.Normal, () =>
    {
        switch (args.Status)
        {
            case PositionStatus.Ready:
                GpsStatusTextBlock.Text += "GPS device: Ready\n";
                break;
            case PositionStatus.Initializing:
                GpsStatusTextBlock.Text += "Geolocation: Initializing\n";
                break;
            case PositionStatus.NoData:
                GpsStatusTextBlock.Text += " Geolocation: No data\n";
                break;
            case PositionStatus.Disabled:
                GpsStatusTextBlock.Text += " Geolocation: Disabled\n";
                break;
            case PositionStatus.NotInitialized:
                GpsStatusTextBlock.Text += " Geolocation: Not initialized\n";
                break;
            case PositionStatus.NotAvailable:
                GpsStatusTextBlock.Text += " Geolocation: Not available\n";
                break;
            default:
                GpsStatusTextBlock.Text += " Geolocation: Unknown\n";
                break;
        }
    });
}
```

After instantiating a *Geolocator* object, you can optionally leverage the *DesiredAccuracy* property to indicate the accuracy level at which the *Geolocator* provides location updates. You should set the *DesiredAccuracy* property to *High* only if your app requires the most accurate data available. Otherwise, set it to *Default* to save battery life. Consider, however, that setting the *DesiredAccuracy* property does not guarantee improvement of the accuracy of data, which depends on several other factors.

The *StatusChanged* event is raised when the capability of the *Geolocator* to provide location data changes. The status of the *Geolocator* is expressed by the *LocationStatus* property of the *PositionChangedEventArgs* supplied to the event handler as parameter. The *LocationStatus* property can assume one of the following values (expressed by the *PositionStatus* enum):

- ***Ready*** Location data is available.
- ***Initializing*** The location provider is initializing, looking for the required number of satellites in view to obtain an accurate position.
- ***NoData*** No location data is available from any location provider. After data becomes available, the *LocationStatus* property will change from the *NoData* state to the *Ready* state.

- ***Disabled*** The user has not granted the application permission to access location. Make sure that your app can handle this kind of scenario gracefully. For further details about handling device errors,refer to Objective 6.2, "Handling device capability errors" in Chapter 6.
- ***NotInitialized*** Neither the *GetGeopositionAsync* method has been called nor has an event handler for the *PositionChanged* event been registered yet.
- ***NotAvailable*** The Windows Sensor and Location platform is not available on this system.

The current status of the location provider can be checked at any time by inspecting the *LocationStatus* property of the *Geolocator* class.

To retrieve the user's current location, the only thing you have to do is to call the *GetGeopositionAsync* method using the *async/await* pattern. The method returns a *Geoposition* instance containing the required data. More specifically, the *Geoposition* class contains two kinds of data concerning the user's location.

The first type of data is exposed through the *Coordinate* property (of type *Geocoordinate*). This data represents geographic coordinates, such as longitude and latitude, and other data associated with the geographic location, such as altitude (expressed in meters above sea level), current heading (in degrees relative to true north), speed (meters per second), accuracy of the measurements, and a timestamp indicating the time at which the location was determined. The availability of some of this data, such as altitude and speed, depends on the implementation of the GPS device, so before using them you should check for *null* values.

NOTE **WINDOWS LOCATION PROVIDER LIMITATIONS**

The Windows Location Provider does not provide information about heading, speed, or altitude; only information about latitude and longitude coordinates, and accuracy.

The *Geoposition* class also exposes a *CivicAddress* property, which represents the civic address data associated with a geographic location. However, this information is not available unless a Civic Address provider has been installed. If no Civic Address provider is installed, the API returns the regional information accessible through Control Panel. Windows 8 does not include a Civic Address provider (as of this writing), nor are third-party providers available at this time. If your app needs to translate geographic coordinates into civic addresses, consider taking advantage of external services, such as the Bing Maps Geocode service.

NOTE **BING MAPS GEOCODE SERVICE**

For further information about the Bing Maps Geocode service, visit *http://msdn.microsoft.com/en-us/library/cc966793.aspx.*

The *Geolocator* class also exposes an overloaded version of the *GetGeopositionAsync* that accepts two *TimeSpan* objects as parameters. The first parameter indicates the maximum acceptable age of cached location data, whereas the second parameter represents the time-out to complete the operation.

EXAM TIP

According to the official MSDN documentation, if the *GetGeopositionAsync* method is called, and the *Geolocator* instance cannot find any sensor within the next seven seconds, the call will time out. As a result, the *StatusChanged* event handler will be called, and the *PositionStatus* property of the *StatusChangedEventArgs* passed to the handler will be *NoData*.

Tracking the user's position

Besides determining the user's current location, you can use the *Geolocator* class to track the user's movements through the *PositionChanged* event. This event is raised every time the location p rovider detects a change in the user's geographical location. Listing 2-24 shows how to leverage the *PositionChanged* event to track the user's movements and display updated information on the screen.

LISTING 2-24 Tracking user position

```
private async void TrackPosition_Click(object sender, RoutedEventArgs e)
{
    try
    {
        this._geoLocator.DesiredAccuracy = PositionAccuracy.Default;
        this._geoLocator.MovementThreshold = 5.0;

        this._geoLocator.PositionChanged += GeoLocator_PositionChanged;

        var position = await this._geoLocator.GetGeopositionAsync();
        this.DisplayPosition(position);
    }
    catch (Exception)
    {
        // handle exception
    }
}

private void GeoLocator_PositionChanged(Geolocator sender,
    PositionChangedEventArgs args)
{
    this.DisplayPosition(args.Position);
}
```

If your app does not track even the smallest change in the user's position, you can leverage the *MovementThreshold* property to set the distance of required movement, in meters, for the location provider to raise the *PositionChanged* event (the default value for this property is zero).

Listing 2-25 shows the XAML definition for the MainPage.xaml file you can use to test the code presented in this section.

LISTING 2-25 XAML definition of the main page used for this sample

```
<Page
    x:Class="GeolocationSample.MainPage"
    xmlns="http://schemas.microsoft.com/winfx/2006/xaml/presentation"
    xmlns:x="http://schemas.microsoft.com/winfx/2006/xaml"
    xmlns:local="using:GeolocationSample"
    xmlns:d="http://schemas.microsoft.com/expression/blend/2008"
    xmlns:mc="http://schemas.openxmlformats.org/markup-compatibility/2006"
    mc:Ignorable="d">

    <Grid Background="{StaticResource ApplicationPageBackgroundThemeBrush}">
        <StackPanel>
            <StackPanel Orientation="Horizontal">
                <Button Content="Track Position" Click="TrackPosition_Click"
                    FontSize="28" Height="Auto" Width="Auto" Margin="20" />
                <Button Content="Get Location" Click="GetLocation_Click"
                    FontSize="28" Height="Auto" Width="Auto" Margin="20"/>
            </StackPanel>
            <TextBlock Margin="5" FontSize="28" Width="Auto" Height="Auto"
                Name="GpsStatusTextBlock" TextWrapping="Wrap" />
            <StackPanel x:Name="TrackPositionPanel" Visibility="Collapsed">
                <TextBlock Margin="5" FontSize="28" Width="Auto" Height="Auto"
                    Name="LatitudeTextBlock" />
                <TextBlock Margin="5" FontSize="28" Width="Auto" Height="Auto"
                    Name="LongitudeTextBlock" />
                <TextBlock Margin="5" FontSize="28" Width="Auto" Height="Auto"
                    Name="AccuracyTextBlock" />
                <TextBlock Margin="5" FontSize="28" Width="Auto" Height="Auto"
                    Name="HeadingTextBlock" />
                <TextBlock Margin="5" FontSize="28" Width="Auto" Height="Auto"
                    Name="SpeedTextBlock" />
                <TextBlock Margin="5" FontSize="28" Width="Auto" Height="Auto"
                    Name="AltitudeTextBlock" />
                <TextBlock Margin="5" FontSize="28" Width="Auto" Height="Auto"
                    Name="TimestampTextBlock" />
            </StackPanel>
        </StackPanel>
    </Grid>
</Page>
```

Figure 2-14 shows the sample app running on the Windows 8 Simulator.

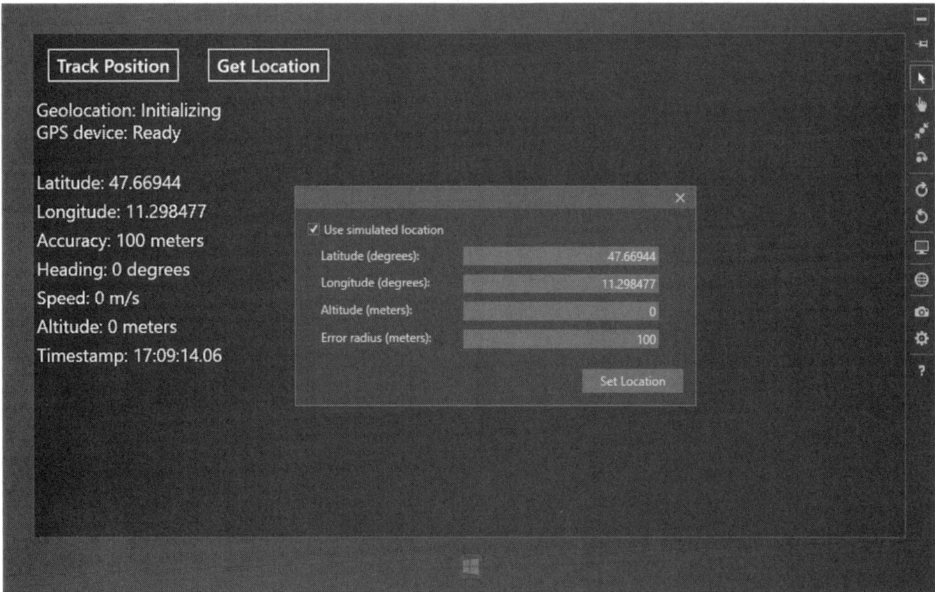

FIGURE 2-14 The sample app in the Windows 8 Simulator, showing the coordinates of a simulated location

Thought experiment

Determining the current heading

In this thought experiment, apply what you've learned about this objective. You can find answers to these questions in the "Answers" section at the end of this chapter.

You are developing an app to for hikers and trekkers. The app keeps track of the user's movements by recording a track that can be traced back to the original location at a later time. The app leverages a device's GPS sensor and uses the GPS data to determine the current heading. However, if the user is not moving, the data coming from the GPS sensor is not precise enough to display the direction the user is currently facing. For example, the user might stop walking and turn her head—and her device—from right to left and vice versa, trying to figure out which direction to take.

1. What kind of sensor could you leverage to gain more precise information about the direction in which the user is currently pointing the device, even if she is not moving?
2. How would you use the data to improve the user experience?

Objective summary

- The *Windows.Devices.Sensors* namespace includes support for a variety of sensors: accelerometer, gyrometer, compass, orientation, inclinometer, and light sensors.
- All corresponding APIs use similar patterns. First, you get a reference to the sensor through the *GetDefault* static method of the corresponding sensor class (such as *Accelerometer, Gyrometer, Compass*, and so on). Then you set the *ReportInterval* property of the sensor to let the system know how many resources need to be allocated for the sensor. (This step is not required for the *SimpleOrientationSensor* class.)
- To retrieve data from the sensor, you can follow an event-driven approach and subscribe to one of the events provided by the sensor class to notify when a new reading is available.
- Most sensor classes expose an almost identical *ReadingChanged* event, whereas the *Acceleration* class also exposes a *Shaken* event. The *SimpleOrientationSensor* exposes an *OrientationChanged* event.
- Alternatively, you can opt for a polling strategy, interrogating the sensor at regular intervals through the *GetCurrentReading* method exposed by all sensor classes (with the exception of the *SimpleOrientationSensor* class, which exposes a *GetCurrentOrientation* method).
- The *Windows.Devices.Geolocation* namespace exposes a Location API that enables retrieving the user's location through a location provider, which uses Wi-Fi triangulation and IP address data to determine the position, or a more precise GPS sensor, when available. The *Geolocator* class enables you to take advantage of these functionalities while hiding most of the inner work.

Objective review

Answer the following questions to test your knowledge of the information in this objective. You can find the answers to these questions and explanations of why each answer choice is correct or incorrect in the "Answers" section at the end of this chapter.

1. Which class does not expose any *ReportInterval*?

A. *Accelerometer* class

B. *Gyrometer* class

C. *Inclinometer* class

D. *SimpleOrientationSensor* class

2. What kind of data is provided by the *Gyrometer* class?
   - **A.** The acceleration of the device along the three axes
   - **B.** The rotation angles of a device around the three axes
   - **C.** The quadrant orientation of the device
   - **D.** The heading in degrees relative to magnetic north
3. What information is provided by the Windows Location Provider based on Wi-Fi triangulation and IP data analysis?
   - **A.** Latitude
   - **B.** Altitude
   - **C.** Heading
   - **D.** Speed

Objective 2.3: Enumerate and discover device capabilities

Sometimes you need to query a system to retrieve the set of available devices. You might need to check whether certain devices are connected and enabled, or whether more devices of the same kind, such as microphones and cameras, are available at the same moment (and therefore let the user decide which device to use). The *DeviceInformation* class, exposed by the *Windows.Devices.Enumeration* namespace, provides two ways of enumerating devices, represented by two static methods that can be used to retrieve information about the devices available on the system.

The first way leverages the *FindAllAsync* static method to perform a one-time search for available devices. This option is best suited for Windows Store apps that do not need to be notified when one of the existing devices changes or is removed from the system, or when new devices are added. The second way relies on the *DeviceWatcher* class, which not only enumerates all available devices but also raises specific events any time the device collection changes. In this section, you learn how to implement both strategies.

This objective covers how to:

- Discover the capabilities of a device (for example, GPS, accelerometer, near field communication, and camera)

Enumerating devices

The code in Listing 2-26 uses the *FindAllAsync* method to retrieve all available devices. More precisely, the method returns a *DeviceInformationCollection* object, which represents a collection of *DeviceInformation* instances, each of which allows accessing device properties. Then, for each device in the collection, the code creates a new custom *DeviceItem* object to hold some of the device information gathered, such as the device's name and unique ID, the thumbnail image that represents the device, and the device's glyph (the graphic symbol associated to that particular type of device). These two last pieces of information, thumbnail and glyph, can be retrieved through two specific methods: *GetThumbnailAsync* and *GetGlyphThumbnailAsync*, respectively. The collection of devices is then bound to the *ListView* control and displayed on the screen.

LISTING 2-26 Retrieving the collection of available devices through the *FindAllAsync* method

```
using System;
using System.Collections.Generic;
using System.IO;
using System.Linq;
using Windows.Devices.Enumeration;
using Windows.Foundation;
using Windows.Foundation.Collections;
using Windows.UI.Xaml;
using Windows.UI.Xaml.Controls;
using Windows.UI.Xaml.Controls.Primitives;
using Windows.UI.Xaml.Data;
using Windows.UI.Xaml.Input;
using Windows.UI.Xaml.Media;
using Windows.UI.Xaml.Media.Imaging;
using Windows.UI.Xaml.Navigation;

namespace EnumeratingDevices
{
    public sealed partial class MainPage : Page
    {
        public MainPage()
        {
            this.InitializeComponent();
        }

        private async void EnumerateDevices_Click(object sender, RoutedEventArgs e)
        {
            var list = new List<DeviceItem>();

            var devices = await
                Windows.Devices.Enumeration.DeviceInformation.FindAllAsync();
```

```
            if (devices != null && devices.Count > 0)
            {
                foreach (DeviceInformation device in devices)
                {
                    var glyph = await device.GetGlyphThumbnailAsync();
                    var thumb = await device.GetThumbnailAsync();

                    list.Add(new DeviceItem(device, thumb, glyph));
                }
            }
            DeviceListView.ItemsSource = list;
        }

        public class DeviceItem
        {
            public String DeviceName { get; set; }
            public String DeviceId { get; set; }
            public BitmapImage DeviceThumb { get; set; }
            public BitmapImage DeviceGlyph { get; set; }

            public DeviceItem(
                DeviceInformation deviceInterface,
                DeviceThumbnail thumbnail,
                DeviceThumbnail glyph)
            {
                this.DeviceName =
                    (String)deviceInterface.Properties["System.ItemNameDisplay"];
                this.DeviceId = String.Format("Device ID: {0}", deviceInterface.Id);
                this.DeviceThumb = new BitmapImage();
                this.DeviceThumb.SetSource(thumbnail);
                this.DeviceGlyph = new BitmapImage();
                this.DeviceGlyph.SetSource(glyph);
            }
        }
    }
}
```

Listing 2-27 includes the XAML definition of the MainPage.xaml page that you can use to test the presented code.

LISTING 2-27 The complete XAML definition of the main page for this sample

```
<Page
    x:Class="EnumeratingDevices.MainPage"
    xmlns="http://schemas.microsoft.com/winfx/2006/xaml/presentation"
    xmlns:x="http://schemas.microsoft.com/winfx/2006/xaml"
    xmlns:local="using:EnumeratingDevices"
    xmlns:d="http://schemas.microsoft.com/expression/blend/2008"
    xmlns:mc="http://schemas.openxmlformats.org/markup-compatibility/2006"
    mc:Ignorable="d">
```

```
    <UserControl.Resources>
        <DataTemplate x:Key="InterfaceItemTemplate">
            <StackPanel Margin="0,0,0,20">
                <TextBlock FontWeight="Bold" Style="{StaticResource SubheaderTextStyle}"
                    Text="{Binding Path=DeviceName}" />
                <TextBlock Style="{StaticResource BasicTextStyle}"
                    Text="{Binding Path=DeviceId}" />
                <StackPanel Orientation="Horizontal">
                    <TextBlock VerticalAlignment="Center"
                        Style="{StaticResource BasicTextStyle}" Text="Thumbnail:" />
                    <Image Width="256" Height="256" Source="{Binding Path=DeviceThumb}"
                        Margin="15,0,0,0"/>
                </StackPanel>
                <StackPanel Orientation="Horizontal">
                    <TextBlock VerticalAlignment="Center"
                        Style="{StaticResource BasicTextStyle}"
                        Text="Glyph Thumbnail:" />
                    <StackPanel Background="Blue" Margin="15,0,0,0">
                        <Image Width="54" Height="54"
                            Source="{Binding Path=DeviceGlyph}" />
                    </StackPanel>
                </StackPanel>
            </StackPanel>
        </DataTemplate>
    </UserControl.Resources>
    <ScrollViewer>
        <Grid Background="{StaticResource ApplicationPageBackgroundThemeBrush}">
            <StackPanel>
                <Button Click="EnumerateDevices_Click" Width="300" Height="50"
                    Content="Enumerate Devices" />
                <ListView x:Name="DeviceListView"
                    ItemTemplate="{StaticResource InterfaceItemTemplate}" />
            </StackPanel>
        </Grid>
    </ScrollViewer>
</Page>
```

If you now run the app, you should see a result similar to Figure 2-15. (Your device enumeration will most likely be different.)

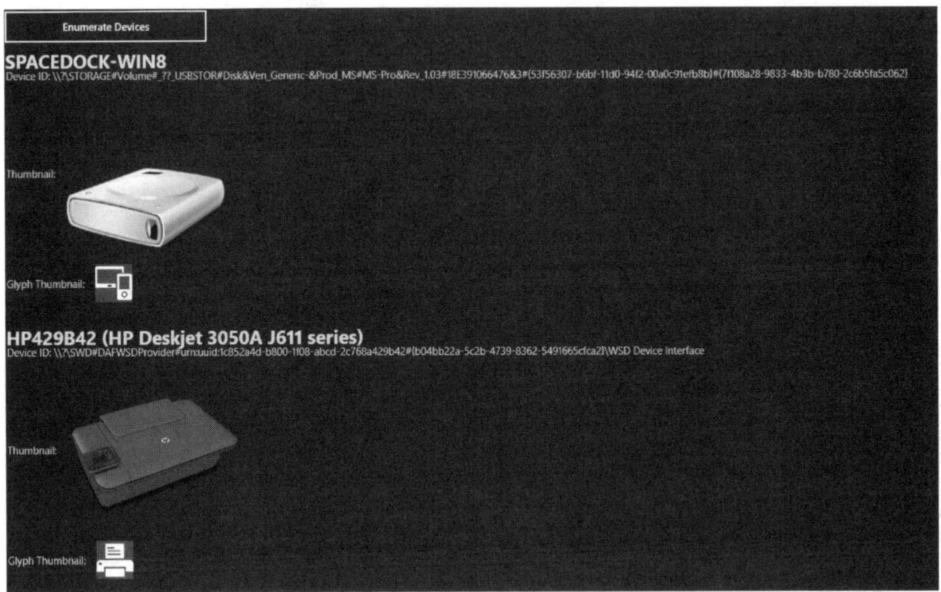

FIGURE 2-15 Enumerating the available devices

The *DeviceInformation* class exposes various overloaded versions of the *FindAllAsync* method that enable you to specify what type of device you are looking for. The first version accepts as a parameter a *DeviceClass* object that indicates the type of devices to enumerate. The *DeviceClass* enum can assume one of the following values:

- ***All*** Indicates that the user wants to enumerate all the devices
- ***AudioCapture*** Indicates that the user wants to enumerate all audio capture devices
- ***AudioRender*** Indicates that the user wants to enumerate all audio rendering devices
- ***PortableStorageDevice*** Indicates that the user wants to enumerate all portable storage devices
- ***VideoCapture*** Indicates that the user wants to enumerate all video capture devices

The following C# code excerpt shows a revised version of the code presented in Listing 2-26 that enumerates only the portable storage devices present on the system:

```
private async void EnumerateDevices_Click(object sender, RoutedEventArgs e)
{
    var list = new List<DeviceItem>();

    var devices = await Windows.Devices.Enumeration.DeviceInformation
        .FindAllAsync(DeviceClass.PortableStorageDevice);
```

```
    if (devices != null && devices.Count > 0)
    {
        foreach (DeviceInformation device in devices)
        {
            var glyph = await device.GetGlyphThumbnailAsync();
            var thumb = await device.GetThumbnailAsync();

            list.Add(new DeviceItem(device, thumb, glyph));
        }
    }
    DeviceListView.ItemsSource = list;
}
```

If you run the app, you should see a result similar to Figure 2-16.

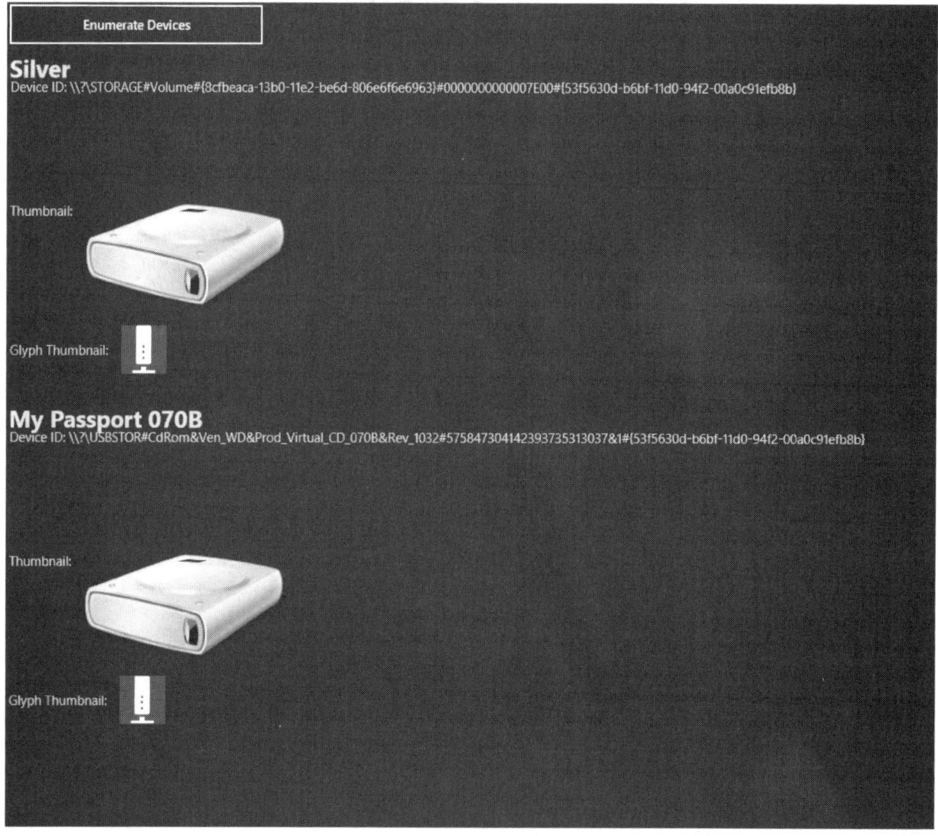

FIGURE 2-16 Enumerating only the storage devices

The other two overloaded versions of the *FindAllAsync* method accept different parameters that allow you finer control over the device to look for. Both of these methods accept an Advanced Query Syntax (AQS) string as parameter, a particular query syntax that Windows uses internally to refine and narrow search parameters. (One of these two methods also accepts, as a second parameter, an array of strings to specify additional properties for the device that you are looking for; you will learn more about this method shortly).

> ***MORE INFO*** **ADVANCED QUERY SYNTAX (AQS)**
>
> **You can find more information on this topic at *http://msdn.microsoft.com/en-us/library/windows/desktop/bb266512(v=vs.85).aspx.***

You can use this string to specify the device interface class implemented by the device you are looking for. In fact, any driver of a physical, logical, or virtual device must supply a name that uniquely identifies the device. Starting with Windows 2000, device drivers make use of a device interface class that represents a way of exposing internal functionalities to other system components. Each device interface class is associated with a globally unique identifier (GUID).

The following code snippet shows a revised version of Listing 2-25 that uses the AQS string to query for all devices implementing the device interface class for printers (represented by the GUID enclosed in curly brackets):

```
private async void EnumerateDevices_Click(object sender, RoutedEventArgs e)
{
    var list = new List<DeviceItem>();

    var selector =
        "System.Devices.InterfaceClassGuid:=\"{0ECEF634-6EF0-472A-8085-5AD023ECBCCD}\"";

    var devices = await DeviceInformation.FindAllAsync(selector);

    if (devices != null && devices.Count > 0)
    {
        foreach (DeviceInformation device in devices)
        {
            var glyph = await device.GetGlyphThumbnailAsync();
            var thumb = await device.GetThumbnailAsync();

            list.Add(new DeviceItem(device, thumb, glyph));
        }
    }
    DeviceListView.ItemsSource = list;
}
```

If you run the app, you should see a result similar to Figure 2-17.

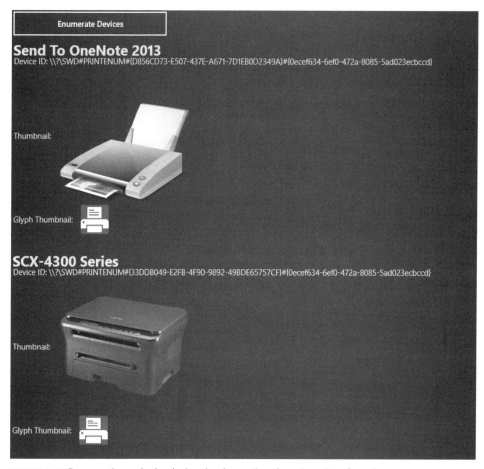

FIGURE 2-17 Enumerating only the devices implementing the printer interface class

Finally, notice that besides an ASQ string, the last overloaded version of the *FindAllAsync* method accepts an array of strings that enables you to specify which additional properties you want to retrieve from the devices you are looking for. By default, when retrieved by the *FindAllAsync* method (or by the *CreateWatcher* method discussed in the next section), a *DeviceInformation* object contains only a little information encapsulated in five properties.

EXAM TIP

DeviceInformation **object properties correspond to the ID and the name of the device (accessible through, respectively, the *Id* and *Name* properties of the *DeviceInformation* class), whether the device is enabled (represented by the *IsEnabled* property), whether the device is also the default device for certain operations (corresponding to the *IsDefault* property), and a path to the physical device location (*EnclosureLocation* property).**

To retrieve more information about the device, supply the *FindAllAsync* method with an array of strings, as shown in the following code snippet. The code specifically asks to retrieve two more properties: the container ID of the device and a Boolean value indicating whether the device is enabled.

```
var selector =
    "System.Devices.InterfaceClassGuid:=\"{0ECEF634-6EF0-472A-8085-5AD023ECBCCD}\"";
var properties = new String[] { "System.Devices.ContainerId",
    "System.Devices.InterfaceEnabled" };
var devices = await DeviceInformation.FindAllAsync(selector, properties);
```

> ***MORE INFO*** ***FINDALLASYNC*** **AND** ***CREATEWATCHER*** **METHODS**
>
> **The complete list of properties that can be retrieved through the *FindAllAsync* method (or the *CreateWatcher* method discussed in the next section), visit *http://msdn.microsoft.com/en-us/library/windows/apps/hh464997.aspx*. Some of these properties refer to devices, some to device interfaces, and some to device containers.**

Using the *DeviceWatcher* class to be notified of changes to the device collection

The *DeviceWatcher* class is responsible for enumerating devices dynamically; raising specific events every time devices are added, removed, or changed after the initial enumeration is completed. The events exposed by the *DeviceWatcher* class are these:

- ***Added*** Raised when a device is added to the collection enumerated by the *DeviceWatcher* class
- ***EnumerationCompleted*** Raised when the enumeration of devices is completed
- ***Removed*** Raised when a device is removed from the collection of enumerated devices
- ***Stopped*** Raised when the enumeration operation has been stopped
- ***Updated*** Raised when a device is updated in the collection of enumerated devices

To enumerate devices dynamically, obtain a reference to a *DeviceWatcher* class by calling the *CreateWatcher* static method of the *DeviceInformation* class. Then, you can begin the search for devices by calling the *Start* method.

NOTE ADDING FILTERS TO THE QUERY FOR THE DEVICE COLLECTION

The *CreateWatcher* method presents three overloaded versions that allow filtering and narrowing of devices that enumerated and kept under observation by the watcher. These overloaded versions use the same parameters as the *FindAllAsync* discussed in the previous section. For example, the following code adds removable storage devices to the device enumeration:

```
DeviceWatcher watcher = DeviceInformation.
    CreateWatcher(DeviceClass.PortableStorageDevice);
```

During the initial enumeration, the *DeviceWatcher* raises an *Added* event for each device found until the enumeration is complete and the *EnumerationCompleted* event is raised. From this point on, the watcher continues to raise *Added*, *Removed*, and *Updated* events every time a device is added, removed, or updated, respectively.

When you no longer need to be notified of any change in the device collection, you can stop the watcher by calling the *Stop* method. Listing 2-28 shows an example of its usage.

LISTING 2-28 Dynamically enumerating devices by using a *DeviceWatcher* object

```
public sealed partial class MainPage : Page
{
    private DeviceWatcher _watcher;
    private List<DeviceInformation> _deviceInfoList = new List<DeviceInformation>();

    public MainPage()
    {
        this.InitializeComponent();

        this._watcher = DeviceInformation
            .CreateWatcher(DeviceClass.PortableStorageDevice);

        this._watcher.Added += Watcher_Added;
        this._watcher.Updated += Watcher_Updated;
        this._watcher.Removed += Watcher_Removed;
        this._watcher.EnumerationCompleted += Watcher_EnumerationCompleted;
    }

    private async void StartWatcher_Click(object sender, RoutedEventArgs e)
    {
        if (this._watcher.Status != DeviceWatcherStatus.Started &&
            this._watcher.Status != DeviceWatcherStatus.Stopping)
        {
            try
            {
                await Dispatcher.RunAsync(Windows.UI.Core.CoreDispatcherPriority.Normal,
                    () =>
                {
                    this._watcher.Start();
                    WatcherStatusTextBlock.Text +=
                        "The Device Watcher has been started.\n";
                });
```

```
        }
        catch (Exception ex)
        {
            // handle exception
        }
    }
}

private async void Watcher_EnumerationCompleted(DeviceWatcher sender, object args)
{
    await Dispatcher.RunAsync(Windows.UI.Core.CoreDispatcherPriority.Normal, () =>
    {
        WatcherStatusTextBlock.Text += "Enumeration completed.\n";
        DeviceCounterTextBlock.Text = String.Format(
            "{0} removable storage devices found on your system.",
            this._deviceInfoList.Count);
    });
}

private async void Watcher_Removed(DeviceWatcher sender,
    DeviceInformationUpdate args)
{
    await Dispatcher.RunAsync(Windows.UI.Core.CoreDispatcherPriority.Normal, () =>
    {
        this._deviceInfoList.RemoveAll((e) => e.Id == args.Id);
        WatcherStatusTextBlock.Text +=
            "A removable storage device has been removed.\n";
        DeviceCounterTextBlock.Text = String.Format(
            "{0} removable storage devices found on your system.",
            this._deviceInfoList.Count);
    });
}

private async void Watcher_Updated(DeviceWatcher sender,
     DeviceInformationUpdate args)
{
    await Dispatcher.RunAsync(Windows.UI.Core.CoreDispatcherPriority.Normal, () =>
    {
        WatcherStatusTextBlock.Text += "A device has been updated.\n";
    });
}

private async void Watcher_Added(DeviceWatcher sender, DeviceInformation args)
{
    await Dispatcher.RunAsync(Windows.UI.Core.CoreDispatcherPriority.Normal, () =>
    {
        this._deviceInfoList.Add(args);
        var name = (String)args.Properties["System.ItemNameDisplay"];
        WatcherStatusTextBlock.Text += String.Format(
            "The following device has been added: {0}\n", name);
        DeviceCounterTextBlock.Text = String.Format(
            "{0} removable storage devices found on your system.",
            this._deviceInfoList.Count);
    });
}
```

```
    private async void StopWatcher_Click(object sender, RoutedEventArgs e)
    {
        try
        {
            await Dispatcher.RunAsync(Windows.UI.Core.CoreDispatcherPriority.Normal,
                () =>
            {
                this._watcher.Stop();
                WatcherStatusTextBlock.Text += "The Watcher has been stopped.\n";
            });
        }
        catch (Exception ex)
        {
            // handle exception
        }
    }
}
```

To test the code, you can use the following XAML code excerpt as a reference for your app's main page:

```
<Page
    x:Class="DeviceWatcherSample.MainPage"
    xmlns="http://schemas.microsoft.com/winfx/2006/xaml/presentation"
    xmlns:x="http://schemas.microsoft.com/winfx/2006/xaml"
    xmlns:local="using:DeviceWatcherSample"
    xmlns:d="http://schemas.microsoft.com/expression/blend/2008"
    xmlns:mc="http://schemas.openxmlformats.org/markup-compatibility/2006"
    mc:Ignorable="d">
    <Grid Background="{StaticResource ApplicationPageBackgroundThemeBrush}">
        <StackPanel>
            <StackPanel Orientation="Horizontal" Margin="20">
                <Button Click="StartWatcher_Click" Content="Start Watcher"
                    FontSize="26" Width="Auto" Height="Auto" Margin="10" />
                <Button Click="StopWatcher_Click" Content="Stop Watcher"
                    FontSize="26" Width="Auto" Height="Auto" Margin="10"/>
            </StackPanel>
            <TextBlock x:Name="DeviceCounterTextBlock" Width="Auto" Height="Auto"
                FontSize="26" Margin="20" />
            <TextBlock x:Name="WatcherStatusTextBlock" Width="Auto" Height="Auto"
                FontSize="26" Margin="20" TextWrapping="Wrap" />
        </StackPanel>
    </Grid>
</Page>
```

Figure 2-18 shows the sample app reacting to changes in the collection of removable storage devices connected to the system.

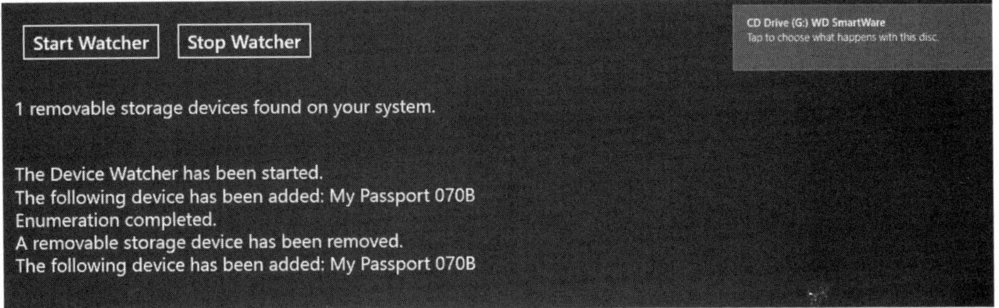

FIGURE 2-18 The sample app being notified of any change in the collection of removable storage devices connected to the system

The code illustrated in Listing 2-28 uses the *DeviceWatcherStatus* enum to check the state of the watcher before starting or stopping the watcher. The *DeviceWatcherStatus* enum can assume one of the following values:

- ***Created*** The initial state of a *Watcher* instance. During this state, clients can register event handlers.
- ***Started*** After the *Start* method has been called, the watcher starts enumerating the initial collection.
- ***EnumerationCompleted*** The watcher has finished enumerating the initial collection. Items can still be added, updated, or removed from the collection.
- ***Stopping*** The *Stop* method has been invoked by the client, and the watcher is still in the process of stopping. Events can still be raised during this state.
- ***Stopped*** The watcher has stopped. No subsequent events will be raised.
- ***Aborted*** The watcher has aborted its operations. No subsequent events will be raised.

The *Start* method cannot be called when *DeviceWatcher* is in the Started or Stopping state. The *Stop* method, on the other hand, raises the *Stopped* event, and the watcher state transitions to the Stopping state. The watcher will pass to the Stopped state after all events that are already in the process of being raised have completed. Figure 2-19 illustrates the complete flow of transitions between the states.

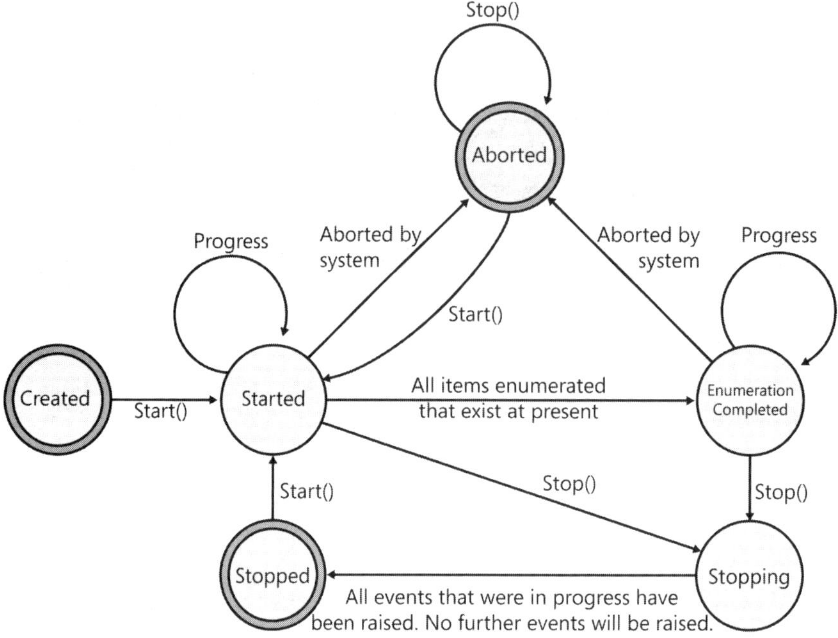

FIGURE 2-19 Diagram illustrating state transitions
Source: Adapted from MSDN documentation, *http://i.msdn.microsoft.com/dynimg/IC557460.png*

Enumerating Plug and Play (PnP) devices

The *Windows.Devices.Enumeration.PnP* namespace enables you to enumerate devices, device interfaces, device interface classes, and device containers. A device interface is a symbolic link to a Plug and Play (PnP) device that an application can use to access the device. A device interface class is the interface that represents functionalities exposed by a class of devices. A device container represents the physical device as seen by the user. The device container enables you to access information that pertains to the entire device hardware product, rather than only one of its functional interfaces. Examples of device container properties are manufacturer or model name.

The *Windows.Devices.Enumeration.PnP* namespace provides a *PnpObject* class that presents the same properties and methods of the *DeviceInformation* class discussed in the preceding sections, with a few differences. For example, for both the *FindAllAsync* and *CreateWatcher* methods exposed by the *PnpObject* class, you have to provide an instance of the *PnpObjectType* enum to indicate what kind of object you are looking for. The *PnpObjectType* enum can assume one of the following values:

- ***Unknown*** Indicates an object of unknown type. This value is not normally used.
- ***DeviceInterface*** Indicates a device interface.
- ***DeviceContainer*** Indicates a device container.
- ***DeviceInterfaceClass*** Indicates a device interface class.

For example, the following C# code snippet searches only the device containers available on the system:

```
string[] properties = {
    "System.ItemNameDisplay",
    "System.Devices.ModelName",
    "System.Devices.Connected",
    "System.Devices.FriendlyName",
    "System.Devices.Manufacturer",
    "System.Devices.ModelNumber" };

var deviceContainers = await PnpObject.FindAllAsync(
    PnpObjectType.DeviceContainer,
    properties);
```

For each *PnpObject* retrieved and added to the collection, the code also retrieves the device display name, the model name, the connection status, the friendly name, the manufacturer, and the model number.

> ***MORE INFO*** **DEVICE CONTAINER**
>
> **For further information about device containers and container IDs, visit *http://msdn.microsoft.com/en-us/library/windows/hardware/ff549447(v=vs.85).aspx*.**

The *PnpObject* class also provides the possibility of leveraging a *PnpDeviceWatcher* object (which is practically identical to the *DeviceWatcher* class) to monitor changes in the device collection. For the *FindAllAsync* method, this option follows the same pattern already illustrated in the preceding section. The following code snippet shows an example of its usage:

```
string[] properties = {
    "System.ItemNameDisplay",
    "System.Devices.ModelName",
    "System.Devices.Connected",
    "System.Devices.FriendlyName",
    "System.Devices.Manufacturer",
    "System.Devices.ModelNumber" };

this._watcher = PnpObject.CreateWatcher(PnpObjectType.DeviceInterfaceClass, properties);

this._watcher.Added += Watcher_Added;
this._watcher.Updated += Watcher_Updated;
this._watcher.Removed += Watcher_Removed;
this._watcher.EnumerationCompleted += Watcher_EnumerationCompleted;

this._watcher.Start();
```

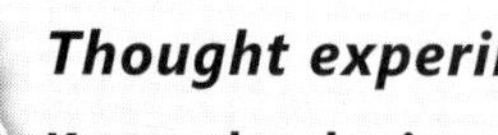

Thought experiment

Know the device you are working with

In this thought experiment, apply what you've learned about this objective. You can find answers to these questions in the "Answers" section at the end of this chapter.

You are developing a Windows Store app for video capturing. The app enables the user to apply several video effects on the recorded stream. In order to apply them, you need to know the manufacturer and the model of the camera.

Which steps do you have to perform to retrieve this kind of information from the system?

Objective summary

- The *DeviceInformation* class provides two ways of enumerating devices, represented by two static methods that can be used to retrieve information about the devices available on the system: the *FindAllAsync* method and the *DeviceWatcher* class.
- The *FindAllAsync* static method performs a one-time search for available devices. This method returns a collection of devices that can be inspected and enumerated. Overloaded versions of this method enable you to provide different search parameters to narrow down the resulting devices.
- The *DeviceWatcher* class, instantiated through the *CreateWatcher* method of the *DeviceInformation* class, not only enumerates available devices but also raises specific events any time the device collection changes.
- Use the *Start* method of the *DeviceWatcher* instance to start retrieving the collection of devices. Use the *Added*, *Updated*, and *Removed* events to be notified of changes in the device collection. Call the *Stop* method when you no longer need to be notified of changes in the devices.
- You can leverage the *PnpObject* class of the *Windows.Devices.Enumeration.PnP* namespace to enumerate Plug And Play (PnP) devices, device interfaces, and device containers. Use the *FindAllAsync* method for a one-time search for available PnP devices, or create a *PnpDeviceWatcher* object to be notified of any change in the collection.

Objective review

Answer the following questions to test your knowledge of the information in this objective. You can find the answers to these questions and explanations of why each answer choice is correct or incorrect in the "Answers" section at the end of this chapter.

1. Which parameter can be passed to the *FindAllAsync* method of the *DeviceInformation* class to retrieve all video capture devices available on a system?
   - **A.** A string with the content "VideoCapture"
   - **B.** An instance of the *DeviceClass* enum
   - **C.** An instance of the *PnpObjectType*
   - **D.** An instance of the *DeviceWatcher* class
2. Which class raises the *Added* event when a new device is added to the collection of available devices?
   - **A.** *PnpObject* class
   - **B.** *DeviceInformation* class
   - **C.** *DeviceWatcher* class
   - **D.** *DeviceThumbnail* class
3. Which of the following capabilities must be declared in the application manifest before enumerating the devices?
   - **A.** Location capability
   - **B.** Webcam capability
   - **C.** Removable Storage capability
   - **D.** None; no declaration needs to be added

Chapter summary

- To capture pictures or video, you can use the *CameraCaptureUI* class that encapsulates all the low-level details and provides the standard UI for simple operations.
- Use the *MediaCapture* class instead of *CameraCaptureUI* whenever you want complete control over the entire process of audio and video capturing, including customization of the UI.
- The *Windows.Devices.Sensors* namespace includes support for a variety of sensors: accelerometer, gyrometer, compass, orientation, inclinometer, and light sensors. All corresponding APIs use similar patterns. To retrieve data from a sensor, you can follow an event-driven approach and subscribe to the event specifically provided by the sensor's class (usually the *ReadingChangedEvent*) and be notified when a new reading is available, or you can opt for a polling strategy (interrogating the sensor at regular intervals).

- The *Windows.Devices.Geolocation* namespace exposes a Location API that enables retrieving the user's location through a location provider, which uses Wi-Fi triangulation and IP address data to determine the position, or a more precise GPS sensor, when available. Use the *Geolocator* class to take advantage of these functionalities.
- The *DeviceInformation* class, under the *Windows.Devices.Enumeration* namespace, provides two ways of enumerating devices. The *FindAllAsync* static method performs a one-time search for available devices, whereas the *DeviceWatcher* class not only enumerates all available devices but also raises specific events any time the device collection changes.
- You can leverage the *PnpObject* class of the *Windows.Devices.Enumeration.PnP* namespace to enumerate PnP devices, device interfaces, and device containers.

Answers

This section contains the solutions to the thought experiments and answers to the lesson review questions in this chapter.

Objective 2.1: Thought experiment

A possible approach is to use the *CameraCaptureUI* API to display the webcam preview using the standard Windows 8 UI. After the picture has been taken, you have to retrieve the picture stream and then show the picture to the user to enable her to insert the additional information. This way, the app uses the well-known standard interface, improving the overall user experience.

Unfortunately, this approach suffers from some limitations. First, the user could do something during the capture of the photo that is not allowed by the standard UI. Second, you still have to solve the problem of recording audio comments to associate to a particular photo. The *CameraCaptureUI* API enables a user to record video and capture photos. Audio is recorded only as part of the video stream coming from the webcam, which means you cannot handle audio and video separately when using the *CameraCaptureUI* API.

The second, more sophisticated approach is to use the *MediaCapture* API to display the webcam preview using a custom UI. This way, you can achieve finer-grained control over the entire flow. You can use the *MediaCapture* class to take pictures from the video stream, display the picture in the same form, and add text information. Then you can use the *MediaCapture* class again to record audio comments to associate to a photo, all without leaving the current page. Besides, by using the *MediaCapture* class, you can enable the user to add some video or audio effects, such as video stabilization or other custom effects.

Objective 2.1: Review

1. **Correct answer:** B

   A. **Incorrect:** You can set the media format.

   B. **Correct:** *VideoSettings* is the property to use to set the media format.

   C. **Incorrect:** *MaxResolution* is not designed to set the media format.

   D. **Incorrect:** The *CameraCaptureUIMode* parameter does not set the media format; it sets the type of capture.

2. **Correct answer:** D

   A. **Incorrect:** When an error occurs during media capture, the *Failed* event is raised.

   B. **Incorrect:** When the app does not have permission to use the capture device, an *UnauthorizedAccessException* is raised.

   C. **Incorrect:** No event is raised when the user stops recording the stream.

   D. **Correct:** The *RecordLimitationExceeded* event is raised when the record limit is exceeded.

3. **Correct answer:** A

   A. **Correct:** The *MediaCaptureInitializationSettings* class contains initialization settings for the *MediaCapture* object that can be passed as parameters to the *InitializeAsync* method.

   B. **Incorrect:** The *CameraCaptureUIPhotoFormat* enum determines the format for storing photos captured through the *CameraCaptureUI* API.

   C. **Incorrect:** The *CameraCaptureUIVideoCaptureSettings class* provides settings for capturing videos through the *CameraCaptureUI* API.

   D. **Incorrect:** The *CameraOptionsUI* class provides access to the UI setting for the webcam.

Objective 2.2: Thought experiment

1. You can leverage the compass sensor to determine which direction the device is pointing. This sensor lets you know the direction your device is facing, expressed in degrees relative to magnetic north and, when available, to geographic (or true) north.

2. You should use the data gathered by the compass sensor to adjust the orientation of the map displayed on the screen according to the user's current heading. Doing so aligns what the user sees on the displayed map with what he sees in front of him in the real world.

Objective 2.2: Review

1. **Correct answer:** D

   A. **Incorrect:** The *Accelerometer* class exposes a *ReportInterval* property.

   B. **Incorrect:** The *Gyrometer* class exposes a *ReportInterval* property.

   C. **Incorrect:** The *Inclinometer* class exposes a *ReportInterval* property.

   D. **Correct:** The *SimpleOrientationSensor* class does not expose a *ReportInterval* property.

2. **Correct answer:** B

   A. **Incorrect:** The acceleration of the device along the three axes is measured by the *Accelerometer* class.

   B. **Correct:** The rotation angles of a device around the three axes (also known as yaw, pitch, and roll) are measured by the *Gyrometer* class.

   C. **Incorrect:** The quadrant orientation of the device is measured by the *SimpleOrientationSensor* class.

   D. **Incorrect:** The heading in degrees relative to magnetic north is measured by the *Compass* class.

3. **Correct answer:** A

   A. **Correct:** The location provider uses Wi-Fi triangulation and IP address data to determine latitude and longitude coordinates.

   B. **Incorrect:** The altitude is not provided by the location provider, only by the GPS sensor.

   C. **Incorrect:** The current heading is not provided by the location provider, only by the GPS sensor or the compass sensor.

   D. **Incorrect:** Current speed is not provided by the location provider, only by the GPS sensor.

Objective 2.3: Thought experiment

Manufacturer or model information, together with all other information related to the hardware of the device, is generally exposed through device containers, which represent the physical devices as seen by the user.

The best option to retrieve information about manufacturer and model of a media capture device is to use the *FindAllAsync* method of the *PnpObject* class to retrieve all pertinent information exposed by the various device containers available on the system. You can also explicitly look only for devices manufactured by certain vendors. To do that, you have to supply the appropriate Advanced Query Syntax (AQS) string to the *FindAllAsync* method. When doing so, be sure to specify the right properties to retrieve.

For example, the following code uses one of the overloaded versions of the *FindAllAsync* method to retrieve all device containers that satisfy the provided condition, expressed through an AQS string that asks only for devices manufactured by Microsoft Corporation. The array of strings specifies which properties should be returned by the query, including device interface class ID, manufacturer, and model number:

```
string[] properties = {
    "System.ItemNameDisplay",
    "System.Devices.InterfaceClassGuid",
    "System.Devices.ModelName",
    "System.Devices.Connected",
    "System.Devices.FriendlyName",
    "System.Devices.Manufacturer",
    "System.Devices.ModelNumber"};

var selector = "System.Devices.Manufacturer:=\"Microsoft Corporation\"";
var containers = await
    PnpObject.FindAllAsync(PnpObjectType.DeviceContainer, properties, selector);
```

Objective 2.3: Review

1. **Correct answer:** B
   - **A. Incorrect:** To retrieve all video capture devices available on the system, you have to provide the *FindAllAsync* method of the *DeviceInformation* class with a *DeviceClass* instance.
   - **B. Correct:** To retrieve all video capture devices available on the system, you have to provide the *FindAllAsync* method of the *DeviceInformation* class with an instance of the *DeviceClass* enum (more precisely, the *DeviceClass.VideoCapture* value) to the *FindAllAsync* method.
   - **C. Incorrect:** The *PnpObjectType* enum is part of the *Windows.Devices.Enumeration.PnP* namespace.
   - **D. Incorrect:** The *DeviceWatcher* class is used to enumerate the devices available on the system and to be notified of any change in the collection.
2. **Correct answer:** C
   - **A. Incorrect:** The *PnpObject* class is used for a one-time search of available devices.
   - **B. Incorrect:** The *DeviceInformation* class is used for a one-time search of available devices.
   - **C. Correct:** The *DeviceWatcher* class raises the *Added* event when a new device is added to the collection of available devices.
   - **D. Incorrect:** The *DeviceThumbnail* class represents the image of a device.

3. **Correct answer:** D
   A. **Incorrect:** The Location capability is required to access data about a user's location.
   B. **Incorrect:** The Webcam capability is required to access the device's webcam.
   C. **Incorrect:** The Removable Storage capability is required to access a device's removable storage.
   D. **Correct:** You do not need to add declarations to enumerate available devices.

CHAPTER 3

Program user interaction

In this chapter, you learn how to implement the Print contract, which handles the entire printing flow, in your Windows Store apps. The chapter also focuses on the Play To contract, which enables users to stream a media element from a Windows Store app to any Play To–certified receiver connected to the network. You learn how to implement a Play To receiver application to receive a media element streaming from other Windows Store apps. Finally you deal with the Windows Push Notification Service (WNS) and learn how to authenticate to the service; how to code against the library to create, request, and save the notification channel; and how to interact with the service and send notifications to users.

Objectives in this chapter:

- Objective 3.1: Implement printing by using contracts and charms
- Objective 3.2: Implement Play To by using contracts and charms
- Objective 3.3: Notify users by using Windows Push Notification Service (WNS)

Objective 3.1: Implement printing by using contracts and charms

By default, a Windows Store app does not allow the user to access the Windows print system to print content. If you activate the Devices charm in the charms bar, a message appears: This app can't send to other devices right now.

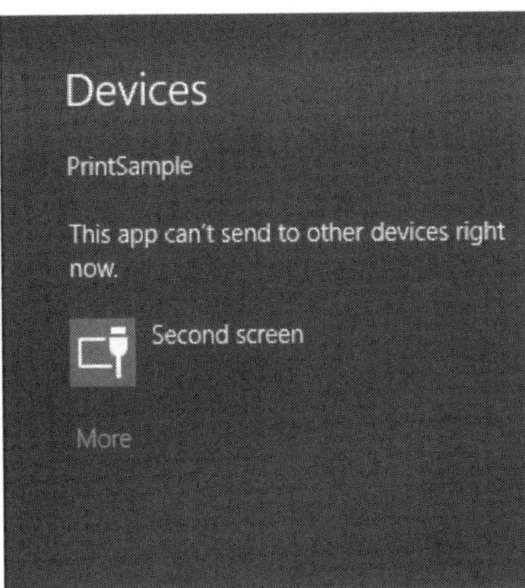

To be able to print, a Windows Store app needs to implement the Print contract. Unlike most of the other Windows 8 contracts, the Print contract requires a considerable amount of effort to be implemented. You not only need to paginate and format the content you want to be printed but you also have to handle numerous events raised at different stages of the printing process. In the following sections, you learn how to manage all the required steps, from generating print previews to handling content pagination and print settings.

This objective covers how to:

- Implement the Print contract
- Create a custom print template
- Construct a print preview
- Handle print pagination
- Expose printer settings within your app
- Implement in-app printing

Registering a Windows Store app for the Print contract

Registering a Windows Store app for the Print contract requires three steps. First, obtain a reference to a *PrintManager* instance for each view that you want users to be able to print. Second, implement a *PrintTask* instance representing the actual printing operation. Third, create a *PrintDocument* instance to hold a reference to the content that you want to print and handle the events raised during the printing process.

> ***NOTE*** **REQUIRED TYPES FOR THE PRINTING PROCESS**
>
> **Most of the types required by the printing process are included in two namespaces: *Windows.Graphics.Printing* and *Windows.UI.Xaml.Printing*.**

The *PrintManager* class is responsible for managing and orchestrating the complete printing process for a Windows Store app. A *PrintManager* instance cannot be shared across different pages, but must be specific for each view that you want your users to be able to print. You have to invoke the *GetForCurrentView* static method of the *PrintManager* class in the *OnNavigatedTo* method of the page that you want to print. Then you have to subscribe to the *PrintTaskRequested* event, as shown in the following code:

```
protected override void OnNavigatedTo(NavigationEventArgs e)
{
    PrintManager printManager = PrintManager.GetForCurrentView();
    printManager.PrintTaskRequested += PrintManager_PrintTaskRequested;
}
```

NOTE **CENTRALIZING CODE FOR THE PRINTING PROCESS**

We recommend that you centralize the code that handles the printing process in a base page class, from which all pages that need to print can inherit.

After you obtain a reference to the *PrintManager* object for a specific view in its *OnNavigatedTo* method, you must remember to unsubscribe the event before leaving that page, as shown in the following code snippet (or else you get an exception):

```
protected override void OnNavigatedFrom(NavigationEventArgs e)
{
    PrintManager printManager = PrintManager.GetForCurrentView();
    printManager.PrintTaskRequested -= PrintManager_PrintTaskRequested;
}
```

The *PrintTaskRequested* event is raised by the system when the user requests a print operation by activating the Devices charm in the charms bar.

The event handler for the *PrintTaskRequested* event is where your code needs to create the *PrintTask* object that represents a specific printing operation for a Windows Store app. It includes the content to be printed (in the form of a *PrintDocument* object) and information describing how that content is to be printed.

Listing 3-1 shows the basic implementation of the *PrintTaskRequested* event handler.

LISTING 3-1 Implementing the *PrintTaskRequested* event handler

```
private void PrintManager_PrintTaskRequested(PrintManager sender,
    PrintTaskRequestedEventArgs args)
{
    PrintTask printTask = null;

    printTask = args.Request.CreatePrintTask("Windows 8 Print Sample",
       (sourceRequested) =>
    {
        // code omitted
    });
}
```

The *PrintTask* object is created by invoking the *CreatePrintTask* method exposed by the *Request* property. (The *Request* property is an instance of the *PrintTaskRequest* class that can be accessed from the *PrintTaskRequestedEventArgs* object passed to the *PrintTaskRequested* event.)

This method requires two parameters: the name for the task and a *PrintTaskSourceRequestedHandler* delegate. The first parameter represents the name that appears in the print queue.

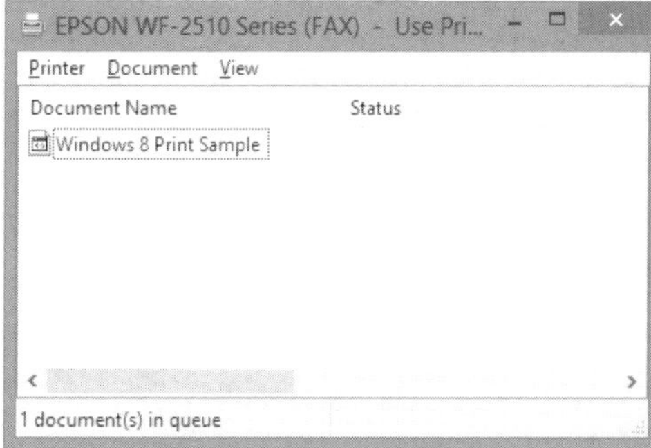

The delegate passed as the second parameter holds a reference to the method that is called when the user is ready to begin the printing process. In the preceding code excerpt, the delegate is represented by an anonymous method.

If you launch the app in Microsoft Visual Studio 2012 and activate the Devices charm, the flyout shows that your app is now registered to the Windows print system (see Figure 3-1).

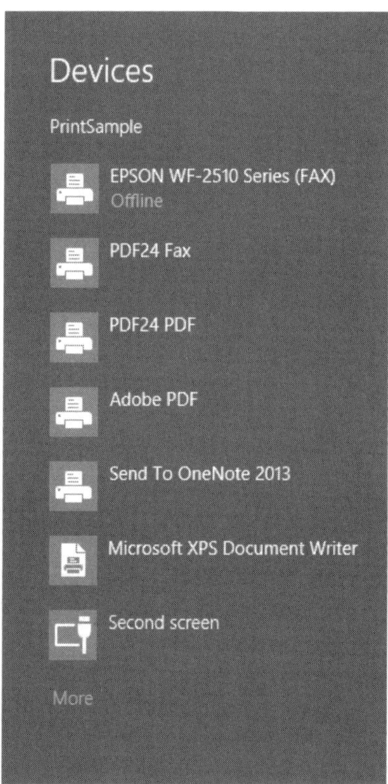

FIGURE 3-1 The Devices flyout available through Windows 8

If you select a print target, the system displays a message: The app didn't provide anything to print (see Figure 3-2).

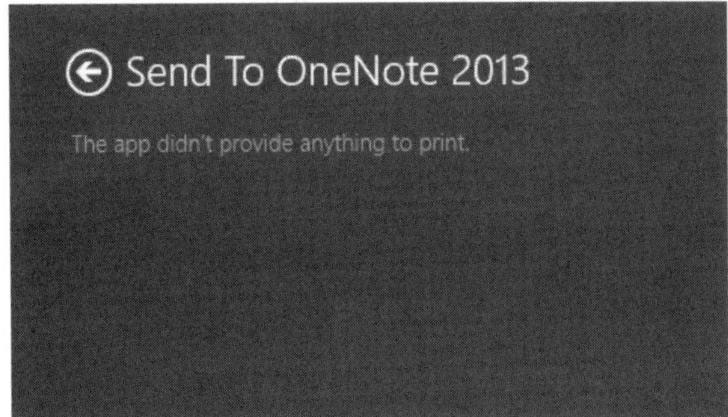

FIGURE 3-2 The error message displayed when the user selects a print target and your app has not provided any content to print yet

After creating the *PrintTask*, you need to provide some content to be printed. To implement the *PrintTask*, provide it with a reference to an object implementing the *IPrintDocumentSource* interface by invoking the *SetSource* method exposed by the *PrintTaskRequestedEventArgs*. The object passed to this method points to the actual content that will be printed as soon as the delegate is invoked. (See "Creating a custom print template" later in the chapter for more details.) Listing 3-2 shows the revised *PrintTaskRequested* event handler originally shown in Listing 3-1, with changes shown in bold.

LISTING 3-2 The *PrintTaskRequested* event handler using the *SetSource* method

```
private void PrintManager_PrintTaskRequested(PrintManager sender,
    PrintTaskRequestedEventArgs args)
{
    PrintTask printTask = null;

    printTask =
        args.Request.CreatePrintTask("Windows 8 Print Sample", (sourceRequested) =>
    {
        sourceRequested.SetSource(this._documentSource);
    });
}
```

The *PrintTaskRequestedEventArgs* also exposes a *GetDeferral* method that can be used whenever you need to perform a lengthy operation. In Windows Store apps, this kind of operation must be performed asynchronously and needs a deferral in combination with the *async/await* pattern. The Windows Runtime (WinRT) waits for the content to be retrieved until the deferral is marked as completed by invoking the *Complete* method of the deferral object. The following code shows the basic pattern for this scenario:

```
    private void PrintManager_PrintTaskRequested(PrintManager sender,
     PrintTaskRequestedEventArgs args)
{
     PrintTask printTask = null;

     var deferral = args.Request.GetDeferral();
```

```
        printTask = args.Request.CreatePrintTask("Windows 8 Print Sample",
            async (sourceRequested) =>
        {
            // perform some async operation here
            // Use the await keyword
        });
        deferral.Complete();
    }
```

You must initialize the document source that will be supplied to the *SetSource* method. In the *OnNavigatedTo* method, add the lines of code shown in bold:

```
private PrintDocument _printDocument;
private IPrintDocumentSource _documentSource;

protected override void OnNavigatedTo(NavigationEventArgs e)
{
    this._printDocument = new PrintDocument();
    this._documentSource = this._printDocument.DocumentSource;

    PrintManager printMan = PrintManager.GetForCurrentView();
    printMan.PrintTaskRequested += PrintManager_PrintTaskRequested;
}
```

The *PrintDocument* type, as its name suggests, is the actual document that is printed after you have supplied it with some content, represented by an object implementing the *IPrintDocumentSource* interface.

> ***NOTE IPRINTDOCUMENTSOURCE***
>
> ***IPrintDocumentSource* is currently just an empty interface, but it is open to future implementations.**

If you now launch the application and select a print target, the print window attempts to retrieve the preview of the document, as shown in Figure 3-3. Because you have not yet provided any actual content, there is nothing to display and the preview eventually displays a blank page.

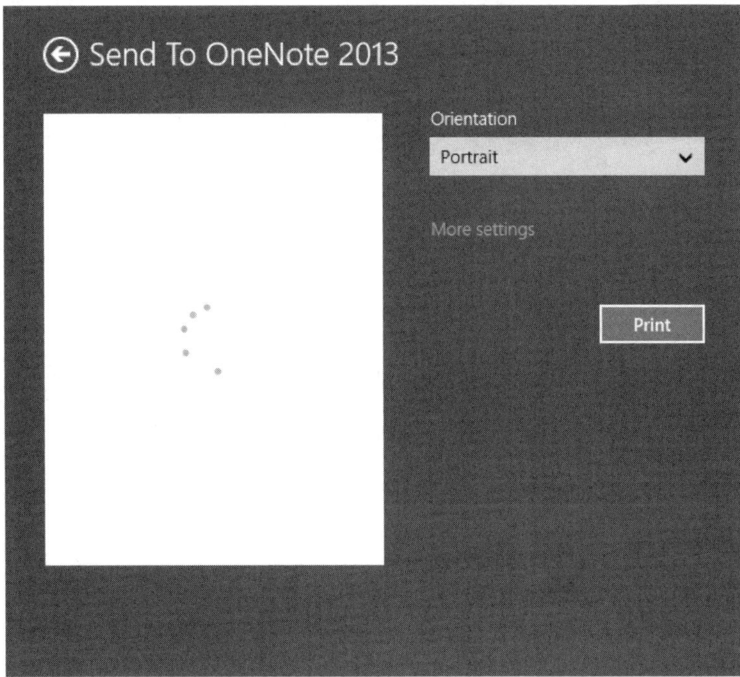

FIGURE 3-3 Print window attempting to load a document into the preview pane

In the following sections, you learn how to paginate content and respond to different events exposed by the *PrintDocument* object. First, there are a few things to know about the *PrintTask* class.

Handling *PrintTask* events

After the *PrintTask* instance has been created, your application can optionally subscribe to the events exposed by this class. These events are raised by the system at different stages of the printing process and can be used to provide feedback to the user:

- ***Previewing*** Raised when the system initializes the preview mode of the printing process
- ***Progressing*** Raised to provide progress information about how much of the printed content has been submitted to the print system
- ***Completed*** Fired when the printing operation is finished
- ***Submitting*** Raised when the print task begins submitting content to the print subsystem

Regarding the *Completed* event, it is important to understand that a task is marked as completed not only when the content has been actually submitted to the system for printing but also when the task has been canceled by the user, has failed, or has been abandoned.

You should consider using the *Completed* event to provide the user with a feedback about the result of the printing task by accessing the *Completion* property of the *PrintTaskCompletedEventArgs* object passed as parameter to the event handler. In particular, the *Completion* property (of type *PrintTaskCompletion*) can assume one of the following values:

- ***Abandoned*** The task has been abandoned.
- ***Canceled*** The task has been canceled.
- ***Failed*** The task has failed.
- ***Submitted*** The task has been submitted.

The following code excerpt shows the *Completed* event handler informing the user that the print task has failed:

```
private async void OnPrintTaskCompleted(PrintTask sender,
    PrintTaskCompletedEventArgs args)
{
    if (args.Completion == PrintTaskCompletion.Failed)
    {
        await Dispatcher.RunAsync(Windows.UI.Core.CoreDispatcherPriority.Normal, () =>
        {
            MessageBox.Text = "Print Task failed";
        });
    }
}
```

In the *PrintTaskRequested* event handler, you can subscribe to the *Completed* event as follows:

```
printTask = args.Request.CreatePrintTask("Windows 8 Print Sample", (SourceRequested) =>
{
    printTask.Completed += OnPrintTaskCompleted;

    (code omitted)
}
```

Adding the user interface

It is time to add a basic user interface (UI) that displays some sample text that the user can print. (As you will see in the "Creating a custom print template" section, however, this is not the actual content that you will print.) Listing 3-3 shows the complete definition of the MainPage.xaml file.

NOTE MAINPAGE CLASS

Remember to derive the *MainPage* class from the custom base class if you centralized the code for implementing the Print contract.

LISTING 3-3 Complete XAML definition of the main page

```
<Page
    x:Class="PrintSample.MainPage"
    xmlns="http://schemas.microsoft.com/winfx/2006/xaml/presentation"
    xmlns:x="http://schemas.microsoft.com/winfx/2006/xaml"
    xmlns:local="using:PrintSample"
    xmlns:d="http://schemas.microsoft.com/expression/blend/2008"
    xmlns:mc="http://schemas.openxmlformats.org/markup-compatibility/2006"
    mc:Ignorable="d">
    <Grid VerticalAlignment="Center" x:Name="PrintableArea" Width="Auto" Height="Auto"
          Margin="50">
        <Grid.RowDefinitions>
            <RowDefinition Height="*"/>
            <RowDefinition Height="Auto" />
        </Grid.RowDefinitions>
        <TextBlock x:Name="DocumentBody"
                       Foreground="White"
                       FontSize="22"
                       TextWrapping="Wrap"
                       FontFamily="Segoe UI"
                       HorizontalAlignment="Left"
                       VerticalAlignment="Top"
                       IsTextSelectionEnabled="True"
                       Grid.Row="0">
               Lorem ipsum dolor sit amet, consectetur adipiscing elit. Fusce in metus
               dui, a scelerisque neque. Morbi eget sapien lectus, hendrerit semper
               orci. Donec elit sem, pharetra in ornare ac, dictum sed massa. Donec
               rhoncus consequat urna. Sed non enim ut quam aliquet adipiscing. Ut a
               enim a sem blandit lobortis. Donec non volutpat orci. In at massa nunc,
               vel lobortis leo. Fusce vel erat sit amet justo sollicitudin varius.
        </TextBlock>
        <TextBlock x:Name="MessageBox"
                   FontSize="18"
                   FontFamily="Segoe UI"
                   HorizontalAlignment="Center"
                   Grid.Row="1"/>
    </Grid>
</Page>
```

The result should look similar to Figure 3-4.

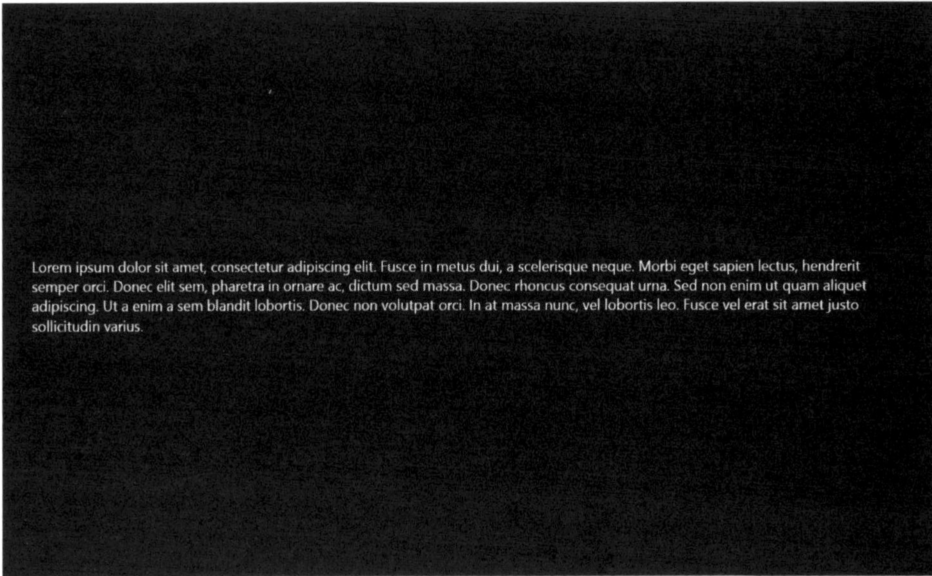
Lorem ipsum dolor sit amet, consectetur adipiscing elit. Fusce in metus dui, a scelerisque neque. Morbi eget sapien lectus, hendrerit semper orci. Donec elit sem, pharetra in ornare ac, dictum sed massa. Donec rhoncus consequat urna. Sed non enim ut quam aliquet adipiscing. Ut a enim a sem blandit lobortis. Donec non volutpat orci. In at massa nunc, vel lobortis leo. Fusce vel erat sit amet justo sollicitudin varius.

FIGURE 3-4 Sample text in the UI

Creating a custom print template

Whenever your Windows Store app needs to print some content, you cannot directly manipulate the Extensible Application Markup Language (XAML) page displayed to the user because any change in the page's content is displayed not only in the print window but also on the screen. What you actually send to the print system is a sort of "clone" of the page currently displayed on the screen that you can tailor based on the specific properties of the print target selected by the user in the Devices charm.

There are many ways to implement this scenario; for the sake of simplicity, the next sample uses a secondary page that includes the content of the page displayed to the user, but specifically formatted for print.

Listing 3-4 contains the complete definition of the secondary page supplied to the Windows print system.

LISTING 3-4 Complete XAML code for the secondary page that represents the actual content to be printed

```
<Page
    x:Class="PrintSample.PrintDocumentSample"
    xmlns="http://schemas.microsoft.com/winfx/2006/xaml/presentation"
    xmlns:x="http://schemas.microsoft.com/winfx/2006/xaml"
    xmlns:local="using:PrintSample"
    xmlns:d="http://schemas.microsoft.com/expression/blend/2008"
    xmlns:mc="http://schemas.openxmlformats.org/markup-compatibility/2006"
    mc:Ignorable="d">
```

```xml
    <Grid VerticalAlignment="Center" x:Name="PrintableArea" Width="800" Height="Auto"
          Margin="5">
        <Grid.RowDefinitions>
            <RowDefinition Height="Auto" />
            <RowDefinition Height="*"/>
            <RowDefinition Height="Auto" />
        </Grid.RowDefinitions>
        <StackPanel x:Name="DocumentHeader"  Grid.Row="0" VerticalAlignment="Top"
                    Visibility="Collapsed">
            <TextBlock Foreground="Black"
                       FontSize="16"
                       TextAlignment="Left"
                       FontFamily="Segoe UI">
                Windows 8 Print Sample Header
            </TextBlock>
        </StackPanel>
        <TextBlock x:Name="DocumentBody"
                   Foreground="Black"
                   FontSize="18"
                   FontFamily="Segoe UI"
                   TextWrapping="Wrap"
                   HorizontalAlignment="Left"
                   VerticalAlignment="Center"
                   IsTextSelectionEnabled="True"
                   Grid.Row="1">
                Lorem ipsum dolor sit amet, consectetur adipiscing elit. Fusce in metus
                dui, a scelerisque neque. Morbi eget sapien lectus, hendrerit semper
                orci. Donec elit sem, pharetra in ornare ac, dictum sed massa. Donec
                rhoncus consequat urna. Sed non enim ut quam aliquet adipiscing. Ut a
                enim a sem blandit lobortis. Donec non volutpat orci. In at massa nunc,
                vel lobortis leo. Fusce vel erat sit amet justo sollicitudin varius.
        </TextBlock>
        <StackPanel x:Name="DocumentFooter"
                    Grid.Row="2"
                    VerticalAlignment="Top"
                    Visibility="Collapsed">
            <TextBlock Foreground="Black"
                       FontSize="16"
                       TextAlignment="Left"
                       FontFamily="Segoe UI">
                    Windows 8 Print Sample Footer
            </TextBlock>
        </StackPanel>
    </Grid>
</Page>
```

The XAML code of the page is quite similar to the one displayed in the default page. The main exception is represented by two *StackPanel* controls. The "Reacting to changes in the print options" section later in this chapter shows you how to manipulate the controls.

Now that the app has a custom template specifically tailored for printing, you can assign the new page to a global variable of type *FrameworkElement* that represents the first page of the document to be printed:

```
private FrameworkElement _firstPage;
private void PreparePrintContent()
{
    if (this._firstPage == null)
    {
        this._firstPage = new PrintDocumentSample();
        this._firstPage.InvalidateMeasure();
        this._firstPage.UpdateLayout();
    }
}
```

In the *OnNavigatedTo* method, you can add a call to the *PreparePrintContent* method (changes are highlighted in bold):

```
protected override void OnNavigatedTo(NavigationEventArgs e)
{
    this._printDocument = new PrintDocument();
    this._documentSource = this._printDocument.DocumentSource;

    PrintManager printManager = PrintManager.GetForCurrentView();
    printManager.PrintTaskRequested += PrintManager_PrintTaskRequested;

    this.PreparePrintContent();
}
```

If you try to execute the app at this point, you still won't see the preview in the print window. In fact, you still have to prepare the preview for the print system. Before doing that, however, you need to understand how to manage the print options and format your content accordingly.

Understanding the print task options

Most of the options exposed by the print target selected by the user in the preview window can be accessed via the *Options* property of the *PrintTask* class. This property (of type *PrintTaskOptions*) can be used to customize the print user experience through a rich set of print options (such as color, number of pages, orientation, print quality, and so on) that define how the content passed to the *PrintTask* should to be formatted during the printing.

Although each of those options presents its specific set of values, they all share three common values (which represent three common scenarios):

- *DefaultValue*
- *NotAvailable*
- *PrintCustom*

The semantics of these values might be slightly different depending on whether they are acquired from the print target or set from code.

When the *Default* value is retrieved by accessing the corresponding print target property, it means the actual value for that property has not been determined. On the contrary, setting an option to the *Default* value instructs the target device to use its default value (whatever it might be) for that property. If the selected print target has no default value for that option, no changes are made (that is, the selected target keeps its original value).

EXAM TIP

When a *NotAvailable* value is retrieved, it means the specific option is not available for the current print target. Setting an option to *NotAvailable* is not allowed and results in an *ArgumentException*.

Most of these options can be used to either set a specific value to display in the print window or retrieve the information provided by the print device currently selected by the user.

For example, you can leverage the *PrintTaskOptions* class to set the initial value of one or more options for the preview window. If you try to set an option that is not supported by the print target, that option is simply ignored and not displayed to the user. Listing 3-5 shows how to provide some default values to the print system. (Changes from Listing 3-2 are highlighted in bold.)

LISTING 3-5 Setting the print option initial values

```
private void PrintManager_PrintTaskRequested(PrintManager sender,
    PrintTaskRequestedEventArgs args)
{
    PrintTask printTask = null;

    printTask =
        args.Request.CreatePrintTask("Windows 8 Print Sample", (sourceRequested) =>
    {
        printTask.Completed += OnPrintTaskCompleted;

        printTask.Options.Orientation = PrintOrientation.Landscape;
        printTask.Options.ColorMode = PrintColorMode.Grayscale;
        printTask.Options.MediaSize = PrintMediaSize.IsoA4;

        sourceRequested.SetSource(this._documentSource);
    });
}
```

Figure 3-5 shows the preview window with the values provided via the *PrintTask* object. The default orientation is now set to Landscape and the color mode to Monochrome.

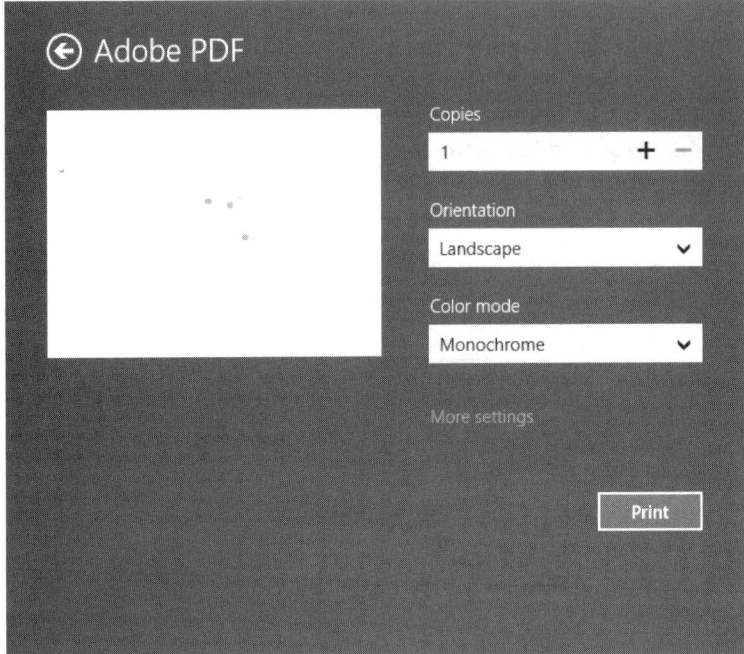

FIGURE 3-5 A print preview window displaying the new default options

In the next section, you learn how to retrieve these values from the selected device and how to format your content accordingly. Later in the chapter, you also learn how to define what options to display in the print preview and how to create custom options to fine-tune your content.

Paginating and previewing the document

Formatting, paginating, and previewing content for the Windows print system can be time-consuming. You need to adjust the format of the content the user wants to print based on the specific settings exposed by the print target, such as page dimensions, supported colors, paper orientation, and so on. Then you have to split the content exceeding the size of a single page into multiple pages and add each page to the collection that is sent to the print system. You also have to provide on request the preview of the page that is shown in the print window. To accomplish all these tasks, the *PrintDocument* class relies on three events, which constitute the "core" of the entire printing process:

- ***Paginate*** Raised when the user activates the Devices charm and selects a print target from the list of available device. The *PrintManager* requests the collection of pages to be shown in the preview window.
- ***GetPreviewPage*** Fired when the *PrintManager* requests a particular page to be shown in the preview window.

- ***AddPages*** Occurs when the *PrintManager* requests the final collection of pages to send to the printer; that is, when the user clicks the Print button in the preview window.

The following snippet shows the *OnNavigatedTo* method revised with the handlers for these three events:

```
protected override void OnNavigatedTo(NavigationEventArgs e)
{
    this._printDocument = new PrintDocument();
    this._documentSource = this._printDocument.DocumentSource;

    this._printDocument.Paginate += PrintDocument_Paginate;
    this._printDocument.GetPreviewPage += PrintDocument_GetPreviewPage;
    this._printDocument.AddPages += PrintDocument_AddPages;

    PrintManager printManager = PrintManager.GetForCurrentView();
    printManager.PrintTaskRequested += PrintManager_PrintTaskRequested;

    this.PreparePrintContent();
}
```

The *Paginate* event is raised when the user selects a print target in the Devices charm. In the corresponding event handler, several things occur. First, you need to format the page that you want to print based on the settings retrieved from the print target selected by the user.

The following code snippet shows how to format the content of the sample page according to the size of the "paper" used by the target device, represented by the *ImageableRect* property of the *PrintPageDescription* class. To retrieve these measures, you can leverage the *GetPageDescription* method exposed by the *PrintTaskOptions* object (which, in turn, can be obtained by casting the *PaginatedEventArgs* object passed as parameter):

```
PrintTaskOptions printingOptions = ((PrintTaskOptions)e.PrintTaskOptions);
PrintPageDescription pageDescription = printingOptions.GetPageDescription(0);

this._firstPage.Width = pageDescription.ImageableRect.Width;
this._firstPage.Height = pageDescription.ImageableRect.Height;
```

The next step is to resize the "printable area" of the sample page (represented by the *Grid* control) to leave some white space between the text and the paper's borders. The following code excerpt shows how to modify the size of the *Grid* control (retrieved using the *FindName* method of the *Framework* class) by applying a simple algorithm that calculates the margins to be left based on the paper size:

```
Grid printableArea = (Grid)this._firstPage.FindName("PrintableArea");
double marginWidth = Math.Max(
    pageDescription.PageSize.Width - pageDescription.ImageableRect.Width,
    pageDescription.PageSize.Width * marginLeft * 2);
double marginHeight = Math.Max(
   pageDescription.PageSize.Height - pageDescription.ImageableRect.Height,
   pageDescription.PageSize.Height * marginTop * 2);
printableArea.Width = this._firstPage.Width - marginWidth;
printableArea.Height = this._firstPage.Height - marginHeight;
```

After you customize the print document template based on the properties exposed by the print target, your application needs to handle the potential content overflow that might result and split the original content into different pages.

Handling and processing the content overflow can be particularly complex and time-consuming. For the sake of simplicity, the example does not have overflow to handle and there is only one page to print, whatever the size of the "paper" used by the print target might be.

MORE INFO **A DETAILED PRINT SAMPLE WITH OVERFLOW**

If you want a more detailed sample that shows how to paginate the content dynamically depending on the properties of the print target and how to handle the resulting overflow, you can download the official Windows 8 SDK Print Sample here: *http://code.msdn.microsoft.com/windowsapps/Print-Sample-c544cce6*.

Because the sample application has only one page to print, you can directly add it to the collection of pages that will be shown in the preview window and invoke the *SetPreviewPageCount* method to let the system know the number of pages for the preview, as follows:

```
this._pageList.Add(this._firstPage);
this._printDocument.SetPreviewPageCount(this._pageList.Count,
    PreviewPageCountType.Intermediate);
```

Listing 3-6 shows the code of the *Paginate* event handler used for this introductory example.

LISTING 3-6 Complete code for the *Paginate* event handler

```
private List<UIElement> _pageList = new List<UIElement>();
private void PrintDocument_Paginate(object sender, PaginateEventArgs e)
{
    var marginLeft = 0.1;
    var marginTop = 0.08;

    this._pageList.Clear();

    PrintTaskOptions printingOptions = ((PrintTaskOptions)e.PrintTaskOptions);
    PrintPageDescription pageDescription = printingOptions.GetPageDescription(0);

    this._firstPage.Width = pageDescription.ImageableRect.Width;
    this._firstPage.Height = pageDescription.ImageableRect.Height;

    Grid printableArea = (Grid)this._firstPage.FindName("PrintableArea");

    double marginWidth = Math.Max(
        pageDescription.PageSize.Width - pageDescription.ImageableRect.Width,
        pageDescription.PageSize.Width * marginLeft * 2);
```

```
    double marginHeight = Math.Max(
        pageDescription.PageSize.Height - pageDescription.ImageableRect.Height,
        pageDescription.PageSize.Height * marginTop * 2);

    printableArea.Width = this._firstPage.Width - marginWidth;
    printableArea.Height = this._firstPage.Height - marginHeight;

    this._pageList.Add(this._firstPage);
    this._printDocument.SetPreviewPageCount(
        this._pageList.Count, PreviewPageCountType.Intermediate);
}
```

As mentioned previously, the *GetPreviewPage* event is raised by the print system each time the user navigates from one page to another in the preview window. In the corresponding event handler, you have to supply the print system with the requested page, as follows:

```
private void PrintDocument_GetPreviewPage(object sender, GetPreviewPageEventArgs e)
{
    this._printDocument.SetPreviewPage(1, this._pageList[e.PageNumber - 1]);
}
```

The *GetPreviewPageEventArgs* object exposes a *PageNumber* property that indicates what page has been requested by the print system to be shown in the preview window.

Finally, in the *AddPages* event handler, you have to add all the pages resulting from the preceding operations to the final collection that is sent to the print target when the user clicks the Print button in the preview window.

To accomplish this task, call the *AddPage* method of the *PrintDocument* object. After all the pages are added, you can signal the system that the collection is ready to be printed by invoking the *AddPagesComplete* method:

```
private void PrintDocument_AddPages(object sender, AddPagesEventArgs e)
{
    for (int i = 0; i < this._pageList.Count; i++)
    {
        this._printDocument.AddPage(this._pageList[i]);
    }

    this._printDocument.AddPagesComplete();
}
```

After you run the application, activate the Devices charm, and select a print device, the result should look similar to Figure 3-6.

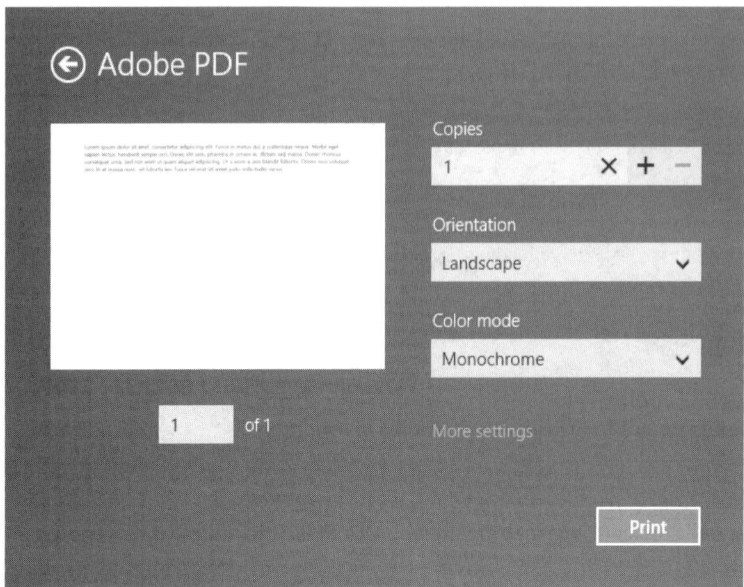

FIGURE 3-6 Print preview window displaying a document in the preview pane

Choosing options to display in the preview window

You can define the options that display in the preview window, and in which order. To do so, obtain a reference to the *PrintTaskOptionDetails* object for the current task and add the options one by one to the collection of options to be displayed, as shown in Listing 3-7.

LISTING 3-7 Choosing print options to display in the preview window

```
private void PrintManager_PrintTaskRequested(PrintManager sender,
    PrintTaskRequestedEventArgs args)
{
    PrintTask printTask = null;
    printTask = args.Request.CreatePrintTask(
        "Windows 8 Print Sample", (sourceRequested) =>
    {
        printTask.Completed += OnPrintTaskCompleted;

        PrintTaskOptionDetails detailedOptions =
            PrintTaskOptionDetails.GetFromPrintTaskOptions(printTask.Options);
        IList<string> displayedOptions = detailedOptions.DisplayedOptions;

        displayedOptions.Clear();

        displayedOptions.Add(StandardPrintTaskOptions.Orientation);
        displayedOptions.Add(StandardPrintTaskOptions.ColorMode);
        displayedOptions.Add(StandardPrintTaskOptions.MediaSize);
```

```
        printTask.Options.Orientation = PrintOrientation.Landscape;
        printTask.Options.ColorMode = PrintColorMode.Grayscale;
        printTask.Options.MediaSize = PrintMediaSize.NorthAmericaLegal;

        sourceRequested.SetSource(this._documentSource);
    });
}
```

After you obtain a reference to the detailed options for the current print task by invoking the *GetFromPrintTaskOptions* static method, you have to get a reference to the *DisplayedOptions* property, clear the collection, and add the options you want to display in the preview window one by one (and in the right order).

After you run the application, activate the Devices charm, and select a print target, the three options added to the collection display in the preview window. If any of the options added to the collection is not supported by the print target selected by the user, that option is ignored. Figure 3-7 shows the orientation and size options but not the color mode option, which is not supported by the print target.

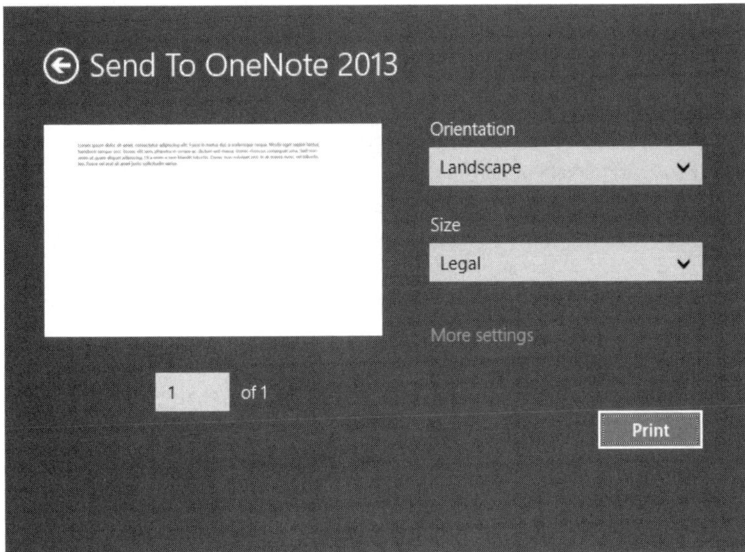

FIGURE 3-7 Print preview window with two of the three options added by using the *DisplayedOptions* property

Reacting to print option changes

Because the user can change the values in the print window, you might want your application to react to those changes and modify the formatted document accordingly. To do so, you can leverage the *OptionChanged* event, which is raised every time the user changes one of the properties of the print target. In the following listing, changes are highlighted in bold:

```
private void PrintManager_PrintTaskRequested(PrintManager sender,
    PrintTaskRequestedEventArgs args)
{
        (code omitted)

        detailedOptions.OptionChanged += OnOptionChanged;

        e.SetSource(this._documentSource);
    });
}
```

In the corresponding event handler, you can leverage the *InvalidatePreview* method exposed by the *PrintDocument* object to invalidate the current print preview. The system raises the *Paginate* event and the preview process starts over. The following code shows the implementation of the event handler:

```
private async void OnOptionChanged(PrintTaskOptionDetails sender,
    PrintTaskOptionChangedEventArgs args)
{
    string optionId = args.OptionId as string;

    if (string.IsNullOrEmpty(optionId))
        return;

    await Dispatcher.RunAsync(Windows.UI.Core.CoreDispatcherPriority.Normal, () =>
    {
        this._printDocument.InvalidatePreview();
    });
}
```

> ***NOTE*** **ADDING A FILTER**
>
> **Because any change in the printing options can raise the *OnOptionChanged* event, you might want to add a filter before invoking the *InvalidatePreview*. Be sure that not all the changes can trigger the code—only those that you are prepared to cope with.**

By subscribing to this event, you can modify your preview layout any time the user changes a particular option in the preview window. For example, you might decide to print the header and/or the footer of the document only in specific scenarios, as shown in Listing 3-8.

LISTING 3-8 Reacting to the changes in the print options

```
private void PrintDocument_Paginate(object sender, PaginateEventArgs e)
{
    (code omitted)

    printableArea.Width = this._firstPage.Width - marginWidth;
    printableArea.Height = this._firstPage.Height - marginHeight;

    var header = (StackPanel)this._firstPage.FindName("DocumentHeader");
    var footer = (StackPanel)this._firstPage.FindName("DocumentFooter");
```

```
    header.Visibility = Windows.UI.Xaml.Visibility.Collapsed;
    footer.Visibility = Windows.UI.Xaml.Visibility.Collapsed;

    if (printingOptions.Orientation == PrintOrientation.Landscape)
        footer.Visibility = Windows.UI.Xaml.Visibility.Visible;
    else if (printingOptions.Orientation == PrintOrientation.Portrait)
        header.Visibility = Windows.UI.Xaml.Visibility.Visible;

    this._pageList.Add(this._firstPage);

    this._printDocument.SetPreviewPageCount(
        this._pageList.Count, PreviewPageCountType.Intermediate);
}
```

The first time you activate the preview window, the *Orientation* property is set to *Landscape* by default, and only the document footer is visible. If you change the value to *Portrait*, a new preview page with a header on top of it and no footer displays (see Figure 3-8).

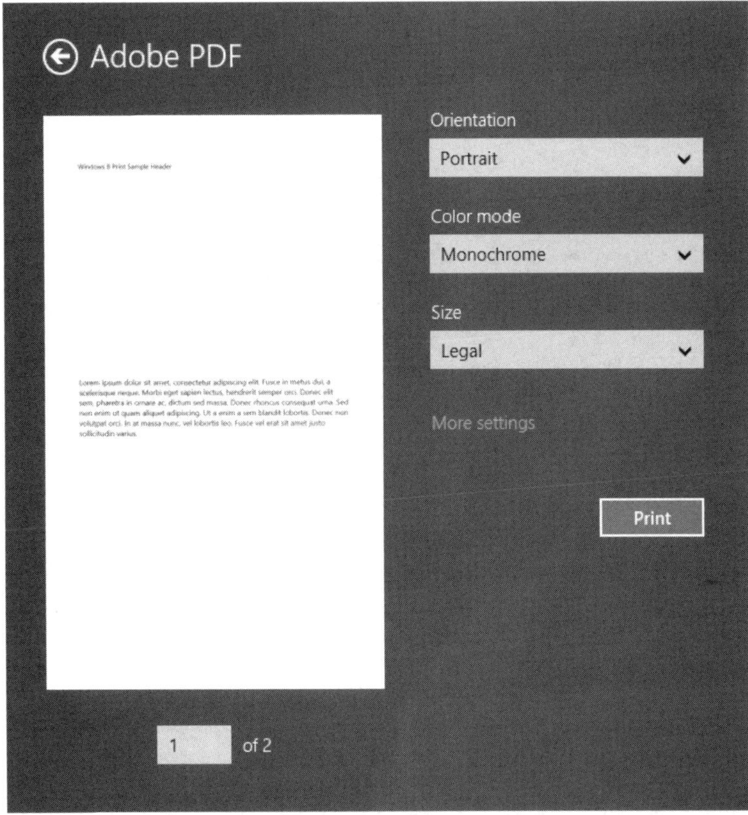

FIGURE 3-8 The preview window with the custom template for the portrait orientation

Adding custom print options

So far, you have been dealing with the print options exposed by the print target. Now it is time to learn how to create custom properties to gain some extra control over the pages you want to be printed. Listing 3-9 shows how to create a custom option to display in a preview window.

LISTING 3-9 Creating a custom option to display in a preview window

```
private void PrintManager_PrintTaskRequested(
    PrintManager sender, PrintTaskRequestedEventArgs args)
{
    PrintTask printTask = null;

    printTask = args.Request.CreatePrintTask("Windows 8 Print Sample", (e) =>
    {
        printTask.Completed += OnPrintTaskCompleted;

        PrintTaskOptionDetails detailedOptions =
            PrintTaskOptionDetails.GetFromPrintTaskOptions(printTask.Options);
        IList<string> displayedOptions = detailedOptions.DisplayedOptions;

        displayedOptions.Clear();

        (code omitted)

        PrintCustomItemListOptionDetails pageFormat =
            detailedOptions.CreateItemListOption("Watermark", "Watermark");
        pageFormat.AddItem("Visible", "Show watermark");
        pageFormat.AddItem("Collapsed", "Hide watermark");

        displayedOptions.Add("Watermark");

        detailedOptions.OptionChanged += OnOptionChanged;

        e.SetSource(this._documentSource);
    });
}
```

The code in Listing 3-9 uses the *CreateItemListOption* method of *PrintTaskOptionDetails* to create a new custom option called "Watermark." It then adds the two possible values for that option ("Visible" and "Collapsed") with the text to show in the corresponding drop-down list displayed in the preview window.

You can later retrieve the selected value by calling the *GetFromPrintTaskOptions* method of the same *PrintTaskOptionDetails* class, as follows:

```
PrintTaskOptionDetails printDetailedOptions =
    PrintTaskOptionDetails.GetFromPrintTaskOptions(printingOptions);
string wm = (printDetailedOptions.Options["Watermark"].Value as string)
    .ToLowerInvariant();
```

After you retrieve the value, you can update your print document accordingly. Figure 3-9 shows the preview window with the new custom option displayed.

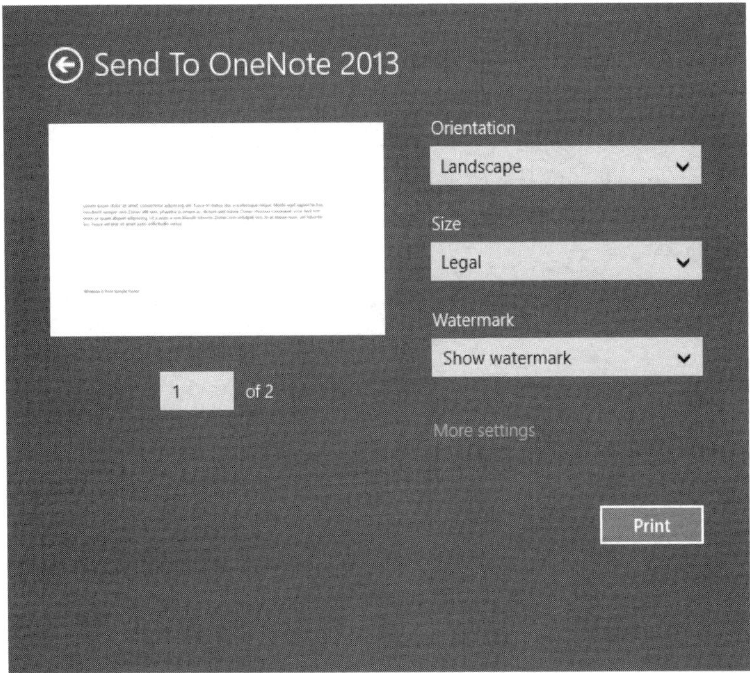

FIGURE 3-9 The preview window with the custom print option

Implementing in-app printing

Normally, the user starts the printing process by manually activating the Devices charm in the charms bar (which, in turn, fires the *PrintTaskRequested* event). The Devices charm can also be "triggered" via code, by leveraging the *ShowPrintUIAsync* method of the *PrintManager* class:

```
private async void Button_Click(object sender, RoutedEventArgs e)
{
    await PrintManager.ShowPrintUIAsync();
}
```

Before calling this method, however, make sure the application has already retrieved the *PrintManager* and registered a listener for *PrintTaskRequested*. The method returns a Boolean value that indicates the success or failure of the procedure.

Keep in mind that Microsoft official documentation explicitly discourages the use of this method in generic applications, in which you should let users start the printing process via the Devices charm. However, the *ShowPrintUIAsync* method can be used in scenarios in which you want to provide guidance to users to help them print some content, such as a ticket purchase, a flight check-in, or a boarding pass.

Thought experiment

Adding a custom print option for your app

In this thought experiment, apply what you've learned about this objective. You can find answers to these questions in the "Answers" section at the end of this chapter.

You want to implement a custom print option for your app that enables your customers to select what pages to print. For example, you might give your users the following printing options: the whole document, the current page only, or all the pages within a certain range.

If the user chooses to print only a subset of the total pages (only the selected page or a specific page range), how should you present the selected content in the print preview?

Objective summary

- To be able to print, a Windows Store app must implement the Print contract. To register with the Windows print system, you have to get a reference to the *PrintManager* object associated with the current view, subscribe to the *PrintTaskRequested* event, and create a print task representing a specific printing operation in the corresponding event handler.
- Handle the print document pagination and preview by implementing the Paginate, *GetPreviewPage*, and *AddPages* events exposed by the *PrintDocument* class.
- Retrieve and/or set the printer settings by leveraging the *PrintTaskOptions* class and create your custom print options to be displayed in the preview window via the *PrintTaskOptionDetails* class.
- Provide your users with in-app printing guidance by invoking the *ShowPrintUIAsync* static method.

Objective review

Answer the following questions to test your knowledge of the information in this objective. You can find the answers to these questions and explanations of why each answer choice is correct or incorrect in the "Answers" section at the end of this chapter.

1. What class is responsible for orchestrating the complete printing process for a Windows Store app?
    - **A.** *PrintManager* class
    - **B.** *PrintDocument* class
    - **C.** Any object implementing the *IPrintDocumentSource* interface
    - **D.** *PrintTask* class

2. What event is raised when the user requests a print operation by activating the Devices charm in the charms bar (before selecting a print target)?

   A. *Paginate* event exposed by the *PrintDocument* class.

   B. *PrintTaskRequested* event exposed by the *PrintManager* class.

   C. *Completed* event exposed by the *PrintTask* class.

   D. No events are raised until the user selects a print target from the list of available targets.

3. What does the delegate passed to the *CreatePrintTask* method as a second parameter hold a reference to?

   A. The method called when the user is ready to begin the printing process

   B. The method called when the *Submitting* event of the *PrintTask* instance is raised

   C. The method that notifies the user of the outcome of the printing operation

   D. The method that paginates the content for the preview window

4. In which event handler are you supposed to add all the preview pages to the final collection that is sent to the print target when the user clicks the Print button in the preview window?

   A. *Paginate* event handler

   B. *GetPreviewPage* event handler

   C. *AddPages* event handler

   D. *OptionChanged* event handler

Objective 3.2: Implement Play To by using contracts and charms

The Play To feature enables you to stream multimedia elements (such as movies, music, and photos) from a Windows Store app to other networked devices (such as TVs, Xbox 360s, speakers, and other receivers). For example, if you are watching a video on your tablet, with a simple gesture you can decide to stream it to your TV in the living room, sharing the experience with your family and friends. Besides streaming toward other devices, a Windows Store app can also receive that stream by implementing the Play To receiver contract.

This objective covers how to:

- Register your app for Play To
- Use *PlayToManager* to stream media assets
- Register your app as a *PlayToReceiver*

Introducing the Play To contract

All native Windows 8 apps that are focused on media, such as Music, Video, Photos, and even Internet Explorer 10, implement the Play To contract. The Play To feature is designed to work with Windows-certified Play To devices. Certified devices compatible with this feature expose the Windows 8/Windows RT logo. At the time of this writing, the manufacturers that offer compatible devices include Microsoft (Xbox 360), Samsung, Sony, and Western Digital.

For the Play To feature to work, the user must enable the Sharing option when connecting to a network. After the sharing feature is enabled, Windows automatically finds and installs all the supported devices connected to the network. You can check the list of available devices in the PC Settings | Devices panel, as shown in Figure 3-10.

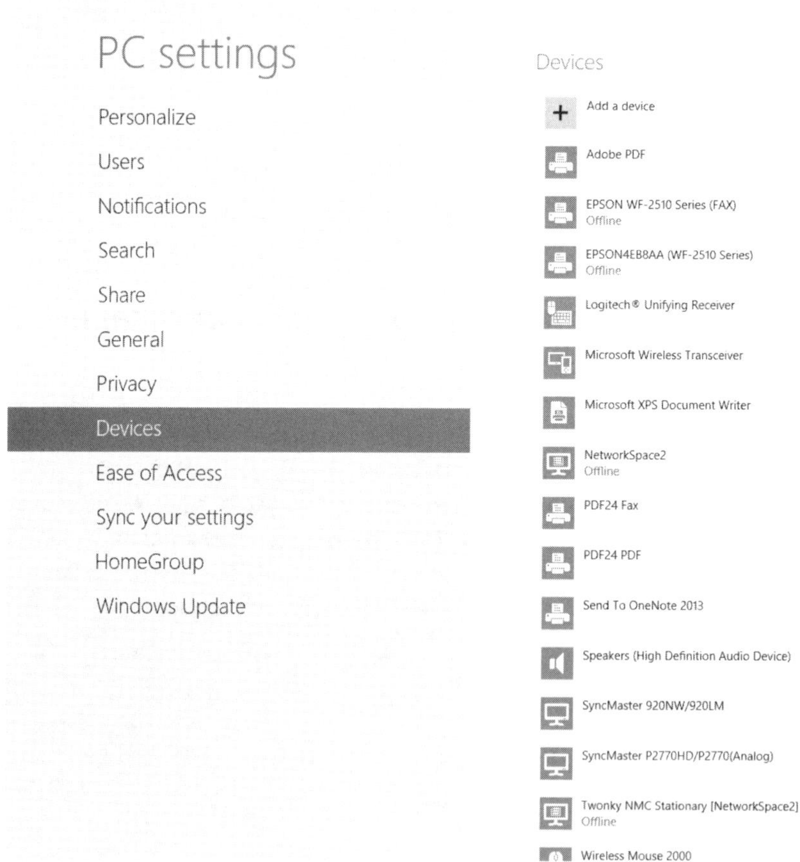

FIGURE 3-10 The PC Settings panel listing all the available devices

If there are no Play To devices connected to your network or if you have turned off the network sharing option, the message shown in Figure 3-11 appears when you click the Devices charm.

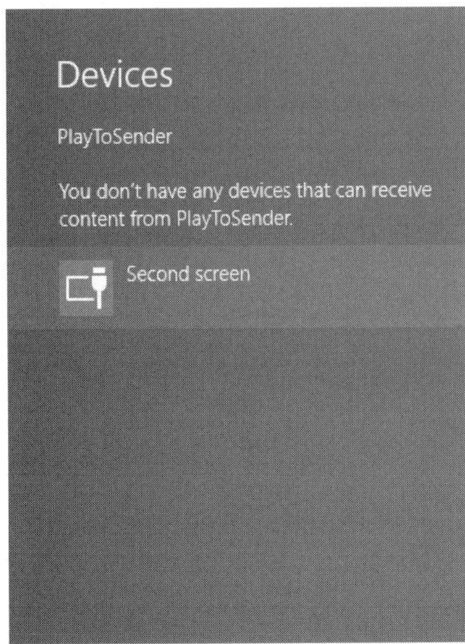

FIGURE 3-11 The Devices pane indicating that no Play To device is available

It is important to understand that any Windows 8 app containing media elements has the Play To feature enabled by default. If a user selects the Devices charm while running the app and clicks a target device, Play To streams the media from the first audio, video, or image element on the current page.

You might wonder why you should implement the Play To contract if your app can leverage this functionality out of the box. The answer is that the built-in capability to stream media content is best suited for individual media elements. If you want to provide your application with more sophisticated interactions with users, such as playlists or slide shows, you need to implement the Play To contract.

> ***NOTE*** **DISABLING THE DEFAULT BEHAVIOR OF THE PLAY TO FEATURE**
>
> **You can disable the default behavior of the Play To feature by setting the *DefaultSourceSelection* of the *PlayToManager* class to *false*.**

The Play To contract introduces a high level of abstraction from the underlying streaming technologies, formats, and protocols, making the implementation of this feature in your Windows 8 app plain and simple, as shown in the following code:

```
private Windows.Media.PlayTo.PlayToManager _ptm;
protected override void OnNavigatedTo(NavigationEventArgs e)
{
        this._ptm = Windows.Media.PlayTo.PlayToManager.GetForCurrentView();
        this._ptm.SourceRequested += ptm_SourceRequested;
}

private void ptm_SourceRequested(Windows.Media.PlayTo.PlayToManager sender,
    Windows.Media.PlayTo.PlayToSourceRequestedEventArgs args)
{
        try
        {
            args.SourceRequest.SetSource(mediaElement.PlayToSource);
        }
        catch (Exception ex)
        {
            lbErrorMessage.Text = "Something went wrong: " + ex.Message;
        }
}
```

The basic code to implement the contract in your source application is quite straightforward. First, get a reference to the *Windows.Media.PlayTo.PlayToManager* instance for the current view by calling the static method *PlayToManager.GetForCurrentView.* After you have a reference to the *PlayToManager* instance, register your application for the *SourceRequested* event exposed by the *PlayToManager* class.

In the corresponding event handler, you have to pass the media element that you want to stream to the *SetSource* method of the *PlayToSourceRequestedEventArgs* object as a parameter to the event handler.

When the user activates the Devices charm in the charms bar, the system raises the *SourceRequested* event. Then, when the user selects one of the Play To devices enumerated in the Devices panel, the *PlayToManager* starts streaming the media element passed to the *SetSource* method to the device selected by the user.

The Play To feature continues to stream the media element to the target device, even if the application has been moved to the background, because the user has launched another app. An app that is currently streaming to other devices using the Play To feature is not suspended by the system as long as the Play To receiver is still playing video or music, or new images are continuously sent to the receiver.

In other words, the system automatically keeps the app running while a Play To session is active. According to the official documentation on MSDN, an application has about 10 seconds to send another audio or video file after the current one has ended, or to send a new image after the current one is displayed, before being suspended by the system.

Testing sample code using Windows Media Player on a different machine

Before implementing a basic source application, you need to set up your development environment to be able to test an application.

The Play To feature works between two or more devices on the local network. If you do not have any Play To–certified target device at hand to test your application, you can always use Windows Media Player on another computer connected to the network (PC, notebook, tablet, or virtual machine) as a target device to test the behavior. To do so, launch Windows Media Player on the target device. In the Stream menu, enable the Allow remote control of my Player option, as shown in Figure 3-12. Do not close the Windows Media Player instance.

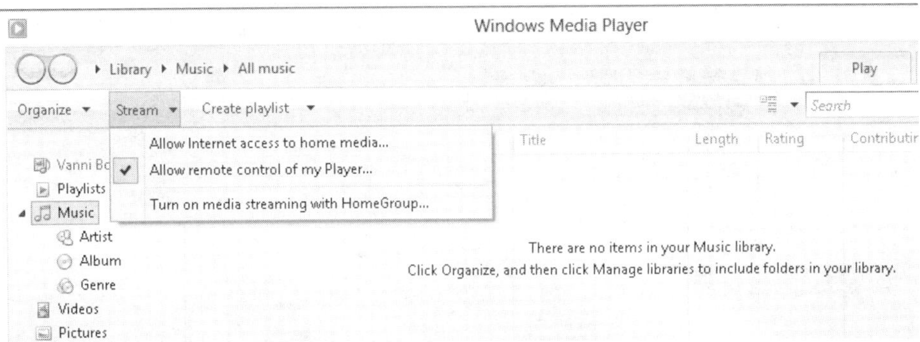

FIGURE 3-12 Windows Media Player Stream options

Go back to your local machine; in the PC Settings panel, click the **Devices** menu item. Windows should find and install the new device as soon as it becomes available. If you do not see the remote instance of Windows Media Player, click the **Add Device** button in the top-right side of the panel. Figure 3-13 shows a Windows Media Player instance running on a virtual machine.

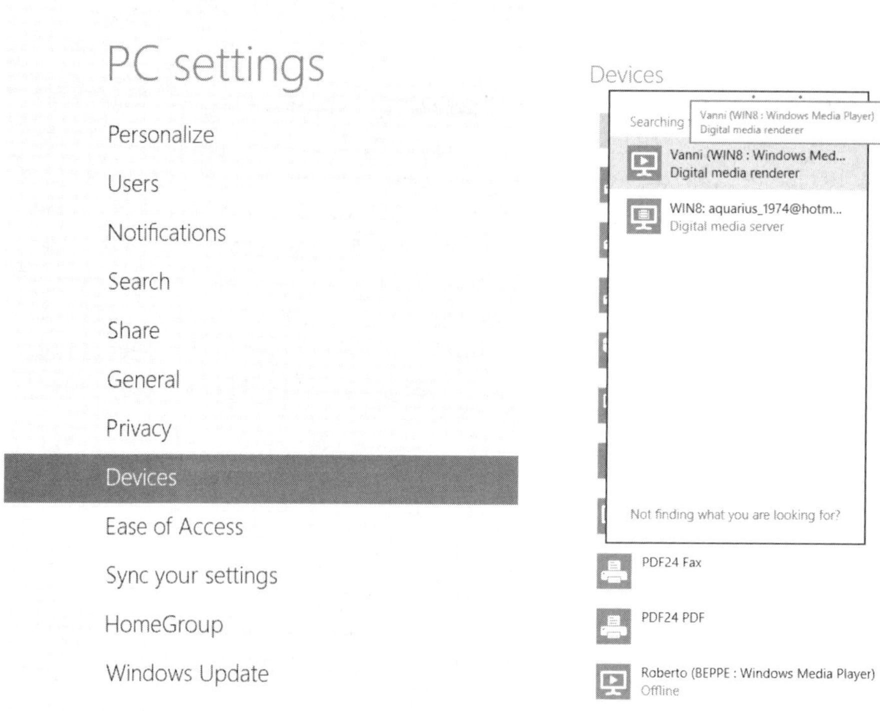

FIGURE 3-13 The Windows Media Player instance in the available device list

Now you can use the Play To feature to stream a media element to the remote machine. In the Windows 8 Start screen, launch one of the native Windows 8 apps that support the Play To feature, such as Photos or Videos; select a media element from your libraries; activate the Devices charm; and select the Windows Media Player instance running on the remote machine. Figure 3-14 shows an example of an image streaming from the local machine to the remote instance of Windows Media Player running on a virtual machine equipped with Windows 8.

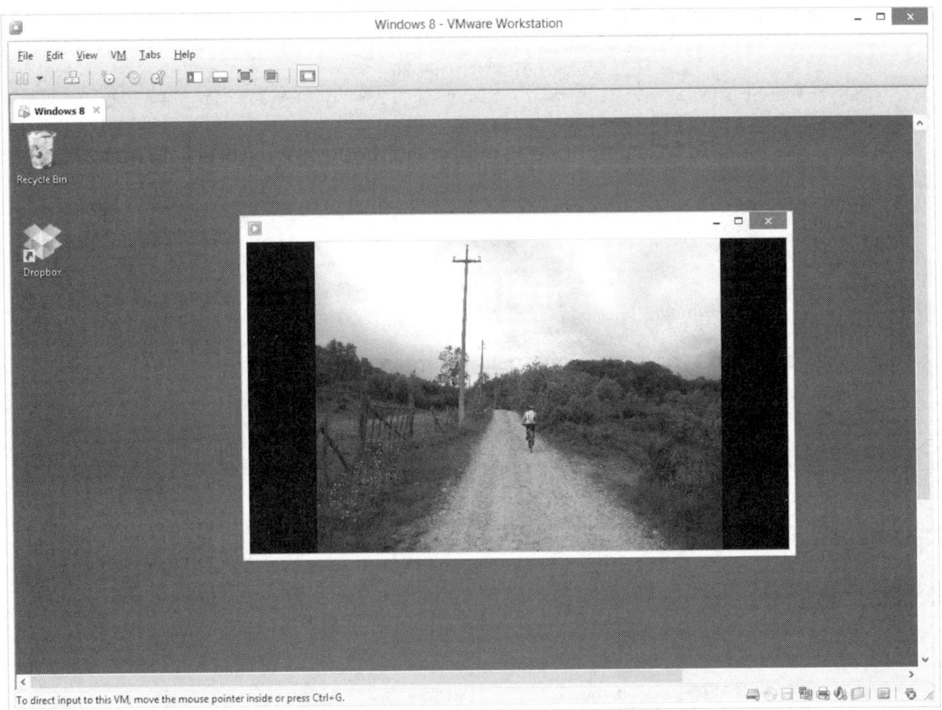

FIGURE 3-14 Streaming an image to a remote instance of Windows Media Player

Implementing a Play To source application

In this section, you learn how to implement a basic Windows Store application that leverages the Play To feature to stream a video to a Play To–certified device.

To begin, add a few controls to the MainPage.xaml to display the video on the screen. Listing 3-10 shows the complete definition of the default page used in this sample.

LISTING 3-10 Displaying video using XAML

```
<Page
    x:Class="PlayToSource.MainPage"
    xmlns=http://schemas.microsoft.com/winfx/2006/xaml/presentation
    xmlns:x=http://schemas.microsoft.com/winfx/2006/xaml
    xmlns:local="using:PlayToSource"
    xmlns:d=http://schemas.microsoft.com/expression/blend/2008
    xmlns:mc=http://schemas.openxmlformats.org/markup-compatibility/2006
    mc:Ignorable="d">

    <StackPanel>
        <Button x:Name="StartPlaying"
                Click="StartVideoButton_Click"
                Content="Start Video"
                Margin="20" />
```

```
        <Button x:Name="ButtonToggleStreaming"
                Click="ButtonToggleStreaming_Click"
                Content="Toggle streaming" Margin="20" />
        <MediaElement x:Name="VideoPlayer" Width="640" Height="480" Margin="20" />
        <TextBlock x:Name="MessageTextBlock"
                   Width="400"
                   Height="Auto"
                   FontSize="16"
                   Margin="20" />
    </StackPanel>

</Page>
```

To make the code work, you need something to stream. In this case, the source application plays the first video file available in the user's Videos library. (Make sure to have at least one video in your library if you want to try this sample.) Because the application accesses the user's libraries, you must declare the corresponding capability in your Package.appxmanifest file (or else an *UnauthorizedAccessException* occurs).

Figure 3-15 illustrates the application manifest with the declared capability.

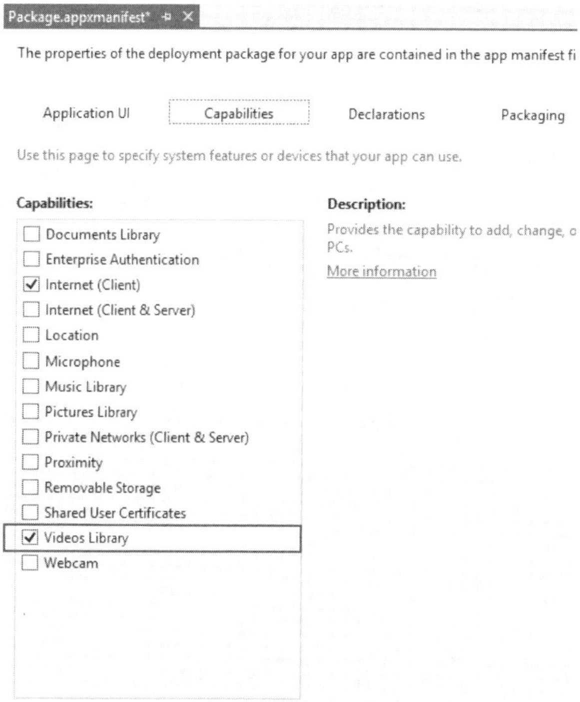

FIGURE 3-15 The Package.appxmanifest file with the required declaration

NOTE MANIFEST DECLARATIONS

In this case, the declaration in the manifest is required because the application will access the user library without asking the user's permission. If you decide to let the user choose which file to stream by using a file picker (as you probably would do in a real application), a specific declaration is not necessary.

In Listing 3-11, the button click handler loads the first video found in the user's Videos library by leveraging the *GetFilesAsync* of the *VideosLibrary* class and then plays it in a loop by setting the *IsLooping* property of the *MediaElement* object to *true*.

LISTING 3-11 Playing the first video available in the user's Videos library

```
private async void StartVideoButton_Click(object sender, RoutedEventArgs e)
{
    try
    {
        IReadOnlyList<Windows.Storage.StorageFile> resultsLibrary =
            await Windows.Storage.KnownFolders.VideosLibrary.GetFilesAsync();

        if (resultsLibrary != null && resultsLibrary.Count > 0)
        {
            MessageTextBlock.Text += "Playing video: " + resultsLibrary[0].Name + "\n";
            Windows.Storage.Streams.IRandomAccessStream videoStream =
                await resultsLibrary[0].OpenAsync(Windows.Storage.FileAccessMode.Read);

            String mimeType = resultsLibrary[0].FileType;

            VideoPlayer.SetSource(videoStream, mimeType);
            VideoPlayer.IsLooping = true;
            VideoPlayer.Play();
        }
        else
            MessageTextBlock.Text = "There's nothing to play";
    }
    catch (Exception ex)
    {
        MessageTextBlock.Text = "Something went wrong: " + ex.Message;
    }
}
```

The *OnNavigatedTo* method gets a reference to the *PlayToManager* class for the current page by invoking the *GetForCurrentView* static method; it then wires up both the events of the *PlayToManager* instance—*SourceRequested* and *SourceSelected*:

```
protected override void OnNavigatedTo(NavigationEventArgs e)
{
    this._ptm = Windows.Media.PlayTo.PlayToManager.GetForCurrentView();
    this._ptm.SourceRequested += ptm_SourceRequested;
    this._ptm.SourceSelected += ptm_SourceSelected;
}
```

The *SourceRequested* event is raised when the user activates the Devices charm but before the selection of the target device. In the corresponding event handler, the code uses the *SourceRequest* property of the *PlayToSourceRequestedEventArgs* class to pass a media element (in the form of a *PlayToSource* object) to Play To during the *SourceRequested* event. The *SourceRequest* property is an instance of the *PlayToSourceRequest* class and, as its name suggests, it represents a request to connect a media element with a Play To target device. Listing 3-12 shows the procedure.

LISTING 3-12 The *SourceRequested* event handler

```
private async void ptm_SourceRequested(PlayToManager sender,
    PlayToSourceRequestedEventArgs args)
{
    var deferral = args.SourceRequest.GetDeferral();

    await Dispatcher.RunAsync(Windows.UI.Core.CoreDispatcherPriority.Normal, () =>
    {
        PlayToSource controller = VideoPlayer.PlayToSource;

        controller.Connection.Error += PlayToConnectionError;
        controller.Connection.StateChanged += PlayToConnectionStageChanged;
        controller.Connection.Transferred += PlayToConnectionTransferred;

        args.SourceRequest.SetSource(controller);

        deferral.Complete();
    });
}
```

The Windows Runtime gives your application a slice of 200 milliseconds (ms) to provide the media element to stream; otherwise, the *SourceRequested* event times out and the Devices charm does not display any Play To targets for your app. To avoid this problem, you can leverage the *GetDeferral* method of the *PlayToSourceRequest* class to create a deferral before making an asynchronous call to retrieve the media element. Then the Windows Runtime waits for the media element until the deferral is marked as complete.

> ***NOTE DEADLINE* PROPERTY**
>
> **You can verify the time left to supply the Play To source element by checking the *Deadline* property.**

The *PlayToSource* object passed to the *SetSource* method represents the media element to stream to the Play To target. Its *Connection* property (of type *PlayToConnection*) provides some useful information about the state of the connection with the device. In this sample, you use the three events exposed by the *PlayToConnection* class to be notified of any variation in the communication with the target device. More specifically, the *Error* event is raised when an error is encountered for the Play To connection (for example, the target device is not responding, is locked, or has encountered an error). The *StateChanged* event occurs when the state of the Play To connection has changed. The possible values of the connection are Disconnected, Connected, and Rendering. Finally, the *Transferred* event is raised every time the Play To connection is transferred to the next Play To source. Listing 3-13 shows the three handlers for the events exposed by the *PlayToConnection* class.

LISTING 3-13 Handling the *PlayToConnection* events

```
private async void PlayToConnectionError(PlayToConnection connection,
    PlayToConnectionErrorEventArgs e)
{
    if (e.Code == PlayToConnectionError.DeviceError ||
        e.Code == PlayToConnectionError.DeviceNotResponding)
    {
        await Dispatcher.RunAsync(Windows.UI.Core.CoreDispatcherPriority.High, () =>
        {
            this.MessageTextBlock.Text += "Error occurred. Disconnecting....\n";
        });
    }
}

private async void PlayToConnectionStageChanged(PlayToConnection connection,
    PlayToConnectionStateChangedEventArgs e)
{
    await Dispatcher.RunAsync(Windows.UI.Core.CoreDispatcherPriority.High, () =>
    {
        this.MessageTextBlock.Text += "State changed: PreviousState = " +
            e.PreviousState.ToString() + "\n";
        this.MessageTextBlock.Text += "State changed: CurrentState = " +
            e.CurrentState.ToString() + "\n";
    });
}

private async void PlayToConnectionTransferred(PlayToConnection connection,
    PlayToConnectionTransferredEventArgs e)
{
    await Dispatcher.RunAsync(Windows.UI.Core.CoreDispatcherPriority.High, () =>
    {
        this.MessageTextBlock.Text += "Transferred: PreviousSource = " +
            e.PreviousSource.ToString() + "\n";

        this.MessageTextBlock.Text += "Transferred: CurrentSource = " +
            e.CurrentSource.ToString() + "\n";
    });
}
```

Figure 3-16 shows a portion of the app's window, which displays different states of the connection with the target device during the streaming.

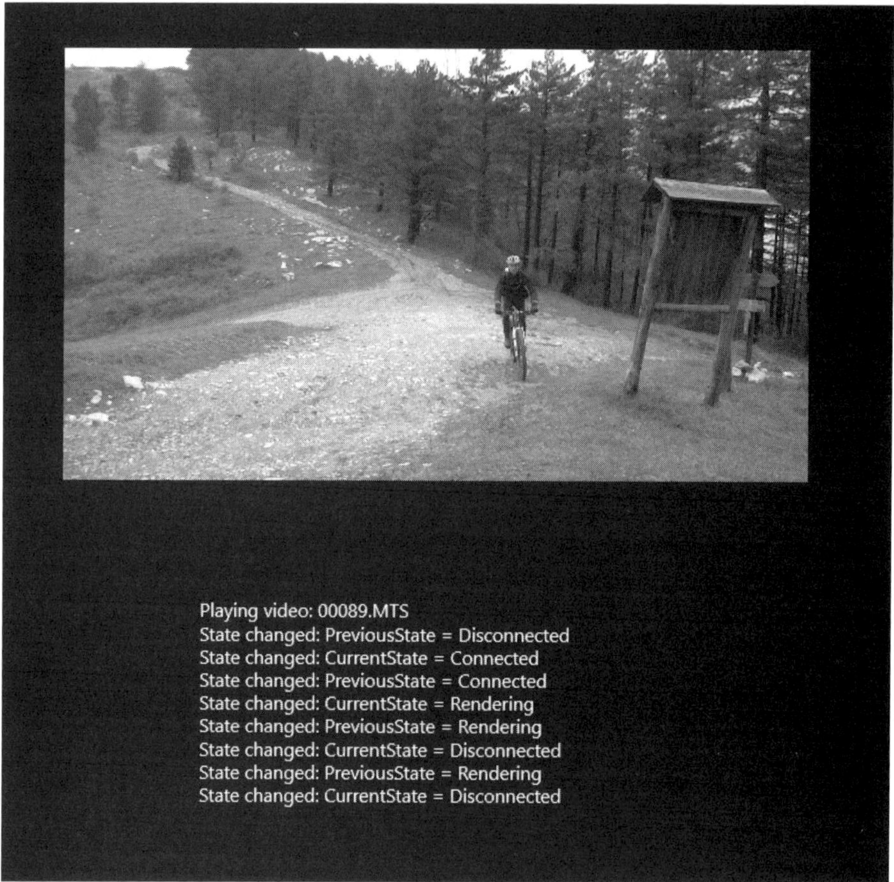
Playing video: 00089.MTS
State changed: PreviousState = Disconnected
State changed: CurrentState = Connected
State changed: PreviousState = Connected
State changed: CurrentState = Rendering
State changed: PreviousState = Rendering
State changed: CurrentState = Disconnected
State changed: PreviousState = Rendering
State changed: CurrentState = Disconnected

FIGURE 3-16 Changes in the connection state of the target device

The *SourceSelected* event is fired when the user selects the target device, so if the user leaves the Devices charm without selecting any device, the event is not raised. The corresponding event handler can be the right place to make sure that the device selected as a Play To target actually supports the specific media element provided for the stream, as illustrated in the following code snippet:

```
private void ptm_SourceSelected(PlayToManager sender,
    PlayToSourceSelectedEventArgs args)
{
    if (!args.SupportsVideo)
    {
        this.MessageTextBlock.Text = args.FriendlyName +
            "does not support streaming videos. Please select a different device";

        return;
    }
}
```

The *FriendlyName* property of the *PlayToSourceSelectedEventArgs* object passed as parameter to the *SourceSelected* event handler identifies the Play To target device on the local network.

To start the streaming of a media element (as well as stop it and disconnect the target device), you have to rely on the Play To flyout that can be activated by clicking the Devices charm. Although you cannot start streaming or disconnect the target device programmatically, you can take advantage of the *ShowPlayToUI* static method exposed by the *PlayToManager* class. Calling this method results in the visualization of the previously mentioned Play To flyout.

For example, in the following code excerpt, the method *ShowPlayToUI* is wired to a button click's event handler that provides the user with a "shortcut" to toggle the Devices charm:

```
private void ButtonToggleStreaming_Click(object sender, RoutedEventArgs e)
{
    Windows.Media.PlayTo.PlayToManager.ShowPlayToUI();
}
```

Registering your app as a Play To receiver

Now that you have seen how to implement the Play To contract that enables a Windows Store app to stream multimedia files to a certified device, let's move on to build a Windows 8 application that can receive and display the streams coming from a client source. Although the implementation of the Play To contract in a source application relies on the *PlayToManager* class, a Windows 8 Play To receiver application has to leverage the *PlayToReceiver* class.

First, you must update the Package.appxmanifest file to enable the target application to act as a server on the private network, as shown in Figure 3-17.

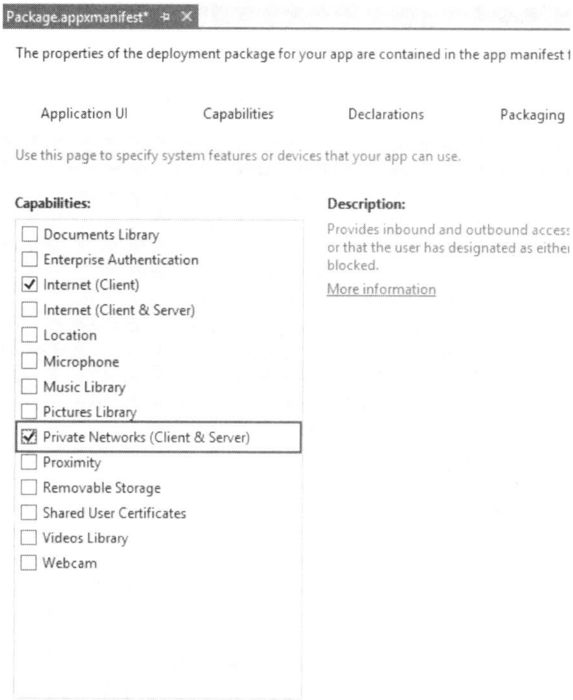

FIGURE 3-17 Selecting Private Networks (Client & Server) in the Package.appmanifest file

The Private Networks (Client & Server) capability provides inbound and outbound access to private networks through the firewall. This capability is typically used for games and apps that share data across the network.

If you forget to add the declaration mentioned previously, when you try to start the receiver by calling the *StartAsync* method of the *PlayToReceiver* class, you end up with an *UnauthorizedAccessException*.

Now that the required capability is declared in the application manifest, you can start coding the target application. First, you need to add few XAML controllers to show the video streaming from the source application. This is the complete definition of the MainPage.xaml file:

```
<Page
    x:Class="VideoPlayToReceiver.MainPage"
    xmlns="http://schemas.microsoft.com/winfx/2006/xaml/presentation"
    xmlns:x="http://schemas.microsoft.com/winfx/2006/xaml"
    xmlns:local="using:VideoPlayToReceiver"
    xmlns:d="http://schemas.microsoft.com/expression/blend/2008"
    xmlns:mc="http://schemas.openxmlformats.org/markup-compatibility/2006"
    mc:Ignorable="d">

    <StackPanel Background="{StaticResource ApplicationPageBackgroundThemeBrush}">
        <Button x:Name="btnStopReceiving"
                Click="StopReceivingButton_Click"
                Content="Stop receiving" />
```

```
        <MediaElement x:Name="VideoPlayerReceiver"
                      Width="680"
                      Height="480"
                      AutoPlay="True" />
        <TextBlock x:Name="tbMessage"
                   Text="Your target application is ready to receive..."
                   FontSize="18" />
    </StackPanel>
</Page>
```

To be able to act as a Play To receiver, the application needs to instantiate a *PlayToReceiver* object to handle the communication with Play To client devices. The application can then display the content streamed from those devices using your own media elements or controls.

The *StartReceivingButton_Click* handler method in Listing 3-14 shows how to perform this operation.

LISTING 3-14 Registering an app as a Play To receiver

```
private PlayToReceiver _receiver;
private async void StartReceivingButton_Click(object sender, RoutedEventArgs e)
{
    this._receiver = new PlayToReceiver();

    this._receiver.FriendlyName = "MyPlayToReceiver";

    // Wiring up the PlayToReceiver's events
    this._receiver.CurrentTimeChangeRequested += receiver_CurrentTimeChangeRequested;
    this._receiver.MuteChangeRequested += receiver_MuteChangeRequested;
    this._receiver.PauseRequested += receiver_PauseRequested;
    this._receiver.PlaybackRateChangeRequested += receiver_PlaybackRateChangeRequested;
    this._receiver.PlayRequested += receiver_PlayRequested;
    this._receiver.SourceChangeRequested += receiver_SourceChangeRequested;
    this._receiver.StopRequested += receiver_StopRequested;
    this._receiver.TimeUpdateRequested += receiver_TimeUpdateRequested;
    this._receiver.VolumeChangeRequested += receiver_VolumeChangeRequested;

    // Supported media type
    this._receiver.SupportsVideo = true;
    this._receiver.SupportsAudio = false;
    this._receiver.SupportsImage = false;

    // Start receiving the stream from the source
    await this._receiver.StartAsync();

    this.StopReceivingButton.IsEnabled = true;
    this.StartReceivingButton.IsEnabled = false;


    this.MessageTextBlock.Text = "Your target application is ready to receive as " +
        this._receiver.FriendlyName;
}
```

Let's review the code in more detail. After creating an instance of the *PlayToReceiver* class, the code sets its *FriendlyName* property. Setting this property is fundamental because it identifies the name of the Play To receiver as it appears on the network (see Figure 3-18).

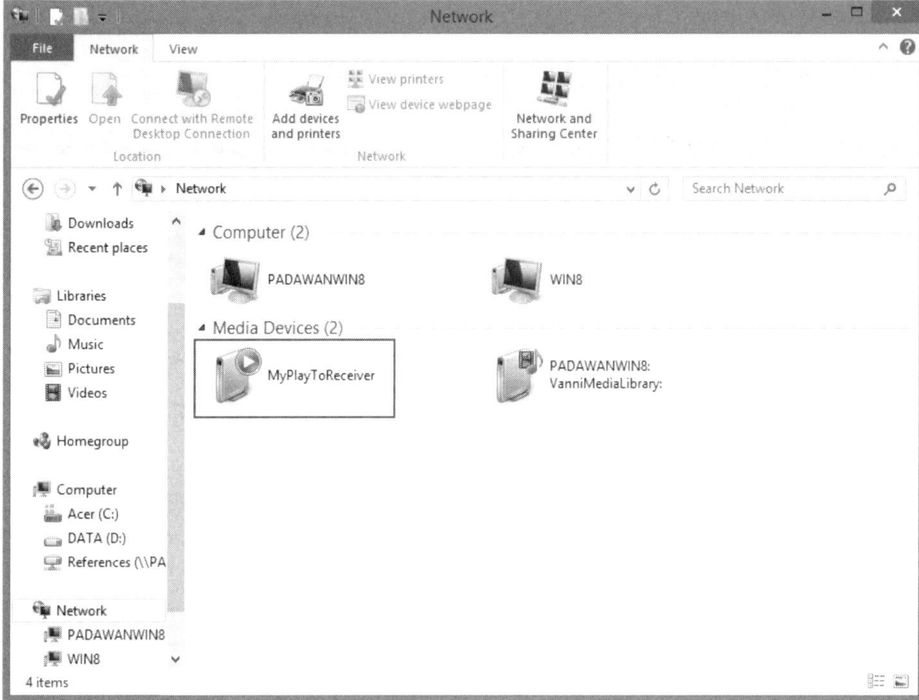

FIGURE 3-18 The Play To target app as it appears on the network

After the *PlayToReceiver* class is instantiated and a friendly name assigned, you have to subscribe to the various events exposed by that class. These events are fired by the system in response to the actions performed by the user on the client application. Here is the complete list of events exposed by the *PlayToReceiver* class:

- ***CurrentTimeChangeRequested*** The playback time location has changed.
- ***MuteChangeRequested*** The audio has been (un)muted.
- ***PauseRequested*** The playback has been paused.
- ***PlaybackRateChangeRequested*** The rate of the playback has changed.
- ***PlayRequested*** The playback has started.
- ***SourceChangeRequested*** The media source for the Play To receiver has changed.
- ***StopRequested*** A request has been made for the Play To receiver to stop playing the streamed media.
- ***TimeUpdateRequested*** The current playback position has changed.
- ***VolumeChangeRequested*** The volume has changed.

If you forget to subscribe to even one of the preceding events, when you invoke the *StartAsync* method to start receiving the stream, you get an *InvalidOperationException* informing you that A Method Was Called At An Unexpected Time. The same exception is raised in case you have forgotten to assign a friendly name to the receiver.

For this reason, it is crucial to remember to subscribe to *all* the events exposed by the *PlayToReceiver* class, even if some of them make sense only for certain types of media elements, such as videos and music. This behavior might seem a little odd at first, but if the streaming target application did not respond to all the events raised by the source application, it would result in a poor user experience (although the exception raised could have been a little more informative).

> ***NOTE* HANDLERS**
>
> **Consider that you can always decide not to implement the handlers of the events that do not relate to the media elements that your receiver application is targeting. For example, if your receiver is targeting only images, implementing *MuteChangeRequested* does not make much sense.**

To filter the type of media that your receiver application can stream, you can leverage the three Boolean properties at the end of the previous code snippet (that is, *SupportsAudio*, *SupportsVideo*, and *SupportsImage*). They indicate to the system what kind of media element the receiver actually supports (in this example, just audio elements).

Finally, the *StartAsync* method of the *PlayToReceiver* class starts the Play To receiver and advertises it on the network as a digital media renderer, ready to receive streams from a source application:

```
await this._receiver.StartAsync();
```

Analogously, when you want your target application to stop receiving the streaming from the source application, you can invoke the *StopAsync* method of the *PlayToReceiver* class and remove all the event handlers:

```
private async void StopReceivingButton_Click(object sender, RoutedEventArgs e)
{
    if (this._receiver != null)
    {
        await this._receiver.StopAsync();

        // Remove Play To Receiver events
        (code omitted)

        this.StopReceivingButton.IsEnabled = false;
        this.StartReceivingButton.IsEnabled = true;

        this.MessageTextBlock.Text =
            "Your target application is no longer receiving...";
    }
}
```

The next step is to implement the handlers for the events exposed by the *PlayToReceiver* class, so the target application can react to the actions performed on the client application. Because the communication between the client and the target application is two-way, you can also notify the client about a change in the Play To receiver by using one of the *Notify** methods exposed by the *PlayToReceiver* class, as shown in Listing 3-15.

LISTING 3-15 *Notify** methods exposed by the *PlayToReceiver* class

```
private async void receiver_VolumeChangeRequested(PlayToReceiver sender,
    VolumeChangeRequestedEventArgs args)
{
    await Dispatcher.RunAsync(Windows.UI.Core.CoreDispatcherPriority.Normal, () =>
    {
        this.VideoPlayerReceiver.Volume = args.Volume;
        this._receiver.NotifyVolumeChange(this.VideoPlayerReceiver.Volume,
        this.VideoPlayerReceiver.IsMuted);
    });
}

private async void receiver_TimeUpdateRequested(PlayToReceiver sender, object args)
{
    await Dispatcher.RunAsync(Windows.UI.Core.CoreDispatcherPriority.Normal, () =>
    {
        if (this.VideoPlayerReceiver.Position != null)
        {
            this._receiver.NotifyTimeUpdate(this.VideoPlayerReceiver.Position);
        }
    });
}

private async void receiver_StopRequested(PlayToReceiver sender, object args)
{
    await Dispatcher.RunAsync(Windows.UI.Core.CoreDispatcherPriority.Normal, () =>
    {
        this.VideoPlayerReceiver.Stop();
        this._receiver.NotifyStopped();
    });
}

private async void receiver_SourceChangeRequested(PlayToReceiver sender,
    SourceChangeRequestedEventArgs args)
{
    if (args.Stream != null)
    {
        await Dispatcher.RunAsync(Windows.UI.Core.CoreDispatcherPriority.Normal, () =>
        {
            this.VideoPlayerReceiver.SetSource(args.Stream, args.Stream.ContentType);
            this.VideoPlayerReceiver.Play();
        });
    }
}
```

```
private async void receiver_PlayRequested(PlayToReceiver sender, object args)
{
    await Dispatcher.RunAsync(Windows.UI.Core.CoreDispatcherPriority.Normal, () =>
    {
        this.VideoPlayerReceiver.Play();
        this._receiver.NotifyPlaying();
    });
}

private async void receiver_PlaybackRateChangeRequested(PlayToReceiver sender,
    PlaybackRateChangeRequestedEventArgs args)
{
    await Dispatcher.RunAsync(Windows.UI.Core.CoreDispatcherPriority.Normal, () =>
    {
        this.VideoPlayerReceiver.PlaybackRate = args.Rate;
    });
}

private async void receiver_PauseRequested(PlayToReceiver sender, object args)
{
    await Dispatcher.RunAsync(Windows.UI.Core.CoreDispatcherPriority.Normal, () =>
    {
        this.VideoPlayerReceiver.Pause();
        this._receiver.NotifyPaused();
    });
}

private async void receiver_MuteChangeRequested(PlayToReceiver sender,
    MuteChangeRequestedEventArgs args)
{
    await Dispatcher.RunAsync(Windows.UI.Core.CoreDispatcherPriority.Normal, () =>
    {
        this.VideoPlayerReceiver.IsMuted = args.Mute;
        this._receiver.NotifyVolumeChange(VideoPlayerReceiver.Volume, true);
    });
}

private async void receiver_CurrentTimeChangeRequested(PlayToReceiver sender,
    CurrentTimeChangeRequestedEventArgs args)
{
    if (this.VideoPlayerReceiver.CanSeek)
    {
        await Dispatcher.RunAsync(Windows.UI.Core.CoreDispatcherPriority.Normal, () =>
        {
            this.VideoPlayerReceiver.Position = args.Time;
            this._receiver.NotifySeeking();
        });
    }
}
```

The same pattern can be used to notify the source application that something has happened in the client. The following code excerpt shows the handler for the *MediaFailed* event exposed by the *MediaElement* class as an example:

```
private void VideoPlayerReceiver_MediaFailed(object sender, ExceptionRoutedEventArgs e)
{
    if (this._receiver != null)
    {
        this._receiver.NotifyError();
    }
}
```

Thought experiment

Interacting with a Play To target app

In this thought experiment, apply what you've learned about this objective. You can find answers to these questions in the "Answers" section at the end of this chapter.

Suppose you are developing a Windows Store app that presents the user's pictures in a slide show. It can also stream those images to a Play To receiver app by implementing the Play To contract. When the slide show is playing only locally, it has a timer that triggers a new photo to be displayed at regular intervals. When streaming to the target device, however, your app needs to know whether the target device has already finished rendering the preceding image before sending a new image to the target.

How can you implement this behavior? What event can you leverage to verify that the target app is ready for a new stream?

Objective summary

- By implementing the Play To contract, a Windows Store app can stream media elements to any Play To–certified device connected to the same private network (source app), as well as receive a stream from another Windows Store app (receiver app).
- To stream media elements to a Play To target, you have to get a reference to the *PlayManager* object for the current view, subscribe to the *SourceRequested* event, and provide a media element to stream.
- To implement a Play To receiver app, you have to instantiate a *PlayToReceiver* object to handle the communication with Play To client devices and display the content streamed from those devices using your own media elements or controls.
- Before starting to receive the stream by calling the *StartAsync* method of the *PlayToReceiver* instance, remember to set the *FriendlyName* property (which will broadcast over the network) and wire up all the events exposed by the *PlayToReceiver* class.

Objective review

Answer the following questions to test your knowledge of the information in this objective. You can find the answers to these questions and explanations of why each answer choice is correct or incorrect in the "Answers" section at the end of this chapter.

1. What is the first thing step of implementing the Play To contract in a source application?
   - **A.** Instantiate a new *PlayToManager* object in the constructor of the page.
   - **B.** Define a *PlayToManager* static variable that can be shared among the pages of the app.
   - **C.** You do not need any reference to a *PlayToManager* object; just use its static methods as needed.
   - **D.** Get a reference to the *PlayToManager* instance for the current view by calling the static method *PlayToManager.GetForCurrentView.*
2. In a Play To source app, what event is raised when the user activates the Devices charm (but before selecting the target device)?
   - **A.** *SourceRequested* event of the *PlayToManager* class.
   - **B.** *SourceSelected* event of the *PlayToManager* class.
   - **C.** *StateChanged* event of the *PlayToSource* class.
   - **D.** No event is raised.
3. In a Play To receiver app, what happens if you do not set a value for the *FriendlyName* property of the *PlayToReceiver* instance?
   - **A.** In the Devices charm, the receiver appears as Unknown Device.
   - **B.** The receiver app is simply ignored and cannot receive the stream.
   - **C.** The receiver app raises an *InvalidOperationException* as soon as the *StartAsync* method of the *PlayToReceiver* instance is invoked.
   - **D.** The receiver raises an *InvalidOperationException* as soon as you launch the application.
4. In a Play To receiver app, which of the following capabilities must be declared in the Package.appxmanifest file to be able to receive the stream?
   - **A.** Internet (Client)
   - **B.** Internet (Client & Server)
   - **C.** Music library and/or Videos library, depending on the type of the media element
   - **D.** Private Networks (Client & Server)

Objective 3.3: Notify users by using Windows Push Notification Service (WNS)

The WNS enables an application to send toasts or tile and badge updates to a Windows 8 user. The service, hosted in the cloud, manages the communication mechanism to the user's device in a transparent and efficient way. To bring the notification to the correct address, the client application needs to request a notification channel to the client application programming interfaces (APIs) and send the returned uniform resource identifier (URI) to the application back end. This URI represents the client univocally and lets the back end send notifications to the desired device.

This objective covers how to:

- Request, create, and save a notification channel
- Authenticate to the WNS
- Call and poll the WNS

Requesting and creating a notification channel

A notification channel is represented by a URI and is used to send notifications to the user via the WNS.

A client application can request the channel URI to the Windows Runtime and send it to a back-end service that stores it in a persistent storage (independent from the WNS), and can use it to send toasts or tile and badge updates. For example, a weather app can request the channel to the Windows Runtime and send it to the application back end together with some user preferences, such as favorite cities and temperature thresholds. This data can be used by the back-end logic to alert the user if the temperature is going higher than a user-entered value or simply update the application tile with the current temperature.

A *channel* represents a single user on a single device for a specific application, which means that two applications on the same device never share the notification channel. If the user uses two devices with the same application installed, the user receives two different channels. The back-end service needs to manage these situations. For example, the back-end service can simply store two channels for a user who works with the weather application on two devices.

To begin working with the push notification APIs, you do not need to add any reference to the main project. If you want, add the *Windows.Networking.PushNotification* namespace.

To create a channel, you can use the *CreatePushNotificationChannelForApplicationAsync* method, which creates and returns the notification channel in the form of a *PushNotificationChannel* instance. Always put the call to this method inside a *try/catch* block, as in the following code:

```
PushNotificationChannel channel = null;

try
{
    channel = await PushNotificationChannelManager.
        CreatePushNotificationChannelForApplicationAsync();

    var dialog = new MessageDialog(channel.Uri);
        dialog.ShowAsync();
}

catch (Exception ex)
{
    // Cannot create the channel.
}
```

The *PushNotificationChannel* exposes the *Uri* property that represents the channel's unique URI, to which notifications are sent. The result of the presented code is shown in Figure 3-19.

https://db3.notify.windows.com/?token=AgYAAADZblUV%2bSzmrvflch1Xm84kEB6aq9m0cmDWyBn7lU%2flNsHLtl3YE5Jj%2brgQrLMNsna2YIlEm3jKqDZ9FndxBkD441Kg9zpXcfg86OlGmFztdrFp7TUFrQ%2b807B7hZhSbp8%3d

Close

FIGURE 3-19 Notification channel URI in a message dialog box

The application needs to send the URI to the application back end in a secure way. If you send this information to a web service, consider using a form of encryption of the message or at least use HTTPS as the transport.

EXAM TIP

The application needs to request a channel each time the application is launched and update the back end when the URI changes.

Because the application needs to request a channel URI on launch, the app can compare the returned information with the previous channel. If the channel URI is different from the previous one, the application must send the new channel to the back end. If the channel is the same, the application does not need to send the channel URI to the server. The application can send the channel to the back end to perform this check, but it is more convenient to store the channel locally to avoid useless roundtrips.

Best practices suggest performing the following steps during the first application launch:

1. Request a channel to the Windows Runtime.
2. Store the channel in the local storage for later check.
3. Send the channel URI to the back end.

When the application is launched, the code can check local storage for a previous channel URI and compare the value with the new one. If the channel is the same, no other actions are required. If the channel is different, the app sends the new channel URI to the back end. Remember to include logic to send a new channel if the following are true:

- The application has never requested a channel.
- The application has never sent the channel URI to the server.
- The last attempt to send the channel URI was not successful.

An application can have multiple valid channels at the same time without any problems. Moreover, each channel remains valid until it expires: There is no need to delete channels or perform any sort of operations.

It is highly important to request a channel every time the application starts because a channel expires in 30 days. There are more chances to work with a fresh channel if the user does not work with the app for some time.

If you are concerned that the user might not launch the application for 30 days, you can implement a background task to request the channel and perform the described operations on a regular basis.

MORE INFO **BACKGROUND TASKS**

For more information on background tasks, see Chapter 1, "Develop Windows Store apps."

If the Internet is not available when the application is launched, and a channel is requested using *CreatePushNotificationChannelForApplicationAsync*, an exception is thrown. The best way to handle this exception is to retry the operation three times in 30 seconds (with a delay of 10 seconds each time). If all three attempts fail, there are few chances to obtain a channel; the application should wait for the next application launch to try the described flow again.

Once the application no longer needs a notification channel, the related code can call the *Close* method of the *PushNotification* instance to close the channel. If the notification channel is used to update the tile, after closing the channel, the application can clear the corresponding tile calling the *Clear* method of the *TileUpdater* class.

Sending a notification to the client

The back end that receives the notification channel URI is responsible for storing this information and making it available to the code that sends the notification on the channel.

For example, the web service can store the channel URI in an SQL Azure database or in a Windows Azure Storage Account table together with the user preferences. The business logic of the back end can inspect the user preferences and use the URI to send to the WNS the notification message that will be delivered to the client.

> ***NOTE*** **CLIENT AND SERVICE ARE DECOUPLED**
>
> **There is no direct connection between the back end and the client; the WNS manages the communication transparently.**

The back end can send tile updates, badge updates, and/or toasts to the client using the corresponding XML syntax. This syntax is identical to the one the client application uses to perform the same operation locally. For example, to send a toast with some text in it, the XML payload might look like this:

```
<toast launch="">
  <visual lang="en-US">
    <binding template="ToastText01">
      <text id="1">The weather is changing to cloudy</text>
    </binding>
  </visual>
</toast>
```

If you need to include an image in the toast, you can use the corresponding template:

```
<toast launch="">
  <visual lang="en-US">
    <binding template="ToastImageAndText01">
      <image id="1" src="Cloudy.jpg" />
      <text id="1"> The weather is changing to cloudy </text>
    </binding>
  </visual>
</toast>
```

The same applies to tiles and badges: Use the same template you normally use in the client code.

> ***NOTE*** **XML**
>
> **In your client code, you have probably used the *NotificationExtensions* library that hides all the XML details. This library creates the XML under the hood.**

The XML fragment must be sent using HTTPS to the WNS using an authentication token provided by the Windows Live service. Therefore, the first thing the server code needs to do is ask for the token to the Windows Live service.

To request the authentication token, you need to use the *HttpClient* class and make a roundtrip to the *login.live.com* authentication service, as shown in the following code:

```
var encSecret = HttpUtility.UrlEncode(secret);
var encSid = HttpUtility.UrlEncode(sid);

var body = String.Format("
    grant_type=client_credentials&client_id={0}&client_secret={1}&scope=notify.
    windows.com",
    encSid,
    encSecret);
```

```
string response;
using (var client = new WebClient())
{
    client.Headers.Add("Content-Type", "application/x-www-form-urlencoded");
    response = client.UploadString("https://login.live.com/accesstoken.srf", body);
}
```

The code encodes the "password" (called the *secret*) and the security identifier (SID), and builds up the string to provide this information to the Windows Live service for the *notify.windows.com* scope. In practice, the code asks for a token to be used on the scope for the secret and SID provided.

To authenticate the request to the Windows Live service, you need to provide the SID and the secret you receive during the WNS subscription. Store them in a secure place.

The Windows Live services response is in JavaScript Object Notation (JSON) format and directly contains the authentication token. You can deserialize the response by using this code:

```
using (var ms = new MemoryStream(Encoding.Unicode.GetBytes(response.ToString())))
{
    var ser = new DataContractJsonSerializer(typeof(OAuthToken));
    var oAuthToken = (OAuthToken)ser.ReadObject(ms);
    return oAuthToken;
}
```

The code uses a *MemoryStream* to encapsulate the JSON string contained in the response. It then instantiates the *DataContractJsonSerializer* to read the stream and transform it in the OAuth authentication token.

You need to define the *OAuthToken* class as follows:

```
[DataContract]
public class OAuthToken
{
    [DataMember(Name = "access_token")]
    public string AccessToken { get; set; }

    [DataMember(Name = "token_type")]
    public string TokenType { get; set; }
}
```

The *OAuthToken* exposes a property called *AccessToken* that represents the authentication header to be passed to the service to authenticate the back end during the notification request.

The complete HTTP message is similar to the one presented in the following code:

```
POST https://db3.notify.windows.com/?token=AfUAABBCQmGg7OMlCg%2fK0K8rBPcBqHuy%2b1rTSNPM
uIzF6BtvpRdT7DM4j%2fs%2bNNm8z5l1QKZMtyjByKW5uXqb9V7hIAeA3i8FoKR%2f49ZnGgyUkAhzix%2fuSua
sL3jalk7562F4Bpw%3d HTTP/1.1
Authorization: Bearer agFaAQDAAAAEgAAACoAAPzCGedIbQb9vRfPF2Lxy3K//QZB78mLTgK
X-WNS-RequestForStatus: true
X-WNS-Type: wns/toast
ContentType: text/xml
Host: db3.notify.windows.com
Content-Length: 189
<toast launch="">
  <visual lang="en-US">
    <binding template="ToastImageAndText01">
      <image id="1" src="Cloudy.jpg" />
      <text id="1"> The weather is changing to cloudy </text>
    </binding>
  </visual>
</toast>
```

Assuming that the code to request the token is refactored in a *GetOAthToken* method, the complete code to create a notification and send it to the service can be similar to the following:

```
var token = GetOAthToken(secret, sid);
byte[] contentInBytes = Encoding.UTF8.GetBytes(toastXML);

HttpWebRequest request = HttpWebRequest.Create(uri) as HttpWebRequest;
request.Method = "POST";
request.Headers.Add("X-WNS-Type", notificationType);
request.ContentType = contentType;
request.Headers.Add("Authorization", String.Format("Bearer {0}",
    token.AccessToken));

using (Stream requestStream = request.GetRequestStream())
    requestStream.Write(contentInBytes, 0, contentInBytes.Length);

using (HttpWebResponse webResponse = (HttpWebResponse)request.GetResponse())
    return webResponse.StatusCode.ToString();
```

The code asks for the token, as explained previously, and uses it to create an authentication header for the request to the WNS. The notification type is expressed by another HTTP header called X-WNS-Type. The code performs an HTTP POST to the service using the content of the XML representation of the notification.

To request the SID and the secret, the developer must register the application with the WNS using the Windows Store Dashboard (see Figure 3-20).

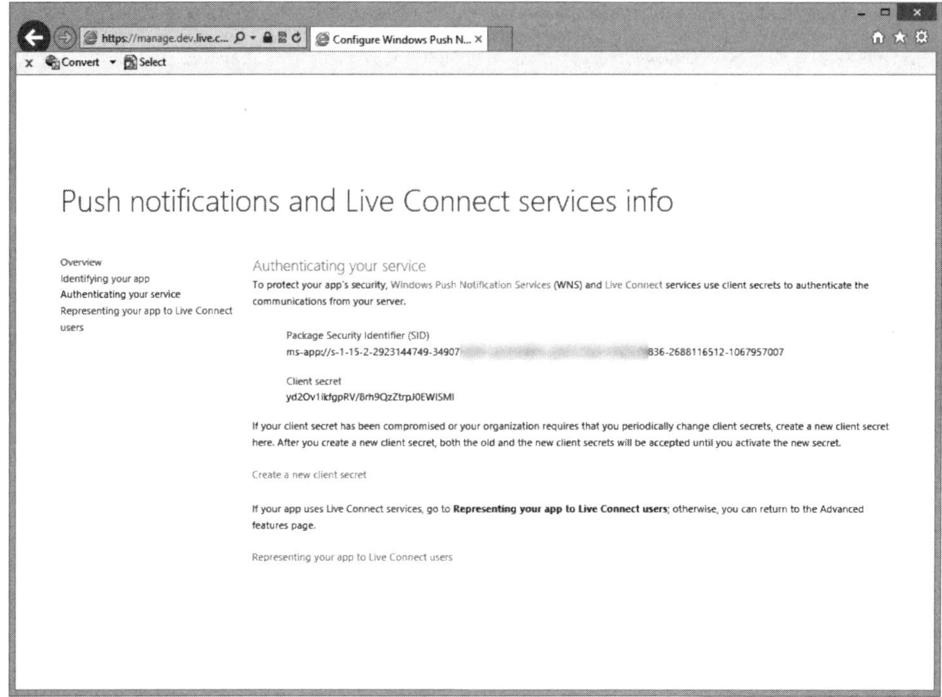

FIGURE 3-20 Notification channel URI in a message dialog box

After creating the application in the Windows Store App Development portal, you have to go to Advanced Features and then select Push notification and live connect services info.

> ***NOTE*** **PACKAGE UPLOAD**
>
> **You do not need to upload the application package. It is sufficient to reserve the application name.**

On this page, select the Identifying Your App link and then the Authenticating Your Service link to display the package SID and the client secret (Figure 3-20 shows the dashboard).

The complete list of request parameters for authenticating the cloud service to a Windows Live service is shown in Table 3-1.

TABLE 3-1 Parameters for authenticating a cloud service to a Windows Live service

Parameter	Description
grant_type	Must be set to *client_credentials*
client_id	Package SID for the cloud service
client_secret	Secret key for the cloud service
scope	Must be set to *notify.windows.com*

The request receives an HTTP status of 200 OK if everything is okay, and the response contains the access token. If something went wrong, the error codes are described in the OAuth 2.0 protocol (in draft at the time of this writing). If the authentication fails, you receive a 400 Bad Request HTTP status code.

The response parameters are described in Table 3-2.

TABLE 3-2 Response parameters for authentication to a Windows Live service

Parameter	Description
access_token	The access token that the cloud service uses use when it sends a notification
token_type	Always returned as *bearer*

A sample successful response can be the following:

```
HTTP/1.1 200 OK
 Cache-Control: no-store
 Content-Length: 422
 Content-Type: application/json

 {
     "access_token":"FgBaAQMBAAAALYAAY/c+Huwi3Fv4Ck10UrKNmtxRO6Njk2MgA=",
     "token_type":"bearer"
 }
```

You can use a class similar to the one provided in the following code to deserialize the response:

```
public class OAuthToken
{
    public string AccessToken { get; set; }

    public string TokenType { get; set; }
}
```

To avoid roundtrips, you can cache the received token, but be sure to catch the exception for an expired token, as shown in the following code:

```
catch (WebException webException)
    {
        string exceptionDetails = webException.Response.Headers["WWW-Authenticate"];
        if (exceptionDetails.Contains("Token expired"))
        {
            GetAccessToken(secret, sid);

            // Retry. Set a maximum retry policy
         }
    }
```

> ***MORE INFO*** **WNS REQUEST AND RESPONSE PARAMETERS**
>
> **For a complete list of request and response parameters to the WNS, visit** ***http://msdn.microsoft.com/en-us/library/windows/apps/xaml/hh868245.aspx.***

If the application is up and running when the notification is sent to the device, the application can intercept the notification and handle it in many ways. The app can intercept the notification before a toast is displayed, or the tile or badge is updated, and then update the notification using internal logic. The app can also suppress the notification. For example, if a weather application receives the current temperature from the WNS as a toast, but the user is already watching the current temperature on the app page, the app can simply intercept and suppress the toast.

The following code intercepts the notification:

```
PushNotificationChannel channel = null;

try
{
    channel = await PushNotificationChannelManager.
    CreatePushNotificationChannelForApplicationAsync();

    channel.PushNotificationReceived += OnPushReceived
}

catch (Exception ex)
{
    // Cannot create the channel.
}
```

The corresponding event handler is shown in Listing 3-16.

LISTING 3-16 Event handler for receiving a push notification

```
private async void OnPushReceived(PushNotificationChannel sender,
    PushNotificationReceivedEventArgs e)
{
    String notificationContent = String.Empty;

    switch (e.NotificationType)
    {
        case PushNotificationType.Badge:
            notificationContent = e.BadgeNotification.Content.GetXml();
            break;

        case PushNotificationType.Tile:
            notificationContent = e.TileNotification.Content.GetXml();
            break;

        case PushNotificationType.Toast:
            notificationContent = e.ToastNotification.Content.GetXml();

            // Some logic to decide to suppress the notification
            e.Cancel = true;  // Supress the Toast
            break;

        case PushNotificationType.Raw:
            notificationContent = e.RawNotification.Content;
            break;
    }
}
```

The code tests the *NotificationType* property of the received *PushNotificationEventArgs* and the type using the WinRT *PushNotificationType* enum. For each kind of notification, it retrieves the corresponding XML that can eventually be evaluated to perform some action. For toast notification, the application performs some logic (probably on the XML content) and decides to suppress the notification.

You can use a raw notification, which is a type of push notification, to send short messages from the app's cloud service to an app through the WNS. Unlike the XML payload of other push notification types (tile, toast, badge), the payload contained in a raw notification is strictly app-defined and is not used to convey UI data.

The background task needs to be registered in the application manifest as usual. Use the *pushNotification* value for the type of the task, as follows:

```
<Extension Category="windows.backgroundTasks">
  <BackgroundTasks>
    <Task Type="pushNotification"/>
  </BackgroundTasks>
</Extension>
```

The application registers the task by using a *PushNotificationTrigger* as the trigger to fire the task:

```
var builder = new BackgroundTaskBuilder();

builder.Name = "PushBGTask";
builder.TaskEntryPoint = "Task.DevLeapBackgroundTask";
builder.SetTrigger(new Windows.ApplicationModel.Background.PushNotificationTrigger());
BackgroundTaskRegistration task = builder.Register();
```

The task is activated when a raw notification arrives from the WNS. You can use *TriggerDetails* to retrieve the instance of the raw notification and use the related *Content* property to inspect the content of the notification. Use the following code as a reference:

```
using Windows.ApplicationModel.Background;
using Windows.Networking.PushNotifications;

namespace Tasks
{
    public sealed class ExampleBackgroundTask : IBackgroundTask
    {
        public void Run(IBackgroundTaskInstance taskInstance)
        {
            RawNotification notification = (RawNotification)taskInstance.TriggerDetails;
            string content = notification.Content;
            // Analyze the string content
        }
    }
}
```

Thought experiment

Receiving notifications

In this thought experiment, apply what you've learned about this objective. You can find answers to these questions in the "Answers" section at the end of this chapter.

You are developing a simple gaming application that needs to receive notifications from the cloud when a player beats your best score.

What should be the application data flow from the application to the WNS?

Objective summary

- Push notifications are a powerful and lightweight way to send toasts to the user or to update tiles and badges.
- The application asks the Windows Runtime library for a channel and sends the related URI to the application back end.
- The back end uses the channel URI to send notification to the device using an HTTP request to the WNS.

Objective review

Answer the following questions to test your knowledge of the information in this objective. You can find the answers to these questions and explanations of why each answer choice is correct or incorrect in the "Answers" section at the end of this chapter.

1. What class creates a channel from the back end of a Windows Store app?
   - **A.** *PushNotificationChannelManager* class.
   - **B.** Every class derived from *PushNotificationChannelManager.*
   - **C.** There is no need to create a channel.
   - **D.** *PushNotificationChannel* class.
2. Where can you find the SID to authenticate a request to send a notification to the client?
   - **A.** The information is in the WNS Authentication Service login page available at *https://db3.notify.windows.com.*
   - **B.** You receive this info from the Windows Store Dashboard.
   - **C.** You do not need the SID to send a notification because the client already received the channel.
   - **D.** The SID is not for authentication; it is the security identifier in the received token.
3. Is it possible to activate a background task when a notification arrives to the application?
   - **A.** Yes, if the application is up and running, it can activate a background task.
   - **B.** No, the application can receive a notification only when it is not up and running, so it cannot activate a background task.
   - **C.** Yes, but only for lock screen–enabled applications.
   - **D.** Yes, by registering the task with a *PushNotificationTrigger.*

Chapter summary

- The Print contract enables a Windows Store app to access the Windows print system. First, you need to obtain a reference to a *PrintManager* instance for each view that you want users to be able to print. Second, you need to implement a *PrintTask* instance representing the actual printing operation. Third, you have to create a *PrintDocument* instance to hold a reference to the content that you want to print and handle the events raised during the printing process.

- The Play To feature enables you to stream multimedia from a Windows Store app to other Play To–certified devices, such as TVs, Xbox 360s, speakers, and other receivers. Besides streaming toward other devices, a Windows Store app can also receive that stream by implementing the Play To receiver contract.
- The Windows Push Notification Service (WNS) sends notifications to the user by using toasts. The client application requests a channel to the API and sends the returned channel to some back end, probably a cloud-based service. The back end can then store the channel to use it later to send notification to the user.

Answers

This section contains the solutions to the thought experiments and answers to the lesson review questions in this chapter.

Objective 3.1: Thought experiment

If the user decides to print only a subset of the pages, there are several ways to show the content to be printed. The following list presents a few examples:

- In the print preview, show all the pages, regardless of whether a specific page or a page range is specified. In this case, you do not need to update the print preview, only the collection of pages to be sent to the print system.
- In the print preview, show only the pages selected by the user. In this case, you also need to update the preview whenever the user changes the page range (you can leverage the *InvalidatePreview* method of the *PrintDocument* class) to display only the selected pages.
- Show all the pages in print preview, but shade the pages that are not in page range selected by the user. In this case, you need to update the preview whenever the user changes the page range. You also need to modify the XAML template of the print document to shade the pages that are not selected for printing.

Objective 3.1: Review

1. **Correct answer:** A
   - **A. Correct:** This is the class responsible for orchestrating the entire printing process.
   - **B. Incorrect:** This class defines a reusable object that sends output to a printer.
   - **C. Incorrect:** An object implementing the *IPrintDocumentSource* interface points to the source for the print document.
   - **D. Incorrect:** This class represents a specific printing operation.

2. **Correct answer: B**
   A. **Incorrect:** This event is raised when the user activates the Devices charm and selects a print target from the list of available devices.
   B. **Correct:** This event is raised by the system when the user requests a print operation by activating the Devices charm in the charms bar.
   C. **Incorrect:** This event is fired when the printing operation is completed.
   D. **Incorrect:** When the user activates the Devices charm, the system raises the *PrintTaskRequested* event.
3. **Correct answer:** A
   A. **Correct:** The *PrintTaskSourceRequestedHandler* delegate passed as a second parameter to the *CreatePrintTask* method holds a reference to the method that is called when the user is ready to begin the printing process.
   B. **Incorrect:** The *Submitting* event of the *PrintTask* instance is raised when a print task begins submitting content to the print subsystem to be printed.
   C. **Incorrect:** To notify the user about the outcome of the printing operation, you can use the *Completed* event exposed by the *PrintTask* class.
   D. **Incorrect:** You have to paginate the content for the preview window in the *Paginate* event handler.
4. **Correct answer:** C
   A. **Incorrect:** In this event handler, you need to format the page that you want to print based on the settings retrieved from the print target selected by the user. The resulting pages can then be added to the collection of preview pages to be displayed in the preview window.
   B. **Incorrect:** In this event handler, you have to supply the print system with the requested page to be displayed in the preview window.
   C. **Correct:** In this event handler, you have to add all the pages resulting from the preceding operations to the final collection to be sent to the print target. To accomplish this task, you have to call the *AddPage* method of the *PrintDocument* object. After all the pages are added, you can signal the system that the collection is ready to be printed by invoking the *AddPagesComplete* method.
   D. **Incorrect:** In this event handler, you can leverage the *InvalidatePreview* method exposed by the *PrintDocument* class to invalidate the current print preview every time the user changes one of the properties of the print target.

Objective 3.2: Thought experiment

To understand whether the target device has finished rendering the streamed image before sending a new one, you can leverage the *StateChanged* event exposed by the *Connection* property of the *PlayToSource* media file being streamed. When this event occurs, you can check the *PreviousState* and *CurrentState* properties of *PlayToConnectionStateChangedEventArgs*. For example, if the previous state was Rendering and the new state is now Disconnected, you can assume that the target device has finished rendering the current image and it is now ready to receive a new stream. On the other hand, if the current state is Connected and the previous state was Disconnected, the image that raised the event has just been connected to the Play To receiver, and you should wait before sending a new stream. You can also detect whether the slide show on the target device was paused by the user. In this case, the previous state was Rendering, and the current state is Connected. When the slide show on the target device is unpaused, the current state is Rendering, and the previous state was Connected.

> ***NOTE*** **PLAY TO CONTRACT**
>
> **You can find a more sophisticated case study that goes through all the possible combinations at *http://msdn.microsoft.com/en-us/library/windows/apps/xaml/hh770870.aspx*.**

Objective 3.2: Review

1. **Correct answer:** D
   - **A. Incorrect:** You cannot instantiate a *PlayToManager* object by using the *new* keyword.
   - **B. Incorrect:** The *PlayToManager* object cannot be shared among pages.
   - **C. Incorrect:** You need to get a reference to the *PlayToManager* instance for the current view.
   - **D. Correct:** Each view needs a reference to its own specific *PlayToManager* instance that can be retrieved by calling the *GetForCurrentView* static method of the *PlayToManager* class.
2. **Correct answer:** A
   - **A. Correct:** The *SourceRequested* event of the *PlayToManager* class is fired as soon as the user activates the Devices charm in the charms bar.
   - **B. Incorrect:** This event is fired when the user selects the target device, and the corresponding event handler can be the right place to make sure that the device selected as a Play To target actually supports the specific media element provided for the stream.

C. **Incorrect:** This event occurs when the state of the Play To connection changes.

D. **Incorrect:** When the user activates the Devices charm in the charms bar, the system raises the *SourceRequested* event.

3. **Correct answer:** C

A. **Incorrect:** As soon as the *StartAsync* method is invoked, the code throws an *InvalidOperationException*. Without a valid call to the *StartAsync* method, your app is not registered on the network.

B. **Incorrect:** As soon as the receiver app tries to start receiving, if the *FriendlyName* property has not been set, the system raises an *InvalidOperationException*.

C. **Correct:** The receiver app raises an *InvalidOperationException* as soon as the *StartAsync* method of the *PlayToReceiver* instance is invoked.

D. **Incorrect:** Until the *StartAsync* method is invoked, no exceptions are raised.

4. **Correct answer:** D

A. **Incorrect:** This capability provides outbound access to the Internet and public networks through the firewall, whereas the Play To feature requires a Play To device connected to the same private network.

B. **Incorrect:** This capability provides inbound and outbound access to the Internet and public networks through the firewall, whereas the Play To feature requires a Play To device connected to the same private network.

C. **Incorrect:** These two capabilities provide programmatic access to the user's Music and Videos libraries, and have nothing to do with the Play To feature.

D. **Correct:** This capability provides inbound and outbound access to home and work networks through the firewall. This capability is typically used for games that communicate across the local area network (LAN) and for apps that share data across a variety of local devices, including Play To devices.

Objective 3.3: Thought experiment

During application launch, the application requests a channel to the Windows Runtime, stores the channel in local storage for later check, and sends the channel URI to the back end.

The back end stores the channel URI in remote storage, assigning it to the player name or id (the unique key that represents a player).

For the first game run, the application stores the reached point in the local store and sends it to the remote back end that, in turn, records this information with the channel URI in the player's "record."

For each subsequent game run, the application compares the score with the one stored locally. If the score is less than the previous one, no action is required. If the score is greater, the app sends the score to the remote back end to store the "record" server side.

The remote back end compares the new score with the record of every other player. If the new score is the game record (that is, the value is greater than any other user record), it sends to the WNS an XML message representing a toast with a message stating that a new record has been reached by another user.

Objective 3.3: Review

1. **Correct answer:** C
    - **A. Incorrect:** This class is used in the client application.
    - **B. Incorrect:** There is no need to derive this class.
    - **C. Correct:** The server code uses a simple HTTP request to send notification to the client.
    - **D. Incorrect:** This class is used in the client application.
2. **Correct answer:** B
    - **A. Incorrect:** This URL represents the WNS service to send notification; it is not a logon page.
    - **B. Correct:** The Windows Store Dashboard provides the SID and the client secret to authenticate a request to the WNS.
    - **C. Incorrect:** You need the SID and the client secret to send a notification request to WNS.
    - **D. Incorrect:** The SID is one of two pieces of information needed to authenticate the request to the WNS.
3. **Correct answer:** D
    - **A. Incorrect:** A background task can be activated regardless of application states.
    - **B. Incorrect:** A background task can be activated regardless of application states.
    - **C. Incorrect:** A background task can be activated for every kind of application.
    - **D. Correct:** It is the only thing to do to activate a background task for push notifications.

CHAPTER 4

Enhance the user interface

In this chapter, you learn how to use asynchronous techniques to improve the user interface (UI) responsiveness, how to define and use animations and transitions to enhance the user experience, and how to create custom controls to centralize and reuse some portions of the UI.

Finally, you examine an often overlooked area: globalization and localization. Planning for globalization and localization can help you create apps that have a much wider user base. Although globalizing and localizing applications takes some time, it can greatly improve your app's usability.

Objectives in this chapter:

- Objective 4.1: Design for and implement UI responsiveness
- Objective 4.2: Create animations and transitions
- Objective 4.3: Create custom controls
- Objective 4.4: Design Windows Store apps for globalization and localization

Objective 4.1: Design for and implement UI responsiveness

Prior to the release of Windows 8 and the Microsoft .NET Framework 4.5, many application programming interfaces (APIs) were exposed mainly through synchronous methods. Asynchronous methods were available for accessing data, calling remote web services, and using some of the input/output (I/O) operations on the file system. The implementations of the asynchronous methods were not the same for all the .NET libraries. For example, the data access methods implement the *IAsyncResult* interface, whereas Microsoft Silverlight and Windows Phone follow the *Async* pattern.

Implementing asynchronous code invoking methods available only synchronously was challenging. In that case, you had to write asynchronous wrappers and choose the right pattern at your own risk. Today, you more easily work with asynchronous code due to the .NET Framework improvements.

This objective covers how to:

- Choose an asynchronous strategy for your app
- Implement the Task Parallel library for multiprocessor utilization
- Convert asynchronous operations to tasks

Understanding .NET asynchronous patterns

Suppose that you have a remote service that exposes a *Save* method that receives an *id* and a description to persist it somewhere.

Calling a remote service synchronously blocks the thread until a response comes back on the network. If both the service and the network are responsive, the user can see the result immediately. If the response is slow, the user will suffer the block of the UI for some time. In .NET, since the first version, the UI is managed by only one thread: the thread that creates forms and controls. This thread is probably the one the framework uses to start the application. If this thread is busy because it's calling the remote service, the thread cannot do anything else. The UI won't refresh, listening for Windows events such as mouse clicks or keyboard strokes. In other words, the application does not respond.

To avoid this problem, you can start a new thread and perform some operations in the background. The following .NET 1.0 code starts a new thread to perform some operations:

```
Thread myThread = new Thread(new ThreadStart(MyWorkerThread));
myThread.Start();
private void MyWorkerThread()
{
    // Performs async work
}
```

The code executes the code of the *MyWorkerThread* method. This way, the UI is not blocked and the user can continue working with it, such as moving the window on the screen, clicking a button to stop the current operation, or performing some other operation. Using a different thread for each operation lets the application performs many tasks simultaneously.

The code is simple but there are several things to consider:

- How to handle the exception
- How to perform some work at the end of the method call
- How to synchronize multiple operations
- How to access variables defined in the first method from the second thread
- How to pass results to the main thread

Since version 1.0, the .NET Framework has tried to simplify these topics by providing an asynchronous version of some methods (the ones that worked with remote resources) that hides many of these complexities.

For example, the client-side service reference enables you to call the method both synchronously or asynchronously.

The code in Listing 4-1 calls the *Save* method of the *SalesmanManager* web service reference from a Windows Form application and displays the result (a string) in a label of the form.

LISTING 4-1 Invoking the synchronous version of a web service method

```
using System;
using System.Collections.Generic;
using System.ComponentModel;
using System.Data;
using System.Drawing;
using System.IO;
using System.Linq;
using System.Text;
using System.Threading.Tasks;
using System.Windows.Forms;

namespace WindowsFormsApplication1
{
    public partial class Form1 : Form
    {
        public Form1()
        {
            InitializeComponent();
        }

        private void btnSyncCode_Click(object sender, EventArgs e)
        {
            SalesmanManagerWS ws = new SalesmanManagerWS();
            String result = ws.Save("rob", "Roberto Brunetti");
            lbl.Text = result;
        }
    }
}
```

The code is easy to follow, even if the developer does not have deep knowledge of the language syntax. A web services proxy created by Microsoft Visual Studio or the Wsdl.exe command-line utility creates the asynchronous version of every method using the Microsoft standard interface *IAsyncResult*. The following code uses the asynchronous pattern to call the same method:

```
private void btnAsyncCodeIAsyncResult_Click(object sender, EventArgs e)
{
    SalesmanManagerWS ws = new SalesmanManagerWS();
    IAsyncResult ar = ws.BeginSave("rob", "Roberto Brunetti",
        new AsyncCallback(SavedCallback), ws);

    lbl.Text = result;
}

private void SavedCallback(IAsyncResult ar)
{
```

```
    SalesmanManagerWS ws = ar.AsyncState as SalesmanManagerWS;
    if (ws != null)
    {
        String result = ws.EndSave(ar);
        // lbl.Text = result;
    }
}
```

The code is becoming more complex to read and to be maintained. There is nothing difficult to understand in the code, but it is not as simple and straightforward as the synchronous version. You have to call the *BeginSave* method, passing the same parameter as the synchronous version, and then pass the callback you want to be called at the end of the method call. The .NET Framework handles all the magic behind it: The framework starts a new thread, makes the call to the remote service from the new thread, and activates the callback at the end.

The call to the callback is made by the secondary thread. This behavior denies the possibility to modify any of the form controls because no other thread but the owner (also called a UI thread) can access the user control. If you uncomment the line that assigns the result to the label, you will encounter an exception of type *InvalidOperationException* with the following message:

```
"Cross-thread operation not valid: Control 'lbl' accessed from a
thread other than the thread it was created on."
```

You can overcome the problem using the *Dispatcher* object that asks the main thread to perform the operation on behalf of the secondary thread, as shown in the following code:

```
private void SavedCallback(IAsyncResult ar)
{
    SalesmanManagerWS ws = ar.AsyncState as SalesmanManagerWS;

    if(ws != null)
    {
        String result = ws.EndSave(ar);
        lbl.BeginInvoke(new updateLabel(UpdateLabel), new { result });
    }
}

private delegate void updateLabel(String message);

private void UpdateLabel(String message)
{
    lbl.Text = message;
}
```

This extra work is worth the effort because an operation made by the principal thread blocks the UI until the call is completed.

In more recent versions of .NET, you can simplify the syntax a bit by replacing the use of a delegate with a lambda expression, but things work the same way, and the code is complex to read and to maintain.

In real code, you also need to catch exceptions that can be thrown during the call of the remote method. These exceptions can be caught only in the callback because you have no control on the thread that activates the remote call.

Understanding the asynchronous method in .NET 2.0

To try to simplify the code, .NET 2.0 introduced a new pattern for web service calls. The following code uses the *async/method* pattern to call the remote method:

```
private void btnAsyncCodeIAsyncResult_Click(object sender, EventArgs e)
{
   SalesmanManagerWS ws = new SalesmanManagerWS();
   ws.SaveCompleted += this.SaveCompleted;
   ws.SaveAsync("rob", "Roberto Brunetti";
}

private void SaveCompleted(object sender, SaveCompletedEventArgs e)
{
    // Note the Typed Result (SaveCompletedEventArgs)
    String result = e.Result;
}
```

The code is much simpler. An event is provided automatically by the proxy. You just need to bind a method to the event and provide the code that will be executed at the end of the web service call.

The method will receive a typed argument, created during the creation of the web service proxy that exposes the typed result in the *Result* property.

The code is simpler compared to the *IAsyncResult* pattern, but just few a classes in the .NET Framework 2.0 implement this new pattern. In practice, you have to use the *IAsyncResult* pattern for everything but web service calls, and you need to use it if you want to write more sophisticated code. For example, you have to use the *IAsyncResult* interface if you need to wait for multiple operations, or if you want to know whether the operation has been completed synchronously or asynchronously.

When Silverlight and then Windows Phone appeared on the market, Microsoft chose to use the simplified pattern instead of the more sophisticated one.

In .NET 2.0, Microsoft released a new library called *PageTask*, available only for ASP.NET applications, to simplify the construction of pages that use many calls to remote resources and need to wait for all of them, before returning the content to the user.

Today you have many choices for .NET applications, each of which has its own advantages (and complexity) and disadvantages (and simplicity).

Even if .NET reduces the complexity to call some methods, the problem of creating and managing threads remains for all those operations that are not provided as asynchronous methods by the platform.

Converting operations to tasks

In previous versions of Windows and .NET, many APIs were exposed mainly through synchronous methods; rarely were asynchronous methods available. Thus, when you needed to implement asynchronous code, even while invoking methods available only synchronously, you had to write asynchronous wrappers and choose the right pattern at your own risk.

For example, to read the content of a text file in a string variable, you could have written this code in a traditional Windows application in .NET:

```
void Operation()
{
    string content;
    using (StreamReader sr = new StreamReader("document.txt"))
    {
        content = sr.ReadToEnd();
    }
    DisplayContent(content);
}
```

Because the *ReadToEnd* call is synchronous, if the time required to access the file took a long time, and the code was embedded in an event connected to, for example, the click of a button or a menu item selection, the UI of the entire application would have been frozen for the full duration required to read the content from the document.txt file.

To avoid this issue, the code would ideally read the file in an asynchronous way in the background, returning control immediately to the application that handles the UI and avoiding problems. To do that, the method attached to the UI event had to return as soon as possible. Performing an operation in an asynchronous manner means that the caller of a function does not need to wait for its completion before continuing, but will obtain the result of the completed operation later, after that operation has finished executing. Because the function *ReadToEnd* did not expose an asynchronous pattern, to prevent the interface from freezing. it was necessary to wrap the *ReadToEnd* call in a separate task that executed in a different thread. The code used the *Task* class introduced with the Task Parallel Library (TPL) in .NET 4.0.

This was the event pattern required in .NET Framework 4.0 (2010), which resulted in code similar to the following:

```
void Operation()
{
    Task.Factory.StartNew( () =>
        {
            using (StreamReader sr = new StreamReader("document.txt"))
            {
                return sr.ReadToEnd();
            }
        })
        .ContinueWith(
           (t) => DisplayContent(t.Result)
           );
}
```

The Windows Runtime (WinRT) offers a simpler syntax for creating a *Task* object compared to traditional Windows applications. Each function that might result in a long response time offers an asynchronous version, which returns a *Task<T>* object. The same code can be written in .NET Framework 4.5 as follows:

```
void Operation()
{
    StreamReader sr = new StreamReader(@"document.txt");
    Task<string> readTask = sr.ReadToEndAsync();
    readTask.ContinueWith((t) => DisplayContent(t.Result));
}
```

The code of the asynchronous example in .NET 4.5 is not functionally identical to the synchronous code. In fact, the *using* statement disappeared and the side effect is that the document.txt file will be kept open much longer than required. To avoid that, you should write the following code:

```
void Operation()
{
    StreamReader sr = new StreamReader(@"document.txt");
    Task<string> readTask = sr.ReadToEndAsync();
    readTask.ContinueWith( (t) =>
        {
            sr.Close();
            return t.Result;
        })
        .ContinueWith( (t) => DisplayContent(t.Result));
}
```

Another difference between this code and the initial version is, if an exception occurs, it doesn't immediately close the file. The closing occurs when the *sr* instance of the *StreamReader* class is collected by the garbage collector.

For these reasons, it is important to use the asynchronous pattern based on the *await* keyword.

You can use the new *async* and *await* keywords available in C# 5.0. The *await* keyword executes the block of code that follows as a subsequent method call in a separate task, which is executed in a way similar to the *ContinueWith* call. Because the method containing an *await* statement no longer executes all the lines of code before returning to the caller, it has to return a *Task*, which will have a completed result as soon as all the lines of the original method are executed. For this reason, it is marked with the *async* statement—transforming a *void* method into a method returning a *Task* object, whereas the *async* statement applied to a method returning a string would result in a method returning a *Task<string>*.

```
static async void Asynchronous2_Ok()
{
    string content;
    using (var sr = new StreamReader(@"document.txt"))
    {
        content = await sr.ReadToEndAsync();
    }
    DisplayContent(content);
}
```

The importance of *await* and *async* statements becomes evident when you realize that WinRT APIs offer only asynchronous versions of the API for each method that might have a response time higher than 50 milliseconds. In practice, any API performing an I/O operation either in an explicit or implicit way will result in this category because the response time of an I/O operation is not always predictable.

The code in Listing 4-2 uses the call inside a click event handler for a button. The UI enables you to see how the synchronous and asynchronous patterns will affect the user experience.

LISTING 4-2 XAML definition of the main page used for this sample

```
<Page
    x:Class="DisplayFile.MainPage"
    xmlns="http://schemas.microsoft.com/winfx/2006/xaml/presentation"
    xmlns:x="http://schemas.microsoft.com/winfx/2006/xaml"
    xmlns:local="using:DisplayFile"
    xmlns:d="http://schemas.microsoft.com/expression/blend/2008"
    xmlns:mc="http://schemas.openxmlformats.org/markup-compatibility/2006"
    mc:Ignorable="d">
    <Grid Background="{StaticResource ApplicationPageBackgroundThemeBrush}">
        <StackPanel>
            <Button Click="ChooseFile_Click" Content="Choose File" />
            <TextBlock x:Name="Result " Height="600" />
        </StackPanel>
    </Grid>
</Page>
```

The *TextBlock* control fills with the content of the file selected by the user through the *FileOpenPicker* picker. The button simply fires the code to start the picker, reads the file in a string, and puts it in the *TextBlock*.

The code-behind for the page uses the *async* keyword as the first attribute of the *ChooseFile_Click* method. Doing so lets you use the *await* keyword to use the new asynchronous pattern, as follows:

```
private async void ChooseFile_Click(object sender, RoutedEventArgs e)
{
    var picker = new Windows.Storage.Pickers.FileOpenPicker();
    picker.FileTypeFilter.Add("*");
    var file = await picker.PickSingleFileAsync();
    string content = await Windows.Storage.FileIO.ReadTextAsync(file);
    this.Result.Text = content;
}
```

The first three lines of code create an instance of the *FileOpenPicker* class, which is addressed in Chapter 5, "Manage data and security."

Then the code uses the *PickSingleFileAsync* method to select just one file. This call is marked as *async*, so the remaining part of the method will be executed after the user selects a file. However, *ChooseFile_Click* immediately returns control to its caller, which is the Windows message pump, so any other user interaction with this application will be handled correctly.

The value returned by *PickSingleFileAsync* is of type *Task<Windows.Storage.StorageFile>*, but because the *await* keyword was used, it can be used as a *Windows.Storage.StorageFile* class within a method marked with the *async* keyword. All the code required to get the value from the *Result* property of a *Task* instance and to create a new *Task* every time a new asynchronous call is performed is automatically created by the compiler, thanks to the *await* and *async* keywords.

When a user has chosen a file, the code continues, reading the file content by calling the static method named *FileIO.ReadTextAsync*, which internally handles the required opening and closing of the file, removing the need to make the call within a *using* statement. Listing 4-3 illustrates the point.

LISTING 4-3 Code-behind for the main page used in this sample

```
using System;
using System.Threading.Tasks;
using Windows.System.Threading;
using Windows.UI.Xaml;
using Windows.UI.Xaml.Controls;

namespace DisplayFile
{
    public sealed partial class MainPage : Page
    {
        public MainPage()
        {
             this.InitializeComponent();
        }

        private async void ChooseFile_Click(object sender, RoutedEventArgs e)
        {
             var picker = new Windows.Storage.Pickers.FileOpenPicker();
             picker.FileTypeFilter.Add("*");
             var file = await picker.PickSingleFileAsync();
             string content = await Windows.Storage.FileIO.ReadTextAsync(file);
             this.Result.Text = content;
        }
    }
}
```

Figure 4-1 shows the UI for the main page of the application after reading a sample text document.

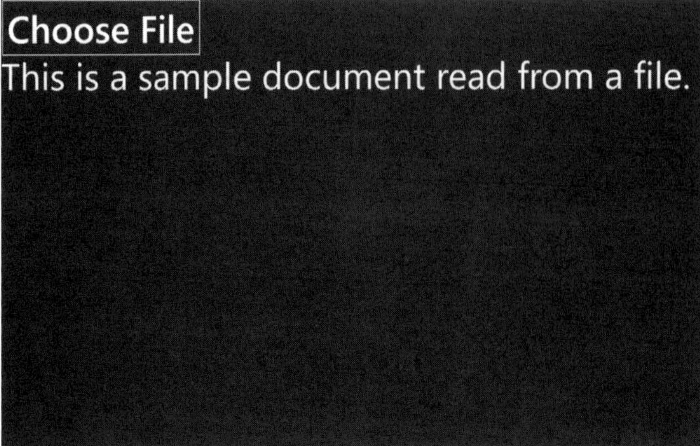

FIGURE 4-1 Content read from a file

Writing methods using *async* techniques

As described in the previous section, handling an event in an asynchronous way is straightforward. You simply have to do the following:

- Include the *async* keyword in the declaration of the method attached to the event.
- Inside the method body, write one or more *await* keywords corresponding to each call to other methods made through asynchronous patterns.

It is important to understand that the method for an event is always called in a synchronous way and does not release control to the message pump until the first call with *await* is executed. Thus, you have to evaluate whether you are executing code that could require a significant amount of time to be executed. You could consider that such a condition exists for any operation that might require more than 50 milliseconds to be completed, adopting the same metric used for WinRT APIs.

For example, suppose that you need to make a calculation that could require a few seconds, such as the following *LongCalculation* method that simulates a long calculation by looping for the number of seconds specified in the parameter:

```
public static void LongCalculation(int seconds)
{
    DateTime exitTime = DateTime.Now.AddSeconds(seconds);
    while (DateTime.Now < exitTime) ;
}
```

If you call this method before any *await* call in an *async* method handling an event, the application will become unresponsive until code execution reaches the first await call. For example, consider what would happen if you call *LongCalculation* in the first line of the *ChooseFile_Click* method of the previous code example, resulting in the following version of the code:

```
private async void ChooseFile_Click(object sender, RoutedEventArgs e)
{
    LongCalculation(5);
    var picker = new Windows.Storage.Pickers.FileOpenPicker();
    picker.FileTypeFilter.Add("*");
    var file = await picker.PickSingleFileAsync();
    string content = await Windows.Storage.FileIO.ReadTextAsync(file);
    this.Result.Text = content;
}
```

If you run this code and click the Choose File button, the application stops responding for five seconds (the value passed as a parameter to *LongCalculation*). The UI to choose the file will display only after that calculation completes. This is because the call to *ChooseFile_Click* is synchronous until execution encounters the first *await*, so it returns control to the message pump after calling the *PickSingleFileAsync* method.

To avoid such problems, you should write the *LongCalculation* method using the asynchronous pattern, so that you can call it with the *await* keyword in the *ChooseFile_Click* method. If you add just the *async* keyword in the *LongCalculation* definition, as follows, you'll get an error message:

```
public static async void LongCalculation(int seconds)
```

The error message that displays is this:

```
DisplayFile.MainPage.LongCalculationAsync(int) does not return a
Task and cannot be awaited. Consider changing it to return Task.
```

What you should understand is that the *async* keyword does not actually make a method asynchronous—*async* is just a keyword that enables (and forces) the use of *await* within the method. To be called with *await*, a method must implement the following asynchronous pattern:

- If the method is void, the asynchronous method must return a *Task*.
- If the method returns a type *T*, the asynchronous method must return a *Task<T>*.

In other words, assume that you have the following methods:

```
public static void Sample1();
public static int Sample2();
public static string Sample3();
```

They would have the following corresponding asynchronous signatures:

```
public static async Task Sample1();
public static async Task<int> Sample2();
public static async Task<string> Sample3();
```

A simple way to transform a CPU-intensive function into an asynchronous function is to change its signature according to the previous pattern and to embed its body within a *Task* action, as in the following example:

```
public static async Task LongCalculationAsync(int seconds)
{
    await Task.Factory.StartNew( () =>
    {
        DateTime exitTime = DateTime.Now.AddSeconds(seconds);
        while (DateTime.Now < exitTime) ;
    });
}
```

> ***NOTE*** **EVENT METHODS AND *TASK* OBJECTS**
>
> **The reason why an event method (such as the previous *ChooseFile_Click* method) does not need to return a *Task* object is because it is not called through *await* but by using a fire-and-forget approach. In other words, there is no code waiting for the end of the asynchronous part of the event method.**

However, remember that creating a new *Task* might execute code in a different thread, introducing a possible race condition caused by execution of code in parallel threads. You will see how to synchronize execution of your code in the proper context later in this chapter. In general, if your code has slow response times because it is calling other APIs or libraries, always favor the call of existing asynchronous versions of the methods of a library by using the *await* call and create new *Task* objects only when you cannot rely on existing asynchronous methods.

Implementing asynchronous methods

This section walks through an implementation of an asynchronous method that prevents the UI from becoming unresponsive while the method executes a long-running operation.

The code in Listing 4-4 uses a button, a label, and a *ProgressBar* control. Engaging the button fires the code, the label displays the result, and the progress bar is useful for verifying the responsiveness of the UI during long operations.

LISTING 4-4 XAML definition of the main page

```
<Page
    x:Class="DisplayFile.MainPage"
    xmlns="http://schemas.microsoft.com/winfx/2006/xaml/presentation"
    xmlns:x="http://schemas.microsoft.com/winfx/2006/xaml"
    xmlns:local="using:DisplayFile"
    xmlns:d="http://schemas.microsoft.com/expression/blend/2008"
    xmlns:mc="http://schemas.openxmlformats.org/markup-compatibility/2006"
    mc:Ignorable="d">
```

```
    <Grid Background="{StaticResource ApplicationPageBackgroundThemeBrush}">
        <StackPanel>
            <Button Click="ChooseFile_Click" Content="Choose File" />
            <ProgressBar x:Name="Progress" HorizontalAlignment="Left"
                         Height="10" Width="1024"/>
            <TextBlock x:Name="Result" Height="600" />
        </StackPanel>
    </Grid>
</Page>
```

The *ProgressBar* control is updated through the following code, which implements continuous updates. The progress bar is an indicator that the message pump is running, and the application is responsive. If the message pump is blocked, the update of the progress bar freezes for the duration of the unresponsiveness state.

```
private void InitializeProgressBar()
{
    var ui = System.Threading.SynchronizationContext.Current;
    ThreadPoolTimer.CreatePeriodicTimer((timer) =>
    {
        ui.Post((a) =>
        {
            this.Progress.Value = (this.Progress.Value >= 100)
                ? 0 : this.Progress.Value + 1;
        }, null);
    }, new TimeSpan(0, 0, 0, 0, 100));
}
```

You can place the previous code in the following page constructor:

```
public MainPage()
{
    this.InitializeComponent();
    InitializeProgressBar();
}
```

You can then use the following code to simulate the long calculation:

```
public static void LongCalculation(int seconds)
{
    DateTime exitTime = DateTime.Now.AddSeconds(seconds);
    while (DateTime.Now < exitTime) ;
}
```

The *LongCalculation* code can be called by the *ChooseFile_Click* method before any other operation, as follows:

```
private async void ChooseFile_Click(object sender, RoutedEventArgs e)
{
    LongCalculation(5);

    var picker = new Windows.Storage.Pickers.FileOpenPicker();
    picker.FileTypeFilter.Add("*");
    var file = await picker.PickSingleFileAsync();
    string content = await Windows.Storage.FileIO.ReadTextAsync(file);
    this.Result.Text = content;
}
```

If you run the application, the progress bar continuously changes its state. When you click the Choose File button, the progress bar freezes for five seconds, which means that the application has become unresponsive. The result is a state similar to that shown in Figure 4-2. The progress bar freezes at the point when the code reaches the long calculation.

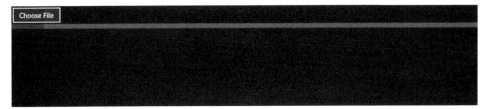

FIGURE 4-2 Progress bar during long operation

After five seconds, the UI for selecting a file appears, which indicates that the long calculation is finished and the system has run the remaining lines of code.

To transform the call to an asynchronous one, you can use the C# code shown in Listing 4-5.

LISTING 4-5 Implementing the asynchronous version of the *LongCalculation* method

```
using System;
using System.Threading.Tasks;
using Windows.System.Threading;
using Windows.UI.Xaml;
using Windows.UI.Xaml.Controls;

namespace DisplayFile
{
    public sealed partial class MainPage : Page
    {
        public MainPage()
        {
            this.InitializeComponent();
            InitializeProgressBar();
        }

        private void InitializeProgressBar()
        {
            var ui = System.Threading.SynchronizationContext.Current;
            ThreadPoolTimer.CreatePeriodicTimer((timer) =>
            {
                ui.Post((a) =>
                {
                    this.Progress.Value =
                        (this.Progress.Value >= 100) ? 0 : this.Progress.Value + 1;
                }, null);

            }, new TimeSpan(0, 0, 0, 0, 100));
        }
```

```
        private async void ChooseFile_Click(object sender, RoutedEventArgs e)
        {
            await LongCalculationAsync(5);
            var picker = new Windows.Storage.Pickers.FileOpenPicker();
            picker.FileTypeFilter.Add("*");
            var file = await picker.PickSingleFileAsync();
            string content = await Windows.Storage.FileIO.ReadTextAsync(file);
            this.Result.Text = content;
        }

        public static async Task LongCalculationAsync(int seconds)
        {
            await Task.Factory.StartNew( () =>
            {
                DateTime exitTime = DateTime.Now.AddSeconds(seconds);
                while (DateTime.Now < exitTime) ;
            } );
        }
    }
}
```

The code is embedded in a lambda expression passed to the *Task.Factory.StartNew* method, called by using the *await* keyword. The method declaration contains the *async* and returns a *Task* class. The last modification is the *await* keyword before the *LongCalculationAsync* call.

If you run the application with the new code, the progress bar will continue to update. This is because the message pump is not blocked, and the application is still responsive even if a long operation is executed before asking to the user to select a file.

Waiting for an event in an asynchronous way

The previous section explored how to call a long-running operation without blocking the responsiveness of an app's UI. However, the long operation was still called in a synchronous way in respect to the operation performed by the user. In fact, the file picker UI was displayed only five seconds after the initial click. What if you want to perform the operation during the file picker operation, without stopping it? To do that, you have to execute the operation in an asynchronous way without using the *await* keyword, by directly manipulating the *Task* object returned by the asynchronous call you make.

In practice, if you save the result of an asynchronous call into a *Task* object, you can write an *await* statement targeting such an object to stop the code flow of a method until the corresponding asynchronous call has been terminated. In practice, if you write the following, the *InputData* call is made after the *LongCalculationAsync* has been completed, and the only reason why you are using *await* is because you want to avoid the UI becoming unresponsive:

```
await LongCalculationAsync(5);
InputData();
DisplayData();
```

However, you can move the *await* statement after the *InputData* call and before the line calling *DisplayData*, as follows:

```
Task longCalculation = LongCalculationAsync(5);
InputData();
await longCalculation;
DisplayData();
```

In this case, the *LongCalculationAsync* call will be executed at the same time as *InputData*, and the *DisplayData* method will be called only after both *LongCalculationAsync* and *InputData* are completed.

> ***NOTE*** **USAGE CAVEAT**
>
> **This technique is attractive, especially when you have long-running calculations that have to be performed before showing results to the user. However, you have to be careful because executing code in such a way might determine race conditions. If both *LongCalculationAsync* and *InputData* access shared data, you have to protect the data structures from possible inconsistencies caused by one method writing data when the other is reading the same memory. This is the classical problem you have to handle in multithreading programming, which is beyond the scope of this book. Be aware that if you directly manipulate *Task* objects in your code, you are no longer using the "safe" synchronous programming paradigm and must manage all behind-the-scenes aspects yourself. You also have to apply all the knowledge of multithreaded programming to avoid race conditions.**

Implementing asynchronous calls

In this section, you will see how to implement an asynchronous call to an asynchronous method to execute parallel actions in your UI, without having to wait for a background action to complete.

Let's examine the following code:

```
await LongCalculationAsync(5);
```

As you have learned, the code waits for the completion of the long calculation, without blocking the UI, and then proceeds to the next line of code. The program cannot execute other operations during the long calculation.

If you want to enable the possibility to perform some other action, you can remove the *await* keyword from the call and save the result returned from the call in a variable of type *Task*, so that the line becomes the following:

```
Task longTask = LongCalculationAsync(5);
```

Then you can *await* the task completion after some other lines of code.

For example, if you insert a wait for *longTask* completion after the read of the file using the *FileOpenPicker* class, the code will not wait for task completion before opening the picker. Such a wait must be done by using the *await* keyword and without using a call to one of the wait methods of the *Task* class (such as *WaitOne*), which might cause a deadlock of the application.

The resulting code of the method should look like the following (changes made to previous examples are highlighted in bold):

```
private async void ChooseFile_Click(object sender, RoutedEventArgs e)
{
    Task longTask = LongCalculationAsync(40);
    var picker = new Windows.Storage.Pickers.FileOpenPicker();
    picker.FileTypeFilter.Add("*");
    var file = await picker.PickSingleFileAsync();
    string content = await Windows.Storage.FileIO.ReadTextAsync(file);
    await longTask;
    this.Result.Text = content;
}
```

If you run the application with the modified code, click the Choose File button within 40 seconds, and then click Open within 40 seconds, you will experience a delay before the file content is displayed on the screen. This is because the content will be displayed only after at least 40 seconds from the click of the Choose File button, waiting for completion of the *LongCalculationAsync* call.

Cancelling asynchronous operations

When an asynchronous operation needs to be canceled, you must include a way to communicate the break of an operation to the code that might be executing in another thread. This could be done by using a simple *Boolean* flag and having a part of the method called asynchronously that polls such a flag and exits from the running function as soon as it finds that flag active.

However, because a method can call other methods that can run other asynchronous operations, there is a need for a standard pattern that transfers the request to inner asynchronous methods. In this way, a request for cancel can be propagated to inner asynchronous method calls, and the latency between cancel request and execution break is the lowest possible.

The internal asynchronous interfaces used by the Windows Runtime are mapped to the standard Task-based Asynchronous Pattern (TAP), which uses .NET classes such as *CancellationToken* and *CancellationTokenSource* to provide a way to cancel an asynchronous operation by propagating the request to any depth of asynchronous call. The basic idea is to pass a *CancellationToken* object that contains the request for the cancellation, so if an asynchronous method has to call another method in an asynchronous way, the same token is used, and the cancellation automatically propagates through the call chain.

Because the standard asynchronous methods provided by .NET returns an *IAsyncInfo* interface, in order to simplify the wrapping in a Task class containing the desired *CancellationToken*, you must call the *AsTask* method passing the *CancellationToken* instance as a parameter. For example, if you want to provide a *CancellationToken* to the *PickSingleFileAsync* method, you have to convert this line:

```
var file = await picker.PickSingleFileAsync();
```

into the following one:

```
var file = await picker.PickSingleFileAsync().AsTask(cancelPickSingleFile.Token);
```

where the *cancelPickSingleFile* instance has been declared in this way:

```
CancellationTokenSource cancelPickSingleFile = new CancellationTokenSource();
```

The *cancelPickSingleFile* can be used to cancel the asynchronous operation to which the token is assigned. The *CancellationTokenSource* class offers a *Cancel* method to forward the request for an cancelling operation to the related asynchronous call.

Cancelling an operation in asynchronous calls

Now let's find out how to add an automatic cancellation of the file picker operation if the user did not make a selection within 10 seconds after clicking the Choose File button.

First, define a method that sets a time-out in seconds:

```
private static async void SetTimeoutOperation(int seconds, CancellationTokenSource cts)
{
    await Task.Delay(seconds * 1000);
    cts.Cancel();
}
```

Then use the following code as a reference to add the declaration of a *CancellationTokenSource* that is passed as a parameter to the *AsTask* call over the *PickSingleFileAsync* result. Changes made to the previous example are highlighted in bold:

```
private async void ChooseFile_Click(object sender, RoutedEventArgs e)
{
    try
    {
        var picker = new Windows.Storage.Pickers.FileOpenPicker();
        picker.FileTypeFilter.Add("*");

        CancellationTokenSource cancelPickSingleFile = new CancellationTokenSource();
        SetTimeoutOperation(5, cancelPickSingleFile);

        var file = await
            picker.PickSingleFileAsync().AsTask(cancelPickSingleFile.Token);

        string content = await Windows.Storage.FileIO.ReadTextAsync(file);
        this.Result.Text = content;
    }
```

```
    catch (Exception ex)
    {
        this.Result.Text = ex.Message;
    }
}
```

If you run the application, click the Choose File button, and then wait until the UI for picking a file disappears, the initial window appears again. It displays the following message:

```
A task was cancelled
```

To cancel the asynchronous operation, a *TaskCanceledException* exception is thrown and it propagates to the *catch* statement in the *ChooseFile_Click* method. Such an exception emerges in the *ChooseFile_Click* method corresponding to the *await* call to the *PickSingleFileAsync*. In this way, the remaining lines in the same *try* block (the call to *ReadTextAsync* and the assignment to the Result text box) are not executed because the control is transferred directly to the *catch* statement.

You can cancel an asynchronous operation made by WinRT classes by passing a *CancellationToken* to the *Task* obtained with the *AsTask* method from a WinRT asynchronous call. The best way to generate and interact with a *CancellationToken* is to create a *CancellationTokenSource*, which is a class that offers methods to request the cancellation of an operation bind to the corresponding *CancellationToken* instance.

Tracking operation progress

During the progress of an asynchronous operation, you might need to display the progress state. WinRT asynchronous calls can be wrapped in a *Task* object that offers the *IProgress<T>* interface, which standardizes the communication of advancement states of an asynchronous operation in the TAP:

```
public interface IProgress<in T>
{
    void Report( T Value );
}
```

By providing an object implementing *IProgress* to an asynchronous operation, it is possible to receive notifications about the state of the operation. All WinRT functions that return an *IAsyncActionWithProgress<TProgress>* object can be attached to code that displays progress of the operation by using the *AsTask* syntax:

```
IProgress<TProgress> progress = ...;
await SomeMethodAsync().AsTask(progress);
```

To obtain an object implementing the *IProgress<T>* interface, the easiest way is to create an instance of the *Progress<T>* class. For example, if you have a function that provides progress information through an *int* type, you have to pass a lambda function as a parameter to the *Progress<int>* constructor that receives an integer as a parameter, as in the following code:

```
IProgress<int> p = new Progress<int>( (value) =>
{
    // Code that display progress
    // The value parameter is of type int
} );
```

The data type used in the progress interface depends on the asynchronous operation. Refer to WinRT documentation to know which type to use for a specific method.

Tracking progress in asynchronous operations

You can add a method that simulates the execution of some work and report the progress of the ongoing operation through the *IProgress<T>* interface.

In this example, the sample UI uses a *Button* control after the Choose File button, embedding the two buttons in a horizontal *StackPanel*. A *ProgressBar* named *ProgressSomework* is added after the *TextBlock* control, as illustrated in the bolded lines of Listing 4-6.

LISTING 4-6 XAML definition of the main page used in this sample

```
<Page
    x:Class="DisplayFile.MainPage"
    xmlns="http://schemas.microsoft.com/winfx/2006/xaml/presentation"
    xmlns:x="http://schemas.microsoft.com/winfx/2006/xaml"
    xmlns:local="using:DisplayFile"
    xmlns:d="http://schemas.microsoft.com/expression/blend/2008"
    xmlns:mc="http://schemas.openxmlformats.org/markup-compatibility/2006"
    mc:Ignorable="d">

    <Grid Background="{StaticResource ApplicationPageBackgroundThemeBrush}">
        <StackPanel>
            <StackPanel Orientation="Horizontal">
                <Button Click="ChooseFile_Click" Content="Choose File" />
                <Button Click="Start_Click" Content="Run Work" />
            </StackPanel>
            <ProgressBar x:Name="Progress"
                         HorizontalAlignment="Left" Height="10" Width="1024"/>
            <TextBlock x:Name="Result" />
            <ProgressBar x:Name="ProgressSomework"
                         HorizontalAlignment="Left" Height="10" Width="1024"/>
        </StackPanel>
    </Grid>
</Page>
```

The button displaying Run Work calls the *Start_Click* method, whereas the *ProgressSomework* progress bar displays the state of the ongoing operation.

The *Start_Click* method implements the event handler for the Run Work button, as follows:

```
private async void Start_Click(object sender, RoutedEventArgs e)
{
    this.Result.Text = "Start running...";
    await DoSomeWork(
       new Progress<int>( (value) =>
       {
           this.ProgressSomework.Value = value;
       } ));
    this.Result.Text = "Loop finished";
}
```

The method shows that the loop is running and then finishes, calling the asynchronous *DoSomeWorkAsync* method and passing an object implementing *IProgress<int>*. To do that, you need to create an instance of *Progress<int>* and pass a lambda expression that updates the value of the *ProgressSomework* progress bar according to the number received as a parameter. The code in the lambda expression will be executed every time a progress notification is sent from the asynchronous operation to the *Progress* instance. In this case, the value of the progress bar named *ProgressSomework* will be updated every time a notification is received.

The *DoSomeWork* method implements a dummy loop, notifying about progress after a pause of 20 milliseconds for each iteration. The code can be similar to the following:

```
private async Task DoSomeWork(IProgress<int> progress) {
    for (int i = 0; i <= 100; i++) {
        if (progress != null) {
            progress.Report(i);
        }
        await Task.Delay(20);
    }
}
```

The call to the *Report* method in the *progress* object executes the lambda expression passed as a parameter to the *Progress<int>* constructor, called in the code you just examined.

The complete code for a page code-behind is shown in Listing 4-7.

LISTING 4-7 Code-behind of the main page

```
using System;
using System.Threading;
using System.Threading.Tasks;
using Windows.System.Threading;
using Windows.UI.Xaml;
using Windows.UI.Xaml.Controls;

namespace DisplayFile
{
    public sealed partial class MainPage : Page
    {
        public MainPage()
        {
            this.InitializeComponent();
            InitializeProgressBar();
        }
```

```
private void InitializeProgressBar()
{
    var ui = System.Threading.SynchronizationContext.Current;
    ThreadPoolTimer.CreatePeriodicTimer((timer) =>
    {
        ui.Post((a) =>
        {
            this.Progress.Value = (this.Progress.Value >= 100)
                                  ? 0 : this.Progress.Value + 1;
        }, null);
    }, new TimeSpan(0, 0, 0, 0, 100));
}

private static async void SetTimeoutOperation(int seconds,
    CancellationTokenSource cts)
{
    await Task.Delay(seconds * 1000);
    cts.Cancel();
}

private async void ChooseFile_Click(object sender, RoutedEventArgs e)
{
    try
    {
        var picker = new Windows.Storage.Pickers.FileOpenPicker();
        picker.FileTypeFilter.Add("*");

        CancellationTokenSource cancelPickSingleFile = new
            CancellationTokenSource();
        SetTimeoutOperation(5, cancelPickSingleFile);

        var file = await
             picker.PickSingleFileAsync().AsTask(cancelPickSingleFile.Token);
        string content = await Windows.Storage.FileIO.ReadTextAsync(file);
        this.Result.Text = content;
    }
    catch (Exception ex)
    {
        this.Result.Text = ex.Message;
    }
}

private async void Start_Click(object sender, RoutedEventArgs e)
{
    this.Result.Text = "Start running...";
    // Use Progress<T> instance for Progress info (same as WinRT/.NET Calls)
    await DoSomeWork(
        new Progress<int>((value) =>
        {
            this.ProgressSomework.Value = value;
        } ));
    this.Result.Text = "Loop finished";
}
```

```
        private async Task DoSomeWork(IProgress<int> progress)
        {
            for (int i = 0; i <= 100; i++)
            {
                if (progress != null)
                {
                    progress.Report(i);
                }
                await Task.Delay(20);
            }
        }

        public async Task LongCalculationAsync(int seconds)
        {
            await Task.Factory.StartNew(() =>
            {
                DateTime exitTime = DateTime.Now.AddSeconds(seconds);
                while (DateTime.Now < exitTime) ;
            } );
        }

    }
}
```

When you run the code, the first progress bar continuously changes its state. Then, after clicking the Run Work File button, a Start running message displays, and the progress bar below this message starts to be updated, rising from 0 to 100 percent in about two seconds. After that, a Loop finished message appears instead of the Start running message. The resulting state should be similar to that shown in Figure 4-3.

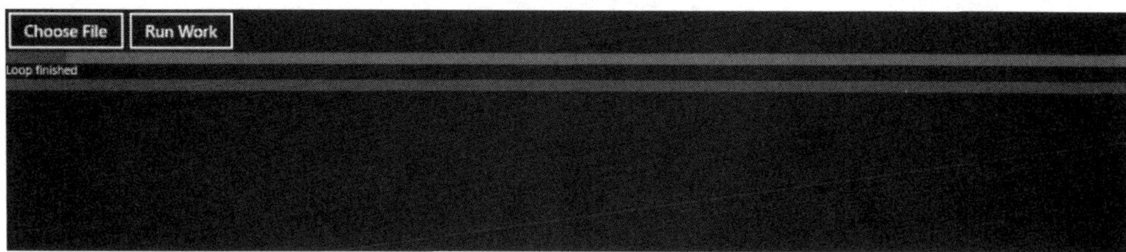

FIGURE 4-3 Progress bars for two concurrent operations

The progress action is always executed in a safe execution context, enabling the UI to be updated. If you are familiar with asynchronous programming in previous versions of .NET, you know that this type of synchronization, which involves an object handling the UI, can be cumbersome. Thanks to the TAP, the code required to execute the code in a proper way is greatly reduced and simplified.

Synchronizing multiple asynchronous calls

When multiple asynchronous calls are active at the same time, there are useful functions that help you write the code that waits for the end of the first call or all pending calls.

For example, consider the following code:

```
await Operation1Async();
await Operation2Async();
await Operation3Async();
```

The total time for executing the three lines of code is equal to the sum of the time required to execute each of the three functions. However, because the three operations are independent, it could be better to use the *Task.WhenAll* function to execute all three functions at the same time. In the best case, the time required to execute the *Task.When* method would correspond to the time required for the longest operation. The code can be written in this way:

```
var t1 = Operation1Async();
var t2 = Operation2Async();
var t3 = Operation3Async();
await Task.WhenAll( t1, t2, t3 );
```

It is also possible to avoid variable creation by putting the asynchronous calls directly in *Task.WhenAll* parameters, like this:

```
await Task.WhenAll(
    Operation1Async(),
    Operation2Async(),
    Operation3Async() );
```

In case of WinRT asynchronous calls, it could be necessary to call the *AsTask*() method to obtain a valid *Task* object for *Task.WhenAll* or *Task.WaitAny*, which you will see shortly.

Thus, if *OperationXAsync* were a WinRT function, the code would be as follows:

```
await Task.WhenAll(
    Operation1Async().AsTask(),
    Operation2Async().AsTask(),
    Operation3Async().AsTask() );
```

In a similar way, it is possible to wait only for the first task to complete in a list of tasks by using the *Task.WhenAny* function, which returns the first call in the list that has been completed. In the following code, the *firstCompleted* variable will be assigned to the first completed task, which will correspond to *t1*, *t2*, or *t3*, depending on the first completed operation:

```
var t1 = Operation1Async();
var t2 = Operation2Async();
var t3 = Operation3Async();
Task firstCompleted = await Task.WhenAny( t1, t2, t3 );
```

It is important to note that *Task.WhenAll* and *Task.WhenAny* should be used instead of the *WaitHandle.WaitAny* and *WaitHandle.WaitAll* methods, even when you have *WaitHandle* objects available. The reason is that the *WaitHandle* static methods ignore the need to use the proper synchronization context (explained in the next section), and they might block the current thread, resulting in a deadlock situation when such a code is mixed with *await* statements.

Waiting for multiple asynchronous calls executed in parallel

This section explores code that waits for completion of all asynchronous calls executed at the same time.

Listing 4-8 defines the UI.

LISTING 4-8 XAML definition of the main page used in this sample

```
<Page
    x:Class="DisplayFile.MainPage"
    xmlns="http://schemas.microsoft.com/winfx/2006/xaml/presentation"
    xmlns:x="http://schemas.microsoft.com/winfx/2006/xaml"
    xmlns:local="using:DisplayFile"
    xmlns:d="http://schemas.microsoft.com/expression/blend/2008"
    xmlns:mc="http://schemas.openxmlformats.org/markup-compatibility/2006"
    mc:Ignorable="d">

    <Grid Background="{StaticResource ApplicationPageBackgroundThemeBrush}">
        <StackPanel>
            <StackPanel Orientation="Horizontal">
                <Button Click="ChooseFile_Click" Content="Choose File" />
                <Button Click="Start_Click" Content="Run Work" />
                <Button Click="WhenAll_Click" Content="WhenAll" />
            </StackPanel>
            <ProgressBar x:Name="Progress"
                         HorizontalAlignment="Left" Height="10" Width="1024"/>
            <TextBlock x:Name="Result" />
            <ProgressBar x:Name="ProgressSomework"
                         HorizontalAlignment="Left" Height="10" Width="1024"/>
        </StackPanel>
    </Grid>
</Page>
```

The button displaying WhenAll calls the *WhenAll_Click* method that fires the following operation in parallel. These methods simulate three operations with different response times (one, two, and three seconds, respectively):

```
private async Task Operation1Async() {
     await Task.Delay(1000);
}

private async Task Operation2Async() {
     await Task.Delay(2000);
}

private async Task Operation3Async() {
     await Task.Delay(3000);
}
```

This code represents the method definition for the button event handler:

```
private async void WhenAll_Click(object sender, RoutedEventArgs e)
{
```

```
    this.Result.Text = "WhenAll starting ...";
    DateTime start = DateTime.Now;
    await Task.WhenAll(
                Operation1Async(),
                Operation2Async(),
                Operation3Async());
    this.Result.Text = String.Format(
        "WhenAll completed in {0} seconds",
        (DateTime.Now - start).Seconds );
}
```

If you run the application and click the WhenAll button, wait until the following message displays:

```
WhenAll completed in 3 seconds
```

The total time required for executing the three operations is three seconds, whereas it would have been six seconds if the three functions were executed sequentially (by using three distinct *await* statements).

Choosing the right *SynchronizationContext* in libraries

The default behavior of the *await* statement is to capture the current *SynchronizationContext* and use it to synchronize the execution of the completion code (the code following the *await* statement) by using such a context. This is why it isn't necessary to write synchronization code when manipulating UI objects in asynchronous methods using the *async* and *await* keywords. However, this behavior is useful in code that directly interacts with the UI, whereas it could be a disadvantage for a library that might be called by code that does not have to interact with the UI.

The following statement will continue execution after task completion in the same execution context of the *await* call:

```
await task;
```

In other words, if you have the following method, the *OtherActivity* method will be called within the same synchronization context of the initial *DoSomeWorkAsync* method, while part of the *OperationAsync* call might be executed in a different synchronization context (in a newly created thread, for example):

```
private async Task DoSomeworkAsync()
{
    await OperationAsync();
    OtherActivity();
}
```

When you write code at the application level, this is usually the expected behavior. However, when you write a library, this behavior might be not optimal for performance reasons. For example, if the *DoSomeWorkAsync* method is called from a service that does not have a UI, or the *OtherActivity* method does not have to interact with the UI in any way, the default behavior that forces synchronization performs a slow operation that is not necessary.

Such an operation can be avoided if the *OtherActivity* method can be executed in a different thread from the one in which *DoSomeWorkAsync* was initially called. By calling the *ConfigureAwait* method, it is possible to change this behavior, requesting execution of the remaining code in the same thread used by the task that completed the activity. The *ConfigureAwait* has to be called as a method of the *Task* that should continue in the same thread, ignoring the existing *SynchronizationContext* when *await* has been called. The changes applied to the previous code are highlighted in the following sample:

```
private async Task DoSomeworkAsync()
{
    await OperationAsync().ConfigureAwait( false );
    OtherActivity();
}
```

Another reason to use *ConfigureAwait(false)* in library code is that libraries can be used by a program with or without a UI. By disabling the use of the current *SynchronizationContext*, the same library will be usable by UI code or services, regardless of the synchronization technique used by the caller.

For example, assume that the first version of the *DoSomeworkAsync* method is used by calling the *WaitOne* method of the *Task* instance it returns. That code could go into a deadlocked state because the *await* within *DoSomeworkAsync* would try to synchronize with the message pump, but the caller might be blocking the message pump. This situation would occur, for example, with the following code handling the click event of a button:

```
async void button1_Click(…)
{
    DoSomeworkAsync().WaitOne();
}
```

It would be better for the caller (*button1_Click*) to use *await* instead of calling *WaitOne*, but the writer of a library might prefer not being considered responsible for a deadlock caused by bad programming habits, so consider using *ConfigureAwait(false)* in library code that does not directly control UI. By doing that, remember that the code following the *await* line could be executed in a different thread, entering in all the concurrent issues (such as race conditions) that are common to multithreading programming.

Thought experiment

Fetching data

In this thought experiment, apply what you've learned about this objective. You can find answers to these questions in the "Answers" section at the end of this chapter.

You are working on a Windows 8 business application that tracks time spent on tasks. You need to issue multiple requests to fetch data from a server with project and client information. In the app, you are processing the data to display it to the user with his personal preferences. This process is quite resource intensive, and you are experiencing performance issues.

Answer the following questions:

1. **How can you optimize data fetching?**
2. **What can you do to improve the performance of the data processing?**
3. **With these answers in mind, what are the main scenarios for using asynchronous methods?**

Objective summary

- The WinRT APIs offer only an asynchronous version of each method that might have a response time higher than 50 milliseconds.
- The .NET Framework *async/await* pattern simplifies dramatically the maintainability of asynchronous code.
- The TPL can be leveraged to perform asynchronous operations.
- Implement your own classes with async code whenever your code could block the UI thread.

Objective review

Answer the following questions to test your knowledge of the information in this objective. You can find the answers to these questions and explanations of why each answer choice is correct or incorrect in the "Answers" section at the end of this chapter.

1. How can you wait for method completion when calling WinRT methods?
   - **A.** Use the callback event handler.
   - **B.** Subscribe to the completion event for the event.
   - **C.** Use the *await* keyword as the first parameter of the method.
   - **D.** Use the *await* keyword in an asynchronous method.

2. How can you handle an exception in an asynchronous method call?
   A. Check for exceptions in the callback.
   B. Use a *try/catch* block in the completion event.
   C. Use a *try/catch* block as you do in synchronous code.
   D. You cannot handle an exception directly because the code is managed by a different thread.
3. How can you stop an asynchronous call?
   A. Use the *IAsyncResult* instance.
   B. Use the completion event handler.
   C. Use the *CancellationTokenSource* class.
   D. Use the *Thread* class.

Objective 4.2: Create animations and transitions

Animations and transitions are an essential part of a Windows 8 app user experience. A fluid interface is defined as one in which everything comes from somewhere and goes somewhere else. Elements shouldn't suddenly appear or disappear. Instead, your animations should tell the story and ensure that your user understands what's happening.

EXAM TIP

There is a slight difference between transitions and animations. You have little or no control over transitions. Animations, on the other hand, usually provide you with more fine-grained control thanks to key frames, interpolation, and easing functions.

You should also be careful not to overuse animations. Using an animation for each and every element could irritate users and hinder them in using your app. Consider animations as a form of communication. You don't want to shout at the user, distract him with a lot of noise, or speak so softly that he can't hear you. Used wisely, animations are an integral part of Windows 8 and can add great value to your app.

This objective covers how to:

- Apply animations from the animation library
- Create and customize animations and transitions, including XAML transitions
- Implement storyboards and transformations
- Utilize built-in animations for controls

Creating and customizing storyboarded animations

A storyboard is not just a way to animate the UI with some fancy transitions. It's more of a way to change the value of a dependency property over time.

> ***NOTE*** **DEPENDENCY PROPERTIES**
>
> **A dependency property is a specialized type of property that is tracked by a dedicated property system that is part of the Windows Runtime. The value of this kind of property depends on the value of other inputs. These inputs can include system properties (such as user preferences), just-in-time properties (such as data binding, animations, and storyboards), templates (such as resources and styles), and so on. For further information on dependency properties, read the "Creating your own dependency properties for a custom control" section in Objective 4.3.**

You can define a storyboarded animation by directly writing XAML code, or you can use tools such as Blend for Microsoft Visual Studio 2012 for Windows 8 to design the storyboard visually, and the tool will take care of producing the corresponding Extensible Application Markup Language (XAML) code for you. It is also possible to programmatically define a storyboarded animation via C# code, but this approach can easily lead to complex and unpleasant code.

> ***MORE INFO*** ***STORYBOARD*** **CLASS**
>
> **The *Storyboard* class derives from the *Timeline* class, which represents the base class not only for storyboards but also for all the Windows Runtime animation types, including those from the animation library and those used for custom animations in visual states or page-level XAML.**

Listing 4-9 shows a simple storyboarded animation that changes the value of the *Opacity* property of the *Rectangle* control from 1.0 (opaque) to 0 (transparent) over the time span specified by the *Duration* property (one second, in this sample). It then starts over from the beginning, according to the *RepeatBehavior* property.

LISTING 4-9 Simple storyboard animation that animates the opacity of a rectangle

```
<Page
    x:Class="StoryboardSample.MainPage"
    xmlns="http://schemas.microsoft.com/winfx/2006/xaml/presentation"
    xmlns:x="http://schemas.microsoft.com/winfx/2006/xaml"
    xmlns:local="using:StoryboardSample"
    xmlns:d="http://schemas.microsoft.com/expression/blend/2008"
    xmlns:mc="http://schemas.openxmlformats.org/markup-compatibility/2006"
    mc:Ignorable="d">
```

```
    <Grid Background="{StaticResource ApplicationPageBackgroundThemeBrush}">
        <Grid.Resources>
            <Storyboard x:Name="SimpleStoryboard">
                <DoubleAnimation Storyboard.TargetName="BlinkingRectangle"
                    Storyboard.TargetProperty="Opacity"
                    From="1.0" To="0.0" Duration="0:0:1"
                    RepeatBehavior="Forever"/>
            </Storyboard>
        </Grid.Resources>
        <Canvas Width="400" Height="300">
            <Rectangle x:Name="BlinkingRectangle" Opacity="1.0" Width="100" Height="100"
                Fill="Orange" />
        </Canvas>
    </Grid>
</Page>
```

Because the animation deals with *Double* values, it uses the *DoubleAnimation* class to determine the intermediate values of the targeted property along the timeline. Only certain types can be manipulated by the framework: *Double*, *Point*, and *Color*. (You will learn how to animate properties of type *Object* in the "Using discrete animations" section.) The logic needed to animate these types is encapsulated, respectively, in the *DoubleAnimation* class, the *PointAnimation* class, and the *ColorAnimation* class.

The *RepeatBehavior* property enables you to repeat the animation from the beginning, after it has reached the end, and accepts one of the following:

- An integer value that specifies the number of times the timeline should play
- A *TimeSpan* value that specifies the total length of the current timeline's active period
- The special value *Forever*, which specifies that the timeline should repeat indefinitely

The animation is connected to the target control through the *TargetName* property, and you have to specify which dependency property will change via the *TargetProperty* property (the opacity of the target object in Listing 4-9). The starting value of the targeted property is set through the *From* property (1.0), whereas the final value of the animated property (that is, the value the property will have at the end of the animation) is set through the *To* property.

> ***NOTE*** **OMITTING THE *FROM* PROPERTY**
>
> **If you omit the *From* property with the starting value of the targeted property, the original value defined in the XAML definition of the control will be used as the starting value.**

Listing 4-10 shows an example of a *ColorAnimation* storyboard that changes the foreground color of an *Ellipse* control over time.

LISTING 4-10 Example of a *ColorAnimation* storyboard

```
<Grid Background="{StaticResource ApplicationPageBackgroundThemeBrush}">
    <Grid.Resources>
        <Storyboard x:Name="ColorStoryboard">
            <ColorAnimation Storyboard.TargetName="MyCircle"
                Storyboard.TargetProperty="(Ellipse.Fill).(SolidColorBrush.Color)"
                To="OrangeRed"
                AutoReverse="True"
                Duration="0:0:3"
                RepeatBehavior="Forever"/>
        </Storyboard>
    </Grid.Resources>
    <Canvas Width="400" Height="100">
        <Ellipse Fill="Yellow" x:Name="MyCircle" Opacity="1.0" Width="200"
            Height="200" />
    </Canvas>
</Grid>
```

In this case, the targeted property is not simply indicated by its name, as in Listing 4-9. That's because the actual property you are trying to change, which is *Color* in this sample, is nested in an object-property relationship. In Listing 4-10, for example, you can't directly pass the new color (*OrangeRed*) to the *Fill* property of the *Ellipse* base class (*Shape*) because it is of type *Brush*. To change this property, you have to drill down until you can reference the right property type that can be animated (*Double*, *Point*, or, in this case, *Color*). To do so, you have to use *indirect targeting*, a technique that uses a syntax known as "property path syntax."

Both sets of parentheses in Listing 4-10 enclose a type name and a property name (the *Ellipse.Fill* property and the *SolidColorBrush.Color* property, respectively). The dot that connects the two sets of parentheses is called step because it represents a "step" into the object model of the first property (*Ellipse.Fill*), to target the specific subproperty indicated in the second set of parentheses (*SolidColorBrush.Color*).

EXAM TIP

If one of the properties involved in the transformation is a collection, you can use an indexer to specify which item in the collection you are looking for, as shown in the following code sample. The code starts from the Fill property of a Shape object and animates the Color of the first GradientStop of the collection:

```
Storyboard.TargetProperty =
    "(Shape.Fill).(GradientBrush.GradientStops)[0].(GradientStop.Color)"
```

For further details about property path syntax, refer to *http://msdn.microsoft.com/en-us/library/windows/apps/jj569302.aspx.*

You can manipulate more than one property at a time within the same storyboard. The next snippet shows revised code from Listing 4-9 where the opacity *and* the color of a rectangle change over time (changes are in bold):

```
<Grid Background="{StaticResource ApplicationPageBackgroundThemeBrush}">
        <Grid.Resources>
            <Storyboard x:Name="SimpleStoryboard">
                <DoubleAnimation Storyboard.TargetName="BlinkingRectangle"
                    Storyboard.TargetProperty="Opacity"
                    From="1.0" To="0.0" Duration="0:0:1"
                    RepeatBehavior="Forever"/>
                <ColorAnimation Storyboard.TargetName="BlinkingRectangle"
                    Storyboard.TargetProperty="(Shape.Fill).(SolidBrushColor.Color)"
                    To="Purple" Duration="0:0:1"
                    RepeatBehavior="Forever"/>
            </Storyboard>
        </Grid.Resources>
        <Canvas Width="400" Height="300">
            <Rectangle x:Name="BlinkingRectangle" Opacity="1.0" Width="100" Height="100"
                Fill="Orange" />
        </Canvas>
    </Grid>
```

After defining the animation in your XAML code, you still have to apply it to the targeted control. The simplest way to start an animation consists of calling the *Begin* method of the *Storyboard* class from the code-behind, as shown in the following code snippet:

Sample of C# code

```
protected override void OnNavigatedTo(NavigationEventArgs e)
{
    SimpleStoryboard.Begin();
}
```

Exploring dependent animations vs. independent animations

So far, a storyboarded animation in a Windows Store app written in C# or C++ looks similar to storyboards in Windows Presentation Foundation (WPF) or Silverlight, but there are a few important differences that are worth noticing.

First, in a Windows Store app, many XAML controls (specifically, the new controls shipped with the Windows Runtime) have their own animations, built in as part of their behavior. Another difference is that, as of this writing, custom easing functions are not supported by the Windows Runtime. Third, in a Windows Store app, developers can take advantage of the standard UI animations and transitions provided by the XAML animation library (discussed in the "Applying animations from the animation library" section) to avoid re-creating common animations and ensure the consistency of the user experience.

Perhaps the most notable difference is that if the Windows Runtime determines that your custom animation can cause performance issues in your UI, such as a layout change, it might prevent the animation from running.

The reason underlying this (apparently) peculiar behavior of the Windows Runtime is simple: Animations require additional work by the main UI thread. The UI thread is the thread responsible for drawing and updating the screen any time new information is displayed. In the XAML framework, there is another thread, called the composition thread, which is dedicated to composing and animating visual elements before they are rendered on the screen.

Having two separate threads for precalculating the layout of a page and for rendering it on the screen helps to achieve a consistent frame rate and fluid animations, even in the presence of complex layouts or other expensive operations. However, as soon as you start animating your UI, things might change a bit. If you animate (that is, change over time) a property that affects the rest of the objects in a scene, the composition thread cannot calculate the layout without additional inputs from the UI thread. The UI thread, in turn, is forced to redraw large areas of the screen at very short time intervals between each refresh to capture the latest property value of the animated property. This kind of animation is called *dependent animation.*

EXAM TIP

As explicitly stated in the MSDN official documentation, you must be aware that dependent animations have performance costs, in terms of responsiveness and fluidity of the UI. You should use them only if you really need them for your UI.

MORE INFO **SMOOTH ANIMATIONS**

You can find useful advice about making your animations smooth at *http://msdn.microsoft.com/en-us/library/windows/apps/hh994638.aspx.*

If a dependent animation is your only option, you can explicitly enable the animation by setting the *EnableDependentAnimation* to *true*, as shown in Listing 4-11.

LISTING 4-11 Sample of a dependent animation

```
<Page
    x:Class="StoryboardSample.MainPage"
    xmlns="http://schemas.microsoft.com/winfx/2006/xaml/presentation"
    xmlns:x="http://schemas.microsoft.com/winfx/2006/xaml"
    xmlns:local="using:StoryboardSample"
    xmlns:d="http://schemas.microsoft.com/expression/blend/2008"
    xmlns:mc="http://schemas.openxmlformats.org/markup-compatibility/2006"
    mc:Ignorable="d">

    <Grid Background="{StaticResource ApplicationPageBackgroundThemeBrush}">
        <Grid.Resources>
            <Storyboard x:Name="ColorStoryboard">
                <DoubleAnimation Storyboard.TargetName="ScenarioRectangle"
                    Storyboard.TargetProperty="Rectangle.Width"
```

```
                From="100" To="300"
                Duration="0:0:3"
                RepeatBehavior="Forever"
                EnableDependentAnimation="True"/>
        </Storyboard>
    </Grid.Resources>
    <Canvas Width="400" Height="100">
        <Rectangle Name="ScenarioRectangle" Width="100" Height="100"
            Fill="Orange" />
    </Canvas>
  </Grid>
</Page>
```

With the *EnableDependentAnimation* property set to its default value (*false*), this animation would not work. Animating the targeted property (*Rectangle.Width*) would require additional work from the UI thread, and the system would prevent the animation from running unless explicitly enabled.

Unlike dependent animations, independent animations can be calculated directly by the composition thread, which is then updated at a consistent rate, ensuring fluidity and responsiveness of the entire user experience.

The distinction between dependent and independent animations depends on several factors. For example, there are animations that, although they affect the UI layout, have minimal impact on the UI thread and therefore can be handled by the composition thread as if they were independent animations.

More precisely, an animation is independent if it has any of these characteristics:

- The duration of the animation is set to zero (also known as zero-duration animations).
- The animation targets the *Opacity* property of the *UIElement* object being animated. (In Listing 4-9, the object being animated is a *Rectangle,* which derives from *UIElement*.)
- The animation targets a subproperty value of the *RenderTransform*, *Projection*, and *Clip* properties of the *UIElement* object.
- The animation targets either the *Canvas.Left* or the *Canvas.Top* properties (as you'll see in Listings 4-13 and 4-14 in the next section).
- The animation targets a *Brush* value and uses a *SolidColorBrush* to animate the *Color* property of the object being animated (as in Listing 4-10).
- The animation is an object animation using key frames (see the next section).

Creating key-frame animations

There are times when you need to create more sophisticated storyboarded animations, for example, animations that use nonlinear behaviors. In this section, you learn how to use key-frame animations and easing functions to animate the UI of your app.

A *key frame* represents a specific point along the animation timeline and enables you to specify different intermediate values for the same property. Each intermediate key-frame value is used as starting value for the next key frame in the sequence, until the last key frame is reached and the final value of the animated property is set.

Listing 4-12 shows a basic example of a key-frame animation.

LISTING 4-12 Key-frame storyboard that uses a combination of color and double animations

```
<Page
    x:Class="AnimationSample.MainPage"
    xmlns="http://schemas.microsoft.com/winfx/2006/xaml/presentation"
    xmlns:x="http://schemas.microsoft.com/winfx/2006/xaml"
    xmlns:local="using:AnimationSample"
    xmlns:d="http://schemas.microsoft.com/expression/blend/2008"
    xmlns:mc="http://schemas.openxmlformats.org/markup-compatibility/2006"
    mc:Ignorable="d">

    <Grid Background="{StaticResource ApplicationPageBackgroundThemeBrush}">
        <Grid.Resources>
            <Storyboard x:Name="SimpleStoryboard">
                <ColorAnimationUsingKeyFrames Storyboard.TargetName="BlinkingRectangle"
                    Storyboard.TargetProperty="(Shape.Fill).(SolidBrushColor.Color)">
                    <LinearColorKeyFrame Value="Violet" KeyTime="0:0:0" />
                    <LinearColorKeyFrame Value="Blue" KeyTime="0:0:2" />
                    <LinearColorKeyFrame Value="Green" KeyTime="0:0:4" />
                </ColorAnimationUsingKeyFrames>
                <DoubleAnimationUsingKeyFrames Storyboard.TargetName="BlinkingRectangle"
                    Storyboard.TargetProperty="Opacity" AutoReverse="True">
                    <LinearDoubleKeyFrame Value="1.0" KeyTime="0:0:0" />
                    <LinearDoubleKeyFrame Value="0" KeyTime="0:0:2" />
                </DoubleAnimationUsingKeyFrames>
            </Storyboard>
        </Grid.Resources>
        <Canvas Width="400" Height="300">
            <Rectangle x:Name="BlinkingRectangle" Opacity="1.0" Width="100" Height="100"
                Fill="Orange"/>
        </Canvas>
    </Grid>
</Page>
```

The first thing to notice is the class that encapsulates the logic to animate a property along a set of key frames. In the first animation, to animate the *Color* value of the *SolidColorBrush* type supplied to the *Fill* property (notice the use of the property path syntax), the code uses a *ColorAnimationUsingKeyFrames* object. To animate the *Opacity* property of the targeted control, which is of type *Double*, the second animation in the code uses the *DoubleAnimationUsingKeyFrames* class. Other classes are the *PointAnimationUsingKeyFrames* class, which animates the values of a *Point* property, and the *ObjectAnimationUsingKeyFrames* class that is used to animate properties of type *Object*. (This class is discussed in more detail in the "Using discrete animations" section.)

The duration of a key-frame animation is implicitly equal to the duration of the highest key time value in the timeline (four seconds, in the example). You can also explicitly set the duration of an animation through the *Duration* property. However, be aware that if the duration set through this property is longer than the implicit duration set by the last *KeyTime*, the exceeding part of the animation will be cut off.

Because all key-frame animation classes derive from the *Timeline* base class, you inherit all the methods exposed by the base class, such as the *AutoReverse* property, which reverses the animation (basically doubling its duration), and the *RepeatBehavior* property discussed in the "Creating and customizing storyboarded animations" section.

A key-frame also enables different interpolation logic; that is, different mathematical methods that allow inferring the intermediate values of a property along the timeline by just knowing the starting value and the final value.

EXAM TIP

When an animation starts, if there are no key frames with *KeyTime* set to *0:0:0*, the starting value is the original value of the property as defined in your XAML code. For example, assume the following line of code is missing:

```
<LinearColorKeyFrame Value="Violet" KeyTime="0:0:0" />
```

Then the starting color of the rectangle will be *Orange* (the one defined in the *Fill* property of the targeted control) instead of *Violet*.

Using interpolations and easing functions in animations

The various interpolation logics you can use to determine the intermediate values between key frames are implemented as different classes. There are three types of interpolation logic you can use to animate your UI: linear interpolation, spline interpolation, or application of an easing function.

Linear interpolation is the simplest method to determine a set of intermediate values between two key fames over a certain duration by simply drawing a straight line between these two values. Depending on the type of property you are animating through linear interpolation, you can use one of the following classes (the first two classes are in Listing 4-12):

- ***LinearColorKeyFrame*** Animates the *Color* value between two key frames using linear interpolation
- ***LinearDoubleKeyFrame*** Animates the *Double* value between two key frames using linear interpolation
- ***LinearPointKeyFrame*** Animates the *Point* value between two key frames using linear interpolation

Spline interpolation creates a nonlinear transition between values according to the value of the *KeySpline* property of the class. This property specifies the first and second control points of a Bézier curve, which describes the acceleration of the animation along the timeline. Each point is defined by two doubles separated by spaces or commas. The first value of each control point represents the time, whereas the second value is the function modifier of the value. Both values should be between 0 and 1 (included).

Depending on the type of property you are animating through spline interpolation, you can use one of the following classes:

- ***SplineColorKeyFrame*** Animates the *Color* value using spline interpolation
- ***SplineDoubleKeyFrame*** Animates a *Double* value using spline interpolation
- ***SplinePointKeyFrame*** Animates a *Point* value using spline interpolation

Listing 4-13 shows an example of a spline interpolation that moves an ellipse along its vertical axis, slow at first, and then the animation accelerates until the *Canvas.Top* property reaches the value of 500 and reverses. (A value of *0,0 1,1* for the *KeySpline* would be equivalent to a linear interpolation.)

LISTING 4-13 Example of spline interpolation

```
<Grid Background="{StaticResource ApplicationPageBackgroundThemeBrush}"
    VerticalAlignment="Top">
    <Grid.Resources>
        <Storyboard x:Name="MyStoryboard">
            <DoubleAnimationUsingKeyFrames Storyboard.TargetName="MyCircle"
                                           Storyboard.TargetProperty="(Canvas.Top)"
                                           AutoReverse="True"
                                           RepeatBehavior="Forever">
                <SplineDoubleKeyFrame KeySpline="0.6,0.0 0.9,0.00" Value="500"
                    KeyTime="0:0:6" />
            </DoubleAnimationUsingKeyFrames>
        </Storyboard>
    </Grid.Resources>
    <Canvas>
        <Ellipse Fill="Yellow" Canvas.Top="0" x:Name="MyCircle" Opacity="1.0"
            Width="200" Height="200"/>
    </Canvas>
</Grid>
```

The third type of interpolation applies built-in easing functions to determine the intermediate values between two subsequent key frames (called "easing key frames"). To apply an easing function to an easing key frame, all you have to do is to set the *EasingFunction* property of the easing key frame, specifying one of the easing function types. The easing functions provided by the framework are exposed through the following classes:

- ***BackEase*** Retracts the motion of an animation slightly before it begins to animate in the path indicated
- ***BounceEase*** Creates a bouncing effect

- ***CircleEase*** Creates an animation that accelerates or decelerates using a circular function
- ***CubicEase*** Creates an animation that accelerates or decelerates using a cubic function
- ***ElasticEase*** Creates an animation that reproduces an oscillation going back and forth until it comes to a stop
- ***ExponentialEase*** Creates an animation that accelerates or decelerates using an exponential formula
- ***PowerEase*** Creates an animation that accelerates or decelerates over time based on the value of the *Power* property
- ***QuadraticEase*** Creates an animation that accelerates or decelerates using the formula $f(t) = t^2$
- ***QuarticEase*** Creates an animation that accelerates or decelerates using the formula $f(t) = t^4$
- ***QuinticEase*** Create an animation that accelerates or decelerates using the formula $f(t) = t^5$
- ***SineEase*** Creates an animation that accelerates or decelerates using a sine formula

Some of the easing functions have properties that enable you to modify the behavior of that particular function over time. For example, the *BounceEase* class exposes two properties, *Bounces* and *Bounciness*, which modify the behavior of the easing function. Listing 4-14 shows how to use this function in combination with a *CubicEase* function. The *Bounces* property is used to make the ellipse bounce five times before reaching a stop.

LISTING 4-14 Bouncing animation using the *BounceEase* function

```
<Grid Background="{StaticResource ApplicationPageBackgroundThemeBrush}"
      VerticalAlignment="Top">
    <Grid.Resources>
        <Storyboard x:Name="MyStoryboard">
            <DoubleAnimationUsingKeyFrames Duration="0:0:10"
                                           Storyboard.TargetProperty="(Canvas.Top)"
                                           Storyboard.TargetName="MyCircle"
                                           EnableDependentAnimation="True">
                <EasingDoubleKeyFrame Value="0" KeyTime="00:00:02">
                    <EasingDoubleKeyFrame.EasingFunction>
                        <CubicEase/>
                    </EasingDoubleKeyFrame.EasingFunction>
                </EasingDoubleKeyFrame>
                <EasingDoubleKeyFrame Value="500" KeyTime="00:00:06">
                    <EasingDoubleKeyFrame.EasingFunction>
                        <BounceEase Bounces="5"/>
                    </EasingDoubleKeyFrame.EasingFunction>
                </EasingDoubleKeyFrame>
            </DoubleAnimationUsingKeyFrames>
        </Storyboard>
    </Grid.Resources>
```

```
    <Canvas>
        <Ellipse Fill="Yellow" Canvas.Top="0" x:Name="MyCircle" Opacity="1.0"
            Width="200" Height="200"/>
    </Canvas>
</Grid>
```

Easing functions can be applied to animations, other than by using easing key frames in a key-frame animation, by setting the *EasingFunction* property of a *ColorAnimation*, *DoubleAnimation*, or *PointAnimation* storyboard, as shown in the following code excerpt.

```
<Grid Background="{StaticResource ApplicationPageBackgroundThemeBrush}"
    VerticalAlignment="Top">
    <Grid.Resources>
            <DoubleAnimation From="30" To="200" Duration="00:00:3"
                Storyboard.TargetName="MyCircle"
                Storyboard.TargetProperty="(Canvas.Top)">
                <DoubleAnimation.EasingFunction>
                    <BounceEase Bounces="2" EasingMode="EaseOut"
                            Bounciness="2" />
                </DoubleAnimation.EasingFunction>
            </DoubleAnimation>
        </Storyboard>
    </Grid.Resources>
    <Canvas>
        <Ellipse Fill="Yellow" Canvas.Top="0" x:Name="MyCircle" Opacity="1.0"
            Width="200" Height="200"/>
    </Canvas>
</Grid>
```

Using discrete animations

A special type of animation is called "discrete key-frame animation" and, unlike the other kinds of animation discussed so far, does not apply any interpolation. When the time value set in the *KeyTime* property is reached, the new value is simply applied, with no transitions.

You use discrete key-frame animations to animate properties that are not *Double*, *Color*, or *Point* types, but rather properties of type *Object*. This kind of animation is provided by the *ObjectAnimationUsingKeyFrames* class. Because the values being changed along the timeline are generic reference types, you cannot rely on interpolation to determine the intermediate values. There is no gradual transition, but only a curt jump between two values. The only way to reduce the twitches in the animation is to increase the number of key frames along the timeline, which decreases the edges between two subsequent key-frame values.

Besides, there is only one type of property being animated (of type *Object*) and no interpolation between key frames, so only one type of key frame can be used in an *ObjectAnimationUsingKeyFrames* animation, represented by the *DiscreteObjectKeyFrame* class.

The default StandardStyles.xaml file, which is automatically added by Visual Studio to any Windows Store project template, offers several examples of *ObjectAnimationUsingKeyFrames* animations. The following XAML code excerpt is taken directly from the StandardStyles.xaml file:

```
<Storyboard>
    <ObjectAnimationUsingKeyFrames Storyboard.TargetName="Text"
        Storyboard.TargetProperty="Foreground">
        <DiscreteObjectKeyFrame KeyTime="0"
            Value="{StaticResource ApplicationPointerOverForegroundThemeBrush}"/>
    </ObjectAnimationUsingKeyFrames>
</Storyboard>
```

You can fill the *Value* property by referencing a *StaticResource* or even by supplying an enum value, as shown in the following XAML code (from the same StandardStyles.xaml file):

```
<Storyboard>
    <ObjectAnimationUsingKeyFrames Storyboard.TargetName="RootGrid"
        Storyboard.TargetProperty="Visibility">
        <DiscreteObjectKeyFrame KeyTime="0" Value="Collapsed"/>
    </ObjectAnimationUsingKeyFrames>
</Storyboard>
```

Applying animations from the animation library

To help developers enhance the UI while avoiding inconsistencies between all the different apps, Microsoft has developed a collection of natural and fluid animations you can use in your Windows Store apps. These animations, included in the *Windows.UI.Xaml.Media.Animation* namespace, are consistent with the typical look and feel of Windows 8 and are conceived to inform the user, without distracting her. In fact, the XAML controls introduced for Windows 8, such as the *GridView*, *ListView*, and *FlipView* controls, already take advantage of this library for animating their transitions.

Table 4-1 lists the animations that are a part of the XAML animation library.

TABLE 4-1 Animations in the XAML animation library

API	Name	Description
EntranceThemeTransition	Page	Animates the contents of a page into or out of view
ContentThemeTransition	Content	Animates one piece or set of content into or out of view
FadeInThemeAnimation *FadeOutThemeAnimation*	Fade in/out	Shows transient elements or controls
FadeInThemeAnimation *FadeOutThemeAnimation*	Crossfade	Refreshes a content area
PointerUpThemeAnimation *PointerDownThemeAnimation*	Pointer up/down	Gives visual feedback of a tap or click on a tile
RepositionThemeAnimation *RepositionThemeTransition*	Reposition	Moves an element into a new position

API	Name	Description
PopInThemeAnimation *PopOutThemeAnimation* *PopupThemeTransition*	Show/Hide popup	Displays contextual UI on top of the view
EdgeUIThemeTransition	Show/Hide edge UI	Slides edge-based UI into or out of view
PaneThemeTransition	Show/Hide panel	Slides large edge-based panels into or out of view
AddDeleteThemeTransition	Add/Delete from list	Adds or deletes an item from a list
DragItemThemeAnimation *DropTargetItemThemeAnimation* *DragOverThemeAnimation*	Start/End a drag or drag-between	Gives visual feedback during a drag-and-drop operation
SwipeHintThemeAnimation	Swipe hint	Hints that a tile supports the swipe interaction
SwipeBackThemeAnimation	Swipe select/deselect	Transitions a tile to a swipe-selected state

Let's examine a few examples of their usage. Page transitions, for example, animate page content during the transition between different pages. This effect is provided by the *EntranceThemeTransition* class, which animates the transition of a control when it first appears. You can use this animation on individual objects or containers of objects. In the latter case, child elements will be animated in the order they are rendered in the view, rather than all at the same time. Listing 4-15 illustrates the point.

LISTING 4-15 Example of a page transition

```
<Grid HorizontalAlignment="Left">
    <Grid.ChildrenTransitions>
        <TransitionCollection>
            <EntranceThemeTransition/>
        </TransitionCollection>
    </Grid.ChildrenTransitions>
    <Grid.RowDefinitions>
        <RowDefinition Height="*"/>
    </Grid.RowDefinitions>
    <Grid.ColumnDefinitions>
        <ColumnDefinition Width="*"/>
        <ColumnDefinition Width="*"/>
        <ColumnDefinition Width="*"/>
    </Grid.ColumnDefinitions>

    <Rectangle Fill="Red" Grid.Row="0" Grid.Column="0"
        Width="100" Height="100" Margin="2"/>
    <Rectangle Fill="Blue" Grid.Row="0" Grid.Column="1"
        Width="100" Height="100" Margin="2"/>
    <Rectangle Fill="Green" Grid.Row="0" Grid.Column="2"
        Width="100" Height="100" Margin="2"/>
</Grid>
```

Content transition animates a piece of content within a page, for example, to show content that was not ready to be displayed when the page was first loaded, or to update content that has changed. The *ContentThemeTransition* class is responsible for providing such animation. The next code snippet shows an example of its usage:

```
<ContentControl x:Name="ContentSample" PointerPressed="ContentSample_PointerPressed">
    <ContentControl.ContentTransitions>
        <TransitionCollection>
            <ContentThemeTransition />
        </TransitionCollection>
    </ContentControl.ContentTransitions>
    <TextBlock FontSize="22">
        Click here for the Content Transition animation
    </TextBlock>
</ContentControl>
```

The transition will be executed as soon as the content of the parent control changes. In the proposed sample, the change is fired by the user's click on the *ContentControl* control. When it happens, the corresponding event handler creates a new *TextBlock* and sets it as the new content of the parent control, as shown in the following code:

Sample of C# code

```
private void ContentSample_PointerPressed(object sender, PointerRoutedEventArgs e)
{
    var tb = new TextBlock();
    tb.FontSize = 22.0;
    tb.Text = "Content transition applied.";
    ContentSample.Content = tb;
}
```

Another general-purpose animation is fade in/out, which show transient elements or controls. The fade in animation brings an item or set of items into place. The *AppBar* control, for example, uses the fade in animation to display its menu items. The fade out animation removes an item or set of items from view. The *ScrollBar* control fades out after some time without user input being detected. The fade in/out animations are provided by the *FadeInThemeAnimation* and the *FadeOutThemeAnimation* classes. The next code snippet applies this transition to a simple *TextBlock*:

Sample of XAML code

```
<StackPanel>
    <StackPanel.Resources>
        <Storyboard x:Name="EnterStoryboard">
            <FadeOutThemeAnimation Storyboard.TargetName="MyContent" />
        </Storyboard>
        <Storyboard x:Name="ExitStoryboard">
            <FadeInThemeAnimation Storyboard.TargetName="MyContent" />
        </Storyboard>
    </StackPanel.Resources>
    <TextBlock x:Name="MyContent"
               FontSize="22"
               Text="Move the mouse here to fade in and out"
               PointerEntered="TextBlock_PointerEntered"
               PointerExited="TextBlock_PointerExited" />
</StackPanel>
```

As soon as the user places the mouse over the text, the code in the corresponding event handler starts the first storyboard, named *EnterStoryboard*, and the *TextBlock* control fades out. When the mouse leaves the region of the screen occupied by the *TextBlock* control, the second event handler starts the second storyboard, and the text fades in. The following snippet shows the code for the two pointer event handlers:

Sample of C# code

```
private void TextBlock_PointerEntered(object sender, PointerRoutedEventArgs e)
{
    EnterStoryboard.Begin();
}

private void TextBlock_PointerExited(object sender, PointerRoutedEventArgs e)
{
    ExitStoryboard.Begin();
}
```

A particular form of fade in/out animation is the crossfade animation, which smoothes the transition when an item's state is changing. This particular animation does not come from a dedicated API, but leverages the fade in and fade out animations with overlapped timing.

Another useful animation is the pointer up/down transition. It gives visual feedback of a tap or click on a UI element. The pointer down animation is played when a user taps or clicks on an item, such as a button or a tile. The animation slightly shrinks the item to indicate that it is pressed. The pointer up animation is played when the tap or click is released. This animation restores the item to its original size, to indicate that it has been released. The classes responsible for providing these animations are *PointerUpThemeAnimation* and *PointerDownThemeAnimation*. The following code sample shows the XAML code to use this transition:

Sample of XAML code

```
<Grid>
    <VisualStateManager.VisualStateGroups>
        <VisualStateGroup x:Name="TapStates">
            <VisualState x:Name="Normal" />
            <VisualState x:Name="PointerDown">
                <Storyboard>
                    <PointerDownThemeAnimation TargetName="MyCircle" />
                </Storyboard>
            </VisualState>
            <VisualState x:Name="PointerUp">
                <Storyboard>
                    <PointerUpThemeAnimation TargetName="MyCircle" />
                </Storyboard>
            </VisualState>
        </VisualStateGroup>
    </VisualStateManager.VisualStateGroups>
    <Ellipse x:Name="MyCircle"
             Width="100"
             Height="100" Fill="Orange"/>
</Grid>
```

The following code-behind toggles between the two states:

Sample of C# code

```
protected override void OnPointerPressed(PointerRoutedEventArgs e)
{
    this.CapturePointer(e.Pointer);
    VisualStateManager.GoToState(this, "PointerDown", true);
}

protected override void OnPointerReleased(PointerRoutedEventArgs e)
{
    VisualStateManager.GoToState(this, "PointerUp", true);
    this.ReleasePointerCapture(e.Pointer);
}
```

> ***MORE INFO*** **ANIMATION LIBRARY**
>
> **For a complete description of all the animations included in the library, visit *http://msdn.microsoft.com/en-us/library/windows/apps/hh452701.aspx*.**

The animations provided by the Microsoft library should be able to cover most scenarios, but there might be situations in which you need to create a custom animation. However, you should be cautious before deciding to diverge from the standard animations. Be sure that none of the animations provided by the XAML library actually suits your needs.

Thought experiment

Creating a complex animation

In this thought experiment, apply what you've learned about this objective. You can find answers to these questions in the "Answers" section at the end of this chapter.

You are developing a game that will include a bouncing ball. You can hit the ball by touching it and then throwing it in some direction. You want to create an animation for your ball so it slowly stops bouncing.

Answer the following questions:

1. **What kind of animation would you use for your bouncing ball?**
2. **How can you factor in the force of the swipe?**
3. **Which properties should you animate?**
4. **Which easing function should you use?**

Objective summary

- Use animations and transitions to help users focus their attention on what is happening in the UI.
- A storyboard enables the value of a dependency property to change as a function of time. However, if the Windows Runtime determines that your custom animation can cause performance issues in your UI, such as a layout change, it might prevent the animation from running. To avoid this issue, you should use independent animations rather dependent ones. If you must use dependent animations, set the *EnableDependentAnimation* property to *true* to prevent the system from blocking the animation. Keep in mind that there will be a price to pay in terms of performance.
- Use a key-frame animation to create more complex animations. To achieve different results, you can choose between linear interpolation, spline interpolation, and easing functions.
- Use a discrete key-frame animation to animate any property that is not of type *Double*, *Point*, or *Color*. Consider, though, that the animation provided by the *ObjectAnimationUsingKeyFrames* class does not apply any interpolation. When the time value set in the *KeyTime* property is reached, the new value is simply applied with no transitions.
- Whenever possible, use the fluid and natural animations provided by the XAML animation library, under the *Windows.UI.Xaml.Media.Animation* namespace, to ensure consistency of the user experience.

Objective review

Answer the following questions to test your knowledge of the information in this objective. You can find the answers to these questions and explanations of why each answer choice is correct or incorrect in the "Answers" section at the end of this chapter.

1. Which of the following animations is not considered an independent animation?

A. A zero-duration animation

B. An animation targeting the *Opacity* property of a control

C. An animation targeting the *Width* property of a control

D. An animation targeting the *Canvas.Left* property of a control

2. Which of the following types cannot be interpolated in a key-frame animation?

A. *Double*

B. *Point*

C. *Color*

D. *Object*

3. Which of the following transitions in the animation library would you use to show transient elements or controls?
   A. Page transition
   B. Content transition
   C. Fade in/out
   D. Reposition

Objective 4.3: Create custom controls

A custom control is a reusable component that extends an existing control with additional features. Custom controls are typically derived from control primitives (such as *Control* and *Panel*) or core controls (such as *Button*), but you can change their behaviors and their visual appearance. A custom control should not be confused with a user control. Custom controls derive from other controls or control primitives, consist of a code file and a default style placed in a dedicated Generic.xaml file, and can be completely restyled with custom templates. A user control derives from the *UserControl* class, and its purpose is to combine multiple existing controls into a reusable group or set of controls. A user control consists of a XAML and a code-behind file and has a static layout.

> ***MORE INFO*** **SOFTWARE DEVELOPMENT KIT (SDK)**
>
> **One of the most common ways to reuse and redistribute a custom control is through a Visual Studio Extension SDK, a collection of APIs that you can reference as a single item in Visual Studio. For further information on the topic, you can refer to *http://msdn.microsoft.com/library/hh768146(v=VS.110).aspx.***

This objective covers how to:

- Choose the appropriate base control to create a custom control template
- Style a control through control templates
- Design the control template to respond to changes in viewstate

Adding a custom control to your Windows Store app

The easiest way to add a custom control to your Windows Store project is to use the provided item template. You can use the Add New Item dialog box of Visual Studio 2012 and select the Templated Control item template, as shown in Figure 4-4.

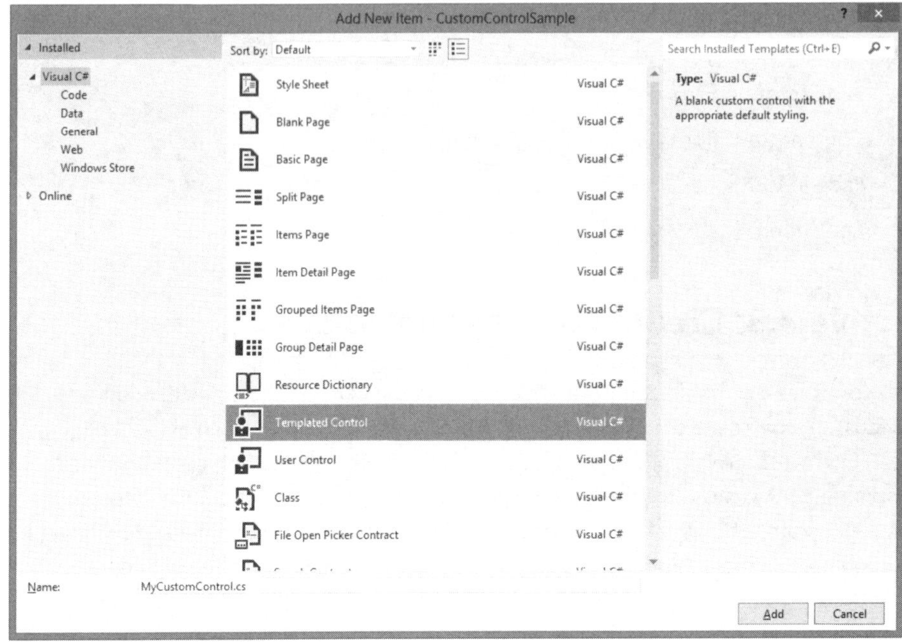

FIGURE 4-4 Add New Item dialog box

Visual Studio then adds three elements for you: a class file containing the logic of the new custom control; a folder named Themes; and, inside the new folder, a Generic.xaml file containing the default template for the control itself. Both the folder name and the file name are required to enable the XAML framework to load the control automatically. Figure 4-5 shows the Solution Explorer in Visual Studio 2012 with the newly added items.

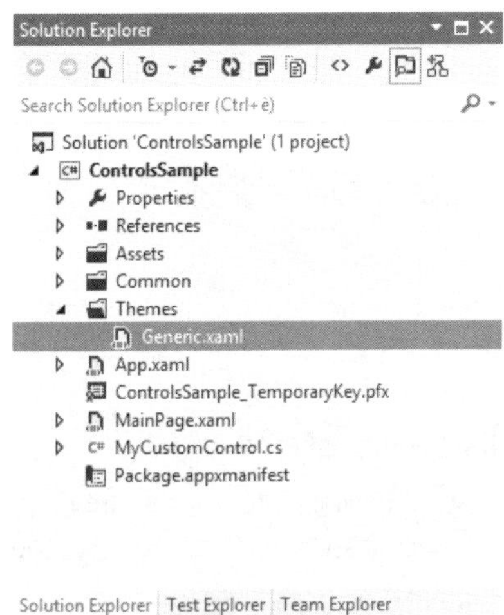

FIGURE 4-5 Solution Explorer

Listing 4-16 shows the default C# definition of a new control.

LISTING 4-16 Default C# definition of the newly added custom control

```
public sealed class MyCustomControl : Control
{
    public MyCustomControl()
    {
        this.DefaultStyleKey = typeof(MyCustomControl);
    }
}
```

The first thing to notice is that, by default, the new custom control inherits directly from the *Control* base class. As already mentioned, you can derive a custom control from any control with the purpose of enriching its functionalities. Whenever you want to create a custom control, it is important to choose the right base class from which you're deriving. This enables you to focus on adding new functionalities rather than reinventing behaviors and features already exposed by other controls.

For example, if you create a custom control that needs to act as a button, just make it derive from the *Button* class to get all the typical properties and events (such as the *Click* event, for example) of a *Button* control, out of the box. The next line of code illustrates this point:

```
public sealed class MyCustomControl : Button
```

The *DefaultStyleKey* property of the *Control* base class tells the framework which style and template should be applied to the custom control. Listing 4-17 shows the default XAML control template provided by the Generic.xaml file, through a *ResourceDictionary*.

LISTING 4-17 Default control template included in the Generic.xaml file

```
<ResourceDictionary
    xmlns="http://schemas.microsoft.com/winfx/2006/xaml/presentation"
    xmlns:x="http://schemas.microsoft.com/winfx/2006/xaml"
    xmlns:local="using:ControlsSample">

    <Style TargetType="local:MyCustomControl">
        <Setter Property="Template">
            <Setter.Value>
                <ControlTemplate TargetType="local:MyCustomControl">
                    <Border
                        Background="{TemplateBinding Background}"
                        BorderBrush="{TemplateBinding BorderBrush}"
                        BorderThickness="{TemplateBinding BorderThickness}">
                    </Border>
                </ControlTemplate>
            </Setter.Value>
        </Setter>
    </Style>
</ResourceDictionary>
```

The style for the custom control is based on a *ControlTemplate* implementing the visual appearance of the control supplied to the *TargetType* property.

In the XAML framework, the *ControlTemplate* class enables you to fine-tune the visual appearance and behavior of a control. In the XAML framework for Windows Store apps, you create a control template when you want to customize a control's visual structure and visual behavior. A control template combines different *FrameworkElement* objects (or derived types) into a single control. It's important to note that a *ControlTemplate* class can have only one *FrameworkElement* as the root element, such as a *Border* element as in the Generic.xaml file.

It's also worth noticing that the values of the *Background*, *BorderBrush*, and *BorderThickness* properties of the control template are in binding with the values of the corresponding properties exposed by the custom control. In other words, the template expects those properties to exist in the custom control.

To use the new control, just declare the namespace under which the control has been defined in the XAML code of your page, as you would do with a *UserControl*. Listing 4-18 illustrates this point.

LISTING 4-18 Using a custom control in the XAML definition of the page

```
<Page
    x:Class="ControlsSample.MainPage"
    xmlns="http://schemas.microsoft.com/winfx/2006/xaml/presentation"
    xmlns:x="http://schemas.microsoft.com/winfx/2006/xaml"
    xmlns:local="using:ControlsSample"
    xmlns:d="http://schemas.microsoft.com/expression/blend/2008"
    xmlns:mc="http://schemas.openxmlformats.org/markup-compatibility/2006"
    mc:Ignorable="d">

    <Grid Background="{StaticResource ApplicationPageBackgroundThemeBrush}">
        <local:MyCustomControl Width="300" Height="300" Background="Orange"
            BorderBrush="OrangeRed" />
    </Grid>
</Page>
```

If you run the app, the result should look similar to the image in Figure 4-6.

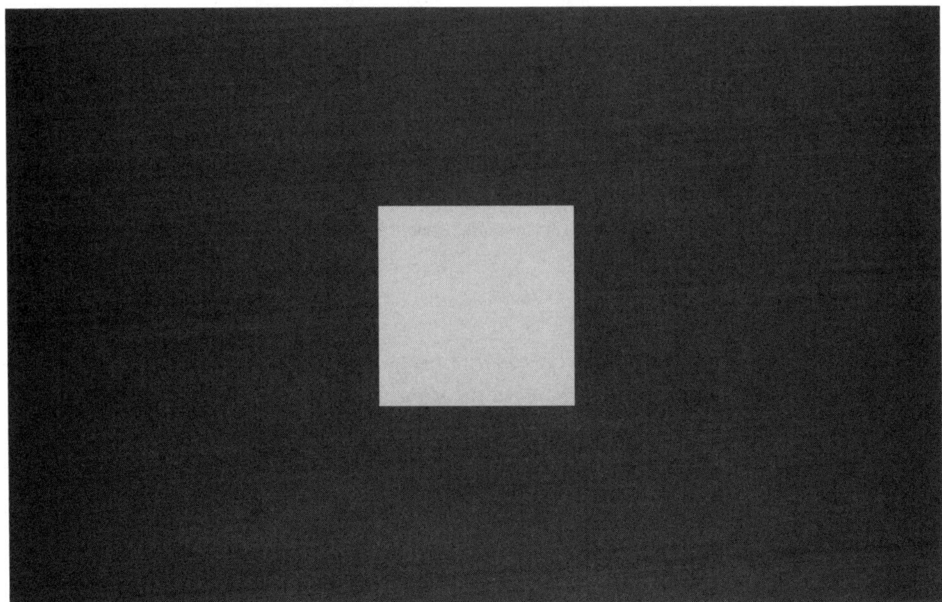

FIGURE 4-6 Custom control

Creating your own dependency properties for a custom control

Custom controls can be extended by providing custom dependency properties. Listing 4-19 shows how to extend the custom control implemented in the last section by adding two custom dependency properties. Changes to Listing 4-18 are in bold.

LISTING 4-19 Adding custom dependency properties to a custom control

```
public sealed class MyCustomControl : Control
{
    public MyCustomControl()
    {
        this.DefaultStyleKey = typeof(MyCustomControl);
    }

    public static readonly DependencyProperty ImagePathProperty =
        DependencyProperty.Register("ImagePath", typeof(ImageSource),
            typeof(MyCustomControl), new PropertyMetadata(null));

    public static readonly DependencyProperty ImageLabelProperty =
        DependencyProperty.Register("ImageLabel", typeof(String),
            typeof(MyCustomControl), new PropertyMetadata(null));
```

```
    public ImageSource ImagePath
    {
       get { return (ImageSource)GetValue(ImagePathProperty); }
       set { SetValue(ImagePathProperty, value); }
    }

    public String ImageLabel
    {
        get { return (String)GetValue(ImageLabelProperty); }
        set { SetValue(ImageLabelProperty, value); }
    }
}
```

The code defines two new *DependencyProperty* instances—*ImagePathProperty* and *ImageLabelProperty*—by registering them with the Windows Runtime property system through the *DependencyProperty.Register* method. This method accepts a string representing the property name, the property type, the owner type (that is, the control type which the new dependency property is being attached to), and the property metadata.

MORE INFO **DEPENDENCY PROPERTIES**

Dependency properties can be used only with *DependencyObject* types. However, because the *DependencyObject* class is a high-level class in the class inheritance hierarchy, most of the classes that deal with the UI can support dependency properties. For more information about dependency properties, refer to the MSDN documentation at *http://msdn.microsoft.com/en-us/library/windows/apps/hh700353.aspx*.

Each dependency property is declared as a *public static readonly* property, whose name also represents the identifier for the dependency property. The suffix "Property" added at the end of the dependency property's name represents a naming convention followed by the XAML framework. For example, the identifier for the *TextBlock.Text* property is *TextBlock.TextProperty*.

Then, the code implements two properties—*ImagePath* and *ImageLabel*—which represent, respectively, the path to an image file that will be used as *ImageSource* and a label that will accompany the image on the screen. These two properties are nothing more than wrappers around the actual dependency properties, and the value of the wrapping property is linked to the value of the wrapped dependency property through the *GetValue* and *SetValue* methods (inherited from the *DependencyObject* class, from which the *Control* class derives).

After the new custom dependency properties have been registered within the system, you can use them in your XAML code like any other property. The next code excerpt shows a revised version of Listing 4-18 (changes in bold):

```
<Page
    x:Class="ControlsSample.MainPage"
    xmlns="http://schemas.microsoft.com/winfx/2006/xaml/presentation"
    xmlns:x="http://schemas.microsoft.com/winfx/2006/xaml"
    xmlns:local="using:ControlsSample"
    xmlns:d="http://schemas.microsoft.com/expression/blend/2008"
    xmlns:mc="http://schemas.openxmlformats.org/markup-compatibility/2006"
    mc:Ignorable="d">

    <Grid Background="{StaticResource ApplicationPageBackgroundThemeBrush}">
        <local:MyCustomControl Width="300" Height="300"
            ImagePath="Assets/devleap.png" ImageLabel="http://www.devleap.com" />
    </Grid>
</Page>
```

Now that you have two more properties you can use to extend the visual appearance of the custom control, you need to modify the control template in the Generic.xaml file. Listing 4-20 shows a revised version of Listing 4-17 (changes in bold).

LISTING 4-20 Control template with the new dependency properties

```
<ResourceDictionary
    xmlns="http://schemas.microsoft.com/winfx/2006/xaml/presentation"
    xmlns:x="http://schemas.microsoft.com/winfx/2006/xaml"
    xmlns:local="using:CustomControlSample">

    <Style TargetType="local:MyCustomControl">
        <Setter Property="Template">
            <Setter.Value>
                <ControlTemplate TargetType="local:MyCustomControl">
                    <Border Background="LightGray" BorderBrush="DarkGray"
                        BorderThickness="2" HorizontalAlignment="Center">
                        <StackPanel HorizontalAlignment="Center">
                            <Image Source="{TemplateBinding ImagePath}" Margin="5"
                                Height="200" />
                            <TextBlock TextAlignment="Center"
                                       Text="{TemplateBinding ImageLabel}"
                                       FontFamily="Segoe UI"
                                       FontWeight="Light"
                                       FontSize="26"
                                       Foreground="Black" />
                        </StackPanel>
                    </Border>
                </ControlTemplate>
            </Setter.Value>
        </Setter>
    </Style>
</ResourceDictionary>
```

Figure 4-7 shows the result.

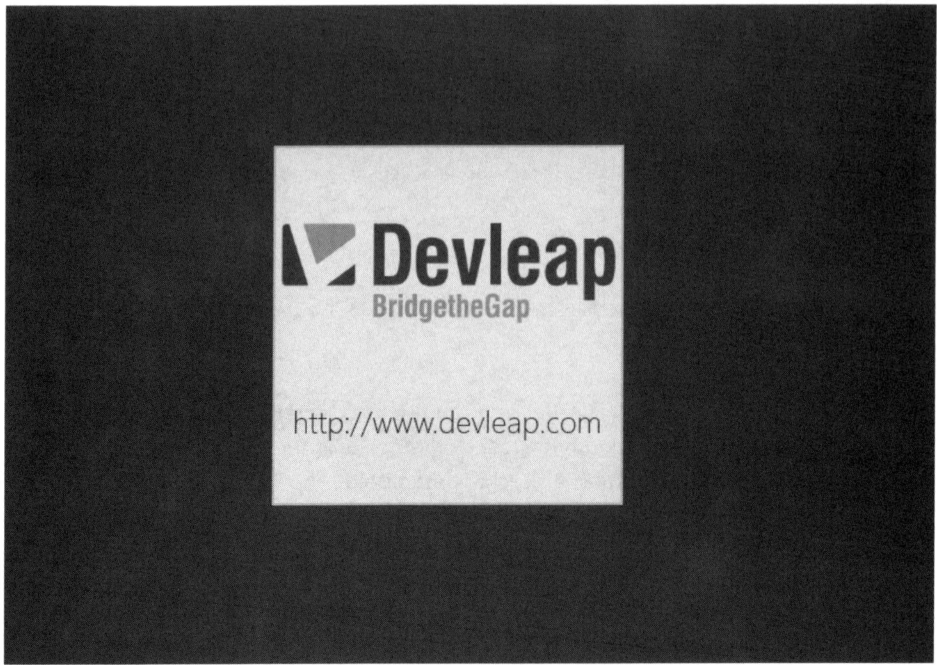

FIGURE 4-7 Custom control taking advantage of the new dependency properties

Reacting to changes in the visual state of the custom control

A visual state can be used within a control template to define the visual appearance of the control when the control is in a specific state. This objective is achieved by the *VisualState* class through a set of storyboarded animations.

> ***NOTE*** **VISUAL STATE ANIMATIONS**
>
> **Animations for visual states use the same syntax as any storyboarded animation. However, animations for visual states should either be zero-duration or otherwise rapid, lasting less than a second.**

Listing 4-21 shows an excerpt of the *Button* control template defined in the default StandardStyles.xaml file as a sample. The *Button* control template leverages *VisualState* objects to determine the visual appearance of the custom control in certain states.

LISTING 4-21 *Button* control template as defined in the StandardStyles.xaml file

```
<ControlTemplate TargetType="Button">
    <Grid x:Name="RootGrid">
        (code omitted)
        <VisualStateManager.VisualStateGroups>
            <VisualStateGroup x:Name="CommonStates">
                <VisualState x:Name="Normal" />
                <VisualState x:Name="PointerOver">
                    <Storyboard>
                        <ObjectAnimationUsingKeyFrames
                            Storyboard.TargetName="BackgroundGlyph"
                            Storyboard.TargetProperty="Foreground">
                            <DiscreteObjectKeyFrame KeyTime="0" Value="{StaticResource
                                BackButtonPointerOverBackgroundThemeBrush}"/>
                        </ObjectAnimationUsingKeyFrames>
                        <ObjectAnimationUsingKeyFrames
                            Storyboard.TargetName="NormalGlyph"
                            Storyboard.TargetProperty="Foreground">
                            <DiscreteObjectKeyFrame KeyTime="0" Value="{StaticResource
                                BackButtonPointerOverForegroundThemeBrush}"/>
                        </ObjectAnimationUsingKeyFrames>
                    </Storyboard>
                </VisualState>
                <VisualState x:Name="Pressed">
                    <Storyboard>
                        <ObjectAnimationUsingKeyFrames
                            Storyboard.TargetName="BackgroundGlyph"
                            Storyboard.TargetProperty="Foreground">
                            <DiscreteObjectKeyFrame KeyTime="0" Value="{StaticResource
                                BackButtonForegroundThemeBrush}"/>
                        </ObjectAnimationUsingKeyFrames>
                        <DoubleAnimation
                            Storyboard.TargetName="ArrowGlyph"
                            Storyboard.TargetProperty="Opacity"
                            To="1"
                            Duration="0"/>
                        <DoubleAnimation
                            Storyboard.TargetName="NormalGlyph"
                            Storyboard.TargetProperty="Opacity"
                            To="0"
                            Duration="0"/>
                    </Storyboard>
                </VisualState>
                <VisualState x:Name="Disabled">
                    <Storyboard>
                        <ObjectAnimationUsingKeyFrames Storyboard.TargetName="RootGrid"
                            Storyboard.TargetProperty="Visibility">
                            <DiscreteObjectKeyFrame KeyTime="0" Value="Collapsed"/>
                        </ObjectAnimationUsingKeyFrames>
                    </Storyboard>
                </VisualState>
            </VisualStateGroup>
```

```
                <VisualStateGroup x:Name="FocusStates">
                    <VisualState x:Name="Focused">
                        <Storyboard>
                            <DoubleAnimation
                                Storyboard.TargetName="FocusVisualWhite"
                                Storyboard.TargetProperty="Opacity"
                                To="1"
                                Duration="0"/>
                            <DoubleAnimation
                                Storyboard.TargetName="FocusVisualBlack"
                                Storyboard.TargetProperty="Opacity"
                                To="1"
                                Duration="0"/>
                        </Storyboard>
                    </VisualState>
                    <VisualState x:Name="Unfocused" />
                    <VisualState x:Name="PointerFocused" />
                </VisualStateGroup>
            </VisualStateManager.VisualStateGroups>
        </Grid>
</ControlTemplate>
```

The default control template includes two groups of visual states: *CommonStates* and *FocusStates*. Each group includes several visual states. For example, the first *VisualStateGroup* contains four visual states: *Normal*, *PointOver*, *Pressed*, and *Disabled*. With the exception of the first visual state, which is just an empty placeholder, the other three visual states use storyboarded animations to handle the transition between different states.

When the control enters one of the specified states, the corresponding storyboard begins. When the control leaves the state, the animation stops. (When a storyboard is used inside a *VisualState*, there is no need to call the *Begin/Stop* methods of the *Storyboard* class to start/stop the animation.) *VisualState* objects are grouped into *VisualStateGroup* objects, which, in turn, are added to the *VisualStateManager.VisualStateGroups* attached property of the root *FrameworkElement* of the *ControlTemplate* (a *Grid* control, in the presented code).

When using visual states, you can decide to react to a change in any given set of properties, not only to changes affecting the custom control. For example, you can use the *VisualState* object to adapt the control's appearance and behavior to different view states. Listing 4-22 shows the visual states used by an *AppBar* button, as defined in the StandardStyles.xaml file.

LISTING 4-22 *AppBar* button control template as defined in the StandardStyle.xaml file

```
(code omitted)
<VisualStateGroup x:Name="ApplicationViewStates">
    <VisualState x:Name="FullScreenLandscape"/>
    <VisualState x:Name="Filled"/>
    <VisualState x:Name="FullScreenPortrait">
        <Storyboard>
            <ObjectAnimationUsingKeyFrames Storyboard.TargetName="TextLabel"
                Storyboard.TargetProperty="Visibility">
                <DiscreteObjectKeyFrame KeyTime="0" Value="Collapsed"/>
            </ObjectAnimationUsingKeyFrames>
```

```
            <ObjectAnimationUsingKeyFrames Storyboard.TargetName="RootGrid"
                Storyboard.TargetProperty="Width">
                <DiscreteObjectKeyFrame KeyTime="0" Value="60"/>
            </ObjectAnimationUsingKeyFrames>
        </Storyboard>
    </VisualState>
    <VisualState x:Name="Snapped">
        <Storyboard>
            <ObjectAnimationUsingKeyFrames Storyboard.TargetName="TextLabel"
                Storyboard.TargetProperty="Visibility">
                <DiscreteObjectKeyFrame KeyTime="0" Value="Collapsed"/>
            </ObjectAnimationUsingKeyFrames>
            <ObjectAnimationUsingKeyFrames Storyboard.TargetName="RootGrid"
                Storyboard.TargetProperty="Width">
                <DiscreteObjectKeyFrame KeyTime="0" Value="60"/>
            </ObjectAnimationUsingKeyFrames>
        </Storyboard>
    </VisualState>
</VisualStateGroup>
```

The *AppBar* button template defines four visual states. The first two (*FullScreenLandscape* and *Filled*) are just empty placeholders with no animation defined. The other two, *FullScreenPortrait* and *Snapped*, use storyboarded animations to define the visual appearance of the control when it is in the corresponding state.

You can also use *VisualTransition* objects to represent the visual behavior that occurs when the control transits from one visual state to another. The *From* and *To* properties enable you to restrict the transition to only certain states. Both properties are optional, so you can achieve different levels of granularity by setting both of them, one of them, or neither, as shown in Table 4-2.

TABLE 4-2 Values of *From* and *To* properties

Granularity of control	Value of *From*	Value of *To*
The transition applies only from a specified state to another specified state.	Set	Set
The transition applies from any state to a specified state.	Not set	Set
The transition applies from a specified state to any state.	Set	Not set
The transition applies from any state to any other state.	Not set	Not set

The *GeneratedDuration* property enables you to define the duration of the transition between two states. (Remember to keep your transitions and animations as short as possible.) Listing 4-23 shows an example of visual transitions for a custom control.

LISTING 4-23 Using visual transitions to animate a custom control

```
<ControlTemplate TargetType="local:MyCustomButton">
    <Border x:Name="MyBorder" Background="LightGray" BorderBrush="DarkGray"
        BorderThickness="2" HorizontalAlignment="Center">
        <VisualStateManager.VisualStateGroups>
            <VisualStateGroup x:Name="CommonStates">
                <VisualStateGroup.Transitions>
                    <VisualTransition To="Normal" GeneratedDuration="0:0:1"/>
                    <VisualTransition To="PointerOver" GeneratedDuration="0:0:1"/>
                </VisualStateGroup.Transitions>
                <VisualState x:Name="Normal">
                    <Storyboard>
                        <ColorAnimation Storyboard.TargetName="MyBorder"
                            Storyboard.TargetProperty="(Border.Background).
                            (SolidColorBrush.Color)" To="LightGray" />
                    </Storyboard>
                </VisualState>
                <VisualState x:Name="PointerOver">
                    <Storyboard>
                        <ColorAnimation Storyboard.TargetName="MyBorder"
                            Storyboard.TargetProperty="(Border.Background).
                            (SolidColorBrush.Color)" To="LightGoldenrodYellow" />
                    </Storyboard>
                </VisualState>
            </VisualStateGroup>
        </VisualStateManager.VisualStateGroups>
        (code omitted)
</ControlTemplate>
```

Thought experiment

Storing user settings

In this thought experiment, apply what you've learned about this objective. You can find answers to these questions in the "Answers" section at the end of this chapter.

You are developing a Windows Store app for instant messaging. The app displays the list of contacts available for a chat. Each contact is represented by a small square icon displaying the photo of the contact, and a counter in the lower-right corner indicating the number of unread messages for that contact. When the user clicks the icon of a contact, the app navigates to a new page and starts a new conversation.

Answer the following questions:

1. To create the control that represents the contact, would you use a custom control or a user control? Why?
2. From which existing control would you derive your new control?
3. Which attached properties would you add to the new control?

Objective summary

- A custom control is a reusable component that extends an existing control with additional features and a custom template. A custom control includes two elements: a class file containing the logic of the new control and a Generic.xaml file containing the control template.
- Custom controls can be extended by registering custom dependency properties with the Windows Runtime property system. Each dependency property must be declared through a *public static readonly* property and wrapped in properties whose values are linked to the corresponding dependency property values through the *GetValue* and *SetValue* methods.
- Visual states define the visual appearance of a UI element when it is in a certain state by using a set of storyboarded animations.
- Use *VisualTransition* objects to represent the visual behavior that occurs when the control transits from one visual state to another.

Objective review

Answer the following questions to test your knowledge of the information in this objective. You can find the answers to these questions and explanations of why each answer choice is correct or incorrect in the "Answers" section at the end of this chapter.

1. Which of the following classes are not suitable for deriving a custom control?
   - **A.** *UserControl* class
   - **B.** *Control* class
   - **C.** *Panel* class
   - **D.** *Button* class
2. Through which kind of property must a *DependencyProperty* instance be exposed?
   - **A.** *private static*
   - **B.** *private static readonly*
   - **C.** *public static*
   - **D.** *public static readonly*
3. Which of the following statements is incorrect?
   - **A.** The default template of a custom control is defined in a Generic.xaml file in the Themes folder.
   - **B.** *VisualTransition* objects represent the visual behavior that occurs when the control transits from one visual state to another.
   - **C.** If you omit both the *From* and *To* properties of the *VisualTransition* instance, the transition will not be applied.
   - **D.** The *GeneratedDuration* property defines the duration of the transition between two visual states.

Objective 4.4: Design Windows Store apps for globalization and localization

The Windows Store helps you reach a large audience. Theoretically, every person on earth can use your application. Large markets such as China or the Middle East can be gold mines for selling an application.

The Windows Store provides support for distributing your app worldwide and takes care of all the financial intricacies. You could choose to create only an English version of your app or an app in your own language, but that would reduce your potential audience.

Fortunately, the Windows Runtime exposes functionality that simplifies the creation of globalized apps. In this objective, you will examine the various options you have for globalizing and localizing your app.

This objective covers how to:

- Implement .resw files to translate text
- Implement collation and grouping to support different reading directions
- Implement culture-specific formatting for dates and times

NOTE **REFERENCE**

The authors want to thank Wouter De Kort, contributor to *MCSD 70-482 Exam Ref: Advanced Windows Store App Development Using HTML5 and JavaScript*. Wouter wrote many of the topics presented in this section; we adapted text and samples to Windows Store apps using C#.

Planning for globalization

Globalization is the process of making sure that your app works well in multiple cultures. It is often confused with localization, which is the process of customizing your app for a specific language and culture.

When you think about a global audience for your app, one of the first things that comes to mind is the text that you display in your app. This is indeed one of the largest visible parts of your application that needs to be translated to other languages.

However, string data is not the only thing you must consider. Some of the things that vary around the world are the representation of dates and times, calendars, numbers, measures and units, phone numbers and addresses, currencies, paper sizes, the way text is sorted, and the direction of text and fonts for specific character sets.

Creating a globalized application means that you don't hard code any of these items. For example, you shouldn't display a date directly on the screen. Instead, you should format it with the current settings of the user. The Windows Runtime contains APIs that can help you display these types of data on the screen in the correct format.

Although globalization is mainly about using the correct APIs, there are other factors you must consider.

Images might contain text that needs to be translated in order for the images to be understood correctly in other parts of the world. Think about road signs. They vary across countries/regions—it's not just a matter of language. For example, Switzerland has 26 cantons (regions). They share road signs but do not have a common language. You have to speak French in Vaud, Italian in Grigioni, and German in Turgovia if you want to be understood.

The same is true for text. Maybe your app uses expressions or phrases that won't be understood by people throughout the world and are difficult to translate. To save money on translation costs, you should try to avoid these expressions and phrases.

When sorting text, don't assume that sorting is always alphabetic. Japanese Kanji characters have the unique property of having more than one pronunciation, depending on the context in which they are used. This means that one character can be sorted in multiple different ways, depending on its use. A special feature called Furigana is used to specify the phonetics for a character and is used for sorting. That's one example, but there are many variations. Some languages sort on the number of pen strokes, for example.

What about text that a user enters in a specific language? In right-to-left environments, the user can switch the text direction on the on-screen keyboard. If you need to display the entered text again, you have to save the text direction with it so you can display it in the correct way.

You should also exercise caution when working with maps. Perhaps you think the borders drawn for countries in a particular map are correct, but someone in another country/region disagrees with you. The official MSDN documentation advises you to refer to "country/region" rather than only "country." Displaying a name in a list of countries that isn't recognized as a country by other countries/regions could cause problems.

Another consideration is the web services you are using. You can use different URLs to get localized content back from a service, or you can specify the language you want through a header or query string parameter.

Language settings in Windows

In Windows, you can configure the languages you want to use. You can add multiple languages and specify your preferred languages. To access language settings, open the **Clock, Language, and Region** applet in Control Panel and then select **Add A Language**. Figure 4-8 shows the Language window.

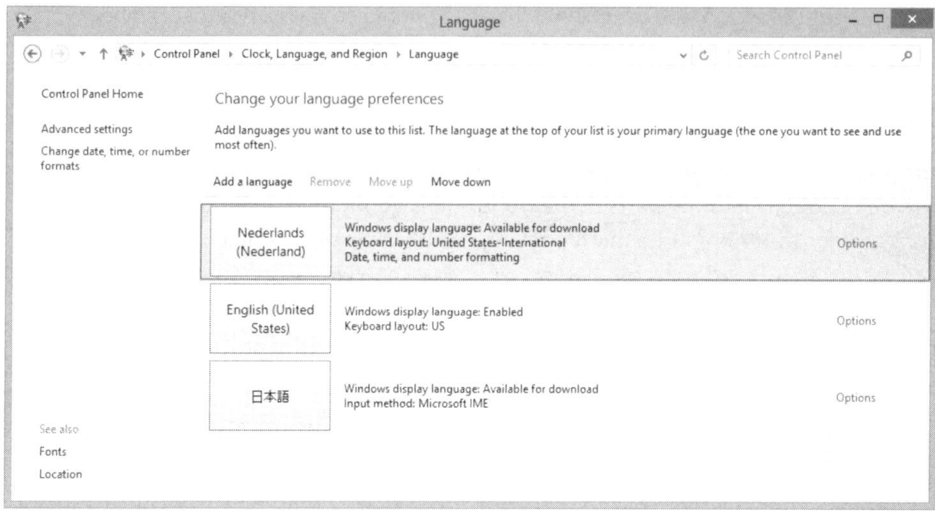

FIGURE 4-8 Language preferences screen in the Language window

In Figure 4-8, three languages are installed: Dutch, English and Japanese. These settings are used by Windows for loading resources in your app. Windows will search for the best matching language, or it will fall back to the default language of the app.

For each language, you can also configure the date, time, and number formats, as shown in Figure 4-9.

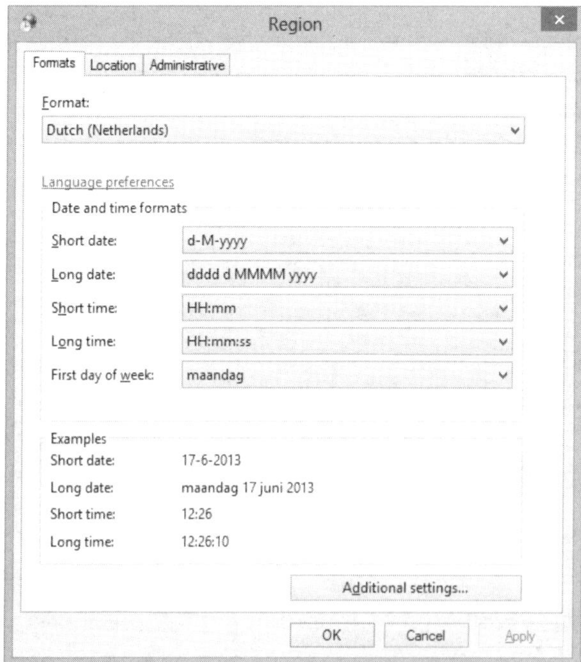

FIGURE 4-9 Regional settings in the Region dialog box

Globalization APIs help you deal with all these settings. You can get these preferences manually by using *Windows.System.UserProfile.GlobalizationPreferences*. Listing 4-24 shows an example of getting the user's globalization preferences.

LISTING 4-24 Using *Windows.System.UserProfile.GlobalizationPreferences*

```
var userLanguages = Windows.System.UserProfile.GlobalizationPreferences.Languages;
var userCalendar = Windows.System.UserProfile.GlobalizationPreferences.Calendars;
var userClock = Windows.System.UserProfile.GlobalizationPreferences.Clocks;
var userHomeRegion = Windows.System.UserProfile.GlobalizationPreferences.
    HomeGeographicRegion;
var userFirstDayOfWeek = Windows.System.UserProfile.GlobalizationPreferences.
    WeekStartsOn;
```

You can also get the specific language tag through the *GlobalizationPreferences* class and then pass this string to a web service to get localized content. Listing 4-25 shows how to do this.

LISTING 4-25 Getting the *LanguageTag*

```
var topUserLanguage = Windows.System.UserProfile.GlobalizationPreferences.Languages[0];
var userLanguage = new Windows.Globalization.Language(topUserLanguage);
var languageTag = userLanguage.LanguageTag;
```

> ***MORE INFO*** **GLOBALIZATION PREFERENCES**
>
> **You can find a globalization preferences sample as a part of the Windows SDK at *http://code.msdn.microsoft.com/windowsapps/Globalization-preferences-6654eb36*.**

Language definition in Windows Store Apps

The developer of a Windows Store app must declare the supported languages in the application manifest. The listed languages are the languages displayed to users in the Windows Store.

The application uses the default language if the user has chosen a language in Control Panel that is not supported by the application.

To set the default language, you can use the Package.appxmanifest in the Visual Studio App Manifest Designer. On the Application UI tab, the chosen language must be the first in the list of supported languages.

Figure 4-10 shows the Visual Studio designer on the Application UI tab.

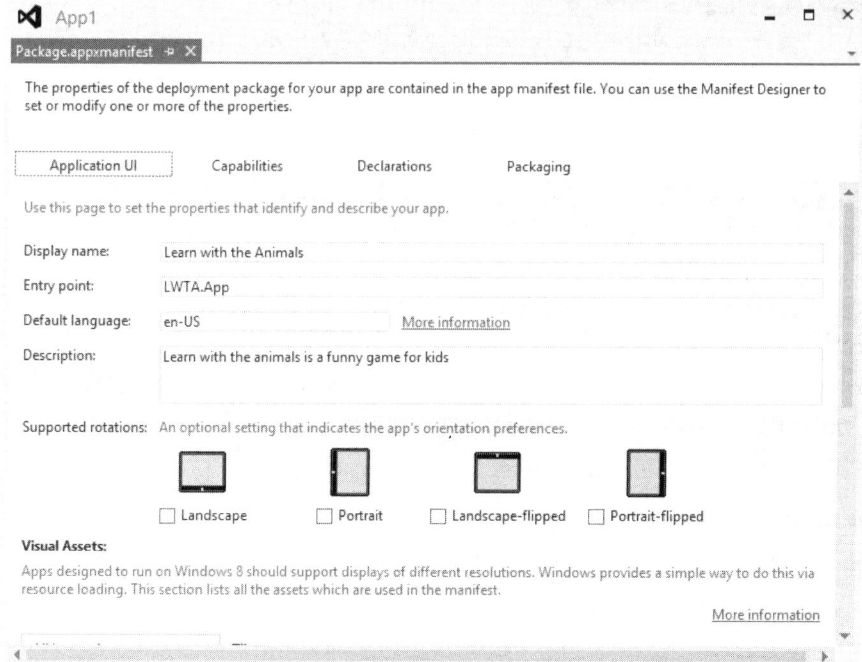

FIGURE 4-10 Visual Studio App Manifest Designer

At runtime, the Windows Runtime determines the language preferences of the user by matching them with the supported language in the application manifest and creating an *application language list*. This list serves to determine the language or languages for application resources, dates, times, numbers, and other objects.

Microsoft recommends that the developer let Windows handle all the intricacies of matching languages because many factors influence the priority of language tags.

> ***MORE INFO*** **LANGUAGE TAGS AND QUALIFY RESOURCES**
>
> **You can find more information as a part of MSDN documentation: *http://msdn.microsoft.com/library/windows/apps/Hh967761(v=win.10).aspx*.**

Localizing your app

Whereas globalization is the process of making sure your app doesn't depend on hard-coded cultural settings, localization is the process of adapting your app for a specific culture and language. To localize an app, you have to translate text, change images, and format data to customize the app for the user preferences.

String data

In your app, you probably use a lot of text data. When building your app, you put your text directly into your XAML and C# code. But when you want to translate your app to another language, you have to move all the strings to separate files called *resource files*.

A resource file has the extension .resw and is placed in a special directory called Strings inside your project. This folder must contain a subfolder for every supported language. The subfolders follow the naming convention for the language/region pattern. For example, en-US means English language in the United States, and en-GB means English language in Great Britain. This pattern is called the BCP-47 language tag. You can also use just the language to force the runtime to use localized resources for every region. For example, if you use a folder named en, the English language will be used for United States as well as Great Britain (and Australia, and so on).

In this subfolder, create a file called Resources.resw. This is the new naming convention for Windows Store apps. If you have an .resx file from a .NET project, copy that file into the new folder structure and rename the file extension to .resw. The format is compatible because the defined schema is the same.

The schema definition defined by Microsoft for resource files is shown in Listing 4-26.

LISTING 4-26 Schema definition for resource files

```
<xsd:schema id="root" xmlns="" xmlns:xsd="http://www.w3.org/2001/XMLSchema"
    xmlns:msdata="urn:schemas-microsoft-com:xml-msdata">
    <xsd:import namespace="http://www.w3.org/XML/1998/namespace" />
    <xsd:element name="root" msdata:IsDataSet="true">
      <xsd:complexType>
        <xsd:choice maxOccurs="unbounded">
          <xsd:element name="metadata">
            <xsd:complexType>
              <xsd:sequence>
                <xsd:element name="value" type="xsd:string" minOccurs="0" />
              </xsd:sequence>
              <xsd:attribute name="name" use="required" type="xsd:string" />
              <xsd:attribute name="type" type="xsd:string" />
              <xsd:attribute name="mimetype" type="xsd:string" />
              <xsd:attribute ref="xml:space" />
            </xsd:complexType>
          </xsd:element>
          <xsd:element name="assembly">
            <xsd:complexType>
              <xsd:attribute name="alias" type="xsd:string" />
              <xsd:attribute name="name" type="xsd:string" />
            </xsd:complexType>
          </xsd:element>
          <xsd:element name="data">
            <xsd:complexType>
              <xsd:sequence>
                <xsd:element name="value" type="xsd:string" minOccurs="0"
                    msdata:Ordinal="1" />
```

```
                <xsd:element name="comment" type="xsd:string" minOccurs="0"
                    msdata:Ordinal="2" />
              </xsd:sequence>
              <xsd:attribute name="name" type="xsd:string" use="required"
                    msdata:Ordinal="1" />
              <xsd:attribute name="type" type="xsd:string" msdata:Ordinal="3" />
              <xsd:attribute name="mimetype" type="xsd:string" msdata:Ordinal="4" />
              <xsd:attribute ref="xml:space" />
            </xsd:complexType>
          </xsd:element>
          <xsd:element name="resheader">
            <xsd:complexType>
              <xsd:sequence>
                <xsd:element name="value" type="xsd:string" minOccurs="0"
                    msdata:Ordinal="1" />
              </xsd:sequence>
              <xsd:attribute name="name" type="xsd:string" use="required" />
            </xsd:complexType>
          </xsd:element>
        </xsd:choice>
      </xsd:complexType>
    </xsd:element>
  </xsd:schema>
```

Visual Studio provides an editor to manage resource files. Figure 4-11 shows the Visual Studio Resource editor for a resource file of a real application.

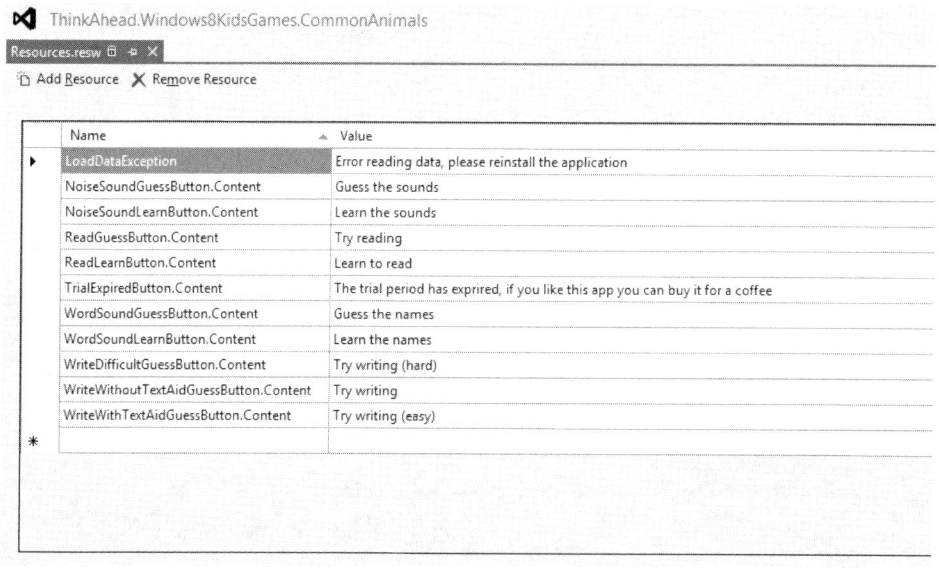

ThinkAhead.Windows8KidsGames.CommonAnimals

Resources.resw

Add Resource Remove Resource

Name	Value
LoadDataException	Error reading data, please reinstall the application
NoiseSoundGuessButton.Content	Guess the sounds
NoiseSoundLearnButton.Content	Learn the sounds
ReadGuessButton.Content	Try reading
ReadLearnButton.Content	Learn to read
TrialExpiredButton.Content	The trial period has exprired, if you like this app you can buy it for a coffee
WordSoundGuessButton.Content	Guess the names
WordSoundLearnButton.Content	Learn the names
WriteDifficultGuessButton.Content	Try writing (hard)
WriteWithoutTextAidGuessButton.Content	Try writing
WriteWithTextAidGuessButton.Content	Try writing (easy)

FIGURE 4-11 Visual Studio Resource editor window

The contents of the resource file are shown in Listing 4-27.

LISTING 4-27 Resource file with English text

```
<?xml version="1.0" encoding="utf-8"?>
<root>
    <resheader name="resmimetype">
         <value>text/microsoft-resx</value>
    </resheader>

    <resheader name="version">
         <value>2.0</value>
    </resheader>
    <resheader name="reader">
         <value>System.Resources.ResXResourceReader, System.Windows.Forms,
          Version=4.0.0.0, Culture=neutral, PublicKeyToken=b77a5c561934e089</value>
    </resheader>

    <resheader name="writer">
         <value>System.Resources.ResXResourceWriter, System.Windows.Forms,
          Version=4.0.0.0, Culture=neutral, PublicKeyToken=b77a5c561934e089</value>
    </resheader>
    <data name="LoadDataException" xml:space="preserve">
         <value>Error reading data, please reinstall the application</value>
    </data>
    <data name="NoiseSoundGuessButton.Content" xml:space="preserve">
         <value>Guess the sounds</value>
    </data>
    <data name="NoiseSoundLearnButton.Content" xml:space="preserve">
         <value>Learn the sounds</value>
    </data>
    <data name="ReadGuessButton.Content" xml:space="preserve">
         <value>Try reading</value>
     </data>
     <data name="ReadLearnButton.Content" xml:space="preserve">
         <value>Learn to read</value>
     </data>
     <data name="WordSoundGuessButton.Content" xml:space="preserve">
         <value>Guess the names</value>
     </data>
     <data name="WordSoundLearnButton.Content" xml:space="preserve">
         <value>Learn the names</value>
     </data>
     <data name="WriteWithoutTextAidGuessButton.Content" xml:space="preserve">
         <value>Try writing</value>
      </data>
      <data name="WriteWithTextAidGuessButton.Content" xml:space="preserve">
          <value>Try writing (easy)</value>
    </data>
    <data name="WriteDifficultGuessButton.Content" xml:space="preserve">
        <value>Try writing (hard)</value>
     </data>
     <data name="TrialExpiredButton.Content" xml:space="preserve">
        <value>The trial period has expired, if you like this app you can buy
            it for a coffee</value>
     </data>
</root>
```

There are two types of resource elements. The first is simply a named resource called *LoadDataException*. In the code, you can reference this resource using the following classes:

```
var loader = new Windows.ApplicationModel.Resources.ResourceLoader();
var string = loader.GetString("LoadDataException");
```

This code is usually placed in the UI layer of your application. The *ResourceLoader* class will use the application language to choose the correct resource file.

The second type of resource has a composite name. The first part represents the name of a user control, and the second part represents the property that will use the value text. The XAML infrastructure of a Windows Store app uses the value of the resource to set the value of the property referenced by the resource item.

The code in Listing 4-28 is taken from the main page of an application titled *Learn with the Animals*.

LISTING 4-28 XAML code per the default page of *Learn with the Animals* app

```
<Grid x:Name="FullScreenGrid">
    <Viewbox Stretch="Uniform">
        <Canvas Width="1366" Height="766"  HorizontalAlignment="Left"
            VerticalAlignment="Top">
            <Button Content="Impara i versi" x:Uid="NoiseSoundLearnButton"
                x:Name="NoiseSoundLearnButton" Click="NoiseSoundLearnButton_Click"
                Style="{StaticResource MenuButtonStyle}" Canvas.Left="52"
                Canvas.Top="44" Foreground="#FF2271B2"  />
            <Button Content="Impara i nomi" x:Uid="WordSoundLearnButton"
                Click="WordSoundLearnButton_Click"
                Style="{StaticResource MenuButtonStyle}"
                Canvas.Left="258" Canvas.Top="192" Foreground="#FF2271B2"/>
                <Button Content="Impara a leggere" x:Uid="ReadLearnButton"
                    Click="ReadLearnButton_Click" HorizontalAlignment="Left"
                    Style="{StaticResource MenuButtonStyle}" Canvas.Left="52"
                    Canvas.Top="318" Foreground="#FF2271B2"/>
                <Button Content="Indovina i versi" x:Uid="NoiseSoundGuessButton"
                    Click="NoiseSoundGuessButton_Click"
                    Style="{StaticResource MenuButtonStyle}" Canvas.Left="533"
                    Canvas.Top="34" Foreground="#FFDC760F"/>
                <Button Content="Indovina i nomi" x:Uid="WordSoundGuessButton"
                    Click="WordSoundGuessButton_Click"
                    Style="{StaticResource MenuButtonStyle}" Canvas.Left="652"
                    Canvas.Top="208" Foreground="#FFDC760F" />
                <Button Content="Prova a leggere" x:Uid="ReadGuessButton"
                    Click="ReadGuessButton_Click"
                    Style="{StaticResource MenuButtonStyle}" Canvas.Left="1122"
                    Canvas.Top="34" Foreground="#FF209107" />
                <Button Content="Prova a scrivere con aiuto"
                    x:Uid="WriteWithTextAidGuessButton"
                    Click="WriteWithTextAidGuessButton_Click"
                    Style="{StaticResource MenuButtonStyle}" Canvas.Left="1001"
                    Canvas.Top="227" Foreground="#FF209107"/>
```

```
                <Button Content="Prova a scrivere senza aiuto"
                    x:Uid="WriteWithoutTextAidGuessButton"
                    Click="WriteWithoutTextAidGuessButton_Click"
                    Style="{StaticResource MenuButtonStyle}" Canvas.Left="879"
                    Canvas.Top="387" Foreground="#FF209107"/>
            </Viewbox>
            <Grid x:Name="TrialPopup" RenderTransformOrigin="0.5,0.5">
                <Grid.RenderTransform>
                    <CompositeTransform ScaleX="1" ScaleY="1" />
                </Grid.RenderTransform>
                <Rectangle x:Name="BackgroundTransparent" Fill="#00F4F4F5"/>
                <Rectangle x:Name="BackgroundPopup" Fill="#FFF4F4F5" Opacity="0.9"
                    Margin="0,0,0,0"/>
                <Button Content="Buy the App" x:Uid="TrialExpiredButton"
                    Click="BuyClick" FontSize="48" HorizontalAlignment="Center"
                    ScrollViewer.VerticalScrollBarVisibility="Disabled" Margin="2"
                    Background="#FF010000"  />
            </Grid>
</Grid>
```

Starting from the bolded line, the button control has an *x:id* set to *NoiseSoundLearnButton*. You can find this key, together with the *Content* property, in the resource file in Figure 4-11. In practice, the XAML framework looks for the name and properties of a control in the resource file and, if a match is found, it uses the value of the resources to set the property of the control. In Figure 4-11 for the presented sample, the *Content* property of the *NoiseSoundLearnButton* button control is set to Learn The Sounds. The XAML code uses Italian for the *Content* property. This value will be overridden because the default language for the application is en-US and there is a corresponding resource file for English (United States).

You can use this system to set the value of many properties of a control. Imagine in German you need to place the button controls in a different position. You can set the *Top* or *Left* properties assigning a different value in the German resource file.

If you create a Dutch translation of the resource file and change the Windows Language settings as explained in the previous section, you will end up with a localized page for the Netherlands.

It's important to translate complete sentences instead of words. For example, the sentence "The task could not be created" translates into Dutch as "De taak kan niet worden aangemaakt." However, the sentence "The document could not be created" translates into "Het document kan niet worden aangemaakt." In English, you can just replace "task" with "document," but in Dutch, you also have to change "de" to "het."

To solve this issue, localize the entire sentence instead of separate words. Doing so might seem like a lot of work, but it will increase the quality of your app. The same is true for reusing words in different contexts. Maybe you can use the same word in your language, but in other languages you might need to use another word.

This method will load resources in the user's default language. If you want to load resources in another language, you can use the *ResourceLoader* class.

When grouping items with the correct collation for a specific language, you can use the *CharacterGroupings* class in the *Windows.Globalization.Collation* namespace. This class gives you the functionality to get a label for any string that you pass in. The following code sample shows how to get the character groupings for the current locale:

```
var characterGroupings = new Windows.Globalization.Collation.CharacterGroupings();
var size = characterGroupings.Count;

if (size > 0)
{
    // Get the first characterGrouping.
    var characterGrouping = characterGroupings[0];
    var first = characterGrouping.First;
    var label = characterGrouping.Label;
}
```

When using the en-US locale, you will get groupings for special characters (such as the ampersand, or &), numbers (0 through 9), and for all letters of the Latin alphabet.

You can then use the *Lookup* method to get the label for a specific string.

Images

You do not have to localize images if they do not contain text or other culture-specific information. Localizing images adds to the download size of your app, which can affect the user experience, so avoid image localization if possible.

If you must localize images, put them in a resource-specific folder. For example, you can place one image in images/en-US and a copy of the same file in images/NL-nl to create both an English and a Dutch version of your image.

Within your XAML, you can reference the image without any qualifiers. It might look like you are pointing to a file on disk, but you are actually loading the image from the package. The resource manager responsible for loading images loads the most appropriate version of the image.

In addition to language, you can specify a scale factor and contrast mode. All of these items are considered when loading an image. The following code shows an example of how to reference an image's location, scale factor, and contrast mode:

```
Images/en-US/homeregion-USA/logo.scale-100_contrast-white.png
```

Use the following to reference the image from your XAML code:

```
Images/logo.png
```

> ***MORE INFO*** **RESOURCE QUALIFIERS**
>
> **For more information on the contrast, scale, and language qualifiers, visit *http://msdn.microsoft.com/en-us/library/windows/apps/hh965372.aspx*.**

If you need to reverse an image for a right-to-left language, you can use the *FlowDirection* property. For example, the following XAML code shows the style applied to images based on cultural settings:

```
<!-- it-IT\localized.xaml -->
<Image ... FlowDirection="LeftToRight" />
<!-- ar-SA\localized.xaml -->
<Image ... FlowDirection="RightToLeft" />
```

Dates and times

As shown in Figure 4-9, there are many possible settings when it comes to working with dates and time. You should never work with a date or time manually to display it on the screen.

Instead, use the *Windows.Globalization.DateTimeFormatting.DateTimeFormatter* class. This class helps you format a date and time easily while following the user's preferences.

When creating an instance of the *DateTimeFormatter* class, you pass it a string that describes the result you want, as follows:

```
DateTimeFormatter shortDateformatter = new DateTimeFormatter("shortdate");
```

Now you can use this formatter to format a date:

```
var sdate = shortDateformatter.Format(DateTime.Now);
```

You can pass all kinds of format strings to your constructor. However, be careful to avoid representations that are not valid in all languages. Specifying that you want a *month day* pattern, for example, is valid in the United States but not in the Netherlands.

Some examples of format templates you can use are:

- *shortdate*
- *shorttime*
- *dayofweek*
- *day*
- *month*
- *year*
- *day month year*
- *hour*
- *minute*
- *second*

> ***MORE INFO*** **FORMAT TEMPLATES**
>
> **For a complete list of format templates and how to combine them, visit *http://msdn.microsoft.com/en-us/library/windows/apps/jj673581.aspx.***

Numbers and currencies

When working with numbers and currencies, you can also use a few built-in formatters:

- ***CurrencyFormatter*** Formats and parses currencies
- ***DecimalFormatter*** Formats and parses decimal numbers
- ***PercentFormatter*** Formats and parses percentages
- ***PermilleFormatter*** Formats and parses permillages

You can use these classes to convert a number to a string or to parse a string to a number. You use these classes by creating a new formatter with or without a language code, and set any necessary properties before calling *format* or *parse*. The following code sample shows how to use the *CurrencyFormatter* to format and parse a number:

```
var userCurrency = Windows.System.UserProfile.GlobalizationPreferences.Currencies[0];
var currencyFormat =
    new Windows.Globalization.NumberFormatting.CurrencyFormatter(userCurrency);
var currencyNumber = 1234.567;
var currencyFormatted = currencyFormat.Format(currencyNumber);
var currency1Parsed = currencyFormat.ParseDouble(currencyFormatted);
```

When working with the formatters, you can set the *IsGrouped* and *FractionDigits* properties. These properties control whether you want to display the group separator and a minimum number of fractional digits you want to display.

Calendars

When working with dates and times, it's important to avoid manual arithmetic. Things can go wrong when another calendar has another number of days in a month (such as the Hebrew calendar) or when you have to deal with adjustments for daylight saving time and leap years. Instead, you should use the *Windows.Globalization.Calendar* class.

You can use the code from Listing 4-29 to display information about the current calendar settings.

LISTING 4-29 Getting calendar data

```
var CalendarIdentifiers = Windows.Globalization.CalendarIdentifiers.Julian;
var ClockIdentifiers = Windows.Globalization.ClockIdentifiers.TwentyFourHour;

var calendarDate = new DateTime();
var cal = new Windows.Globalization.Calendar();
cal.SetDateTime(calendarDate);
var calItems = "User's default calendar: " + cal.GetCalendarSystem() + "\n" +
    "Name of Month: " + cal.MonthAsString() + "\n" +
    "Day of Month: " + cal.DayAsPaddedString(2) + "\n" +
    "Day of Week: " + cal.DayOfWeekAsString() + "\n" +
    "Year: " + cal.YearAsString();
```

When you have an instance of a *Calendar* object, you can use this to perform arithmetic's on a date. A *Calendar* object has methods for adding nanoseconds, seconds, minutes, hours, days, weeks, and years to a date. It can also give you information such as how many days there are in a year or hours in a day. This code snippet shows how to add and subtract a day from a date:

```
var cal = new Windows.Globalization.Calendar();
cal.SetDateTime(new DateTime(2013, 1, 1));
var endDate = cal.Clone();
cal.AddDays(-1);
endDate.AddDays(1);
```

EXAM TIP

You should never perform manual math on a date or time. Always use the built-in classes so you don't introduce mistakes.

Localizing your manifest

When distributing your app to multiple markets, you should localize your manifest. This enables you to show a translated description for your app in the Windows Store.

You can localize several items in your manifest:

- Display name, short name, and description
- Descriptions on the Declarations page
- URIs on the Content URIs page

To set the default language, open the Package.appxmanifest file in Visual Studio Editor. On the Application UI page, specify the default language for your app. This language is used as a fallback language for your app. If the user requests a language that's not available in your app, it switches to the fallback language.

Inside your manifest, use *ms-resource:<identifier>* to reference resource strings. For example, to set your application title, you can add an *app_title* to your resource file and reference it with *ms-resource:app_title*.

MORE INFO **LOCALIZING THE MANIFEST**

For more information on how to localize your manifest, see *http://msdn.microsoft.com/en-us/library/windows/apps/hh454044.aspx*.

Using the Multilingual App Toolkit

One tool you should definitely use is the Multilingual App Toolkit. This toolkit is an extension for Visual Studio that helps you localize your app and manage translations.

MORE INFO MULTILINGUAL APP TOOLKIT

You can find the download for the toolkit at *http://msdn.microsoft.com/en-us/windows/apps/hh848309.aspx*.

After you create a default resource file for your app, you can use the Multilingual App Toolkit to translate your app to other languages. The tool helps you create resource files for other languages and also for a pseudolanguage. The pseudolanguage is helpful for testing your app and making sure that all text is moved to a resource file. The pseudolanguage is also designed to show you any places in your app in which translations can lead to layout errors (because some languages use more characters that can take up more space).

To enable the toolkit, select **Enable Multilingual App Toolkit** from the Tools menu, and then select **Add Translation Languages** from the Project menu.

Some languages support Microsoft automatic translation. This is a machine translation that can get you started with creating a new translation. A human native speaker must still check the translation, but automatic translation can save you a lot of time.

After adding languages and building your project, the toolkit adds resource files for you. By using the supplied editor, you can then execute a machine translation. The tool uses XLF files, which are used by most translators. You can send XLF files to translators, let them translate your resources, and then import their changes into your app.

MORE INFO MULTILINGUAL APP TOOLKIT

A complete discussion of how to use the toolkit can be found at *http://msdn.microsoft.com/en-us/library/windows/apps/jj569303.aspx*.

Thought experiment

Globalizing and localizing your app

In this thought experiment, apply what you've learned about this objective. You can find answers to these questions in the "Answers" section at the end of this chapter.

You created an app that tracks holidays and shows you when your next day off will be. You have built the app for your local language and now you want to translate it. Your app includes a few images.

Answer the following questions:

1. **Which elements should you globalize and localize?**
2. **Why is it important to use the built-in APIs? Which APIs do you plan to use?**
3. **How can you organize your languages?**

Objective summary

- Globalization is the process of ensuring that your app does not depend on a hard-coded language. Instead, you use built-in APIs for formatting numbers, currencies, dates, and so on.
- Localization is the process of translating text and images to a specific locale so your app supports that language.
- You use resource files (.resw) for storing resource strings. You use the *ResourceLoader* class from C# code to retrieve localized resources, the *x:Uid* attribute to bind resources in XAML, and the *CharacterGrouping* class for sorting and grouping string data.
- You can localize images by moving them to a folder that contains the current locale. You reference the image by name as if it were located in the root folder.
- You can use the *DateTimeFormatter* class to format and parse dates and time. You can use the *CurrencyFormatter, DecimalFormatter, PercentFormatter,* and *PermilleFormatter* classes to work with numbers.
- You can translate resources in your manifest to localize content for the Windows Store.
- The Multilingual App Toolkit is a useful tool for translating apps.

Objective review

Answer the following questions to test your knowledge of the information in this objective. You can find the answers to these questions and explanations of why each answer choice is correct or incorrect in the "Answers" section at the end of this chapter.

1. You want to localize an image for Hebrew. What is the best approach?

   A. Put the image in images/IW/<*yourimagename*>.png and reference image/<*yourimagename*>.png from your XAML.

   B. From C#, load the correct image from the images/IW folder and bind that to the *src* property in your XAML.

   C. Use the *FlowDirection* attribute in your XAML to mirror your image controls.

   D. Put the image path in a resource string and use it to load the image.

2. You want to format a number so that it always has two-digit fractions. Which class do you use?

   A. *CurrencyFormatter*

   B. *DecimalFormatter*

   C. *PercentFormatter*

   D. *PermilleFormatter*

3. You want to localize the application manifest. What do you need to do? (Choose all that apply.)
   - **A.** Set the fallback language as the default language.
   - **B.** Set the *ms-resource* keyword using the Visual Studio 2012 App Manifest Designer.
   - **C.** Set the *ms-resource* keyword using an XML editor.
   - **D.** Use the Multilingual App Toolkit.

Chapter summary

- The WinRT APIs offer only an asynchronous version of each method that might have a response time higher than 50 milliseconds.
- The .NET Framework *async/await* pattern greatly simplifies the maintainability of asynchronous code. You do not have to subscribe to events or use the .NET *IAsyncResult* interface directly.
- You can leverage the TPL to perform asynchronous operations, and to track task progresses or handle task cancellation.
- Use animations and transitions to help users to focus their attention on what is happening in the UI, but be careful not to irritate or distract the user.
- Use a storyboard to animate a dependency property over time. Choose independent animations whenever possible to prevent the Windows Runtime from blocking the animation. However, if you must use a dependent animation, remember to set the *EnableDependentAnimation* property to *true*.
- Use a key-frame animation to create more complex animations. To achieve different results, you can choose between linear interpolation, spline interpolation, and easing functions.
- Use the *ObjectAnimationUsingKeyFrames* class to animate any property that is not of type *Double*, *Point*, or *Color*. When the time value set in the *KeyTime* property is reached, the new value is simply applied, with no transitions.
- Whenever possible, use the animations provided by the XAML animation library, under the *Windows.UI.Xaml.Media.Animation* namespace, to ensure consistency of the user experience.
- Use a custom control to extend functionalities of an existing control, or to customize its visual appearance or behavior. Derive it from the control that already exposes properties or events that you might need for your new custom control.
- Use *VisualState* objects to define the visual appearance of a UI element when it is in a certain state. Use *VisualTransition* objects to represent the visual behavior that occurs when the control transits from one visual state to another.

- Use resource files for storing resources and the *ResourceLoader* class to retrieve localized resources.
- Localize images by moving them to a folder that contains the current locale. Reference the image by name as if it were located in the root folder.
- Use the *DateTimeFormatter* class to format and parse dates and time. You can use the *CurrencyFormatter, DecimalFormatter, PercentFormatter,* and *PermilleFormatter* classes to work with numbers.
- Translate resources in your manifest to localize content for the Windows Store.
- Use the Multilingual App Toolkit to translate apps.

Answers

This section contains the solutions to the thought experiments and answers to the lesson review questions in this chapter.

Objective 4.1: Thought experiment

1. Fetching data is an I/O operation that's not CPU bound. You can use the TPL to execute multiple requests in parallel. That way, you bring your fetch time down to the longest request instead of the sum of all requests.
2. You can use the TPL to split the work over multiple threads. Doing so will improve performance, especially on multicore machines, because you can parallelize the CPU-bound processing.
3. Tasks move work to a separate thread. This is useful for CPU-bound work that can be split to multiple cores. It is also useful for moving work out of the UI thread so you don't block that thread for too long, which would make the UI unresponsive.

Objective 4.1: Review

1. **Correct answer:** D
   - **A. Incorrect:** The asynchronous methods in WinRT do not offer callbacks.
   - **B. Incorrect:** The completion event pattern has been dismissed in WinRT APIs.
   - **C. Incorrect:** There is no need to pass an asynchronous parameter.
   - **D. Correct:** You just need to use the *await* keyword in method calls.

2. **Correct answer:** C
   A. **Incorrect:** The asynchronous methods in WinRT do not offer callbacks.
   B. **Incorrect:** In the completion event, you cannot use a *try/catch* block to catch the exception raised from a different thread.
   C. **Correct:** The new *async/await* pattern lets you also use a traditional *try/catch* block for asynchronous calls.
   D. **Incorrect:** You can use a *try/catch* block to catch exceptions in asynchronous code.
3. **Correct answer:** C
   A. **Incorrect:** In the Windows Runtime, this interface is hidden by the framework.
   B. **Incorrect:** You cannot abort a task from the completion handler.
   C. **Correct:** You have to use a *CancellationTokenSource* class of the *System.Threading* namespace to request a cancellation.
   D. **Incorrect:** An asynchronous method does not enable you to access the underlying thread directly.

Objective 4.2: Thought experiment

1. The easiest way to animate the ball is by using an animation with key frames. A transition from the animation library would not be suitable because you have a few different states that you want to use in your animation.
2. The force of the swipe might affect, for example, the length of the animation and/or the number of bounces.
3. You can animate the *Canvas.Top* and *Canvas.Left* attached properties of the bouncing ball (nested within a *Canvas* control). By using different sets of key frames for these two properties, you can easily compose the animation and apply it to your element.
4. For animating the bouncing of the ball, you could use the *BounceEase* easing function. Set the *Bounces* property to the number of bounces and the *EasingMode* property either to *EaseIn*, to describe the motion from top to bottom (slow to fast), or to *EaseOut*, to describe the motion from bottom to top (fast to slow).

Objective 4.2: Review

1. **Correct answer:** C
   A. **Incorrect:** A zero-duration animation is an independent animation.
   B. **Incorrect:** An animation targeting the *Opacity* property of a control is an independent animation.

C. **Correct:** An animation targeting the *Width* property of a control is a dependent animation.

D. **Incorrect:** An animation targeting the *Canvas.Left* property of a control is an independent animation.

2. **Correct answer:** D

   A. **Incorrect:** A property of type *Double* can be interpolated through a linear interpolation, a spline interpolation, or an easing function.

   B. **Incorrect**: A property of type *Point* can be interpolated through a linear interpolation, a spline interpolation, or an easing function.

   C. **Incorrect:** A property of type *Color* can be interpolated through a linear interpolation, a spline interpolation, or an easing function.

   D. **Correct:** A property of type *Object* does not support interpolation.

3. **Correct answer:** C

   A. **Incorrect:** A page transition animates the contents of a page into or out of view.

   B. **Incorrect:** A content transition animates one piece or set of content into or out of view.

   C. **Correct:** A fade in/out transition shows transient elements or controls.

   D. **Incorrect:** A reposition transition moves an element into a new position.

Objective 4.3: Thought experiment

1. The best option is to use a custom control because you need to provide your new control with a custom template, in this case.
2. You should derive your control from the *Button* class (or from the *ButtonBase* class) so you can use all of the button's properties and events out of the box.
3. You could add two dependency properties: an *ImageSource* for the uniform resource identifier (URI) of the contact's picture and an integer counter for keeping track of the unread messages.

Objective 4.3: Review

1. **Correct answer:** A

   A. **Correct:** The *UserControl* class is not suitable for deriving a custom control. The *UserControl* class represents a composition of already existing controls, whereas a custom control must derive from a control, such the *Button* class, or a control primitive, such as the *Control* or the *Panel* class, to extend its appearance or behavior.

   - **B. Incorrect:** By default, a custom control derives from the *Control* class.
   - **C. Incorrect:** A custom control can be derived from the *Panel* class.
   - **D. Incorrect:** A custom control can be derived from the *Button* class.

2. **Correct answer:** D
   - **A. Incorrect:** A dependency property must be exposed through a *public static readonly* property.
   - **B. Incorrect:** A dependency property must be exposed through a *public static readonly* property.
   - **C. Incorrect:** A dependency property must be exposed through a *public static readonly* property.
   - **D. Correct:** A dependency property must be exposed through a *public static readonly* property.

3. **Correct answer:** C
   - **A. Incorrect:** The default template of a custom control is defined in a Generic.xaml file in the Themes folder.
   - **B. Incorrect:** *VisualTransition* objects represent the visual behavior that occurs when the control transits from one visual state to another.
   - **C. Correct:** If you omit both the *From* and *To* properties of the *VisualTransition* instance, the transition will apply from any state to any other state.
   - **D. Incorrect:** The *GeneratedDuration* property defines the duration of the transition between two visual states.

Objective 4.4: Thought experiment

1. You need to globalize all code that deals with date and time functions, both for formatting and parsing. You should also check your images to determine whether they need to be localized. You must create resource files for all text, both in XAML and code, and in your application manifest.
2. The globalization APIs are built to work with all of the user preferences for language settings and for settings that display date, time, number, and currency data. It would be difficult to write this code yourself. You can use the *DateTimeFormatter* class when working with date and time data.
3. You need to organize your languages by moving all resources (both images and text) into specific folders with the locale name in the folder name.

Objective 4.4: Review

1. **Correct answer:** A
   - **A. Correct:** This way, the resource manager can find the correct file for the Hebrew language.
   - **B. Incorrect:** Binding to a localized image can be done from XAML. The resource manager will automatically load the correct version.
   - **C. Incorrect:** This will mirror your image in XAML. It won't load the localized version of your image.
   - **D. Incorrect:** Although this is possible, it is also unwieldy. You can just bind to the image from your XAML and the resource manager will load the correct version.
2. **Correct answer:** B
   - **A. Incorrect:** The *CurrencyFormatter* class is specifically for displaying currencies. It can display them with two-digit fractions, but it will also add the local currency symbol.
   - **B. Correct:** *DecimalFormatter* can be configured to display a number with two-digit fractions.
   - **C. Incorrect:** *PercentFormatter* adds a percent symbol to your formatted number.
   - **D. Incorrect:** *PermilleFormatter* adds a per mille symbol to your formatted number.
3. **Correct answers:** A, C
   - **A. Correct:** You have to set the default language for users who use a language different from the one defined in the application.
   - **B. Incorrect:** The Visual Studio 2012 App Manifest Designer does not let you set a different language.
   - **C. Correct:** You have to use an XML editor to define localized manifest resources.
   - **D. Incorrect:** Although the Multilingual App Toolkit is a useful tool for verifying your application, you cannot use it to define application manifest localized resources.

CHAPTER 5

Manage data and security

In this chapter, you learn how to use the local file system in an efficient and effective way, implement a data-caching strategy, and secure application data using certificates and encryption algorithms.

Objectives in this chapter:

- Objective 5.1: Design and implement data caching
- Objective 5.2: Save and retrieve files from the file system
- Objective 5.3: Secure app data

Objective 5.1: Design and implement data caching

Windows Store applications have various options to store data, and each has its advantages and disadvantages. The right place to store information or cache depends on the application, the scenario in which the user works, and whether the application relies on HTML5/JavaScript or on XAML with C#, Microsoft Visual Basic, or C++.

> **This objective covers how to:**
>
> - Choose which types of items (user data, settings, app data) in an app should be persisted to the cache according to requirements
> - Choose when items are cached
> - Choose where items are cached (Windows Azure, remote storage)
> - Select the caching mechanism

Understanding application and user data

A Windows Store app works with different kinds of data; mainly application data and user data. *Application data* (also referred to as *app data*) represents information that the application creates, updates, and deletes; or, in general terms, uses. This kind of data is bound to the application and has no meaning outside of it: The data cannot live without the application because it has no sense outside of the app. Types of application data include the following:

- **User preferences** Any setting the user can personalize in an application, such as choices for browsing, searching, and receiving notifications. For example, the preferred city for a weather app is a user preference, which has no meaning outside of that application.
- **Runtime state** Data entered by the user and preserved in a page preserved in the navigation state. Runtime state data has meaning only inside the application.
- **Reference content** An item related to the application. For example, the list of cities for a weather application or the list of terms for a translation app is bound to the application.

User data is independent from the application and is usually stored outside the application in a database, nonrelational storage, or file. This kind of data can be used by other applications. Types of user data include these:

- **Entities** The main classes a developer works on. Entities can include invoices, orders, and customer data, such as for an accounting app.
- **Media files** Audio files, videos, and photos.
- **Documents** Files that can be stored via a web service, Microsoft SkyDrive, or Microsoft SharePoint service.

Application data must be stored in a specific per-app, per-user store. This data cannot be shared across users and needs to be placed in an isolated storage that prevents access from other apps and users. If the user installs an application update, this kind of data must be preserved, but the data must be cleaned if the user removes the application from the system. It is important to store this kind of data in a type of storage that provides these features. Fortunately, Microsoft Windows 8 exposes a storage mechanism that perfectly suits these needs.

You cannot use the same storage mechanism for user data, such as application entities or documents, however. You can use user libraries, SkyDrive, or a cloud service to store user data.

Caching application data

The Windows Runtime (WinRT) offers many solutions to store application data in local and remote storage. This section analyzes the most important ones:

- Application data application programming interfaces (APIs)
- IndexedDB
- Extensible Storage Engine (ESE)
- HTML5 Web Storage
- Windows Library for JavaScript (WinJS)–specific classes, such as *sessionState*, *local*, *roaming*

Application data APIs

The WinRT application data APIs provide access to local and roaming data stores. Simply choose the class and the name of the object; these classes can save and retrieve content from both local and roaming data.

Every Windows 8 application, regardless of the language in which it is written, can save settings and unstructured data files to local and roaming storage. The storage also provides a place to store temporary data. This area is subject to clean-up by the system automatically.

LOCAL STORAGE

You can save and retrieve application settings with a single line of code and compose them using either a simple or complex data type. The settings provide a mechanism to store composite types, which are sets of application settings to be managed as a single unit in an atomic operation. The following code references the *LocalSettings* and *LocalFolder* properties of the *ApplicationData* class in a local variable to be used throughout the code:

Sample of C# code

```
Windows.Storage.ApplicationDataContainer localSettings =
   Windows.Storage.ApplicationData.Current.LocalSettings;

Windows.Storage.StorageFolder localFolder =
   Windows.Storage.ApplicationData.Current.LocalFolder;
```

Settings can be saved and retrieved in a synchronous way. File and folder access uses the *async/await* pattern. The following code saves and then retrieves a setting called *PageSize*:

```
localSettings.Values["PageSize"] = "20";

(code omitted)

Object value = localSettings.Values["PageSize"];
```

Settings are limited to 8 kilobytes (KB) per single setting, whereas composite settings are limited to 64 KB. Listing 5-1 demonstrates the use of a composite setting. The *PageSize* and *Title* key-value pair is stored in the *PrintSettings* composite setting.

LISTING 5-1 Saving and retrieving a composite setting

```
Windows.Storage.ApplicationDataContainer localSettings =
    Windows.Storage.ApplicationData.Current.LocalSettings;

Windows.Storage.ApplicationDataCompositeValue composite =
    new Windows.Storage.ApplicationDataCompositeValue();

composite["PageSize"] = 20;
composite["Title"] = "DevLeap Members";

localSettings.Values["PrintSettings"] = composite;

Windows.Storage.ApplicationDataCompositeValue composite =
    (Windows.Storage.ApplicationDataCompositeValue)localSettings
        .Values["PrintSettings "];
```

```
if (composite == null)
{
   // No data stored in the composite setting yet
}
else
{
   // Access data in composite["PageSize"] and composite["Title"]
}
```

If you have a complex settings structure, you can create a container to better understand and manage settings categories. Use the *ApplicationDataContainer.CreateContainer* method to create a settings container. The following code excerpt creates a settings container named *PrintSettingsContainer* and adds a setting value named *PageSize*:

```
Windows.Storage.ApplicationDataContainer localSettings =
    Windows.Storage.ApplicationData.Current.LocalSettings;
Windows.Storage.ApplicationDataContainer container =
    localSettings.CreateContainer("PrintSettingsContainer",
        Windows.Storage.ApplicationDataCreateDisposition.Always);

if (localSettings.Containers.ContainsKey("PrintSettingsContainer"))
{
   localSettings.Containers["PrintSettingsContainer "].Values["PageSize"] = "20";
}
```

The second line of code creates a container named *PrintSettingsContainer* with the s method. The second parameter represents the *ApplicationDataCreateDisposition*. The value of *Always* means the container should be created if it does not exist. The *ApplicationData-CreateDisposition* enum exposes a second value, *Existing*, that activates the container only if the resource it represents already exists.

To reference a container and retrieve its settings values, you can use the *Containers* enum to test for container existence and then reference the object to ask for its settings and relative values. The following code uses the *ContainsKey* method to test for container presence. If the method returns *true*, it retrieves the value for the *PageSize* setting.

```
Windows.Storage.ApplicationDataContainer localSettings =
    Windows.Storage.ApplicationData.Current.LocalSettings;

bool hasContainer = localSettings.Containers.ContainsKey("PrintSettingsContainer");
bool hasSetting = false;

if (hasContainer)
{
   hasSetting = localSettings
       .Containers["PrintSettingsContainer"].Values.ContainsKey("PageSize");
}
```

To delete a setting, you simply call the *Remove* method, as follows:

```
localSettings.Values.Remove("exampleSetting");
```

To delete a container, you can use the *DeleteContainer* method of the *ApplicationData-Container* class:

```
localSettings.DeleteContainer("exampleContainer");
```

Remember that this area of storage is suitable for settings, not user data. Do not store more than 1 megabyte (MB) of data.

If you have a very complex setting structure or you need to store information locally, you can choose to store these values in a local file instead of a local settings container. As you learn in the next section, local storage gives you a simple way to manage files and folders.

For example, if the application wants to track the time the user performs some operations, the settings container becomes very difficult to manage. A plain text file can be a simple but effective solution to store this log information. The code in Listing 5-2 creates a file called log.txt to store the current date and time.

LISTING 5-2 Logging to files in local user storage

```
async void CreateLog()
{
   Windows.Storage. StorageFolder localFolder =
      Windows.Storage.ApplicationData.Current.LocalFolder;

   Windows.Globalization.DateTimeFormatting.DateTimeFormatter formatter =
       new Windows.Globalization.DatetimeFormatting.DateTimeFormatter("longtime");

   StorageFile logFile = await localFolder.CreateFileAsync("log.txt",
       CreationCollisionOption.ReplaceExisting);

   await FileIO.WriteTextAsync(logFile, formatter.Format(DateTime.Now));
}
```

The code creates a file in the local folder storage called log.txt using the *CreateFileAsync* method. Then it references the file in the *WriteTextAsync* method of the *FileIO* class (of the *Windows.Storage* namespace). The *CreationCollisionOption* can be *ReplaceExisting* to create a new file or *FailIfExist* to return an error if the file already exists; *OpenIfExists* to create a new file if it does not exist or open the existing one; and *GenerateUniqueName* to create a new file with an autogenerated number if a file with the same name already exists.

To read a value from a file, use the code in Listing 5-3.

LISTING 5-3 Reading values from files

```
async void ReadLog()
{
   try
   {
       Windows.Storage.StorageFolder localFolder =
           Windows.Storage.ApplicationData.Current.LocalFolder;

      StorageFile logFile = await localFolder.GetFileAsync("log.txt");
      String logDateTime = await FileIO.ReadTextAsync(logFile);
```

```
        // Perform some operation
    }
    catch (Exception)
    {
        // Problems reading the file
    }
}
```

ROAMING STORAGE

Settings and files in local storage can be roamed to "follow" the user on different devices and places. For example, a user can set application printing preferences on his Windows 8 desktop and retrieve the same value on his tablet WinRT device. You do not need to manage data transfers because the Windows Runtime gives you the *RoamingSettings*.

Roaming settings are synchronized by the system that manages the overall process in respect to battery life and bandwidth consumption.

First, you can retrieve the roaming settings or folder reference in a similar way as the local one:

```
Windows.Storage.ApplicationDataContainer roamingSettings =
    Windows.Storage.ApplicationData.Current.RoamingSettings;

Windows.Storage.StorageFolder roamingFolder =
    Windows.Storage.ApplicationData.Current.RoamingFolder;
```

You can then access the settings in a synchronous way. The following code saves and then retrieves a setting called *PageSize*:

```
roamingSettings.Values["PageSize"] = "20";
(code omitted)
Object value = roamingSettings.Values["PageSize"];
```

If you need to store complex values, you can use the same strategy you saw for the local settings in Listing 5-1. Create an *ApplicationDataCompositeValue* instance, assign the values to it, and then use the *RoamingSettings* reference to store the instance. See Listing 5-4.

LISTING 5-4 Composite setting stored in the roaming user profile

```
Windows.Storage.ApplicationDataContainer roamingSettings =
    Windows.Storage.ApplicationData.Current.RoamingSettings;

Windows.Storage.ApplicationDataCompositeValue composite =
    new Windows.Storage.ApplicationDataCompositeValue();

composite["PageSize"] = 20;
composite["Title"] = "DevLeap Members";

roamingSettings.Values["PrintSettings"] = composite;

Windows.Storage.ApplicationDataCompositeValue composite =
    (Windows.Storage.ApplicationDataCompositeValue)roamingSettings
        .Values["PrintSettings"];
```

```
if (composite == null)
{
   // No data stored in the composite setting yet
}
else
{
   // Access data in composite["PageSize"] and composite["Title"]
}
```

You can group roaming settings in containers to manage complex structures easily.

The following code excerpt creates a settings container named *PrintSettingsContainer* and adds a setting value named *PageSize*:

```
Windows.Storage.ApplicationDataContainer roamingSettings =
    Windows.Storage.ApplicationData.Current.RoamingSettings;

Windows.Storage.ApplicationDataContainer container =
    roamingSettings.CreateContainer(
        "PrintSettingsContainer",
        Windows.Storage.ApplicationDataCreateDisposition.Always);

if (roamingSettings.Containers.ContainsKey("PrintSettingsContainer"))
{
   roamingSettings.Containers["PrintSettingsContainer "].Values["PageSize"] = "20";
}
```

The first line of code creates a container *PrintSettingsContainer* using the *CreateContainer* method. The second parameter represents the *ApplicationDataCreateDisposition*. The value of *Always* means the container should be created if it does not exist yet. The enum also contains a second value, *Existing*, that activates the container only if the resource it represents already exists.

To reference a container and retrieve its settings values, you can use the *Containers* enum to test for container existence and then reference the object to ask for its settings and relative values. The following code uses the *ContainsKey* method to test for container presence. If the method returns *true*, it retrieves the value for the *PageSize* setting.

```
Windows.Storage.ApplicationDataContainer roamingSettings =
    Windows.Storage.ApplicationData.Current.RoamingSettings;

bool hasContainer = roamingSettings.Containers.ContainsKey("PrintSettingsContainer");
bool hasSetting = false;

if (hasContainer)
{
   hasSetting = roamingSettings
      .Containers["PrintSettingsContainer"].Values.ContainsKey("PageSize");
}
```

To delete a setting you simply call the *Remove* method:

```
roamingSettings.Values.Remove("exampleSetting");
```

To delete a container, you can use the *DeleteContainer* method of the *ApplicationDataContainer* class:

```
roamingSettings.DeleteContainer("exampleContainer");
```

As for local storage, you can use a class to store a file in the roaming user profile. The code in Listing 5-5 creates a file called log.txt to store the current time in the roaming profile.

LISTING 5-5 Logging to a file in roaming user storage

```
async void CreateLog()
{
   Windows.Storage.StorageFolder roamingFolder =
       Windows.Storage.ApplicationData.Current.RoamingFolder;

   Windows.Globalization.DateTimeFormatting.DateTimeFormatter formatter =
       new Windows.Globalization.DateTimeFormatting.DateTimeFormatter("longtime");

   StorageFile logFile = await roamingFolder.CreateFileAsync("log.txt",
       CreateCollisionOption.ReplaceExisting);

   await FileIO.WriteTextAsync(logFile, formatter.Format(DateTime.Now));
}
```

This code is similar to the code for accessing local storage. It creates a file in roaming storage called log.txt using the *CreateFileAsync* method. Then it references the file in the *WriteTextAsync* method of the *FileIO* class (of the *Windows.Storage* namespace). The *CreateCollisionOption* can be *ReplaceExisting* to create a new file or *FailIfExist* to return an error if the file already exists; *OpenIfExists* to create a new file if it does not exist or open the existing one; and *GenerateUniqueName* to create a new file with an autogenerated number if a file with the same name already exists.

To read a value from a file, use the code shown in Listing 5-6.

LISTING 5-6 Reading values from a file in the roaming profile

```
async void ReadLog()
{
   try
   {
       Windows.Storage.StorageFolder roamingFolder =
           Windows.Storage.ApplicationData.Current.RoamingFolder;

       StorageFile logFile = await roamingFolder.GetFileAsync("log.txt");
       String logDateTime = await FileIO.ReadTextAsync(logFile);

      // Perform some operation
   }
   catch (Exception)
   {
      // Problems reading the file
   }
}
```

Files in the local settings space have no limits, whereas roaming settings are limited to the quota specified by the *RoamingStorageQuota* property of the *ApplicationData* class. If you exceed that limit, synchronization does not occur.

You can be notified when data changes in the roaming profile of the user. Let's say an application on the desktop changes some date in the roaming profile. The application on a different user device can be notified and react to this change, refreshing the user interface.

The following code uses the *DataChanged* event to handle this situation:

```
Windows.Storage.ApplicationData.Current.DataChanged +=
      new TypedEventHandler<ApplicationData, object>(DataChanged);

void DataChanged(Windows.Storage.ApplicationData appData, object o)
{
   // Refresh data or inform the user.
}
```

TEMPORARY STORAGE

If your application needs temporary data, you can use the temporary space reserved by the Windows Runtime to store this information. The code is similar to code for local and roaming storage, but uses different classes to obtain the reference to the store.

Temporary storage is not limited in any way apart from the physical disk space.

Let's say that the log that tracks the time of every operation presented in the previous samples (refer to Listings 5-2 and 5-5) is not permanent; the application simply stores log information that is useful just for a user session on the application. The code in Listing 5-7 uses the *TemporaryFolder* property of the *ApplicationData.Current* class to retrieve the temporary storage folder and then create a file in it.

LISTING 5-7 Writing log files in the temporary folder

```
async void CreateLog()
{
    Windows.Storage.Storage tmpFolder =
        Windows.Storage.ApplicationData.Current.TemporaryFolder;

   Windows.Globalization.DateTimeFormatting.DateTimeFormatter formatter =
       new Windows.Globalization.DateTimeFormatting.DateTimeFormatter("longtime");

   StorageFile logFile = await tmpFolder
       .CreateFileAsync("log.txt", CreationCollisionOption.ReplaceExisting);

   await FileIO.WriteTextAsync(logFile, formatter.Format(DateTime.Now));
}
```

The code is similar to the code for accessing local storage. It creates a file in the temporary storage called log.txt using the *CreateFileAsync* method. Then it references the file in the *WriteTextAsync* method of the *FileIO* class (of the *Windows.Storage* namespace). The *CreationCollisionOption* can be *ReplaceExisting* to create a new file or *FailIfExist* to return an error if the file already exists; *OpenIfExists* to create a new file if it does not exist or open the existing one; and *GenerateUniqueName* to create a new file with an autogenerated number if a file with the same name already exists.

To read a value from a file, use the code shown in Listing 5-8.

LISTING 5-8 Reading a value from a temporary file

```
async void ReadLog()
{
   try
   {
      Windows.Storage.Storage tmpFolder =
          Windows.Storage.ApplicationData.Current.TemporaryFolder;
      StorageFile logFile = await tmpFolder.GetFileAsync("log.txt");
      String logDateTime = await FileIO.ReadTextAsync(logFile);
      // Perform some operation
   }
   catch (Exception)
   {
      // Problems reading the file
   }
}
```

Using temporary storage enables your app to be fast and fluid when the use of a network is limited. For example, a weather application can immediately display weather information that was cached to disk from a previous session. After the latest information is available, the app can update its content gracefully, ensuring that the user has content to view immediately upon launch while waiting for new content updates.

IndexedDB

IndexedDB technology enables a Windows Store app written in HTML and JavaScript to store Indexed Sequential Access Method (ISAM) files that can be read using sequential or indexed cursors. This storage has some limits:

- 250 MB per application
- 375 MB for all applications if the hard drive capacity is less than 30 gigabytes (GB)
- 4 percent of the total drive capacity for disks greater than 30 GB with a limit of 20 GB maximum
- Page's URL must be listed in the *ApplicationContentUriRules* of the application manifest, unless you set the *ms-enable-external-database-usage* meta tag in the application home (start) page

The following JavaScript code demonstrates how to access IndexedDB:

```
try
{
  var db = null;
  var sName = "CustomerDB";
  var nVersion = 1.2;
```

```
  if (window.indexedDB)
{
    var req = window.indexedDB.open( sName, nVersion );
    req.onsuccess = function(evt)
{
       db = evt.target.result;
       doSomething( db );
    }
    req.onerror = handleError( evt );
    req.onblocked = handleBlock( evt );
    req.onupgradeneeded = handleUpgrade( evt );
  }
}
catch( ex ) {
    handleException( ex );
}
```

Extensible Storage Engine (ESE)

This engine provides ISAM storage technology to save and access files. Access can be done using indexed or sequential navigation. ESE can be used in transactional code and provides a robust data consistency with transparent mechanisms to the developer. It also provides for fast data retrieval based on caching technology; it is considered a scalable technology for large files (over 40 GB).

The drawback of this technology is the fact that the API is provided only in C/C++. The call to this API must be wrapped in a WinRT component to be accessed by a Windows Store application written in a language different from C++.

HTML5 Web Storage

Any HTML and JavaScript application; or a Windows Store app using C++, C#, or Visual Basic using the *WebView* control can use HTML5 Web Storage.

These APIs are suitable for storing key-value pairs of strings using the web standard. The APIs are synchronous and enable the application to store 10 MB per single user. The storage is isolated on a per-user and per-app basis, so there is no conflict between apps, and it offers both local and session storage.

You can use the provided *localStorage* class to store data locally if you need lightweight storage in a web context and the Windows Runtime is not available. Be aware that if you use the *sessionStorage* class instead of the *localStorage* class, data exists only in memory and does not survive application termination. The *sessionStorage* can be used for transient data.

WinJS.Application.sessionState

As the name implies, this store is available for Windows Store apps using JavaScript in the local context, and is suitable to store transitory application state during suspension to resume them when the application resumes.

This store can contain JavaScript objects with application-defined properties and is automatically persisted during suspension to the local *ApplicationData* class. There is no size limit.

If you want to use a web standard to store settings that can be shared to non-Windows Store apps, using *WinJS.Application.sessionState* is one of the preferred methods.

WinJS.Application.local

The second storage option dedicated to Windows Store apps using JavaScript is a wrapper for the *ApplicationData* class that makes the use of the local context or web context transparent for the developer. In the local context, the wrapper uses local storage to persist data; in the web context, it falls back to in-memory.

WinJS.Application.roaming

The third storage option dedicated to Windows Store apps using JavaScript is a wrapper for the *ApplicationData* class that makes the use of roaming profiles or the web context transparent for the developer. In the local context, the wrapper uses the roaming storage to persist data; in the web context it falls back to in-memory.

Understanding Microsoft rules for using roaming profiles with Windows Store apps

Microsoft recommends some general guidelines for using roaming profiles with Windows Store apps. Use roaming settings for settings the user can reuse on a different device. Many users commonly work on two or more different devices, such as a desktop at work, a tablet at home, and/or a notebook while traveling. Using roaming settings enables the user to reuse all preferences on every device. When the user installs the application on a secondary device, all user preferences are already available in the roaming profile. Any changes to user settings are propagated to the roaming profile and applied to the settings on all devices.

These considerations apply to session and state information as well. Windows 8 roams all this data, enabling the user to continue to use a session that was closed or abandoned on one device when he uses a secondary device. For example, Vanni is playing his favorite game at home on his desktop. If he leaves the house, he can take his tablet and continue playing the game.

Using user data in a roaming profile is as easy as using local data, with just a few differences in class names. Use roaming data for anything that can be reused on a different device without modifications, such as color preferences, gaming scores, and state data. Do not use roaming profiles for settings that can differ from device to device. For example, be careful about display preferences. It is not practical to store the number of items to be displayed in a list because a desktop screen can easily represent 50 elements in an ordered list when a small tablet screen can become unreadable with just 20 elements.

To give you some examples, use the roaming profile for the following:

- Favorite football team (sports news app)
- First category to display in a page for a news magazine
- Color customization
- View preferences
- Ordering preferences

Some examples of state data include:

- The last page read for an e-book app
- The score for a game and relative level
- Text inserted in a text box

Do not use roaming data for information bound to a specific device, such as the following:

- The number of items to be displayed in a list
- History of visited pages
- Global printing preferences

Do not use roaming data for large amounts of data. Remember that the roaming profile has quota limits. The roaming profile does not work as a synchronization mechanism, either. Windows 8 transfers data from a device to the roaming profile using many different parameters to determine the best time to start a transfer. This is also true for downloading the profile or changing the profile from other devices. This method is not reliable for instantly passing information from one device to another.

Finally, to use roaming profiles, verify that all prerequisites are met:

- The user must have a Microsoft account.
- The user has used the Microsoft account to log on to the device.
- The network administrator has not switched off the roaming feature.
- The user has made the device "trusted."

Caching user data

The following points summarize the complete reference of where to store the different kinds of information and the pros and cons of each storage mechanism.

User data can be stored here:

- Libraries
- SkyDrive
- HTML5 API
- External service, third-party database, and cloud storage

Libraries

Every Windows Store app, whether written in C++, JavaScript, C#, or Visual Basic, can use libraries for storage. Even DirectX apps written in C++ can use libraries.

The *StorageFile* class and file pickers are the primary mechanisms for accessing user libraries. There are no size limitations and all the APIs are asynchronous.

File and folder pickers are useful when you want the user to participate in the selection of library items to manage or create.

Programmatic access requires a capability in the application manifest for each library the application needs to access. In the Downloads library, the code can write any file but can read only the file the app wrote. In practice, you cannot access files downloaded from other applications.

This storage is intended to survive application updates and installation because it represents user libraries, not application libraries. In practice, libraries exist by means of Windows 8. A library can also be used independently from the user that runs the application.

SkyDrive

All Windows Store apps, including DirectX apps written in C++, can use SkyDrive for storage. SkyDrive supports storage for user data in the cloud and can be shared across devices, applications, and even platforms.

SkyDrive is not a relational database; it is a shared storage service for items such as documents, photos, music, and videos. You can use SkyDrive storage to share content with other users and apply a size quota based on the level of the user account.

> ***MORE INFO*** **SKYDRIVE–SUPPORTED FILE FORMATS**
>
> **For a list of supported file formats, see the SkyDrive documentation available at *http://msdn.microsoft.com/en-us/library/live/hh826521.aspx*.**

You can use Live Connect Representational State Transfer (REST) APIs with JavaScript Object Notation (JSON) payloads to work with SkyDrive.

HTML5 File API

Like SkyDrive, all Windows Store apps can use HTML5 File API storage, including DirectX apps. HTML5 File APIs are web standard APIs for uploading and downloading files from a running application. Remember that, as you learned in Chapter 1, an application can be suspended if it's not in the foreground. For transfers that continue while the application is not in the foreground, use the *BackgroundTransfer* class.

HTML5 Application Cache API

A Windows Store app using JavaScript supports AppCache (formerly Application Cache API), as defined in the HTML5 specification, which enables pages to use offline content. AppCache enables web pages to save resources locally, including images, script libraries, style sheets, and other HTML-defined resources. In addition, AppCache enables URLs to be served from cached content using standard uniform resource identifier (URI) notation. By using AppCache to save resources locally, you improve web page performance by reducing the number of requests made to the Internet.

External service, server application, third-party database, and cloud storage

Windows 8 does not provide a native local database for Windows Store apps or a way to interact with data access libraries for a database. You cannot access SQL Azure directly, nor can you access SQL Server or SQL Express locally. There are no relational database APIs in the Windows Runtime.

To overcome this limitation, you can store and access data locally using a third-party solution or you can rely on web services to interact with a service-oriented architecture (SOA)/REST back end. For example, a Windows Communication Foundation (WCF) service can be hosted in the Microsoft Windows Azure platform to bridge an SQL Azure database from Windows Store apps.

If the application uses some form of web service or website, the app can use other ways to store data. For example, if the application makes HTTP calls to a website or web application, it can use the standard web cookie mechanism to share data with each request to the server. Applications written in JavaScript for both web and local context can use cookies directly; applications written in C++, C#, and Microsoft Visual Basic can leverage cookies via the *WebView* control. Any other apps can use cookies via the *IXMLHTTPRequest2* interface.

Cookies are a web standard and well-known technology but have a 4 KB limit per cookie. Cookies in the local context to the web via *XMLHttpRequest* (XHR) are subject to web cross-domain rules.

If a JavaScript-based application reads data from the web, you can leverage the HTML5 AppCache to make data available offline. This is another web standard technique that caches server response content locally and enables prefetching of web-based markup, scripts, CSS, and resources in general that do not contain code.

Any Windows Store app can consume web services using SOAP or REST and become the new user interface for every kind of existing or new solutions.

Thought experiment

Storing user settings

In this thought experiment, apply what you've learned about this objective. You can find answers to these questions in the "Answers" section at the end of this chapter.

Your application needs to store some user settings as the number of items to display in a page. Which kind of storage do you plan to use and why?

Objective summary

- The most important thing to remember is the difference between application data and user data.
- Application data is related to the application and can be stored in local, roaming, or temporary storage using different techniques.
- Use the *LocalSettings* property of the *ApplicationDataContainer* class to store data locally.
- Use the *RoamingSettings* property of the *ApplicationDataContainer* class to store data in the user roaming profile. The APIs hide the complexity of storing data remotely.
- User data has a meaning outside the application: Orders, customers and so on are examples of user data.
- User data is normally stored in outside stores such as databases or via web services.

Objective review

Answer the following questions to test your knowledge of the information in this objective. You can find the answers to these questions and explanations of why each answer choice is correct or incorrect in the "Answers" section at the end of this chapter.

1. Which data types are considered application data? (Choose all that apply.)
   - **A.** User preferences
   - **B.** Application entities such as invoices
   - **C.** All data related to the application itself, such as users and groups
   - **D.** Reference content
2. How can you store application data? (Choose all that apply.)
   - **A.** Via the *ApplicationDataContainer.LocalSettings* property.
   - **B.** Via the *ApplicationDataContainer.RoamingSettings* property.
   - **C.** Via the *ApplicationDataCreateDisposition* enumeration.
   - **D.** There are no classes related to the application data type.

3. Is it possible to store a file locally?
   A. No, Windows Store apps cannot access the file system.
   B. No, Windows Store apps can use only web services to store data.
   C. Yes, you can use the *ApplicationData* class properties to cache data locally.
   D. No, you can only save settings locally.

Objective 5.2: Save and retrieve files from the file system

As you learned in the previous section, Windows 8 applications have various options for storing data and each one has its pros and cons. The right place to store information or to cache it depends on the application and the scenario in which the user works. You can save application data in local, roaming, or temporary storage in the form of application settings dictionary or in files. Storing information in files enables you to organize the data as you want: You can represent complex structures or hierarchical data using XML, for example, or you can store a comma separated value (.csv) file with log information.

This section is dedicated to the different ways the application can leverage WinRT classes to store information in files and folders. You can access the file system to save and retrieve information by using a file picker, by accessing files programmatically, or by accessing the HomeGroup content.

This objective covers how to:

- Handle file streams
- Save and retrieve files by using *StorageFile* and *StorageFolder* classes
- Set file extensions and associations
- Save and retrieve files by using the file picker classes
- Compress files to save space
- Access libraries, including pictures, documents, and videos

Using file pickers to save and retrieve files

Accessing files through pickers enables the user to choose files and folders explicitly during the process. Simply put, the code asks the user to choose a file or a folder to work on, giving control to the default Windows 8 user interface. When the user chooses a file or folder, the Windows Runtime gives control to the calling code to perform one or more operations on the item chosen by the user. In practice, the developer can use an easy and standard way to enable the user to choose the location to perform the I/O operation the code will work with.

Many apps work with individual files or folders (or small lists of files in a folder), so file pickers are often the best choice for providing a unified interface for users to work with file system resources. By using pickers, you can also minimize the application's capability declarations and simplify the process to certify your application for the Windows Store. For example, Figure 5-1 shows a file picker that enables the user to choose a photo from his Pictures library. The user can select images, sort them, navigate back, and open one of them.

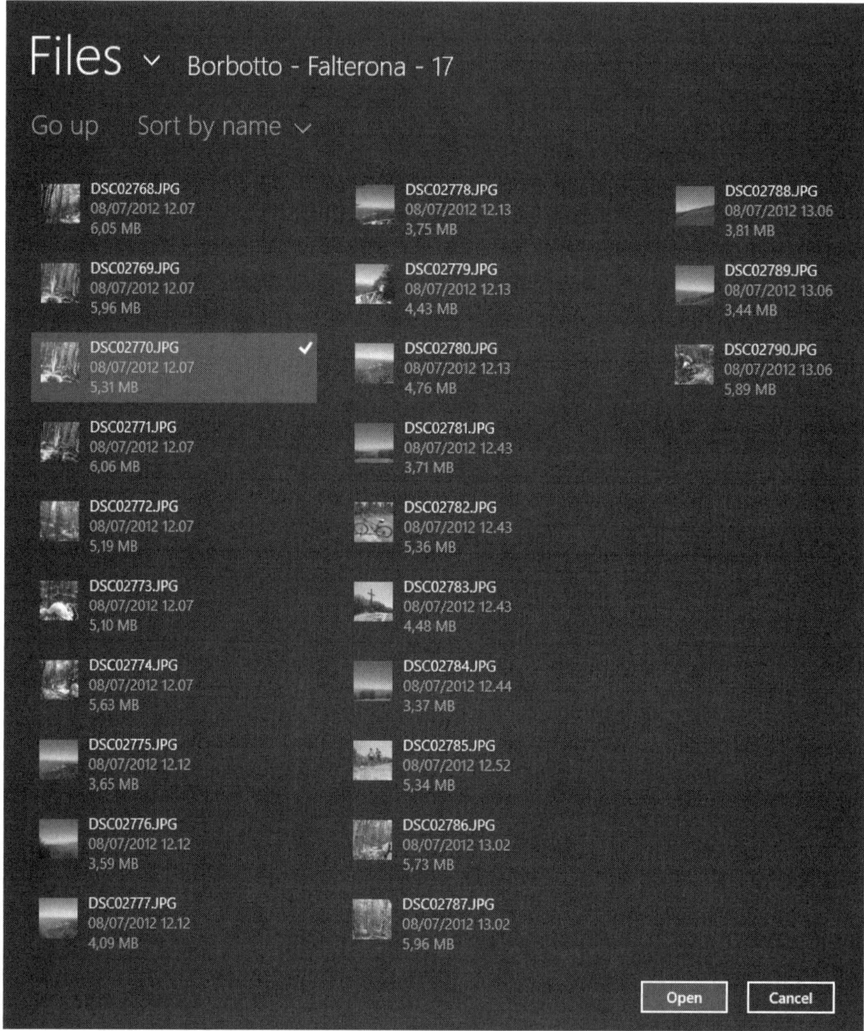

FIGURE 5-1 A file picker enables a user to choose files from libraries

You can use the *FileOpenPicker* class to gain access to files. The methods to work with resources are asynchronous and follow the *async/await* pattern.

The file picker has different areas on the screen:

- Upper left, which is the current location
- Below upper left, which is the command zone with the *Up* command that goes to the previous folder and the type of sorting to choose how to sort the images
- Drop-down list of locations the user can use to browse for files
- An area at the center to select one file or multiple files

The drop-down list also presents some system locations, such as the Music library or the Downloads folder.

The number of available locations list depends on the user profile. For example, if the user has a SkyDrive account, the picker shows the SkyDrive of the user as a possible selection for the libraries. If the user-installed applications registered themselves as pickers (through the Picker contract), they are visible in the drop-down list. Figure 5-2 shows that the user can choose the Bing application in the provided drop-down list and then a photo from a standard picker.

FIGURE 5-2 Example of a file picker

To activate the file picker, you can use a new instance of the *FileOpenPicker* class, asking it to select a single file or multiple files and letting the picker know which kind of files to select. For example, in the following code, the main page contains a simple button that fires the *ChooseFile_Click* event handler:

Sample of XAML code

```
<Page
    x:Class="Pickers.MainPage"
    xmlns="http://schemas.microsoft.com/winfx/2006/xaml/presentation"
    xmlns:x="http://schemas.microsoft.com/winfx/2006/xaml"
    xmlns:local="using:Pickers"
    xmlns:d="http://schemas.microsoft.com/expression/blend/2008"
    xmlns:mc="http://schemas.openxmlformats.org/markup-compatibility/2006"
    mc:Ignorable="d">
```

```
    <Grid Background="{StaticResource ApplicationPageBackgroundThemeBrush}">
        <Button Content="Choose File" Click="ChooseFile_Click" />
    </Grid>
</Page>
```

The code-behind for the main page contains the reference to the *Windows.Storage.Pickers* namespace that contains all the pickers related to the storage and the simplest code to open the file picker on JPEG images. See the C# code in Listing 5-9.

LISTING 5-9 Using the *FilePicker* class

```
using System;
using System.Collections.Generic;
using System.IO;
using System.Linq;
using Windows.Foundation;
using Windows.Foundation.Collections;
using Windows.Storage.Pickers;
using Windows.UI.Xaml;
using Windows.UI.Xaml.Controls;
using Windows.UI.Xaml.Controls.Primitives;
using Windows.UI.Xaml.Data;
using Windows.UI.Xaml.Input;
using Windows.UI.Xaml.Media;
using Windows.UI.Xaml.Navigation;

// The Blank Page item template is documented at
     http://go.microsoft.com/fwlink/?LinkId=234238

namespace Pickers
{
    /// <summary>
    /// An empty page that can be used on its own or navigated to within a Frame.
    /// </summary>
    public sealed partial class MainPage : Page
    {
        public MainPage()
        {
            this.InitializeComponent();
        }

        /// <summary>
        /// Invoked when this page is about to be displayed in a Frame.
        /// </summary>
        /// <param name="e">Event data that describes how this page was reached.  The
        ///   Parameter
        /// property is typically used to configure the page.</param>
        private async void ChooseFile_Click(object sender, RoutedEventArgs e)
        {
            var picker = new FileOpenPicker();
            picker.FileTypeFilter.Add(".jpg");
            var file = await picker.PickSingleFileAsync();
        }
    }
}
```

The *FileTypeFilter* collection cannot be empty, so you have to explicitly set file extensions (each one starting with a period).

To clear the filter or to add every file extension, use the following code:

```
picker.FileTypeFilter.Clear();
picker.FileTypeFilter.Add("*");
```

The *PickSingleFileAsync* follows the async pattern. It is awaitable, so you can manage user selection waiting without blocking the user interface thread.

The result can be null if the user does not select any file or it can be the file in the form of a *StorageFile* class of the *Windows.Storage* namespace.

There are no differences between choosing a file from the file system or from other applications: They are always returned as *StorageFile* objects.

The complete flow is represented by Figure 5-3. The application calls the file picker to enable the user to pick a file or a list of files to open. The system invokes the picker that will display the user interface and present all the available system folders and applications able to provide files. If the user chooses a file, the picker returns the file immediately. If the user selects a file picker application, the system activates the application that will provide its own user interface in the form of a page that the picker presents to select the file.

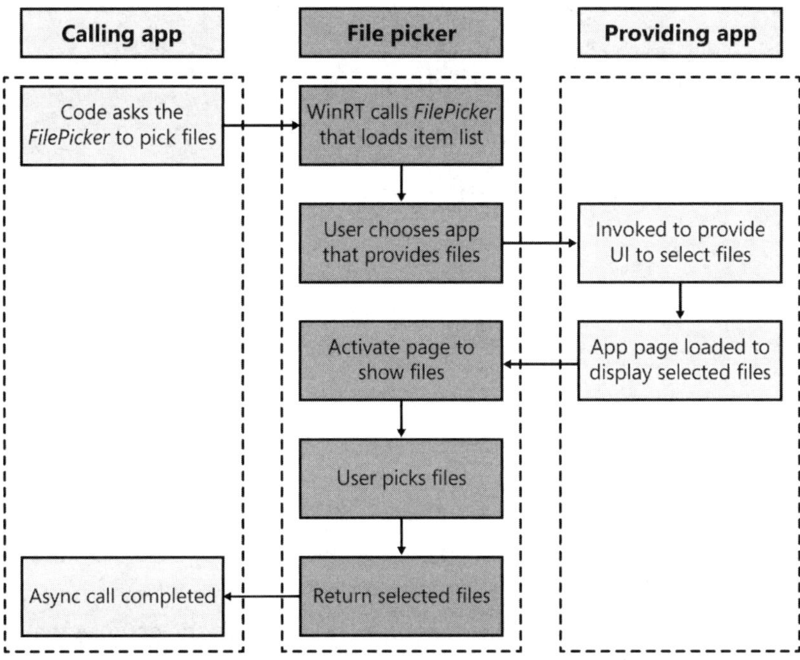

FIGURE 5-3 File pickers flow and contracts

The code can ask the *FileOpenPicker* to select different file types and provide a starting point to the user as well as the type of suggested view. The following code assumes a label (a *TextBlock* control) on the page called ChosenFile:

```
var picker = new FileOpenPicker();
picker.ViewMode = PickerViewMode.Thumbnail;
picker.SuggestedStartLocation = PickerLocationId.PicturesLibrary;
picker.FileTypeFilter.Add(".jpg");
picker.FileTypeFilter.Add(".jpeg");
picker.FileTypeFilter.Add(".png");

StorageFile file = await picker.PickSingleFileAsync();
if (file != null)
{
    ChosenFile.Text = "Picked file: " + file.Name;
}
else
{
    ChosenFile.Text = "Operation cancelled by the user.";
}
```

The code can also request multiple files obtaining an *IReadOnlyCollection<T>* where *T* is a *Windows.Storage.StorageFile* class:

```
private async void ChooseFile_Click(object sender, RoutedEventArgs e)
{
    var picker = new FileOpenPicker();
    picker.FileTypeFilter.Add(".jpg");

    try
    {
        var files = await picker.PickMultipleFilesAsync();
        foreach (var file in files)
        {

        }
    }
    catch (Exception ex)
    {
        new MessageDialog("Cannot open Picker").ShowAsync();
    }
}
```

Use the *FolderPicker* to gain access to folders.

If you try to show a file or folder picker when the application is snapped, the picker does not display, and the system throws an exception that you can catch to inform the user.

The result is shown in Figure 5-4, in which the Learn with Wild Animals app occupies the bigger portion of the screen and the sample picker app appears in the snapped view.

FIGURE 5-4 Snapped application displaying the error during the exception for trying to open the file picker in snapped view

Although this method works well from a developer's perspective, it is better to inform the user before trying to open the picker or unsnapping the application from code before opening the picker.

For example, you can use the following code to try to unsnap the application automatically:

```
bool unsnapped = ((ApplicationView.Value != ApplicationViewState.Snapped) ||
    ApplicationView.TryUnsnap());

if (!unsnapped)
{
    // Notify we are snapped and we cannot unsnap automatically
}
```

You can also save files using pickers. The first thing to do is define and set the *FileSavePicker* instance:

```
FileSavePicker savePicker = new FileSavePicker();
savePicker.SuggestedStartLocation = PickerLocationId.DocumentsLibrary;
savePicker.FileTypeChoices.Add("Text", new List<string>() { ".txt" });
savePicker.SuggestedFileName = "DevLeap Description";
```

Then you can call the *PickSaveFileAsync* method to retrieve the file in which the user wants to save the content:

```
StorageFile file = await savePicker.PickSaveFileAsync();
```

If the user chooses a file, the resulting variable *file* is not null. Before calling the *WriteTextAsync* method of the *FileIO* class, remember to prevent updates to the remote version of the file until the change is completed. The *CachedFileManager* class is very useful to perform this kind of lock:

```
if (file != null)
{
    CachedFileManager.DeferUpdates(file);
    await FileIO.WriteTextAsync(file, file.Name);
    FileUpdateStatus status = await CachedFileManager.CompleteUpdatesAsync(file);
}
```

The code can also access HomeGroup content using the *SuggestedStartLocation* property:

```
Windows.Storage.Pickers.FileOpenPicker picker =
    new Windows.Storage.Pickers.FileOpenPicker();
picker.ViewMode = Windows.Storage.Pickers.PickerViewMode.Thumbnail;
picker.SuggestedStartLocation = Windows.Storage.Pickers.PickerLocationId.HomeGroup;
picker.FileTypeFilter.Clear();
picker.FileTypeFilter.Add("*");
```

Accessing files and data programmatically

Application code can access files and folders in locations such as libraries, devices, and network paths; and can query the file system for files and folders matching the search expression. Before using the code, a Windows Store app must explicitly set the permission to use user libraries in the application manifest. Figure 5-5 shows the application manifest with all the user libraries selected in the capability set.

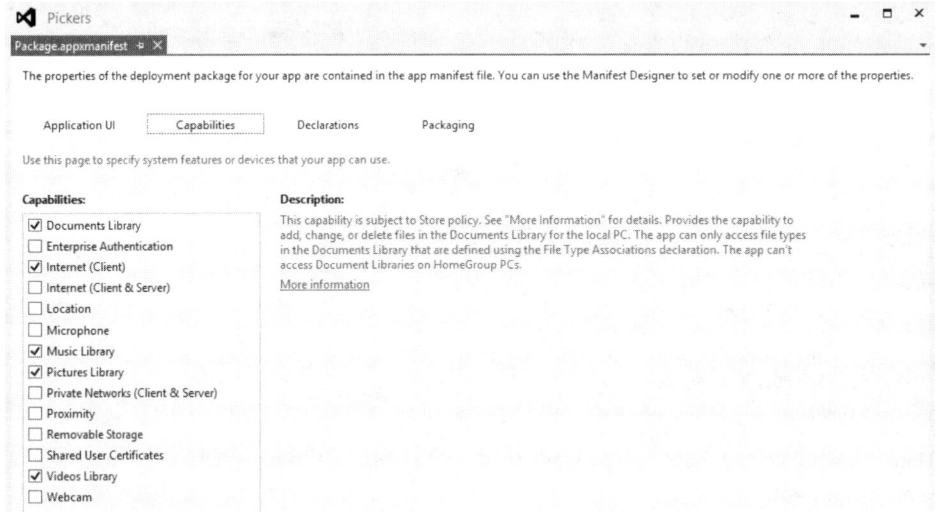

FIGURE 5-5 Application manifest file- and folder-related capabilities

After setting the capabilities (in the Pictures library for example), the code can call the *StorageFolder* class method to work with files. For example, the following code defines a *ListBox* control to show the files:

Sample of XAML code

```
<Page
    x:Class="Pickers.MainPage"
    xmlns="http://schemas.microsoft.com/winfx/2006/xaml/presentation"
    xmlns:x="http://schemas.microsoft.com/winfx/2006/xaml"
    xmlns:local="using:Pickers"
    xmlns:d="http://schemas.microsoft.com/expression/blend/2008"
    xmlns:mc="http://schemas.openxmlformats.org/markup-compatibility/2006"
    mc:Ignorable="d">

    <Grid Background="{StaticResource ApplicationPageBackgroundThemeBrush}">
        <StackPanel>
            <Button Content="Choose File" Click="ChooseFile_Click" />
            <Button Content="List Files" Click="ListFiles_Click" />
            <ListBox x:Name="files" DisplayMemberPath="Name" />
        </StackPanel>
    </Grid>
</Page>
```

The code for the event handler can be similar to the one presented in the following code excerpt:

Sample of C# code

```
private async void ListFiles_Click(object sender, RoutedEventArgs e)
{
    StorageFolder picturesFolder = KnownFolders.PicturesLibrary;

    IReadOnlyList<StorageFile> fileList =
        await picturesFolder.GetFilesAsync();

    files.ItemsSource = fileList;
}
```

You can use the *GetItemsAsync* to retrieve the list of both files and folders.

To query the system for particular files and group them by one of their properties (for example, the year of the shot for a picture), use the *CreateFolderQuery* method of the *StorageFolder* class:

```
StorageFolder picturesFolder = KnownFolders.PicturesLibrary;

StorageFolderQueryResult queryResult =
    picturesFolder.CreateFolderQuery(CommonFolderQuery.GroupByYear);

IReadOnlyList<StorageFolder> folderList =
    await queryResult.GetFoldersAsync();
```

Working with folders, files, and streams

After obtaining a reference to the file or folder, you can perform read and write operations on it. Remember that you need to define the explained capabilities to perform operations on system folders. For example, you can create a file in a folder using the following code:

```
var folder = KnownFolders.DocumentsLibrary;
var logFile = await storageFolder.CreateFileAsync("log.txt");
```

To write some text to the file, use the *WriteTextAsync* method, as in the following code sample:

```
await Windows.Storage.FileIO.WriteTextAsync(logFile, "Operation Logged");
```

To write bytes to a file, you can use the following code:

```
var buffer = Windows.Security.Cryptography.CryptographicBuffer
    .ConvertStringToBinary(
        "DevLeap is a group of professionals . . .",
        Windows.Security.Cryptography.BinaryStringEncoding.Utf8);

var folder = KnownFolders.DocumentsLibrary;
var file = await storageFolder.CreateFileAsync("document.txt");
await Windows.Storage.FileIO.WriteBufferAsync(file, buffer);
```

The code converts the string "DevLeap is a group of professionals . . ." to a binary object and then writes the obtained buffer to the file named document.txt in the *DocumentsLibrary* user folder.

You can also use streams to write text to a file, as follows:

```
var folder = KnownFolders.DocumentsLibrary;
var file = await storageFolder.CreateFileAsync("document.txt");
var stream = await file.OpenAsync(Windows.Storage.FileAccessMode.ReadWrite);

using (var outputStream = stream.GetOutputStreamAt(0))
{
    DataWriter dataWriter = new DataWriter(outputStream);
    dataWriter.WriteString("DevLeap is a group of professionals . . .");
    await dataWriter.StoreAsync();
    await outputStream.FlushAsync();
}
```

The code opens a file in *ReadWrite* mode, builds the output stream using the *GetOutput-StreamAt* method, and then uses the *DataWriter* class to write a string on the stream.

Remember to call *StoreAsync* and *FlushAsync* to save to the file and close the stream. Do not forget to call the *Dispose* method at the end of the work (in the samples in this chapter, the *using* statement performs the disposing).

To read some data from a file, the methods are straightforward:

```
var folder = KnownFolders.DocumentsLibrary;
var file = await folder.GetFileAsync("document.txt");
string text = await Windows.Storage.FileIO.ReadTextAsync(file);
```

To read bytes from a file, you can use the *ReadBufferAsync* method:

```
var folder = KnownFolders.DocumentsLibrary;
var file = await folder.GetFileAsync("document.txt");

var buffer = await Windows.Storage.FileIO.ReadBufferAsync(file);
DataReader dataReader = Windows.Storage.Streams.DataReader.FromBuffer(buffer);

string text = dataReader.ReadString(buffer.Length);
```

To read a stream from a file, use the following code:

```
var folder = KnownFolders.DocumentsLibrary;
var file = await folder.GetFileAsync("document.txt");
var stream = await file.OpenAsync(Windows.Storage.FileAccessMode.ReadWrite);
var size = stream.Size;

using (var inputStream = stream.GetInputStreamAt(0))
{
    DataReader dataReader = new DataReader(inputStream);
    uint numBytesLoaded = await dataReader.LoadAsync((uint)size);
    string text = dataReader.ReadString(numBytesLoaded);
}
```

Setting file extensions and associations

Windows enables an app to register to become the default handler for a certain file type. If the user chooses your app as the default handler for a certain file type, your app is activated every time that type of file is launched.

You should register for a file type only if you expect to handle all file launches for that type of file. If your app needs to use the file type only internally, you do not need to register to be the default handler. If you choose to register for a file type, it is important that you provide the user with the functionality that is expected when your app is activated for that file type. For example, a picture viewer app can register to display a .jpg file.

The first thing to do is declare the functionality in the application manifest, as shown in Figure 5-6.

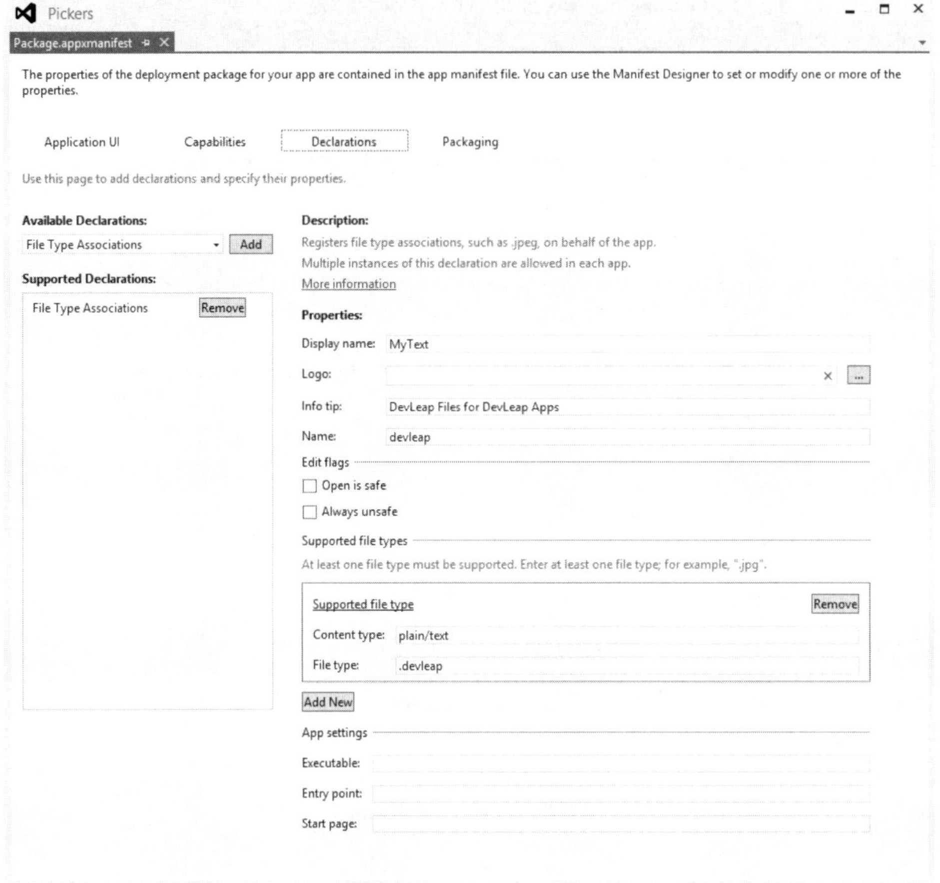

FIGURE 5-6 Application manifest with declarations for file associations and extensions

The corresponding XML settings are displayed in Listing 5-10.

LISTING 5-10 Application manifest with declarations for file associations and extensions

```
<?xml version="1.0" encoding="utf-8"?>
<Package xmlns="http://schemas.microsoft.com/appx/2010/manifest">
  <Identity Name="f512a0c2-b668-4a46-a026-b9090e60717b" Publisher="CN=Roberto"
      Version="1.0.0.0" />
  <Properties>
    <DisplayName>Pickers</DisplayName>
    <PublisherDisplayName>Roberto</PublisherDisplayName>
    <Logo>Assets\StoreLogo.png</Logo>
  </Properties>
  <Prerequisites>
    <OSMinVersion>6.2.1</OSMinVersion>
    <OSMaxVersionTested>6.2.1</OSMaxVersionTested>
  </Prerequisites>
```

```xml
  <Resources>
    <Resource Language="x-generate" />
  </Resources>
  <Applications>
    <Application Id="App" Executable="$targetnametoken$.exe" EntryPoint="Pickers.App">
      <VisualElements DisplayName="Pickers" Logo="Assets\Logo.png"
          SmallLogo="Assets\SmallLogo.png" Description="Pickers" ForegroundText="light"
          BackgroundColor="#464646">
        <DefaultTile ShowName="allLogos" />
        <SplashScreen Image="Assets\SplashScreen.png" />
      </VisualElements>
      <Extensions>
        <Extension Category="windows.fileTypeAssociation">
          <FileTypeAssociation Name="devleap">
            <DisplayName>MyText</DisplayName>
            <InfoTip>DevLeap Files for DevLeap Apps</InfoTip>
            <SupportedFileTypes>
              <FileType ContentType="plain/text">.devleap</FileType>
            </SupportedFileTypes>
          </FileTypeAssociation>
        </Extension>
      </Extensions>
    </Application>
  </Applications>
  <Capabilities>
    <Capability Name="documentsLibrary" />
    <Capability Name="picturesLibrary" />
    <Capability Name="videosLibrary" />
    <Capability Name="internetClient" />
  </Capabilities>
</Package>
```

You need to provide the icon the system will display on these particular custom files. To do this, add the following images to the application package. The icons must match the look of the app tile logo:

- Icon.targetsize-16.png
- Icon.targetsize-32.png
- Icon.targetsize-48.png
- Icon.targetsize-256.png
- smallTile-targetsize-16.png
- smallTile-targetsize-32.png
- smallTile-targetsize-48.png
- smallTile-targetsize-256.png

NOTE **TESTING IMAGES**

Test all the images on a white background.

Implement the *OnFileActivated* method of the application overriding the base class method, as in the following code:

Sample of C# code

```
protected override void OnFileActivated(FileActivatedEventArgs args)
{
    foreach (var file in args.Files)
    {
    }
}
```

Compressing files to save space

The *System.IO.Compression.FileSystem* assembly cannot be referenced from a Windows Store app. You cannot compress and decompress files using the classic *ZipArchive* class. To save disk space, you can compress and decompress files by using the *GZipStream* class or the *DeflateStream* class. You can also leverage the *Compressor* and *Decompressor* classes.

You can use the following method to build your own compression and decompression utility:

```
public async void Compress(StorageFile fileToCompress)
{
    using (var originalFileStream = await fileToCompress.OpenReadAsync())
    {
        var compressedFileStream = await
            KnownFolders.DocumentsLibrary.CreateFileAsync(fileToCompress.Name + ".gz");

        using (var compressedOutput = await
            compressedFileStream.OpenAsync(FileAccessMode.ReadWrite))
        {
            using (var compressor = new
                Windows.Storage.Compression.Compressor
                    (compressedOutput.GetOutputStreamAt(0)))
            {
                var bytesCompressed = await Windows.Storage.Streams.RandomAccessStream.
                    CopyAsync(originalFileStream, compressor);
                var   finished = await compressor.FinishAsync();
            }
        }
    }
}

public async void Decompress(StorageFile fileToDecompress)
{
    using (var compressedFileStream = await
        fileToDecompress.OpenSequentialReadAsync())
    {
        var decompresedFileStream = await
            KnownFolders.DocumentsLibrary.
                CreateFileAsync(fileToDecompress.Name + ".original");
```

```
            using (var decompressedOutput = await
                decompresedFileStream.OpenAsync(FileAccessMode.ReadWrite))
            {
                using (var decompressor = new
                    Windows.Storage.Compression.Decompressor(compressedFileStream))
                {
                    var bytesDecompressed = await
                        Windows.Storage.Streams.RandomAccessStream.
                            CopyAsync(decompressor, decompressedOutput);
                 }
            }
        }
    }
```

Thought experiment

Working with files

In this thought experiment, apply what you've learned about this objective. You can find answers to these questions in the "Answers" section at the end of this chapter.

Your application needs to store a log file locally to store exception information. Which kind of data access technique do you plan to use and why?

Objective summary

- Accessing files through pickers enables the user to choose files and folders explicitly during the process. The contract regulates data interchange from app to app.
- You can access files and folders programmatically in locations such as libraries, devices, and network paths.
- The code can query the file system for files and folders matching a search expression.
- After obtaining a reference to a file or folder, you can perform read and write operations on it as a stream.
- Windows enables an app to register to become the default handler for a certain file type.

Objective review

Answer the following questions to test your knowledge of the information in this objective. You can find the answers to these questions and explanations of why each answer choice is correct or incorrect in the "Answers" section at the end of this chapter.

1. Which type of storage can you access with file pickers? (Choose all that apply.)
   - **A.** Local storage
   - **B.** Cloud storage on SkyDrive
   - **C.** Network storage
   - **D.** Windows Azure storage account
2. Is it possible to set an application as a file handler?
   - **A.** Yes, by declaring it in the application manifest.
   - **B.** Yes, but only for apps written in C# or /VB.
   - **C.** Yes, but only for apps written in C++.
   - **D.** No, it is not possible.
3. Which class do you use to read a file programmatically?
   - **A.** *FileOpenPicker*
   - **B.** *StorageFolder*
   - **C.** *StorageFile*
   - **D.** *ApplicationData*

Objective 5.3: Secure app data

Communications over public networks, such as the Internet, can be easily intercepted by unauthorized third parties who might be interested in reading or tampering with the content transmitted through the communication channel. You can use cryptography to protect data and communications over otherwise unsafe channels. In this objective, you learn about the most fundamental types and methods that help secure your Windows Store app.

> ***NOTE*** **.NET FRAMEWORK SECURITY**
>
> **Discussing security, cryptography, or certificate management in the .NET Framework in detail is beyond the scope of this objective. The purpose of this objective is to illustrate the most important classes and methods you can leverage in a Windows Store app to secure data and communications.**

This objective covers how to:

- Encrypt data by using the *Windows.Security.Cryptography* namespaces
- Enroll and request certificates
- Encrypt data by using certificates

Introducing the *Windows.Security.Cryptography* namespaces

The *Windows.Security.Cryptography* namespaces include types and methods that can be used for secure encoding and decoding of data, hashing, random numbers generation, conversions between byte arrays and buffers, and message authentication. These new libraries replace the .NET libraries included under the *System.Security.Cryptography* namespace, which performs the same operations in the classic .NET world.

Cryptography is used to achieve the following goals:

- **Authentication** Cryptography can be used to ensure that the communication actually originates from a certain source.
- **Confidentiality** Cryptography helps prevent data from being read by unauthorized third parties; confidentiality is ensured by encryption algorithms.
- **Data integrity** Cryptography protects data from being tampered with by unauthorized parties.
- **Nonrepudiation** As a consequence of authentication, confidentiality, and integrity, cryptography also prevents other parties from repudiating their own messages after they have been sent.

It is worth noting that the Bureau of Industry and Security in the United States Department of Commerce regulates the export of technology that uses certain types of encryption. All apps listed in the Windows Store must comply with these laws and regulations because the app files can be stored in the United States.

READERAID **EXPORT RESTRICTIONS**

Further information on export restrictions on cryptography can be found at *http://msdn.microsoft.com/en-us/library/windows/apps/hh694069.aspx*.

Using hash algorithms

According to the Microsoft official documentation definition, "Hash algorithms transform binary values of arbitrary length to smaller binary values of a fixed length, known as hash values. A hash value is a numerical representation of a piece of data."

In other words, when you apply a hash algorithm to a plain text message, what you get is a binary code known as a *message digest*, or just *digest*, representing the "fingerprint" that identifies the message content.

In fact, even the slightest change in the content of the message produces a different hash code. For example, if a single bit of a message is changed, a strong hash function might produce an output that differs by 50 percent. For this reason, hash algorithms can help protect message integrity. To ensure that a certain message has not been tampered with, you can send a message along with its corresponding hash code. The receiver applies the same algorithm used by the sender to the message to produce a new hash code and then compares the two hash codes to verify the integrity of the message.

> ***NOTE*** **PLAIN TEXT**
>
> **Hash algorithms do not prevent someone from reading hashed content because messages are transmitted in plain text. Full security typically requires also digital signatures and encryption.**

Given the digest, you cannot go back to the original document. Hash algorithms are one-way algorithms.

Besides message authentication, cryptographic hash algorithms have many applications, such as indexing data in hash tables, uniquely identifying data, and detecting data corruption.

To perform hash operations, you can leverage the *HashAlgorithmProvider* class, as shown in Listing 5-11.

LISTING 5-11 Hashing a plain text message through the *HashAlgorithmProvider* class

```
public void HashMessage_Click(object sender, RoutedEventArgs args)
{
    String message = "Plain text message to hash";
    String hashAlgorithmName = HashAlgorithmNames.Sha512;
    IBuffer binaryMessage = CryptographicBuffer
        .ConvertStringToBinary(message, BinaryStringEncoding.Utf8);

    HashAlgorithmProvider hashProvider =
        HashAlgorithmProvider.OpenAlgorithm(hashAlgorithmName);

    IBuffer hashedMessage = hashProvider.HashData(binaryMessage);
```

```
    if (hashedMessage.Length != hashProvider.HashLength)
    {
        HashedMessageTextBlock.Text = "There was an error creating the hash";
    }
    HashedMessageTextBlock.Text =
        CryptographicBuffer.EncodeToBase64String(hashedMessage);
}
```

First, convert the original text message in its binary representation by calling the *ConvertStringToBinary* method, which is one of several methods provided by the *CryptographicBuffer* class to perform conversions between the base types involved in cryptographic operations (such as the *EncodeToBase64String/DecodeToBase64String* and the *EncodeToHexString/DecodeToHexString* methods). Second, choose the hash algorithm to use to produce the hash code. You can enumerate all the supported hash algorithms by making use of the *HashAlgorithmNames* static class, as shown in Listing 5-11.

> ***NOTE* WINRT-SUPPORTED HASH ALGORITHMS**
>
> **The first version of the Windows Runtime supports the MD5, SHA1, SHA256, SHA384, and SHA512 hash algorithms.**

The next step is to get a reference to the hash algorithm provider, which encapsulates all the details of the inner mechanisms, by calling the *OpenAlgorithm* method and passing the name of the chosen algorithm (SHA512, in our sample). After you obtain the reference, you can hash the message simply by invoking the *HashData* method. The subsequent *if* statement checks that the length of the produced hash matches the length specified for the algorithm used for hashing (indicated by the *HashLength* property of the *HashAlgorithmProvider* instance).

To test this function, you can add the XAML controls shown in bold in Listing 5-12 within the default *Grid* control of the MainPage.xaml.

LISTING 5-12 The XAML definition of the MainPage.xaml file

```
<Page
    x:Class="CryptoSample.MainPage"
    xmlns="http://schemas.microsoft.com/winfx/2006/xaml/presentation"
    xmlns:x="http://schemas.microsoft.com/winfx/2006/xaml"
    xmlns:local="using:CryptoSample"
    xmlns:d="http://schemas.microsoft.com/expression/blend/2008"
    xmlns:mc="http://schemas.openxmlformats.org/markup-compatibility/2006"
    mc:Ignorable="d">

    <Grid Background="{StaticResource ApplicationPageBackgroundThemeBrush}">
        <StackPanel>
            <StackPanel Orientation="Horizontal">
                <Button Width="Auto"
                        Height="40"
                        Content="Hash message"
```

```
                    VerticalAlignment="Center"
                    FontSize="18"
                    Margin="5"
                    Click="HashMessage_Click" />
                <TextBlock x:Name="HashedMessageTextBlock"
                    Width="Auto"
                    Height="40"
                    Margin="5"
                    FontSize="18" />
            </StackPanel>
        </StackPanel>
    </Grid>
</Page>
```

Figure 5-7 shows the result of the hashing operation.

FIGURE 5-7 The generated hash code

To check whether two hash codes are the same (and therefore the message content has not been tampered with), you can leverage the *Compare* method exposed by the *CrytographicBuffer* class, which returns *true* when the two compared hashes match. The C# code in Listing 5-13 shows how to check hash codes (changes are in bold).

LISTING 5-13 Checking whether two hash codes match

```
public void HashMessage_Click(object sender, RoutedEventArgs args)
{
    (code omitted)

    CryptographicHash reusableHash = hashProvider.CreateHash();
    reusableHash.Append(binaryMessage);

    IBuffer otherMessage = reusableHash.GetValueAndReset();

    if (!CryptographicBuffer.Compare(hashedMessage, otherMessage))
    {
        HashedMessageTextBlock.Text +=
            "CryptographicHash failed to generate the same hash data!\n";

        return;
    }
    HashedMessageTextBlock.Text =
        CryptographicBuffer.EncodeToBase64String(hashedMessage);
}
```

The *CreateHash* method of the *HashAlgorithmProvider* instance enables creating a reusable hash container to hash the data through multiple calls, represented by the *CryptographicHash* class. You can pass the content that needs to be hashed via a call to the *Append* method, which accepts an *IBuffer* object as parameter and returns an instance of the

CryptographicHash class. The hash code can be then retrieved through the *GetValueAndReset* method, which also cleans the *CryptographicHash* object after having retrieved the hash code. At this point, you can compare the two hash codes to check whether they match.

Generating random numbers and data

Random number generation represents an important step in many cryptographic operations, such as in the generation of cryptographic keys or passwords. The *CryptographicBuffer* class enables you to generate random numbers easily by using the *GenerateRandomNumber* method. The following code excerpt shows an example of its usage:

```
private void GenerateRandomNumber_Click(object sender, RoutedEventArgs e)
{
    RandomNumberTextBlock.Text = CryptographicBuffer.GenerateRandomNumber().ToString();
}
```

The *GenerateRandomNumber* method returns a random 32-bit unsigned integer. (Remember, though, that this type is not compliant with the Common Language Specification.) You can use the unsigned integer to perform further cryptographic operations. (You will see an example of its usage in the "Encrypting messages with MAC algorithms" section, later in the chapter.)

Besides random numbers generation, the *CryptographicBuffer* class also provides a *GenerateRandom* method that, as its name suggests, can be used to generate a buffer of random data. In this case, the only thing you have to provide is the length of the buffer in bytes, as shown in the following code snippet:

```
private void GenerateRandomData_Click(object sender, RoutedEventArgs e)
{
    UInt32 length = 32;

    IBuffer rndData = CryptographicBuffer.GenerateRandom(length);

    RandomDataTextBlock.Text = CryptographicBuffer.EncodeToHexString(rndData);
}
```

To test these two methods, just add the lines of code shown in bold in Listing 5-14 to the code illustrated in Listing 5-12.

LISTING 5-14 Updating the MainPage.xaml to display generated random numbers and data

```
<Page
    x:Class="CryptoSample.MainPage"
    xmlns="http://schemas.microsoft.com/winfx/2006/xaml/presentation"
    xmlns:x="http://schemas.microsoft.com/winfx/2006/xaml"
    xmlns:local="using:CryptoSample"
    xmlns:d="http://schemas.microsoft.com/expression/blend/2008"
    xmlns:mc="http://schemas.openxmlformats.org/markup-compatibility/2006"
    mc:Ignorable="d">
```

```
    <Grid Background="{StaticResource ApplicationPageBackgroundThemeBrush}">
        <StackPanel>
            <StackPanel Orientation="Horizontal">
                <Button Width="Auto"
                        Height="40"
                        Content="Hash message"
                        VerticalAlignment="Center"
                        FontSize="18"
                        Margin="5"
                        Click="HashMessage_Click" />
                <TextBlock x:Name="HashedMessageTextBlock"
                           Width="Auto"
                           Height="40"
                           Margin="5"
                           FontSize="18" />
            </StackPanel>
            <StackPanel Orientation="Horizontal">
                <Button Width="Auto"
                        Height="40"
                        Content="Generate random number"
                        Margin="5"
                        FontSize="18"
                        Click="GenerateRandomNumber_Click" />
                <TextBlock x:Name="RandomNumberTextBlock"
                           Width="Auto"
                           Height="40"
                           Margin="5"
                           FontSize="18" />
            </StackPanel>
            <StackPanel Orientation="Horizontal">
                <Button Width="Auto"
                        Height="40"
                        Content="Generate random data"
                        Margin="5"
                        FontSize="18"
                        Click="GenerateRandomData_Click" />
                <TextBlock x:Name="RandomDataTextBlock"
                           Width="Auto"
                           Height="40"
                           Margin="5"
                           VerticalAlignment="Center"
                           FontSize="18"/>
            </StackPanel>
        </StackPanel>
    </Grid>
</Page>
```

Figure 5-8 shows a randomly generated number and some randomly generated data.

FIGURE 5-8 A hash, a random number, and random data

Encrypting messages with MAC algorithms

A special form of hash algorithms is represented by the message authentication code (MAC) algorithms, also known as *keyed hashing algorithms.* A MAC consists of a short set of data that is used not only to ensure the integrity of the transmitted message but also its authenticity. The integrity offered by a MAC algorithm depends on a secret key that both the sender and the receiver know (symmetric encryption). In the more common scenarios, the secret key is used in combination with a hash algorithm (hash-based message authentication code, or HMAC) to produce an encrypted hash code that can be decrypted only by those who possess the secret key. In other, less common scenarios, the secret key is used to encrypt the whole message, and the last bits of the encrypted message are used as keyed hash code (even though no hash algorithms have been actually applied), whereas the rest of the data is discarded.

> ***NOTE*** **SYMMETRIC KEY ALGORITHMS**
>
> **Symmetric-key algorithms use the same cryptographic key for both encrypting and decrypting a message. The key, in practice, represents a shared secret between two or more subjects that can be used to encrypt and decrypt information that must be kept private. The fact that both parties must have access to the secret key represents one of the main drawbacks of symmetric-key encryption, compared with public-key encryption.**

To encrypt a message by using a MAC algorithm, you can leverage the *MacAlgorithmProvider* class, which strictly resembles the *HashAlgorithmProvider* class illustrated in the preceding section. The main difference resides in the presence of a key that is used to encrypt the message, as shown in the C# code in Listing 5-15.

LISTING 5-15 Encrypting a message using a MAC algorithm

```
private IBuffer _macSignature = null;
private String _message = "Plaintext message to sign";
private IBuffer _key = null;

private void GenerateMacSignature_Click(object sender, RoutedEventArgs e)
{
    String macAlgorithmName = MacAlgorithmNames.HmacSha256;
```

```
    MacAlgorithmProvider macProvider =
        MacAlgorithmProvider.OpenAlgorithm(macAlgorithmName);

    this._key = CryptographicBuffer.GenerateRandom(macProvider.MacLength);

    CryptographicKey hmacKey = macProvider.CreateKey(this._key);

    var binaryMessage = CryptographicBuffer
        .ConvertStringToBinary(this._message, BinaryStringEncoding.Utf8);

    this._macSignature = CryptographicEngine.Sign(hmacKey, binaryMessage);

    MacSignatureTextBlock.Text += String.Format("Signature: {0}",
        CryptographicBuffer.EncodeToHexString(this._macSignature));
}
```

The first lines of code are quite similar to the hash sample illustrated in Listing 5-11. First, the code sets the name of the MAC algorithm you want to use by enumerating through the *MacAlgorithmNames* static class. It then obtains a reference to the MAC algorithm provider by calling the *OpenAlgorithm* method and passing the name of the algorithm to use (HmacSha256, in our sample).

> ***NOTE*** **MACALGORITHMPROVIDER**
>
> **The *MacAlgorithmProvider* supports the following algorithm names: *AesCmac*, *HmacMd5*, *HmacSha1*, *HmacSha256*, *HmacSha384*, and *HmacSha512*.**

The next step consists of creating the key to encrypt/decrypt the message. To generate the key, the code leverages the *GenerateRandom* method described in the "Generating random numbers and data" section to create a random buffer of data that is supplied to the *CreateKey* method of the MAC algorithm provider. The code then calls the *Sign* method exposed by the *CryptographicEngine* class to produce an encrypted hash code (signature) based on the provided key.

The authenticity of the keyed hash code can be verified by calling the *VerifySignature* method, which accepts the following parameters: the key used to encrypt the hash code, the message, and the signature to be verified. The method decrypts the signature using the provided key and then compares the hash codes. If they match, the recipient can reasonably be sure that the message comes from the sender and it was not tampered with during transmission. Listing 5-16 shows an example of its usage.

LISTING 5-16 Verifying the authenticity of the secret key

```
private void VerifyMacSignature_Click(object sender, RoutedEventArgs e)
{
    String macAlgorithmName = MacAlgorithmNames.HmacSha256;

    MacAlgorithmProvider macProvider =
        MacAlgorithmProvider.OpenAlgorithm(macAlgorithmName);
```

```
    CryptographicKey hmacKey = macProvider.CreateKey(this._key);

    var binaryMessage = CryptographicBuffer
        .ConvertStringToBinary(this._message, BinaryStringEncoding.Utf8);

    bool IsAuthenticated = CryptographicEngine.VerifySignature(
        hmacKey,
        binaryMessage,
        this._macSignature);

    if (!IsAuthenticated)
    {
        VerificationTextBlock.Text += "The MAC signature does not match";
    }
    else
    {
        VerificationTextBlock.Text += "The MAC signature match";
    }
}
```

The code starts with the same steps followed to sign the message, by obtaining a reference to the MAC algorithm provider and creating a *CryptographicKey* instance based on the same key used to encrypt the hash code. It then leverages the *VerifySignature* method to check whether the signature is valid by supplying it with the key, the message, and the associated signature.

To test this procedure, you can use the XAML code shown in Listing 5-17 as a reference.

LISTING 5-17 Complete definition of the MainPage.xaml file used for this sample

```
<Page
    x:Class="CryptoSample.MainPage"
    xmlns="http://schemas.microsoft.com/winfx/2006/xaml/presentation"
    xmlns:x="http://schemas.microsoft.com/winfx/2006/xaml"
    xmlns:local="using:CryptoSample"
    xmlns:d="http://schemas.microsoft.com/expression/blend/2008"
    xmlns:mc="http://schemas.openxmlformats.org/markup-compatibility/2006"
    mc:Ignorable="d">

    <Grid Background="{StaticResource ApplicationPageBackgroundThemeBrush}">
        <StackPanel>
            <StackPanel Orientation="Horizontal">
                <Button Width="Auto"
                        Height="40"
                        Content="Generate MAC signature"
                        Margin="5"
                        FontSize="18"
                        Click="GenerateMacSignature_Click" />
                <TextBlock x:Name="MacSignatureTextBlock"
                           Width="Auto"
                           Height="40"
                           Margin="5"
                           VerticalAlignment="Center"
                           FontSize="18"/>
            </StackPanel>
```

```
            <StackPanel Orientation="Horizontal">
                <Button Width="Auto"
                        Height="40"
                        Content="Validate MAC signature"
                        Margin="5"
                        FontSize="18"
                        Click="VerifyMacSignature_Click" />
                <TextBlock x:Name="VerificationTextBlock"
                           Width="Auto"
                           Height="40"
                           Margin="5"
                           VerticalAlignment="Center"
                           FontSize="18"/>
            </StackPanel>
        </StackPanel>
    </Grid>
</Page>
```

If you run the app, generate a MAC signature, and then validate the generated signature, the result should resemble Figure 5-9.

FIGURE 5-9 MAC signature generation and validation

Using digital signatures

Digital signatures are conceptually similar to message authentication codes. The difference is that although the latter use a shared secret key (or symmetric key) to sign the message and prevent tampering, digital signatures use asymmetric keys to obtain the same result.

> ***NOTE*** **ASYMMETRIC ENCRYPTION**
>
> **Asymmetric encryption uses a pair of keys mathematically linked to each other: a private key that must be kept secret and a public key that can be made publicly available. Data encrypted using the public key can be decrypted only with the private key, whereas data signed with the private key can be verified only with the public key. It is impossible to discover one of them without knowing the other.**

To sign a message digitally, the sender first applies a hash algorithm to the message to create a digest; then the sender encrypts the digest with the private key to create a signature. Upon receiving the message and signature, the receiver decrypts the signature using the sender's public key to retrieve the digest, computes a new hash of the content, and compares the two hash codes. If the digests match, it means that the message comes from the owner of the private key, and the data has not been tampered with. Listing 5-18 shows an example of a digital signature's usage.

LISTING 5-18 Digitally signing a message

```
private void GenerateDigitalSignature_Click(object sender, RoutedEventArgs e)
{
    CryptographicKey keyPair;
    UInt32 keySize = 256;
    String message = "Plain text message to sign";
    String asymmetricAlgorithmName = AsymmetricAlgorithmNames.EcdsaP256Sha256;

    IBuffer binaryMessage = CryptographicBuffer.
        ConvertStringToBinary(message, BinaryStringEncoding.Utf8);

    var asymmetricKeyProvider = AsymmetricKeyAlgorithmProvider
        .OpenAlgorithm(asymmetricAlgorithmName);

    try
    {
        keyPair = asymmetricKeyProvider.CreateKeyPair(keySize);
    }
    catch (ArgumentException ex)
    {
        DigitalSignatureTextBlock.Text = "Invalid key size for the given algorithm";

        return;
    }

    IBuffer signature = CryptographicEngine.Sign(keyPair, binaryMessage);

    IBuffer publicKeyBuffer = keyPair.ExportPublicKey();

    IBuffer keyPairBuffer = keyPair.Export();

    CryptographicKey keyPublic = asymmetricKeyProvider.ImportPublicKey(publicKeyBuffer);

    if (keyPublic.KeySize != keyPair.KeySize)
    {
        DigitalSignatureTextBlock.Text = "Importing public key failed";

        return;
    }

    keyPair = asymmetricKeyProvider.ImportKeyPair(keyPairBuffer);

    if (keyPublic.KeySize != keyPair.KeySize)
    {
        DigitalSignatureTextBlock.Text = "Importing key pair failed";

        return;
    }
```

```
    if (!CryptographicEngine.VerifySignature(keyPublic, binaryMessage, signature))
    {
        DigitalSignatureTextBlock.Text = "Signature verification failed!";

        return;
    }

    DigitalSignatureTextBlock.Text = String.Format(
        "Signature was successfully verified: {0}",
        CryptographicBuffer.EncodeToBase64String(signature));
}
```

Compared with the code shown in Listing 5-15, the major difference resides in the use of a key pair to sign the message instead of a shared secret key. To create a public/private key pair, the code uses the *CreateKeyPair* method of the *AsymmetricKeyProvider* class. In this case, the code does not use random data to generate the keys because the two keys are mathematically related in asymmetric cryptography.

> ***MORE INFO*** ***ASYMMETRICKEYPROVIDER* CLASS–SUPPORTED ALGORITHMS**
>
> **The list of algorithms supported by the *AsymmetricKeyProvider* class is quite long. You can check the full list at *http://msdn.microsoft.com/en-us/library/windows/apps/windows.security.cryptography.core.asymmetricalgorithmnames.aspx*.**

The private key is then used to sign the message digitally by calling the *CryptographicEngine.Sign* method (refer to Listings 5-15 and 5-18). After you create the encrypted signature with the provided keys, you can export the key pair or just the public portion of a public/private key pair into a buffer by calling, respectively, the *Export* and the *ExportPublicKey* methods of the *CryptographicKey* class (as shown in Listing 5-18 for illustrative purposes). Analogously, you can import a key pair or just the public key by leveraging, respectively, the *ImportKeyPair* and the *ImportPublicKey* methods.

Finally, to verify the signature, you can use the *VerifySignature* method, providing the imported public key, the message, and the digest encrypted using the private key.

You can use the XAML code in Listing 5-19 to test the flow.

LISTING 5-19 Complete XAML definition of the MainPage.xaml file used to test the C# code

```
<Page
    x:Class="DigitalSignatureSample.MainPage"
    xmlns="http://schemas.microsoft.com/winfx/2006/xaml/presentation"
    xmlns:x="http://schemas.microsoft.com/winfx/2006/xaml"
    xmlns:local="using:DigitalSignatureSample"
    xmlns:d="http://schemas.microsoft.com/expression/blend/2008"
    xmlns:mc="http://schemas.openxmlformats.org/markup-compatibility/2006"
    mc:Ignorable="d">

    <Grid Background="{StaticResource ApplicationPageBackgroundThemeBrush}">
        <StackPanel>
```

```
            <Button Click="GenerateDigitalSignature_Click"
                    Height="40"
                    Content="Generate digital signature"
                    Margin="5"
                    FontSize="18" />
            <TextBlock x:Name="DigitalSignatureTextBlock"
                       Width="Auto"
                       Height="40"
                       Margin="5"
                       VerticalAlignment="Center"
                       FontSize="18"
                       TextWrapping="Wrap"/>
        </StackPanel>
    </Grid>
</Page>
```

Figure 5-10 shows the digital signature generated by the code.

FIGURE 5-10 Digital signature

Enrolling and requesting certificates

As mentioned previously, asymmetric cryptography relies on a key pair made up by a public key and a private key. The key pair is used to encrypt and decrypt a message. Whereas the private key must be kept secret, the public key is usually embedded in a binary certificate. A certificate is a signed data structure that binds a public key to a person, computer, or organization.

> ***NOTE*** **X.509 PUBLIC KEY INFRASTRUCTURE (PKI)**
>
> **X.509 PKI is a standard for identifying the base requirements for using certificates. A certificate contains information about one subject, including the subject's public key. A certification authority (CA) issues certificates. All parties involved in a secure communication trust the CA and rely on it to verify the identities of the individuals, systems, or entities that represent the subject. The level of verification can be different based on the level of security required for a particular transaction. The following listing shows the definition of a X.509 certificate:**

```
  -----------------------------------------------------------------
-- X.509 signed certificate
-----------------------------------------------------------------
SignedContent ::= SEQUENCE
{
  certificate        CertificateToBeSigned,
  algorithm          Object Identifier,
  signature          BITSTRING
}

-----------------------------------------------------------------
-- X.509 certificate to be signed
-----------------------------------------------------------------
CertificateToBeSigned ::= SEQUENCE
{
  version                  [0] CertificateVersion DEFAULT v1,
  serialNumber             CertificateSerialNumber,
  signature                AlgorithmIdentifier,
  issuer                   Name
  validity                 Validity,
  subject                  Name
  subjectPublicKeyInfo     SubjectPublicKeyInfo,
  issuerUniqueIdentifier   [1] IMPLICIT UniqueIdentifier OPTIONAL,
  subjectUniqueIdentifier  [2] IMPLICIT UniqueIdentifier OPTIONAL,
  extensions               [3] Extensions OPTIONAL
}
```

The Windows.Security.Cryptography.Certificates namespace contains types and methods that enable you to create certificate requests, as well as to install or import an issued certificate. Listing 5-20 shows C# code for creating a certificate request.

LISTING 5-20 Creating a certificate request

```
public async Task<String> CreateRequestAsync()
{
    CertificateRequestProperties crp = new CertificateRequestProperties();
    crp.FriendlyName = "MyCertificate";
    crp.Subject = "SampleCertificateRequest";
    crp.KeyProtectionLevel = KeyProtectionLevel.NoConsent;
    crp.KeyUsages = EnrollKeyUsages.All;
    crp.Exportable = ExportOption.Exportable;
    crp.KeySize = 2048;

    crp.KeyStorageProviderName = KeyStorageProviderNames.SoftwareKeyStorageProvider;

    KeyStorageProviderTextBlock.Text = String.Format("Key Storage Provider Name: {0}",
        crp.KeyStorageProviderName);
```

```
    HashAlgorithmNameTextBlock.Text = String.Format("Hash Algorithm Name: {0}",
        crp.HashAlgorithmName);

    KeyAlgorithmNameTextBlock.Text = String.Format("Key Algorithm Name: {0}",
        crp.KeyAlgorithmName);

    String request = await CertificateEnrollmentManager.CreateRequestAsync(crp);

    return request;
}
```

The first thing you must do is instantiate a *CertificateRequestProperties* object containing the properties of a certificate request. In particular, the *KeyProtectionLevel* enum indicates the level of protection and accepts one of the following values:

- ***NoConsent*** No strong key protection is required (this is the default value).
- ***ConsentOnly*** The user is notified through a dialog box when the private key is created or used.
- ***ConsentWithPassword*** The user is prompted to enter a password for the key when the key is created or when the key is used.

Figure 5-11 shows the dialog box asking for a password.

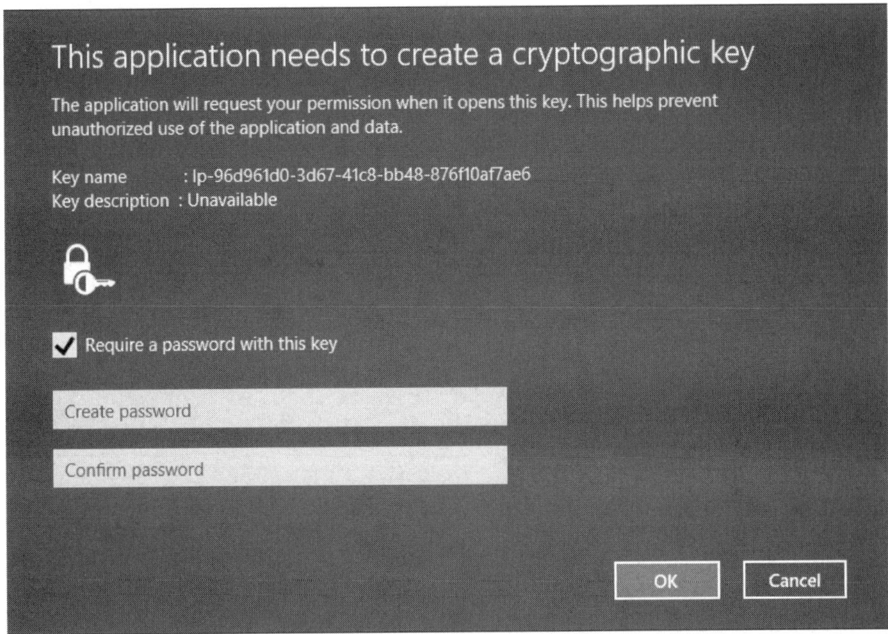

FIGURE 5-11 Dialog box requesting a password

The *KeyUsages* property (of type *EnrollKeyUsage*) indicates what kind of operation can be performed by the private key created for this certificate request. The possible values are the following:

- ***None*** No usage is specified for the key.
- ***Decryption*** The key can be used for decryption.
- ***Signing*** The key can be used for signing (this represents the default value).
- ***KeyAgreement*** The key can be used for secret agreement encryption.
- ***All*** The key can be used for decryption, signing, and key agreement.

The *Exportable* property (of type *ExportOption*) specifies whether the private key created for the request can be exported. (By default, the private key is not exportable for security reasons.) The *KeySize* enables you to specify the size, in bits, of the private key to be generated. (For the RSA and DSA algorithms, the default value is 2,048 bits; whereas for elliptic curve cryptographic (ECC) algorithms, the key size is ignored.)

Another important property is represented by the *KeyStorageProviderName*, which indicates the key storage provider (KSP) that is used to generate the private key. There are three KSPs available for a Windows Store app:

- ***PlatformKeyStorageProvider*** Microsoft Platform Key Storage Provider
- ***SmartcardKeyStorageProvider*** Microsoft Smart Card Key Storage Provider
- ***SoftwareKeyStorageProvider*** Microsoft Software Key Storage Provider (the default value)

Finally, the *KeyAlgorithmName* property specifies the algorithm to be used to generate the public key. The default value is *RSA*.

The *CertificateEnrollmentManager* class also exposes an *InstallCertificateAsync* method that enables you to asynchronously install a certificate chain into the app container on the local computer. Listing 5-21 shows an example of its usage.

LISTING 5-21 Using the InstallCertificateAsync method to install a certificate

```
private async void InstallCertificate_Click(object sender, RoutedEventArgs e)
{
    String response = "";
    String request = await this.CreateRequestAsync();

    if (String.IsNullOrEmpty(request))
    {
        // something went wrong
    }

    try
    {
        response = await SubmitCertificateRequestAndGetResponseAsync(request,
            "http://www.contoso.org/");

        if (String.IsNullOrEmpty(response))
        {
            // Submit request succeeded but the returned response is empty.";
        }
```

```
        // Install the certificate
        await CertificateEnrollmentManager.InstallCertificateAsync(response,
            InstallOptions.None);
    }
    catch (Exception ex)
    {
        // handle exception
    }
}

private Task<String> SubmitCertificateRequestAndGetResponse(
    String certificateRequest,
    String url)
{
    // Submit a certificate request to a Certificate Services and return the response
}
```

After creating a certificate request through the *CreateRequestAsync* method, the code invokes the *SubmitCertificateRequestAndGetResponseAsync* method, which basically creates an HTTP web request, submits the certificate request to the server indicated as second parameter, and then returns the certificate response coming from the server.

After the certificate is retrieved, the code calls the *InstallCertificateAsync* method and passes the encoded certificate as the first parameter, along with an *InstallOption* instance that specifies the certificate installation option (none, in this sample).

In Windows, issued certificates and pending or rejected requests to local computers and devices are stored in the Microsoft certificate store, which consists of the following logical stores:

- **Personal** Contains certificates associated with a private key controlled by the user or computer
- **Trusted Root Certification Authorities** Contains certificates from implicitly trusted CAs
- **Enterprise Trust** Contains certificate trust lists typically used to trust self-signed certificates from other organizations
- **Intermediate Certification Authorities** Contains certificates issued to subordinate CAs in the certification hierarchy
- **Active Directory User Object** Contains the user object certificate or certificates published in Active Directory
- **Trusted Publishers** Contains certificates from trusted CAs
- **Untrusted Certificates** Contains certificates that have been explicitly identified as untrusted
- **Third-Party Root Certification Authorities** Contains trusted root certificates from CAs outside the internal certificate hierarchy
- **Trusted People** Contains certificates issued to users or entities that have been explicitly trusted

- **Other People** Contains certificates issued to users or entities that have been implicitly trusted
- **Certificate Enrollment Requests** Contains pending or rejected certificate requests

Certificates are normally stored in per-user, per-app container locations. A Windows Store app has write access to only its own certificate storage, and read access to only the certificates added by the app. An app can also have the right to read the local machine certificate stores. If the application adds certificates to any of its stores, these certificates cannot be read by other Windows Store apps. Because the certificate store is specific to the Windows Store app, when the app is uninstalled, any certificates specific to it are also removed.

As far as smart cards are concerned, certificates and keys contained on the card are automatically transferred to the user MY store and can be used by any application with full trust rights. To enable groups of principals to access groups of resources, you can leverage the Shared User Certificates capability to enable an app container process to access a specific resource. This capability grants an app container read access to the certificates and keys contained in the user MY store and the Smart Card Trusted Roots store (it is typically used for financial or enterprise apps that require a smart card for authentication). The capability does not grant read access to the user REQUEST store.

Finally, to import a certificate from a Personal Information Exchange (PFX) message asynchronously, you can use the *ImportPfxDataAsync* method of the *CertificateEnrollmentManager* class. Listing 5-22 shows an example of its usage.

LISTING 5-22 Using the ImportPfxDataAsync method to import a certificate

```
private async void ImportCertificate_Click(object sender, RoutedEventArgs e)
{
    try
    {
        string pfxCertificate = new ResourceLoader().GetString("MyCertificate");
        string password = "password";
        string friendlyName = "Pfx Certificate Sample";

        await CertificateEnrollmentManager.ImportPfxDataAsync(
            pfxCertificate,
            password,
            ExportOption.NotExportable,
            KeyProtectionLevel.NoConsent,
            InstallOptions.None,
            friendlyName);
    }
    catch (Exception ex)
    {
        // handle exception
    }
}
```

To import an issued certificate, it is not necessary for the certificate request to have been generated on the importing computer. The certificates included in the response do not need to be chained to trusted root certificates on the importing computer.

MORE INFO CERTIFICATE ENROLLMENT SAMPLE

For a more detailed example of certificate creation and enrollment, see *http://code.msdn.microsoft.com/windowsapps/Certificate-enrollment-84892e0c*.

Protecting your data with the *DataProtectionProvider* class

The *DataProtectionProvider* class (in the *Windows.Security.Cryptography.DataProtection* namespace) exposes methods that can help you to protect sensitive application data by asynchronously encrypting and decrypting static data or data streams.

The *DataProtectionProvider* class has two constructors: a default constructor with no parameters and an overloaded constructor that accepts a string as parameter describing the protection provider to use.

EXAM TIP

The default constructor must be used before starting a decryption operation. Do not use this constructor to start an encryption operation; use the overloaded constructor instead.

NOTE ENTERPRISE AUTHENTICATION CAPABILITY

As stated in the official documentation, for security descriptors and security descriptor definition language (SDDL) strings, you must declare the enterprise authentication capability in the application manifest. The enterprise authentication capability is restricted to Windows Store apps built with company accounts and is subject to additional onboarding validation. You should avoid the enterprise authentication capability unless absolutely necessary.

The following code shows how to use the *ProtectAsync* method of the *DataProtectionProvider* to encrypt some static data:

```
private IBuffer _protectedBuffer = null;
private async void ProtectButton_Click(object sender, RoutedEventArgs e)
{
    String descriptor = "LOCAL=user";
    DataProtectionProvider dpp = new DataProtectionProvider(descriptor);

    IBuffer binaryMessage = CryptographicBuffer
        .ConvertStringToBinary(PlaintextTextBlock.Text, BinaryStringEncoding.Utf8);

    this._protectedBuffer = await dpp.ProtectAsync(binaryMessage);

    EncryptedTextBlock.Text = CryptographicBuffer
        .EncodeToBase64String(this._protectedBuffer);
}
```

To decrypt the protected data, you can leverage the *UnprotectAsync* method, which accepts an *IBuffer* object containing the encrypted message to unprotect, as shown in the following snippet:

```
private async void UnprotectButton_Click(object sender, RoutedEventArgs e)
{
    if (this._protectedBuffer != null)
    {
        DataProtectionProvider dpp = new DataProtectionProvider();

        IBuffer unprotectedBuffer = await dpp.UnprotectAsync(this._protectedBuffer);

        UnprotectedTextBlock.Text = CryptographicBuffer
            .ConvertBinaryToString(BinaryStringEncoding.Utf8, unprotectedBuffer);
    }
}
```

To test this code, use the XAML code in Listing 5-23 as reference for your default page.

LISTING 5-23 The complete XAML definition for the MainPage.xaml

```
<Page
    x:Class="DataProtectionSample.MainPage"
    xmlns="http://schemas.microsoft.com/winfx/2006/xaml/presentation"
    xmlns:x="http://schemas.microsoft.com/winfx/2006/xaml"
    xmlns:local="using:DataProtectionSample"
    xmlns:d="http://schemas.microsoft.com/expression/blend/2008"
    xmlns:mc="http://schemas.openxmlformats.org/markup-compatibility/2006"
    mc:Ignorable="d">

    <Grid Background="{StaticResource ApplicationPageBackgroundThemeBrush}">
        <StackPanel>
            <TextBlock x:Name="PlaintextTextBlock"
                       Text="Message to protect"
                       Margin="5"
                       FontSize="20"
                       Width="Auto"
                       Height="50" />
            <Button x:Name="ProtectButton"
                    Margin="5"
                    Content="Protect Message"
                    Width="Auto"
                    Height="50"
                    Click="ProtectButton_Click" />
            <TextBlock x:Name="EncryptedTextBlock"
                       Margin="5"
                       FontSize="20"
                       Width="Auto"
                       Height="Auto"
                       TextWrapping="Wrap" />
```

```
            <Button x:Name="UnprotectButton"
                    Margin="5"
                    Content="Unprotect Message"
                    Width="Auto"
                    Height="50"
                    Click="UnprotectButton_Click" />
            <TextBlock x:Name="UnprotectedTextBlock"
                       Margin="5"
                       FontSize="20"
                       Width="Auto"
                       Height="Auto"
                       TextWrapping="Wrap" />
        </StackPanel>
    </Grid>
</Page>
```

If you run the application, the result should resemble Figure 5-12.

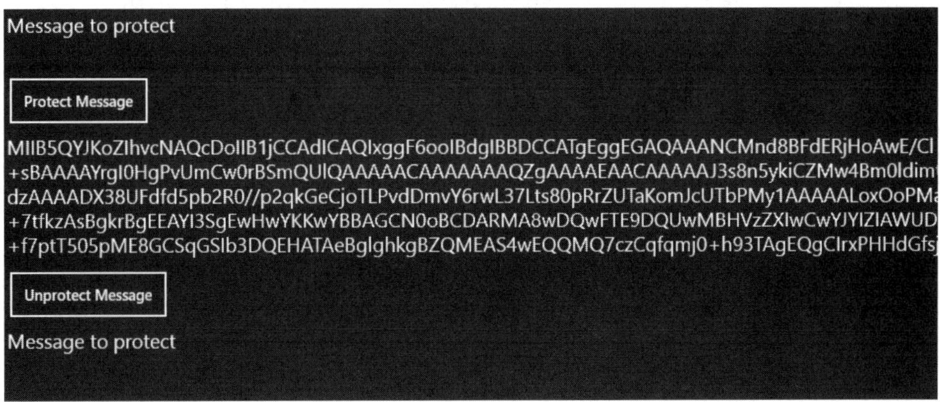

FIGURE 5-12 A message first encrypted and then decrypted using the *DataProtectionProvider* class

You can also leverage the *ProtectStreamAsync* method to perform analogous operations on a stream of data. The method accepts two parameters: an *IInputStream* object representing the stream to protect and an *IOutputStream* object that contains the encrypted stream. Analogously, to decrypt a protected stream, you can call the *UnprotectStreamAsync* method, which also accepts two parameters: an *IInputStream* object that represents the stream to decrypt and an *IOutputStream* that contains the unprotected stream.

> ***NOTE*** ***PASSWORDVAULT*** **CLASS**
>
> **To protect your users' passwords, you should leverage the dedicated *PasswordVault* class in the *Windows.Security.Credentials* namespace.**

Thought experiment

Transmitting shared secret keys

In this thought experiment, apply what you've learned about this objective. You can find answers to these questions in the "Answers" section at the end of this chapter.

You are developing a Windows Store app that needs to share a secret key with a third-party service. For symmetric key cryptography to work for online communications, the secret key must be securely shared with authorized communicating parties and protected from discovery and use by unauthorized parties.

1. **Which of the techniques explained in this objective should you use to protect the confidentiality of the secret key over the Internet?**
2. **Which technique should you leverage to also protect the key's authenticity?**

Objective summary

- Cryptography is used to secure your app and guarantee one or more of the following principles: authentication (the communication actually originates from a certain source), confidentiality (data being read by unauthorized third parties), data integrity (data being tampered with by unauthorized parties), and nonrepudiation (other parties repudiating their own messages after they have been sent).
- You can leverage the *HashAlgorithmProvider* class and use one of the supported algorithms to protect message integrity. To ensure that a certain message has not been tampered with, send a message along with its corresponding hash code.
- Random generation of numbers and data represents an important step in many cryptographic operations, such as in generating cryptographic keys or passwords. To achieve these goals, you can use the *GenerateRandom* and *GenerateRandomNumber* methods exposed by the *CryptographicBuffer* class.
- Encrypt the hash code to ensure not only the integrity of the transmitted message but also its authenticity. Use the *MacAlgorithmProvider* class to encrypt the hash codes by using a shared secret key, or use the *CryptographicEngine.Sign* method to encrypt the hash code by using asymmetric cryptography.
- You can request a certificate from a specific uniform resource identifier (URI) by using the *CreateRequestAsync* method of the *CertificateEnrollmentManager* class. To install the certificate in the app container on the local computer, use the *InstallCertificateAsync* method; or use the *ImportPfxDataAsync* method to import a certificate from a PFX message asynchronously.
- Remember to protect the sensitive data and streams used by your Windows Store app by encrypting them using the *DataProtectionProvider* class. To encrypt/decrypt static data, you can use the *ProtectAsync/UnprotectAsync* methods; use the *ProtectStreamAsync/UnprotectStreamAsync* methods to encrypt/decrypt data streams.

Objective review

Answer the following questions to test your knowledge of the information in this objective. You can find the answers to these questions and explanations of why each answer choice is correct or incorrect in the "Answers" section at the end of this chapter.

1. Which of the following goals does a hash algorithm help protect?
   - **A.** Authentication
   - **B.** Data integrity
   - **C.** Confidentiality
   - **D.** All the above
2. Which method do you need to call to digitally sign (encrypt) a message using a key pair?
   - **A.** *HashData* method of the *HashAlgorithmProvider* class
   - **B.** *InstallCertificateAsync* method of the *CertificateEnrollmentManager* class
   - **C.** *ProtectAsync* method of the *DataProtectionProvider* class
   - **D.** *Sign* method of the *CryptographicEngine* class
3. When do you have to use the default constructor of the *DataProtectionProvider* class?
   - **A.** Before starting a decryption operation, by calling the *UnprotectAsync/Unprotect-StreamAsync* methods.
   - **B.** Before starting an encryption operation, by calling the *ProtectAsync/Protect-StreamAsync* methods.
   - **C.** When you do not want to provide a specific security description and want to use the default descriptor instead.
   - **D.** *DataProtectionProvider* does not expose a default constructor.

Chapter summary

- Application data represents data that is bound to the application and is not useful outside of it. User settings for an application are application data.
- User data represents data that has a meaning outside of the application. This type of data represents entities such as customers, orders, and invoices. It is usually stored outside of the application in a database or some other form of storage.
- To access a file, you can use file pickers or folder pickers in which the user has an active part in the process; or you can rely on WinRT classes programmatically to save and retrieve text, stream, and binary data.
- Remember to define capabilities and declarations in the application manifest.

- Use one of the hash algorithms supported by the *Windows.Security.Cryptography* namespace to protect message integrity. To ensure not only the integrity of the transmitted message but also its authenticity, encrypt the hash code either by using a secret key or leveraging asymmetric cryptography. Generate random numbers and data for your keys and password, or request a certificate and use the key pair to digitally sign the hash code.
- Protect sensitive information managed by your Windows Store app by encrypting it.

Answers

This section contains the solutions to the thought experiments and answers to the lesson review questions in this chapter.

Objective 5.1: Thought experiment

You can use the local or roaming setting. The provided classes enables you store application settings locally in the device or in the live user profile in the cloud. Settings in the cloud follow the user on each of his devices. For example, if you need to store the user's color preference, you can store it in the roaming profile; the user will see the same color on each of his devices. If you have to store the number of items to be displayed in a grid, this value can be stored locally because it can be different from device to device. Or you can store it in the roaming profile and override the value if the user changes it locally.

Objective 5.1: Review

1. **Correct answers:** A, D
    - **A. Correct:** User preferences are related to the application and have no meaning outside of it.
    - **B. Incorrect:** Entities are user data. They are usually stored outside of the application.
    - **C. Incorrect:** Not all application-related data is considered application data: users and groups are considered user data.
    - **D. Correct:** Reference content like the list of cities for a weather application isbound to the application.
2. **Correct answers:** A, B
    - **A. Correct:** Use the *LocalSettings* properties to store application data locally.
    - **B. Correct:** Use the *RoamingSettings* properties to store application data in the user roaming profile.
    - **C. Incorrect:** The *ApplicationDataCreateDisposition* enables you choose only the container creation methods.
    - **D. Incorrect:** The *ApplicationDataContainer* class enables you store application data.

3. **Correct answer:** C
    A. **Incorrect:** Windows Store apps can use the *StorageFolder* class to store data in files.
    B. **Incorrect:** Windows Store apps can store data locally for application and user data.
    C. **Correct:** The *ApplicationData* properties enable you access the local, roaming, or temporary folder to store data and settings.
    D. **Incorrect:** You can create files using the *LocalFolder* property of the *ApplicationData* class.

Objective 5.2: Thought experiment

After obtaining a reference to the file or folder, you can perform read and write operations on it. For example, you can create a file in a folder using the following code:

```
var folder = KnownFolders.DocumentsLibrary;
var logFile = await storageFolder.CreateFileAsync("log.txt");
```

Then, to write some text to the file, use the *WriteTextAsync* method as in the following code sample:

```
await Windows.Storage.FileIO.WriteTextAsync(logFile, "Operation Logged");
```

Remember, you need to define capabilities to perform operations on a system folder.

Objective 5.2: Review

1. **Correct answers:** A, B, C
    A. **Correct:** You can access local storage.
    B. **Correct:** You can access cloud storage on SkyDrive.
    C. **Correct:** You can access network storage.
    D. **Incorrect:** You cannot access the Windows Azure Storage Account with file pickers.
2. **Correct answer:** A
    A. **Correct:** You have to define file extensions and associations in the application manifest.
    B. **Incorrect:** Any Windows Store app can act as a file handler.
    C. **Incorrect:** Any Windows Store app can act as a file handler.
    D. **Incorrect:** You can associate an application as the handler for a particular extension.

3. **Correct answer:** C

   A. **Incorrect:** The *FileOpenPicker* class does not enable you to access files.

   B. **Incorrect:** The *StorageFolder* class does not enable you to access files.

   C. **Correct:** The *StorageFile* class enables you to read a file programmatically.

   D. **Incorrect:** The *ApplicationData* class does not enable you to access files.

Objective 5.3: Thought experiment

1. One way to exchange the secret key over the Internet without compromising the security of the key is encrypting the secret key with the intended recipient's public key. Only the intended recipient can decrypt the secret key because it requires the use of the recipient's private key. Therefore, a third party who intercepts the encrypted, secret key cannot decrypt and use it. The following image illustrates the mechanism.

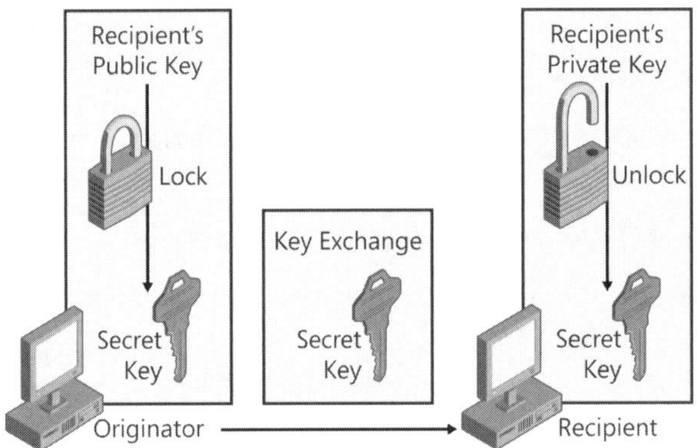

2. Encrypting the secret key using the recipient's public key does not guarantee that the encrypted key comes from the intended sender. A malicious third party could replace the original key and encrypt it with the recipient's public key, for example. To address this issue, you could hash the secret key and then encrypt the hash key using the sender's private key. Only the corresponding sender's public key can decrypt the message. The recipient is guaranteed that the secret key comes from the sender. The hash can also be used to verify data integrity.

Objective 5.3: Review

1. **Correct answer:** B
   - **A. Incorrect:** Message authentication code (MAC) algorithms and digital signatures can help to ensure message authentication.
   - **B. Correct:** A hash code obtained by applying a hash algorithm to binary content represents the fingerprint of that document and prevents unauthorized people from tampering with it, preserving data integrity.
   - **C. Incorrect:** Hash algorithms transform binary values of arbitrary length only to smaller binary values of a fixed length. They do not encrypt the message content itself.
   - **D. Incorrect:** A hash algorithm helps to protect authentication, data integrity, and confidentiality.
2. **Correct answer:** D
   - **A. Incorrect:** The *HashData* method of the *HashAlgorithmProvider* class is used to generate a hash code.
   - **B. Incorrect:** The *InstallCertificateAsync* method of the *CertificateEnrollmentManager* class is used to install a certificate in the app container.
   - **C. Incorrect:** The *ProtectAsync* method of the *DataProtectionProvider* class is used to encrypt static data.
   - **D. Correct:** The *Sign* method of the *CryptographicEngine* class digitally signs (encrypts) a message with the provided key pair.
3. **Correct answer:** A
   - **A. Correct:** You must instantiate the *DataProtectionProvider* class by calling the default constructor before starting a decryption operation through the *UnprotectAsync/UnprotectStreamAsync* methods.
   - **B. Incorrect:** Before starting an encryption operation by calling the *ProtectAsync/ProtectStreamAsync* methods, you have to use the overloaded constructor. The constructor accepts as its only parameter a string, indicating the security descriptor to be used.
   - **C. Incorrect:** The overloaded constructor must be used before starting an encryption operation. The constructor accepts as its only parameter a string indicating the security descriptor to be used. Providing the descriptor is not optional.
   - **D. Incorrect:** The *DataProtectionProvider* exposes a default constructor that must be used to perform decryption operations.

CHAPTER 6

Prepare for a solution deployment

This chapter begins by showing you how to design and implement trial functionality in your Windows Store app, handle licensing scenarios, and perform in-app purchases from your app. From there, you learn how to handle errors and exceptions in a Windows Store app, with a focus on device capability errors and exceptions thrown during asynchronous operations. The chapter also explores designing and implementing a test strategy for your app, which includes the peculiarities of the test framework for Windows Store apps and the Unit Test Library project template. Finally, you learn how to test your app's performance, trace and collect detailed information about your app's behaviors, and generate reports and other analytical information.

Objectives in this chapter:

- Objective 6.1: Design and implement trial functionality in an app
- Objective 6.2: Design for error handling
- Objective 6.3: Design and implement a test strategy
- Objective 6.4: Design a diagnostics and monitoring strategy

Objective 6.1: Design and implement trial functionality in an app

In this section, you learn how to design and implement trial functionality in your Windows Store app, such as timed trials and feature-based trials. You also learn how to handle in-app purchases to offer your customers extra features and products.

> **This objective covers how to:**
> - Set up a timed trial
> - Set up a feature-based trial
> - Set up in-app purchases
> - Transition an app from trial to full

Choosing the right business model for your app

One of the most critical steps of publishing a Windows Store app is determining the right type of license. In the Selling Details section of the Windows Store Dashboard, shown in Figure 6-1, you can enter the price of the app, select a trial period, and choose the countries/regions in which you want to sell the app.

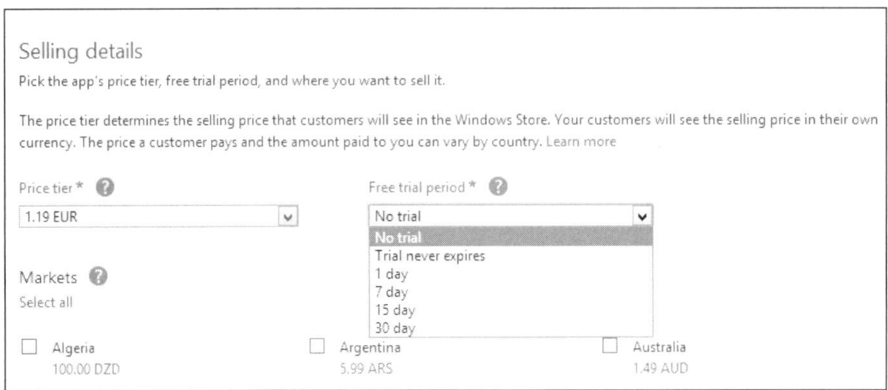

FIGURE 6-1 Choosing app selling details in the Windows Store Dashboard

The simplest but probably least effective possibility is selling your entire application for a certain price. Users can decide whether your app is worth the price only by reading the information and the reviews published on your app's dedicated page in the Windows Store. This approach corresponds to the No trial option shown in Figure 6-1.

A second possibility is to let your customers download and try your app before paying for it. One option is called a *timed trial*, in which you provide a trial version of your app with all the features of the paid version. When the trial period expires, the app simply stops working. In more refined scenarios, the app still works when the trial period ends, but it can ask the users to buy the full license at regular intervals or display commercial ads until the user purchases the full version. In the drop-down list shown in Figure 6-1, you have to choose among four different deadlines for a timed trial: 1, 7, 15, and 30 days.

Another option is the *feature-based trial*, which enables potential customers to access only a subset of your app's functionalities or content unless they decide to buy the full version of the app. Imagine, for example, a game that lets you play only the first levels, or a photo enhancement app that enables you to use only a limited set of filters and effects. In this scenario, the trial period lasts indefinitely and corresponds to the Trial never expires option shown in Figure 6-1.

Figure 6-2 shows the left panel of a feature trial game that enables you to play the first few levels for an indefinite period, but if you want to access the entire content, you must purchase the full version of the app in the Windows Store.

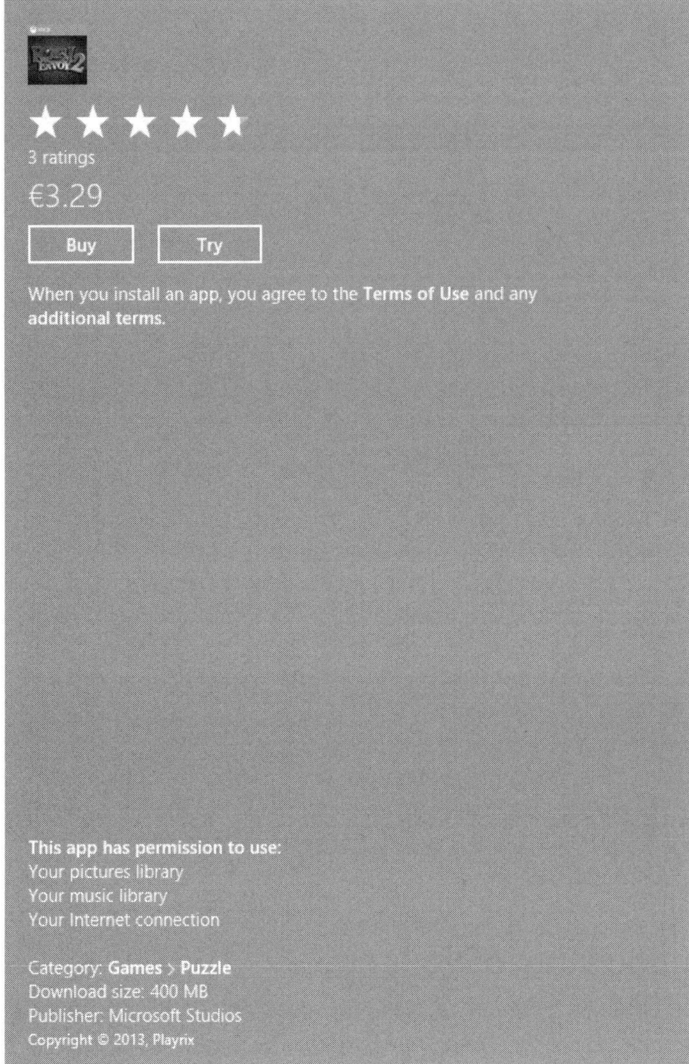

FIGURE 6-2 Buy and Try buttons in a feature-based game

Finally, you can decide to distribute a basic version of your app but give your customers the option to extend it by purchasing advanced functionalities or additional content. This distribution method is referred to as *in-app purchase*. In this case, the app is split into multiple modules that can be purchased separately.

In the Windows Store, you can define which features or products can be purchased by your customers. For each feature or product, you have to pick a price and decide the product lifetime. The feature lifetime describes how long a customer can use the purchased feature. After the time expires, the feature stops working and it must be purchased again. Figure 6-3 shows the various options.

NOTE IN-APP PURCHASES

In-app purchases cannot be offered during a trial version of an app.

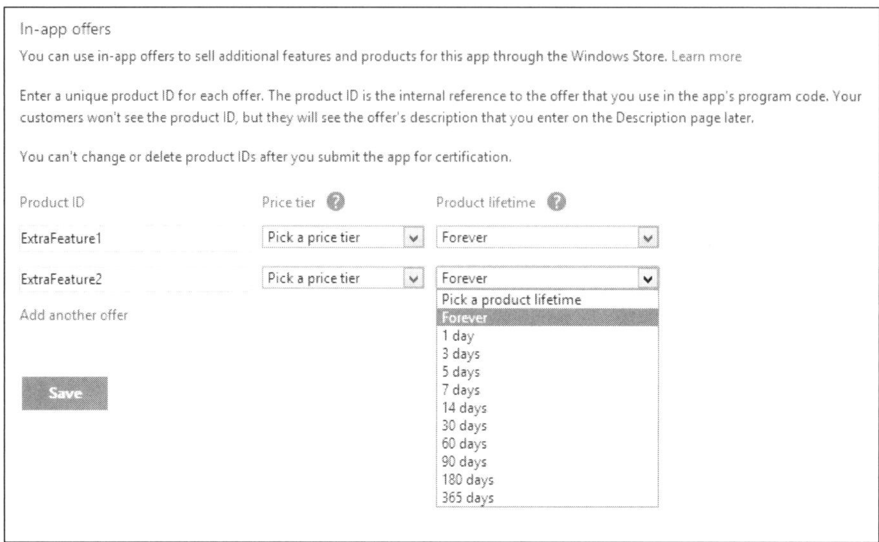
In-app offers
You can use in-app offers to sell additional features and products for this app through the Windows Store. Learn more
Enter a unique product ID for each offer. The product ID is the internal reference to the offer that you use in the app's program code. Your customers won't see the product ID, but they will see the offer's description that you enter on the Description page later.
You can't change or delete product IDs after you submit the app for certification.
Product ID
Price tier
Product lifetime
ExtraFeature1
Pick a price tier
Forever
ExtraFeature2
Pick a price tier
Forever
Add another offer
Save
Pick a product lifetime
Forever
1 day
3 days
5 days
7 days
14 days
30 days
60 days
90 days
180 days
365 days

FIGURE 6-3 In-app offers in the Windows Store Dashboard

Remember to implement all the features and products you want to offer to your customers through in-app purchases before publishing the app in the Windows Store. If you want to add new features or products after your app has been published, you need to submit an updated version of your app to the Windows Store.

Exploring the licensing state of your app

You can use the licensing APIs provided by the *Windows.ApplicationModel.Store* namespace to determine the license state of an app or an in-app purchase feature. The licensing application programming interface (API) enables you to do the following:

- Check the current license status of an app
- Check the expiration date of a trial period
- Check whether an app's feature has been purchased through an in-app purchase
- Perform an in-app purchase

The *LicenseInformation* property exposed by the *CurrentApp* class enables you to access information about the current license state of your app and of other products or features that are enabled when the customer makes an in-app purchase. In particular, the *LicenseInformation* class exposes the following read-only properties:

- ***IsActive*** Describes the current license state of this app. A value of *true* indicates a valid license, regardless of whether the app is in trial mode. A value of *false* indicates that the app's license state is invalid because the license is missing, expired, or has been revoked.
- ***IsTrial*** Indicates whether an app is in trial mode. A value of *false* means that a full version of the app has been bought by the user, whereas a value of *true* indicates that the app is still in trial mode. It is important to understand that this property returns *true* even if the trial period is expired, so you should always check the *IsTrial* property with the *IsActive* property.
- ***ExpirationDate*** Indicates the expiration date for the trial. The date must be expressed in the ISO 8601 format, which is *yyyy-mm-ddThh:mm:ss.ssZ*. For example, the date 2014-06-19T09:00:00.00Z means that the trial will expire on June 19, 2014, at 9:00 A.M.
- ***ProductLicenses*** Contains the list of licenses for the app's features that can be bought through an in-app purchase.

Because the *CurrentApp* class contains data and information retrieved from the Windows Store, you can access them only if your app has been published in the Windows Store. Even in that case, it would be hard to test different behaviors of your app in the local environment by using the *CurrentApp* class because you would be working against the actual Windows Store. When dealing with trials and in-app purchases, you have to use the *CurrentAppSimulator* class, which defines methods and properties that mimic those exposed by the *CurrentApp* class, but in a simulated environment. You can use the methods and properties of the *CurrentAppSimulator* class to get simulated license information (such as the app's ID and license metadata) for testing the app's behaviors in your development environment.

EXAM TIP

Remember to replace the *CurrentAppSimulator* class with the *CurrentApp* class before submitting the app to the Windows Store; otherwise, the app does not pass the certification process.

Listing 6-1 shows how to retrieve a simulated license state via the *CurrentAppSimulator* object to display on the screen.

LISTING 6-1 Retrieving a simulated license state

```
protected override void OnNavigatedTo(NavigationEventArgs e)
{
    this.DisplayLicenseInfo();
}

private async void DisplayLicenseInfo()
{
    var licenseInfo = CurrentAppSimulator.LicenseInformation;

    if (licenseInfo.IsActive)
    {
        if (licenseInfo.IsTrial)
        {
            await Dispatcher.RunAsync(Windows.UI.Core.CoreDispatcherPriority.Normal,
                () =>
            {
                LicenseState.Text = "License current status: Trial license";
                var remainingDays = (licenseInfo.ExpirationDate - DateTime.Now).Days;
                LicenseRemainingDays.Text = String.Format(
                    "Expiration date: {0:MM/dd/yyyy} - Remaining days: {1}",
                    licenseInfo.ExpirationDate, remainingDays);
            });
        }
        else
        {
            await Dispatcher.RunAsync(Windows.UI.Core.CoreDispatcherPriority.Normal,
                () =>
            {
                LicenseState.Text = "License current status: Full license";
                LicenseRemainingDays.Text = "no expiration";
            });
        }
    }
    else
    {
        await Dispatcher.RunAsync(Windows.UI.Core.CoreDispatcherPriority.Normal, () =>
        {
            LicenseState.Text = "License current status: license is expired. Please buy
                the app!";
        });
    }
}
```

The use of the *async/await* pattern in the *DisplayLicenseInfo* method is not necessary at this point, but its purpose becomes clear in the following pages, when you call this method from a different thread. The next step is to add a few Extensible Application Markup Language (XAML) controls to display the retrieved information. The following listing shows the XAML definition of the default page:

Sample of XAML code

```
<Page
    x:Class="Demo.Chapter6.TimedTrial.MainPage"
    xmlns="http://schemas.microsoft.com/winfx/2006/xaml/presentation"
    xmlns:x="http://schemas.microsoft.com/winfx/2006/xaml"
    xmlns:local="using:Demo.Chapter6.TimedTrial"
    xmlns:d="http://schemas.microsoft.com/expression/blend/2008"
    xmlns:"mc=http://schemas.openxmlformats.org/markup-compatibility/2006"
    mc:Ignorable="d">

    <StackPanel Background="{StaticResource ApplicationPageBackgroundThemeBrush}">
        <TextBlock x:Name="LicenseState" FontSize="20" Margin="20, 5" Width="Auto" />
        <TextBlock x:Name="LicenseRemainingDays" FontSize="20, 5" Margin="20"
            Width="Auto" />
    </StackPanel>
</Page>
```

If you execute the application, the result should look similar to Figure 6-4.

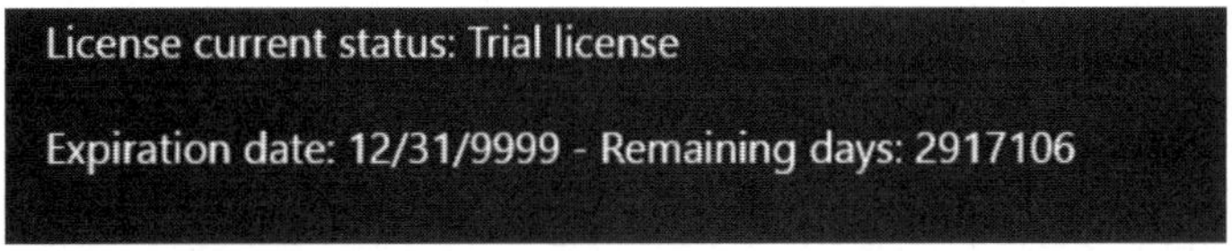

License current status: Trial license

Expiration date: 12/31/9999 - Remaining days: 2917106

FIGURE 6-4 The sample app displaying the license status, expiration date, and remaining days

The information comes from the WindowsStoreProxy.xml file. When using the *CurrentAppSimulator* class, the app's initial license state is defined in the WindowsStoreProxy.xml file that is located in the %userprofile%\appdata\local\packages\<package-moniker>\localstate\microsoft\Windows Store\Apidata folder.

Listing 6-2 shows the autogenerated WindowsStoreProxy.xml file of an app deployed on the local machine.

LISTING 6-2 WindowsStoreProxy.xml file

```
<?xml version="1.0" encoding="utf-16" ?>
<CurrentApp>
    <ListingInformation>
        <App>
            <AppId>00000000-0000-0000-0000-000000000000</AppId>
            <LinkUri>
               http://apps.microsoft.com/webpdp/app/00000000-0000-0000-0000-000000000000
            </LinkUri>
            <CurrentMarket>en-US</CurrentMarket>
            <AgeRating>3</AgeRating>
            <MarketData xml:lang="en-us">
                <Name>AppName</Name>
                <Description>AppDescription</Description>
                <Price>1.00</Price>
                <CurrencySymbol>$</CurrencySymbol>
                <CurrencyCode>USD</CurrencyCode>
            </MarketData>
        </App>
```

```
        <Product ProductId="1" LicenseDuration="0">
            <MarketData xml:lang="en-us">
                <Name>Product1Name</Name>
                <Price>1.00</Price>
                <CurrencySymbol>$</CurrencySymbol>
                <CurrencyCode>USD</CurrencyCode>
            </MarketData>
        </Product>
    </ListingInformation>
    <LicenseInformation>
        <App>
            <IsActive>true</IsActive>
            <IsTrial>true</IsTrial>
        </App>
        <Product ProductId="1">
            <IsActive>true</IsActive>
        </Product>
    </LicenseInformation>
</CurrentApp>
```

Notice that the first section, <ListingInformation>, includes general information about the app, as well as about additional features and products that can be bought separately. Some of this information can be accessed through the corresponding properties of the *CurrentApp* class (or the *CurrentAppSimulator* class in a simulated environment), such as the *AppId* property, which represents the app's unique ID in the Windows Store, and the *Link* property, which represents the link to the listing page in the store.

The other information contained in the <ListingInformation> section includes the name of the app in the store, the age rating, the current market, the app price, and so on. This information can be retrieved from the Windows Store by leveraging the *LoadListingInformationAsync* method of the *CurrentApp* class (or *CurrentAppSimulator*, if you are testing your app in a simulated environment), which returns an instance of the *ListingInformation* class.

> ***NOTE*** **WINDOWSSTOREPROXY.XML FILE**
>
> **The WindowsStoreProxy.xml file is normally created the first time your application tries to access the *CurrentAppSimulator.LicenseInformation* property.**

The C# code in Listing 6-3 displays some of the listing information on the screen.

LISTING 6-3 Displaying listing information

```
protected async override void OnNavigatedTo(NavigationEventArgs e)
{
    this.DisplayListingInformation();
    this.DisplayLicenseInfo();
}
```

```
private async void DisplayListingInformation()
{
    AppId.Text = String.Format("App ID: {0}", CurrentAppSimulator.AppId);
    StoreLink.Text = String.Format("Store Link: {0}", CurrentAppSimulator.LinkUri);

    try
    {
        ListingInformation listingInfo = await
            CurrentAppSimulator.LoadListingInformationAsync();

        AppName.Text = String.Format("App's Name on the Store: {0}", listingInfo.Name);
    }
    catch (Exception ex)
    {
        AppName.Text = String.Format(
            "Listing information unavailable. Exception: {0}", ex.Message);
    }
}
```

To display the app listing information on the screen, modify the XAML code of the page by adding three more *TextBlock* controls, as shown in the following code:

Sample of XAML code

```
<StackPanel Background="{StaticResource ApplicationPageBackgroundThemeBrush}">
        <TextBlock x:Name="AppId" FontSize="20" Margin="20, 5" Width="Auto" />
        <TextBlock x:Name="StoreLink" FontSize="20" Margin="20, 5" Width="Auto" />
        <TextBlock x:Name="AppName" FontSize="20" Margin="20, 5" Width="Auto" />
        <TextBlock x:Name="LicenseState" FontSize="20" Margin="20, 5" Width="Auto" />
        <TextBlock x:Name="LicenseRemainingDays" FontSize="20" Margin="20, 5"
            Width="Auto" />
</StackPanel>
```

If you launch the application, the results should resemble Figure 6-5.

App ID: 00000000-0000-0000-0000-000000000000
Store Link: http://apps.microsoft.com/webpdp/app/00000000-0000-0000-0000-000000000000
App's Name on the Store: AppName
License current status: Trial license
Expiration date: 12/31/9999 - Remaining days: 2917092

FIGURE 6-5 Displaying app listing information

The <ListingInformation> section contains, as its name suggests, specific information about the license state of the app (in the *App* element) and of other products or features that are enabled when the customer makes an in-app purchase (in the *Product* element). As mentioned previously, this information can be retrieved from the store by accessing the *LicenseInformation* object exposed by the *CurrentApp* (or *CurrentAppSimulator*) class.

EXAM TIP

It is important to understand that any modification that alters the license state does not affect the WindowsStoreProxy.xml file, only the object in memory. This means that the next time you launch the app, you will find that the content of the original file has not changed.

Now that you know where the initial licensing information comes from, the next question is why the expiration date corresponds to the *DateTime.Max* value. (The value of this constant is equivalent to December 31, 9999, exactly one 100-nanosecond tick before 00:00:00, January 1, 10000.) The answer is that the default XML definition does not indicate any expiration date. In this case, the *CurrentAppSimulator* object assumes that the trial will never expire (as in a feature-based trial).

Using custom license information

To test your app under different licensing options, you can write your own XML definition file and supply it to the *CurrentAppSimulator* object by leveraging the *ReloadSimulatorAsync* static method. Listing 6-4 shows the custom licensing information used for this sample.

LISTING 6-4 The timed-trial.xml custom file definition

```
<?xml version="1.0" encoding="utf-16"?>
<CurrentApp>
  <ListingInformation>
    <App>
      <AppId>01234567-1234-1234-1234-0123456789AB</AppId>
      <LinkUri>
          http://apps.windows.microsoft.com/app/2B14D306-D8F8-4066-A45B-0FB3464C67F2
      </LinkUri>
      <CurrentMarket>en-US</CurrentMarket>
      <AgeRating>5</AgeRating>
      <MarketData xml:lang="en-us">
        <Name>Basic Timed Trial</Name>
        <Description>Basic Timed trial sample</Description>
        <Price>0.99</Price>
        <CurrencySymbol>$</CurrencySymbol>
      </MarketData>
    </App>
  </ListingInformation>
  <LicenseInformation>
    <App>
      <IsActive>true</IsActive>
      <IsTrial>true</IsTrial>
      <ExpirationDate>2014-06-19T09:00:00.00Z</ExpirationDate>
    </App>
  </LicenseInformation>
</CurrentApp>
```

The *ReloadSimulatorAsync* method accepts the *StorageFile* object, which represents the custom XML file containing the values you want to simulate in a particular scenario. To load and display the custom licensing information, you need to modify the code used in Listing 6-3 as follows:

Sample of C# code

```
protected async override void OnNavigatedTo(NavigationEventArgs e)
{
    await this.LoadCustomSimulator();
    this.DisplayListingInformation();
    this.DisplayLicenseInfo();
}

private async Task LoadCustomSimulator()
{
    StorageFolder proxyDataFolder = await
        Package.Current.InstalledLocation.GetFolderAsync("trial-configs");

    StorageFile proxyFile = await proxyDataFolder.GetFileAsync("timed-trial.xml");

    await CurrentAppSimulator.ReloadSimulatorAsync(proxyFile);
}
```

Figure 6-6 shows the new license information that displays on the screen.

App ID: 01234567-1234-1234-1234-0123456789ab
Store Link: http://apps.windows.microsoft.com/app/2B14D306-D8F8-4066-A45B-0FB3464C67F2
App's Name on the Store: Timed Trial
License current status: Trial license
Expiration date: 06/19/2014 - Remaining days: 440

FIGURE 6-6 Updated license information

Purchasing an app

After you enable trial functionality in your app, the next step is to let customers buy the full version. To accomplish this task, the *CurrentApp* (or *CurrentAppSimulator)* class exposes the *RequestAppPurchaseAsync* static method. This method creates the async operation that enables the user to purchase (or simulate a purchase, in the case of the *CurrentAppSimulator* object) a full license for the current app.

The *RequestAppPurchaseAsync* method accepts a Boolean value as a parameter to indicate whether the method should return a string representing the receipt for the purchase, as shown in Listing 6-5. (You learn how to handle purchase receipts later in this section. For now, use the simplest version of this method by passing *false* as parameter.)

LISTING 6-5 Purchasing an app using the *RequestAppPurchaseAsync* method

```
private async void BuyButton_Click(object sender, RoutedEventArgs e)
{
    try
    {
        await CurrentAppSimulator.RequestAppPurchaseAsync(false);
    }
```

```
    catch (Exception ex)
    {
        PurchaseErrorMessage.Text = String.Format("Unable to buy: {0}", ex.Message);
        PurchaseErrorMessage.Visibility = Windows.UI.Xaml.Visibility.Visible;
    }
}
```

In the XAML page, just add the line of code highlighted in bold:

Sample of XAML code

```
<Page
    x:Class=" Demo.Chapter6.TimedTrial.MainPage"
    xmlns="http://schemas.microsoft.com/winfx/2006/xaml/presentation"
    xmlns:x="http://schemas.microsoft.com/winfx/2006/xaml"
    xmlns:local="using:TimedTrialStep"
    xmlns:d="http://schemas.microsoft.com/expression/blend/2008"
    xmlns:mc="http://schemas.openxmlformats.org/markup-compatibility/2006"
    mc:Ignorable="d">

    <StackPanel Background="{StaticResource ApplicationPageBackgroundThemeBrush}">
        <TextBlock x:Name="AppId" FontSize="20" Margin="20, 5" Width="Auto" />
        <TextBlock x:Name="StoreLink" FontSize="20" Margin="20, 5" Width="Auto" />
        <TextBlock x:Name="AppName" FontSize="20" Margin="20, 5" Width="Auto" />
        <TextBlock x:Name="LicenseState" FontSize="20" Margin="20, 5" Width="Auto" />
        <TextBlock x:Name="LicenseRemainingDays" FontSize="20" Margin="20, 5"
            Width="Auto" />
        <Button x:Name="BuyButton" Click="BuyButton_Click" Content="Buy app" Width="300"
            Height="50" Margin="20, 5" />
       <TextBlock x:Name="PurchaseErrorMessage" FontSize="20" Margin="20, 5"
            Width="Auto" Visibility="Collapsed" />
    </StackPanel>
</Page>
```

If you launch the application and try to buy the app, the *CurrentAppSimulator* displays a Windows Store dialog box (see Figure 6-7), prompting you to select an error code to return. You can choose the result you want to simulate for the current transaction to test whether your code reacts properly to all possible responses, without purchasing the app from the Windows Store. Leave the default value (S_OK, which means the transaction was successful) and click **Continue**.

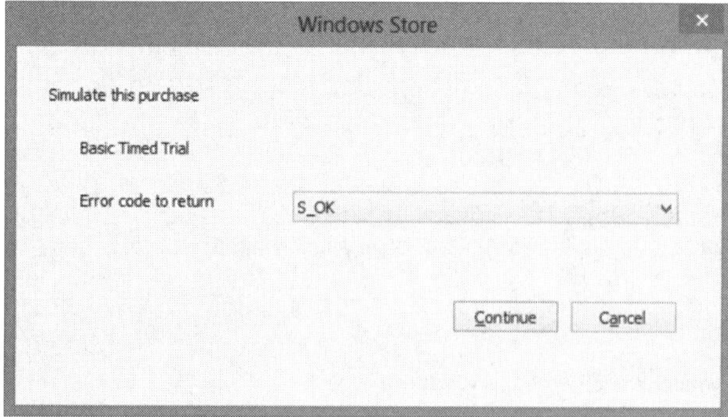

FIGURE 6-7 The Windows Store dialog box prompting for an error code

After the user purchases the full version of the app, you must update the license information to display the new state. The *LicenseInformation* class exposes a *LicenseChanged* event that is raised when the status of the app's license changes. The C# code in Listing 6-6 shows how to handle this event to update the license state displayed on the screen.

LISTING 6-6 Handling the *LicenseChanged* event

```
protected async override void OnNavigatedTo(NavigationEventArgs e)
{
    await this.LoadCustomSimulator();

    this.DisplayListingInformation();

    this.DisplayLicenseInfo();

    CurrentAppSimulator.LicenseInformation.LicenseChanged +=
        LicenseInformation_LicenseChanged;
}

private void LicenseInformation_LicenseChanged()
{
    this.DisplayLicenseInfo();
}

protected override void OnNavigatedFrom(NavigationEventArgs e)
{
    CurrentAppSimulator.LicenseInformation.LicenseChanged -=
        LicenseInformation_LicenseChanged;
}
```

Figure 6-8 shows the updated license state after the user has purchased the full version.

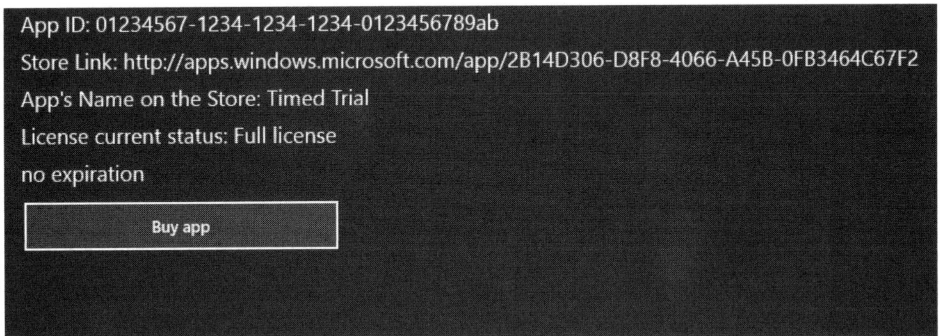

FIGURE 6-8 Updated license information after purchase

> ***NOTE*** **LICENSE STATE MODIFICATION**
>
> **Remember that any modification to the license state does not affect the XML file supplied to the *CurrentAppSimulator* object, only the object in memory.**

So far, you have learned about a timed trial. But what happens if you want to implement a feature-based trial? Depending on the type of trial, the semantics of the *IsActive* and *IsTrial* properties might be slightly different.

If you chose a timed trial, the *IsActive* property tells you if the trial period has already expired (or, in rare cases, if the license is missing or has been revoked). If the property returns *false*, it means the evaluation period is expired and that consequently, your app (in the simplest scenario) should stop working. If the property returns *true*, it means the evaluation period is not over yet, and the app can keep working normally.

EXAM TIP

You should check the *IsTrial* property to verify whether the customer has bought the full version of the app or it is still in trial mode. If in trial mode, you should let your customer know the number of days left before the app stops working.

The following code uses a pattern similar to the timed-trial sample in Listing 6-1:

```
if (licenseInfo.IsActive)
{
    if (licenseInfo.IsTrial)
    {
        // Your app is still in trial mode.
        // Remember to let your customers know the remaining time
        // before the app stops working.
    }
    else
    {
        // The user has bought the full license version of your app.
    }
}
else
{
    // Your app's license is expired (or the license is missing or has been revoked).
    // It means that your app should stop working.
    // Remember to invite your customers to buy the full version of the app
}
```

NOTE ***ISTRIAL*** **PROPERTY**

Remember that the *IsTrial* property returns *true* even if the trial period is expired.

On the contrary, if you offer a feature-based trial, you need to modify the pattern followed in Listing 6-1 because in this case, there is no expiration date that needs to be checked. In a feature-based scenario, the *IsActive* property should return *true* (unless something has gone wrong; remember to handle this scenario as well). In this type of trial, you want to know whether the user has bought the full version of the app to decide what features to enable. This code follows this type of pattern:

```
if (licenseInfo.IsActive)
{
    if (licenseInfo.IsTrial)
    {
        // Your app is in trial mode. Enable only the features available in trial mode.
    }
    else
    {
        // The user has bought the full license for your app.
        // You can now enable all the features.
    }
}
else
{
    // something went wrong: the license is missing or revoked
}
```

Handling errors

When you use the *CurrentApp* class in an application, invoking any methods that access the Windows Store API can result in an exception. For this reason, any call to one of these methods should be wrapped in a *try/catch* block, and you have to be sure that your app is capable of handling these errors gracefully.

You learn how to set up different test strategies in the "Design for error handling" section. For now, keep in mind that in the local environment, you can leverage the *CurrentAppSimulator* class to ensure that your code covers the most common failure scenarios, at a minimum. There are two ways to achieve the same result.

The simplest method is to take advantage of the Windows Store dialog box shown in Figure 6-7 to return different error codes. However, this procedure can be quite time-consuming and, more importantly, it cannot be used in an automated test strategy. The *CurrentAppSimulator* object gives you another way to achieve this objective. When supplying the *CurrentAppSimulator* object with a custom XML definition for the license state, you can leverage the *Simulation* element to specify what error code you want each method to return. Listing 6-7 shows a revised version of the timed-trial.xml supplied to the *CurrentAppSimulator* class (changes are highlighted in bold).

LISTING 6-7 Retrieving a simulated license state

```
<?xml version="1.0" encoding="utf-16"?>
<CurrentApp>
  <ListingInformation>
    <App>
      <AppId>01234567-1234-1234-1234-0123456789AB</AppId>
      <LinkUri>
        http://apps.windows.microsoft.com/app/2B14D306-D8F8-4066-A45B-0FB3464C67F2
      </LinkUri>
      <CurrentMarket>en-US</CurrentMarket>
      <AgeRating>5</AgeRating>
      <MarketData xml:lang="en-us">
```

```
        <Name>Basic Timed Trial</Name>
        <Description>Basic Timed trial sample</Description>
        <Price>0.99</Price>
        <CurrencySymbol>$</CurrencySymbol>
      </MarketData>
    </App>
  </ListingInformation>
  <LicenseInformation>
    <App>
      <IsActive>true</IsActive>
      <IsTrial>true</IsTrial>
      <ExpirationDate>2014-06-19T09:00:00.00Z</ExpirationDate>
    </App>
  </LicenseInformation>
  <Simulation SimulationMode="Automatic">
    <DefaultResponse MethodName="RequestAppPurchaseAsync_GetResult" HResult="E_FAIL"/>
  </Simulation>
</CurrentApp>
```

The *Simulation* element describes how to handle the various method calls. When the *SimulationMode* attribute is set to *Automatic*, the methods specified in the *MethodName* attribute automatically returns the error code indicated in the *HResult* attribute.

> ***NOTE* <SIMULATION> SECTION**
>
> **If you add a <Simulation> section to the custom XML license definition and launch the app, the Windows Store dialog box shown in Figure 6-7 does not appear. In this case, you have already defined the response code to be returned for the method indicated in the *MethodName* attribute.**

Unfortunately, this strategy has significant drawbacks because the *MethodName* attribute supports only the following three methods: *RequestAppPurchaseAsync_GetResult*, *RequestProductPurchaseAsync_GetResult*, and *LoadListingInformationAsync_GetResult*. (The *GetResult* suffix indicates a call to the *GetResults* method exposed by the *IAsyncOperation<TResult>* object to retrieve the result of the asynchronous operation.) For example, if you use the XML definition in Listing 6-7, any call to the *RequestAppPurchaseAsync* method would throw an exception with an E_Fail error code.

This strategy can be used when running automated test cases. In fact, you can leverage the *ReloadSimulatorAsync* method to supply different metadata definitions to your app. For example, you could prepare multiple XML files with different metadata and then feed them to the *CurrentAppSimulator* object to simulate the most common scenarios.

Setting up in-app purchases

You can offer products and features from within your app that your customers can buy. You must first design the app's code to treat these features and products as separate modules so they can be incorporated into your licensing model without effort. Then you can indicate which features or products you want to offer in the in-app section of your Windows Store Dashboard.

> ***MORE INFO*** **IN-APP PURCHASES**
>
> **Deciding what features or products might be worth selling separately to your customers is just the first step. You must design the code of your application so that you can actually treat these features and products as separate modules, so they can be incorporated into your licensing model without effort. You can find some useful tips on this topic at the following address: *http://msdn.microsoft.com/en-us/library/windows/apps/hh694067.aspx#Y959*.**

To begin, you must add a new custom license definition to be supplied to the *CurrentAppSimulator* that includes information about the features and products that can be purchased. It enables you to test the app's behavior in the local environment. Listing 6-8 shows a custom XML license definition to test the in-app purchase feature. For the sake of simplicity, only one extra feature is added.

LISTING 6-8 The in-app-purchase.xml custom file definition to test the in-app purchase feature

```
<?xml version="1.0" encoding="utf-16"?>
<CurrentApp>
  <ListingInformation>
    <App>
      <AppId>01234567-1234-1234-1234-0123456789AB</AppId>
      <LinkUri>
          http://apps.windows.microsoft.com/app/2B14D306-D8F8-4066-A45B-0FB3464C67F2
      </LinkUri>
      <CurrentMarket>en-US</CurrentMarket>
      <AgeRating>5</AgeRating>
      <MarketData xml:lang="en-us">
        <Name>In-app Purchase Sample</Name>
        <Description>In-app Sample</Description>
        <Price>0.99</Price>
        <CurrencySymbol>$</CurrencySymbol>
      </MarketData>
    </App>
    <Product ProductId="feature1">
      <MarketData xml:lang="en-us">
        <Name>Advanced Feature</Name>
        <Price>0.99</Price>
        <CurrencySymbol>$</CurrencySymbol>
        <CurrencyCode>USD</CurrencyCode>
      </MarketData>
    </Product>
  </ListingInformation>
  <LicenseInformation>
    <App>
      <IsActive>true</IsActive>
      <IsTrial>false</IsTrial>
    </App>
```

```
    <Product ProductId="feature1">
      <IsActive>false</IsActive>
    </Product>
  </LicenseInformation>
</CurrentApp>
```

The *IsTrial* element of the <App> section is set to *false* because the in-app purchase feature is not compatible with trial mode. In addition, the *IsActive* property of the offered product is set to *false*, which means the user has not yet purchased the extra feature or product.

After you provide the new custom license definition to the *CurrentAppSimulator* instance, you can retrieve the information contained in the *Product* element within the <ListingInformation> section, such as the feature's name and price, by leveraging the *LoadListingInformationAsync* method. This method returns a read-only dictionary containing all the features and products that can be purchased by the customer. Listing 6-9 shows how to retrieve the listing information concerning the offered feature.

LISTING 6-9 Retrieving listing information of a feature

```
private async void DisplayProductListingInfo()
{
    try
    {
        ListingInformation listingInfo = await
            CurrentAppSimulator.LoadListingInformationAsync();

        var productListing = listingInfo.ProductListings["feature1"];

        InAppPurchaseFeatureName.Text = String.Format(
            "Feature name: {0}", productListing.Name);
        InAppPurchaseFeaturePrice.Text = String.Format(
            "You can buy this feature for {0}", productListing.FormattedPrice);
    }
    catch (Exception ex)
    {
        InAppPurchaseErrorMessage.Text = String.Format(
            "Unable to show feature info. Exception: {0}", ex.Message);
    }
}
```

You can also display the licensing information of the offered feature, as shown in Listing 6-10, in which the code retrieves the *ProductLicense* for the current feature and displays the state of the license.

LISTING 6-10 Displaying licensing information of a feature

```
private void DisplayProductLicenseInfo()
{
    try
    {
        var productLicenses = CurrentAppSimulator.LicenseInformation.ProductLicenses;
        var productLicense = productLicenses["feature1"];
        if (!productLicense.IsActive)
```

```
        {
            Dispatcher.RunAsync(Windows.UI.Core.CoreDispatcherPriority.Normal, () =>
            {
                InAppPurchaseFeatureLicenseStatus.Text = String.Format("Advanced feature
                    license status: inactive. You cannot use this feature");
            });
        }
        else
        {
            Dispatcher.RunAsync(Windows.UI.Core.CoreDispatcherPriority.Normal, () =>
            {
                InAppPurchaseFeatureLicenseStatus.Text = String.Format("Advanced feature
                license status: active. You can now use this feature");
            });
        }
    }
    catch (Exception ex)
    {
        Dispatcher.RunAsync(Windows.UI.Core.CoreDispatcherPriority.Normal, () =>
        {
            InAppPurchaseErrorMessage.Text = String.Format("Unable to show product
               information. Exception: {0}", ex.Message);
        });
    }
}
```

Do not forget to modify the other methods to display the new information, as shown in Listing 6-11 (changes are highlighted in bold).

LISTING 6-11 Modifying methods to display new information

```
protected async override void OnNavigatedTo(NavigationEventArgs e)
{
    await this.LoadCustomSimulator();
    this.DisplayListingInformation();
    this.DisplayLicenseInfo();
    this.DisplayProductListingInfo();
    this.DisplayProductLicenseInfo();

    CurrentAppSimulator.LicenseInformation.LicenseChanged +=
        LicenseInformation_LicenseChanged;
}

private async Task LoadCustomSimulator()
{
    StorageFolder proxyDataFolder = await
        Package.Current.InstalledLocation.GetFolderAsync("trial-configs");

    StorageFile proxyFile = await proxyDataFolder.GetFileAsync("in-app-purchase.xml");
    await CurrentAppSimulator.ReloadSimulatorAsync(proxyFile);
}

private void LicenseInformation_LicenseChanged()
{
    this.DisplayLicenseInfo();
    this.DisplayProductLicenseInfo();
}
```

Now that you have all the information about the features and products offered through this app, you can implement the in-app purchase feature. The *RequestProductPurchaseAsync* method accepts two parameters: a string representing the ID of the feature to be purchased (that must match the name of the product added in the Windows Store Dashboard) and a Boolean value indicating whether to return a receipt for the purchase. The following code excerpt shows the complete code for this method:

Sample of C# code

```
private async void InAppPurchaseButton_Click(object sender, RoutedEventArgs e)
{
    try
    {
        await CurrentAppSimulator.RequestProductPurchaseAsync("feature1", false);
    }
    catch (Exception ex)
    {
        InAppPurchaseErrorMessage.Text = String.Format("Unable to purchase the feature.
            Exception: {0}", ex.Message);
    }
}
```

You can modify the XAML code of the page, as follows, to display the new information:

Sample of XAML code

```
<StackPanel Background="{StaticResource ApplicationPageBackgroundThemeBrush}">
    <TextBlock x:Name="AppId" FontSize="20" Margin="20, 5" Width="Auto" />
    <TextBlock x:Name="StoreLink" FontSize="20" Margin="20, 5" Width="Auto" />
    <TextBlock x:Name="AppName" FontSize="20" Margin="20, 5" Width="Auto" />
    <TextBlock x:Name="LicenseState" FontSize="20" Margin="20, 5" Width="Auto" />
    <TextBlock x:Name="LicenseRemainingDays" FontSize="20" Margin="20, 5"
        Width="Auto" />
    <Button x:Name="BuyButton" Click="BuyButton_Click" Content="Buy app" Width="300"
        Height="50" Margin="20, 5" />
    <TextBlock x:Name="PurchaseErrorMessage" FontSize="20" Margin="20, 5" Width="Auto"
        Visibility="Collapsed" />
    <TextBlock x:Name="InAppPurchaseFeatureName" FontSize="20" Margin="20, 5"
        Width="Auto" />
    <TextBlock x:Name="InAppPurchaseFeatureLicenseStatus" FontSize="20" Margin="20, 5"
        Width="Auto" />
    <TextBlock x:Name="InAppPurchaseFeaturePrice" FontSize="20" Margin="20, 5"
        Width="Auto" />
    <Button x:Name="InAppPurchaseButton" Click="InAppPurchaseButton_Click"
        Content="Buy advanced feature" Width="300" Height="50" Margin="20, 5" />
    <TextBlock x:Name="InAppPurchaseErrorMessage" FontSize="20" Margin="20, 5"
       Width="Auto" Visibility="Collapsed" />
</StackPanel>
```

Running the app displays a screen similar to Figure 6-9. The newly added information is indicated with a callout. The state of the feature's license is set to inactive, which means you do not have access to this feature unless you purchase it.

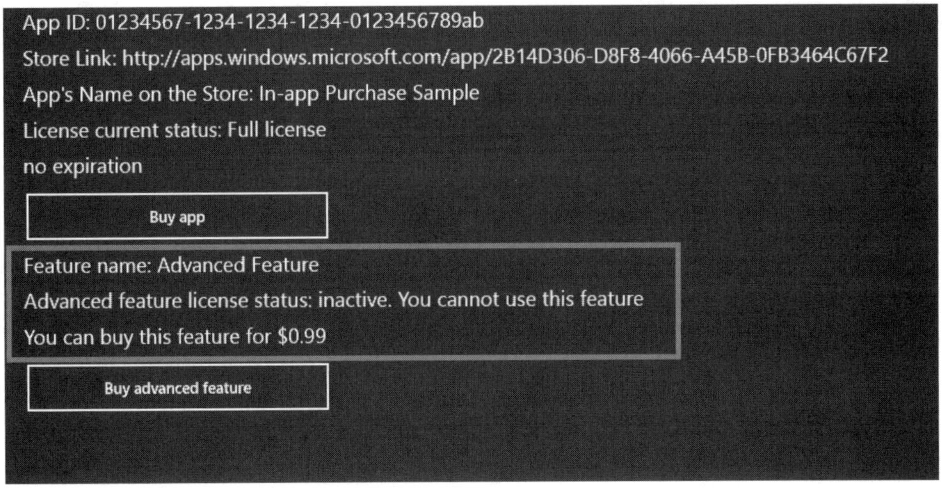

App ID: 01234567-1234-1234-1234-0123456789ab
Store Link: http://apps.windows.microsoft.com/app/2B14D306-D8F8-4066-A45B-0FB3464C67F2
App's Name on the Store: In-app Purchase Sample
License current status: Full license
no expiration
Buy app
Feature name: Advanced Feature
Advanced feature license status: inactive. You cannot use this feature
You can buy this feature for $0.99
Buy advanced feature

FIGURE 6-9 Information about the advanced feature

To step through the transaction, click the **Buy Advanced Feature** button. In the Windows Store dialog box, select the **S_OK** code in the simulator to simulate that the transaction has succeeded. The screen should display the updated license state for the newly purchased advanced feature, as shown in Figure 6-10.

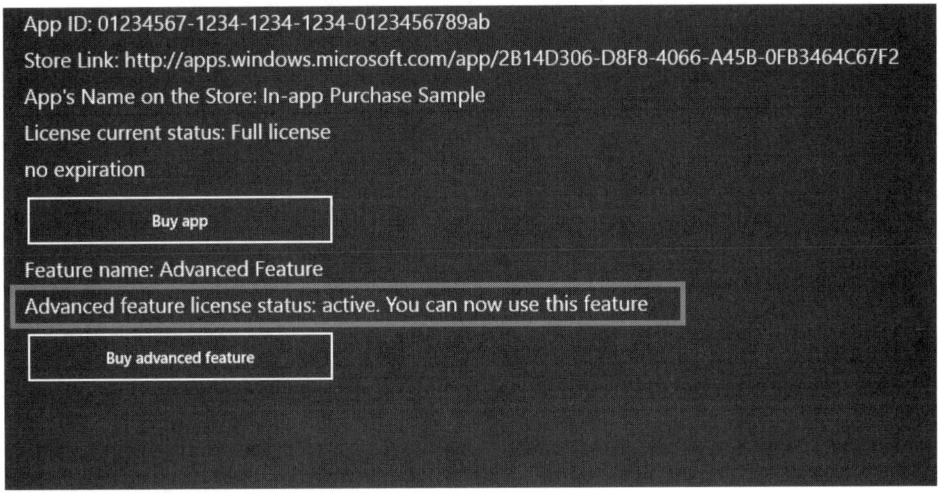

App ID: 01234567-1234-1234-1234-0123456789ab
Store Link: http://apps.windows.microsoft.com/app/2B14D306-D8F8-4066-A45B-0FB3464C67F2
App's Name on the Store: In-app Purchase Sample
License current status: Full license
no expiration
Buy app
Feature name: Advanced Feature
Advanced feature license status: active. You can now use this feature
Buy advanced feature

FIGURE 6-10 Updated license information for the advanced feature

Retrieving and validating the receipts for your purchases

Sometimes, you might need to check the receipt of a transaction to determine whether the user bought the full version of your app or a specific feature or product. The *Windows.ApplicationModel.Store* namespace supports two ways of getting a receipt:

- You can ask for a receipt when you purchase an app. To do that, you need to only pass *true* to the *RequestProductPurchaseAsync* method (as the only parameter) or to the *RequestAppPurchaseAsync* method (as a second parameter).
- You can ask for a receipt at any time by calling the *GetAppReceiptAsync* and *GetProductReceiptAsync* methods.

The receipt for an app or product purchase consists of an XML fragment that contains all the information regarding the transaction, such as the receipt ID, the app ID, the date of the purchase, and the type of license purchased. Listing 6-12 shows an example of an app purchase receipt.

LISTING 6-12 An in-app purchase receipt in XML

```
<?xml version="1.0" encoding="utf-8" ?>
  <Receipt Version="1.0" ReceiptDate="2013-04-09T08:34:52Z" CertificateId=""
      ReceiptDeviceId="db2e1812-c704-4ce9-82b0-dc0910476139">
  <AppReceipt Id="843f7847-faf4-49bc-be5c-ae818216ad57"
    AppId="b1cd9500-216a-496a-b377-d8343aa36f32_16p6bmm8bp4fr"
    PurchaseDate="2013-04-09T08:34:45Z" LicenseType="Full" />
  <ProductReceipt Id="673f1d2a-2518-41e4-883f-b0cb4d2d8f09"
      AppId="b1cd9500-216a-496a-b377-d8343aa36f32_16p6bmm8bp4fr" ProductId="feature1"
      PurchaseDate="2013-04-09T08:34:47Z" ProductType="Durable" />
  <Signature xmlns="http://www.w3.org/2000/09/xmldsig#">
    <SignedInfo>
      <CanonicalizationMethod Algorithm="http://www.w3.org/2001/10/xml-exc-c14n#" />
      <SignatureMethod Algorithm="http://www.w3.org/2001/04/xmldsig-more#rsa-sha256" />
      <Reference URI="">
        <Transforms>
          <Transform
              Algorithm="http://www.w3.org/2000/09/xmldsig#enveloped-signature" />
        </Transforms>
        <DigestMethod Algorithm="http://www.w3.org/2001/04/xmlenc#sha256" />
        <DigestValue>cdiU06eD8X/w1aGCHeaGCG9w/kWZ8I099rw4mmPpvdU=</DigestValue>
      </Reference>
    </SignedInfo>
    <SignatureValue>
          SjRIxS/2r2P6ZdgaR9bwUSa6ZItYYFpKLJZrnAa3zkMylbiWjh9oZGGng2p6... (omitted)
      </SignatureValue>
  </Signature>
</Receipt>
```

The receipt fragment uses the following elements and attributes:

- ***Receipt*** This element contains information about apps and in-app purchases. Its attributes list includes the following:
  - ***CertificateId*** The certificate thumbprint used to sign the receipt.
  - ***ReceiptDate*** When the receipt was signed and downloaded.
  - ***ReceiptDeviceId*** Identifies the device used to request the receipt.
- ***AppReceipt*** This element includes all the information about the purchase of the app. Its attributes are:
  - ***Id*** The unique identifier of the purchase.
  - ***AppId*** A unique name assigned by the operating system to identify the package. Corresponds to the package family name. The *AppId* name is displayed in the Packaging section of the Package.appxmanifest file.
  - ***LicenseType*** The type of license purchased by the user.
  - ***PurchaseDate*** When the app was bought.
- ***ProductReceipt*** This element contains information about in-app purchases. Its attributes include the following:
  - ***AppId*** The app id (see the previous list).
  - ***ProductId*** The product ID.
  - ***PurchaseDate*** When the product was purchased.
  - ***ProductType*** The duration of the license for the product. In theory, *ProductType* can assume two values: *Consumable*, meaning that the purchased product can be used and then can be purchased again (such as credits that can be used to buy items in a game); or *Durable*, meaning that the purchased product cannot be consumed and will last forever. However, the first option does not apply to Windows Store apps (only Windows Phone apps). Remember, though, that a product/feature can have an expiration date.
- ***Signature*** This element contains the digital signature for the receipt you can use to validate the receipt and make sure no tampering took place. See Chapter 5, "Manage data and security," for further details.

> ***MORE INFO*** **RECEIPT AUTHENTICITY VALIDATION**
>
> **For details about receipt authenticity validation, visit *http://msdn.microsoft.com/en-us/library/windows/apps/jj649137.aspx*.**

Thought experiment

Making the purchased feature available on different Windows 8 devices

In this thought experiment, apply what you've learned about this objective. You can find answers to these questions in the "Answers" section at the end of this chapter.

You have developed a Windows Store game that enables users to play a few levels for free; then they have to buy additional levels in exchange for a small fee.

Because the app can be installed on up to five devices, what safe mechanism could you leverage to ensure that the user can play the new levels on a different Windows 8 device after the extra content is purchased?

Objective summary

- Choose the business model that best suits your needs and use the *CurrentAppSimulator* to test your app's behavior. Remember to replace any instance of *CurrentAppSimulator* with the *CurrentApp* instance before publishing your app in the Windows Store.
- Check the state of your app's license by leveraging the *LicenseInformation* property of the *CurrentApp* class. Check the *IsActive* and *IsTrial* properties and act accordingly.
- Let your customers purchase your app and other features and products by using the *RequestAppPurchaseAsync* and *RequestProductPurchaseAsync* methods.
- Retrieve purchase receipts by calling *GetAppReceiptAsync* and *GetProductReceiptAsync*.

Objective review

Answer the following questions to test your knowledge of the information in this objective. You can find the answers to these questions and explanations of why each answer choice is correct or incorrect in the "Answers" section at the end of this chapter.

1. What class should you use to test your app's behaviors in the local environment when dealing with license states and in-app purchases?
   - **A.** Always use the *CurrentApp* class, regardless of whether your app was published in the Windows Store.
   - **B.** Use the *CurrentApp* class, but only if your app was not published in the Windows Store yet.
   - **C.** Use the *CurrentAppSimulator* to test your app locally, and then replace any reference to this class with the *CurrentApp* class before publishing your app.
   - **D.** There is no way to test your app's behaviors before it is published in the Windows Store.

2. In a feature-based trial, what does it mean when the *IsActive* property of the *LicensingInformation* class returns *false*?
   - **A.** The trial period has expired.
   - **B.** The app's license is revoked or missing.
   - **C.** The user has purchased the full version of the app.
   - **D.** The user can no longer purchase the app.
3. What is the meaning of the Boolean parameter passed to the *RequestAppPurchase-Async* method when purchasing a trial app?
   - **A.** It indicates whether the app is performing a real transaction or a simulated purchase.
   - **B.** It indicates whether the app can be purchased for free.
   - **C.** It indicates whether your customer is purchasing all extra features and products, along with the full license version of the app.
   - **D.** It indicates whether you want the method to return the receipt for the app purchase.

Objective 6.2: Design for error handling

In this objective, you learn how to handle errors and exceptions before they reach the user and how to use the *Application* class for catching unhandled exceptions. You also learn how to deal with device capability errors and asynchronous exceptions.

This objective covers how to:

- Design the app so that errors and exceptions never reach the user
- Use the *Application* class for global collection
- Handle device capability errors
- Handle asynchronous exceptions

Handling exceptions in the .NET Framework

All .NET applications, including Windows Store apps, must be able to handle errors and exceptions so they never reach the user directly. The common language runtime (CLR) provides a model for notifying errors in a uniform way. This model states that any .NET Framework operation generally indicates its failure by throwing exceptions. It also means that all the patterns and best practices that usually apply in .NET error handling can and should be proficiently used in handling exceptions in a Windows Store app as well.

MORE INFO CLR EXCEPTION HANDLING

For further details on the topic, you can visit *http://msdn.microsoft.com/en-us/library/2w8f0bss(v=vs.71).aspx.*

The following list summarizes some fundamental guidelines you should follow when designing your Windows Store app:

- Set up a *try/catch* block wherever there's a chance the app might not function as expected, such as when accessing a resource that might be unavailable or missing, or when relying on types and functions over which you don't have any control (third-party libraries, remote services, and so on).
- Use the *finally* block to release any unmanaged resource and perform any necessary clean-up as soon as possible.
- Use multiple *catch* blocks any time the code might throw different types of exceptions. In this case, order exceptions in *catch* blocks from the most specific to the least specific and make sure that the last *catch* block in the sequence is the most generic. Exceptions are caught only if they match the type specified in the *catch* block. For example, in the following code excerpt, the first *catch* block catches only those exceptions that match the type specified in the block (that is, if the exception is of type *UnauthorizedAccessException*). If the types do not match, the exception keeps propagating until it is caught by the second, more generic *catch* block.

  Sample of C# code

  ```
  try
  {
      Geoposition pos = await this._geo.GetGeopositionAsync();
      LatitudeTextBlock.Text = "Latitude: " + pos.Coordinate.Latitude.ToString();
      LongitudeTextBlock.Text = «Longitude: « + pos.Coordinate.Longitude.ToString();
  }
  catch (UnauthorizedAccessException ex)
  {
       ErrorMessageText.Text =
           "This app needs your permission to access to your location";
   }
  catch (Exception ex)
  {
       ErrorMessageText.Text = "Unable to initialize your location";
  }
  ```

- When you create your own custom classes to handle exceptions, derive them from the *Exception* base class or one of its derived classes, and implement all the constructors of the base class, as shown in the following code snippet:

  ```
  public class MyCustomException: Exception
  {
      public MyCustomException()
      {
      }
  ```

```
        public MyCustomException(string message) : base(message)
        {
        }

        public MyCustomException(string message, Exception inner) :
            base(message, inner)
        {
        }
    }
```

- In your methods, you should prefer throwing an exception to indicate that something went wrong instead of returning error codes or other messages. Error codes or null values do not continue to propagate through the system, thus they might go unnoticed. However, you can return *null* for very common error cases (for example, a *GetCustomerById* method that returns *null* when the customer is not found).
- Clean up any intermediate results when throwing an exception. It should be safe for callers to assume that when an exception is thrown from a method, the state of the object involved is not affected.
- When dealing with exceptions at the user interface level, include a localized description string in every exception that will display to the user.

All the patterns and best practices discussed so far apply to any .NET application. When you deal with Windows Store apps, however, there are a few things worth further consideration. First, the XAML framework provides a way to catch exceptions that have not been handled by the application code that you must be aware of. Second, exceptions raised by any device capability not working properly should be addressed in a specific way. These kinds of exceptions are usually raised because your app lacks the permission to access that capability or because it is not present on the system. Third, a significant number of Windows Runtime (WinRT) APIs are based on asynchronous calls. (You will learn how to handle asynchronous exceptions and why you should avoid unobserved exceptions in the "Handling asynchronous errors" section later in this chapter.)

Catching errors and exceptions at the application level

The *Application* class of a Windows Store app, which encapsulates your app and its services, exposes a special event called *UnhandledException* that is fired when the XAML framework encounters exceptions that have not been handled by the application code.

It is important to understand that, as stated in the official MSDN documentation, "this event will only be raised when there is no longer any possibility that application code can catch an exception." For example, an exception raised but not caught during the execution of a function propagates through the XAML framework back to the caller, which is given a chance to catch it. If the caller does not handle the exception, the exception keeps propagating to the next function in the chain of subsequent calls. Only when there are no more chances to handle the exception in the application code is the *UnhandledException* event raised.

Before learning how to handle this event from code, however, it might be interesting to see what happens when an unhandled exception is raised while you debug your app. Listing 6-13 shows the autogenerated code that provides the entry point for your application, such as in Microsoft Silverlight, Windows Presentation Foundation (WPF), or Windows Phone apps.

LISTING 6-13 The autogenerated code

```
//------------------------------------------------------------------------------
// <auto-generated>
//     This code was generated by a tool.
//
//     Changes to this file may cause incorrect behavior and will be lost if
//     the code is regenerated.
// </auto-generated>
//------------------------------------------------------------------------------

namespace MyWindowsStoreApp
{
#if !DISABLE_XAML_GENERATED_MAIN
    public static class Program
    {
        [global::System.CodeDom.Compiler.GeneratedCodeAttribute
            ("Microsoft.Windows.UI.Xaml.Build.Tasks"," 4.0.0.0")]
        [global::System.Diagnostics.DebuggerNonUserCodeAttribute()]
        static void Main(string[] args)
        {
            global::Windows.UI.Xaml.Application.Start((p) => new App());
        }
    }
#endif

    partial class App : global::Windows.UI.Xaml.Application
    {
        [global::System.CodeDom.Compiler.GeneratedCodeAttribute
            ("Microsoft.Windows.UI.Xaml.Build.Tasks"," 4.0.0.0")]
        private bool _contentLoaded;

        [global::System.CodeDom.Compiler.GeneratedCodeAttribute
            ("Microsoft.Windows.UI.Xaml.Build.Tasks"," 4.0.0.0")]
        [global::System.Diagnostics.DebuggerNonUserCodeAttribute()]

        public void InitializeComponent()
        {
            if (_contentLoaded)
                return;

            _contentLoaded = true;

#if DEBUG && !DISABLE_XAML_GENERATED_BINDING_DEBUG_OUTPUT
            DebugSettings.BindingFailed += (sender, args) =>
            {
                global::System.Diagnostics.Debug.WriteLine(args.Message);
            };
```

```
#endif
#if DEBUG && !DISABLE_XAML_GENERATED_BREAK_ON_UNHANDLED_EXCEPTION
            UnhandledException += (sender, e) =>
            {
                if (global::System.Diagnostics.Debugger.IsAttached)
                    global::System.Diagnostics.Debugger.Break();
            };
#endif
        }
    }
}
```

The *Program* class instantiates the *App* class (which wraps your application code) and passes it to the *Windows.UI.Xaml.Application.Start* method. In the *App* class, the autogenerated code subscribes two events: the *BindingFailed* event, which is raised when a binding in the XAML code cannot be resolved, and the *UnhandledException* event. Both the handlers are wrapped in a conditional statement that has those instructions compiled only if the solution is built in debug mode. When an app encounters an unhandled exception during debugging, the autogenerated code puts the debugger in "break" mode. Otherwise, there is no need to break the debugger. The code in the conditional statement is not compiled, the *UnhandledException* event is not handled, and the application is terminated.

If you want to handle the event for yourself, subscribe the *UnhandledException* event in the constructor of your *App* class and take the necessary actions in the corresponding event handler. The following code shows you how:

Sample of C# code

```
public App()
{
    this.InitializeComponent();
    this.Suspending += OnSuspending;

    UnhandledException += App_UnhandledException;
}

void App_UnhandledException(object sender, UnhandledExceptionEventArgs args)
{
    // Handle the event

    // If you want to avoid the app being terminated, set the Handled property to true
    args.Handled = true;
}
```

In the event handler, if you set the *Handled* property of the *UnhandledExceptionEventArgs* to *true*, you tell the framework not to process the exception any further because you handled it. In this case, the app might not be terminated.

Microsoft discourages this practice, however, for at least two reasons:

- The *UnhandledExceptionEventArgs* received by the event handler does not offer enough information to know whether keeping the application up and running is safe. Consider that because you do not know where that exception comes from, parts of your app might be in an inconsistent state when the exception is raised. Besides, any information about type, message, and stack trace of the unhandled exception (exposed through in the *Exception* property of the *UnhandledExceptionEventArgs*) are not guaranteed to match those of the original exception, so you can never be sure about what kind of error you are actually dealing with.

- When exceptions are raised during certain operations, the framework considers these operations as not recoverable because it knows they will leave the system in an inconsistent state. In these scenarios, the app is terminated anyway, regardless of the *Handled* property's value.

For these reasons, you should never leverage this property to avoid termination unless you are certain there will be no consequences. Instead, you should use the *UnhandledException* event handler to perform certain actions, such as logging the exception for tracking purposes or saving temporary data in the local storage, before exiting the application.

It is important to understand that this event suffers from other important limitations that should discourage you from relying too much on it. According to the official MSDN documentation, exceptions that are not connected to the XAML Framework do not fire the *UnhandledException* event (for example, exceptions raised by worker threads do not result in the event being raised).

Handling device capability errors

Some of the capabilities declared in the application manifest file, such as microphone, camera, and location providers, are considered "sensitive devices" because they can reveal personal information that the user might want to be private (such her current location). The first time your Windows Store app needs to access a sensitive device declared in the application manifest, users have to grant their permission before the app can start using the corresponding feature. Figure 6-11 shows an app asking the user's permission to use the webcam.

FIGURE 6-11 Asking permission to use a webcam

After the permission has been granted, a user can revoke it at any time by modifying the Privacy settings in the Permissions flyout, activated through the Settings charm. See Figure 6-12.

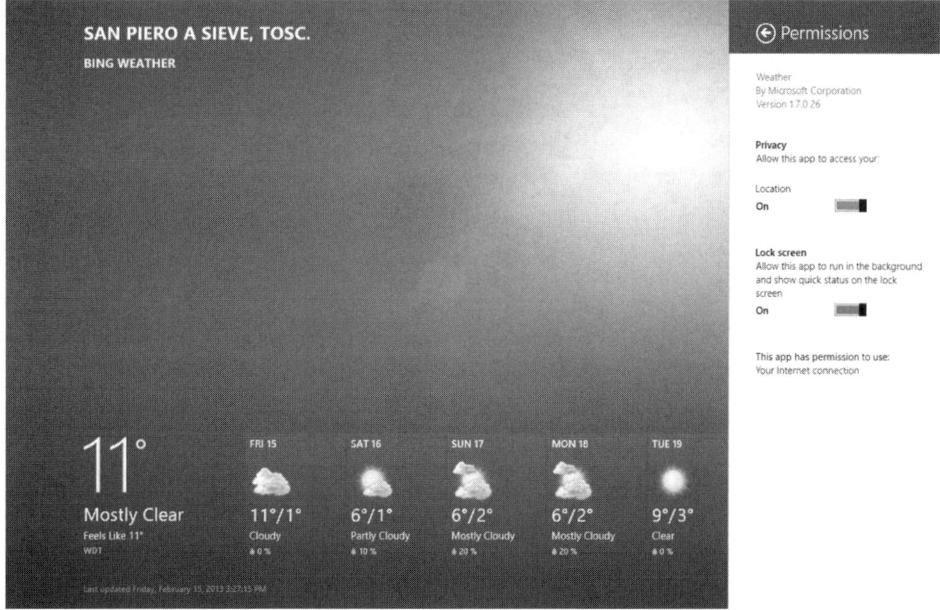

FIGURE 6-12 Privacy settings

> ***NOTE*** **SENSITIVE DEVICE USE**
>
> **Permissions for Windows Store apps to use sensitive devices are specific for each app, on a per-user basis.**

To provide a good user experience when your app needs to access sensitive devices, you need to handle the errors that can occur when trying to access a disabled device capability. Reasons your app might not be able to access a sensitive device include these:

- The user does not grant access to the device capability in the dialog box.
- The user revoked the permission to access the device in the Settings charm.
- The device capability is not present on the system.

Not all WinRT APIs behave in the same manner when trying to access capabilities for which the app does not have permission, however.

For example, if your app uses the *Windows.Media.Capture.MediaCapture* class to preview or capture photos, video, or audio, and the device is not present on the system, any call to the *InitializeAsync* method of the *MediaCapture* instance raises a *System.Exception*. If the device is present, but the user did not grant the app permission to access the device capability (or the permission was revoked), the system raises an *UnauthorizedAccessException*. In both cases, you have to handle the errors gracefully, informing the user that the device capability is not available on the system or that it cannot be used until permission is granted through the Settings charm. Listing 6-14 shows how to handle a simple scenario.

LISTING 6-14 Handling media capture errors

```
private MediaCapture _mediaCaptureManager;

private async void StartMediaCapture_Click(object sender, RoutedEventArgs e)
{
    try
    {
        DeviceInformationCollection devInfoCollection = await
            DeviceInformation.FindAllAsync(DeviceClass.VideoCapture);
        MediaCaptureInitializationSettings settings = new
            Windows.Media.Capture.MediaCaptureInitializationSettings();

        if (devInfoCollection.Count > 0)
        {
            settings.VideoDeviceId = devInfoCollection[0].Id;

            this._mediaCaptureManager = new MediaCapture();
            await this._mediaCaptureManager.InitializeAsync();
            capturePreview.Source = this._mediaCaptureManager;

            await this._mediaCaptureManager.StartPreviewAsync();
        }
        else
            ErrorMessageText.Text = "No device connected";
    }
    catch (UnauthorizedAccessException ex)
    {
        ErrorMessageText.Text = "This app needs your permission to use the webcam";
    }
    catch (Exception ex)
    {
        ErrorMessageText.Text = "Unable to initialize the webcam";
    }
}
```

Before trying to access a media capture device, the code searches for all the available devices looking for a video capture device. If a video capture device is found, the code tries to initialize the device by calling the *InitializeAsync* method.

On the contrary, if you use the *CaptureCameraUI* class, and the webcam capability is turned off, invoking the *CaptureFileAsync* method does not raise an error. Instead, the Camera Capture user interface (UI) displays a message indicating that the webcam capability is turned off and needs user intervention to be enabled, as shown in Figure 6-13.

FIGURE 6-13 Message regarding permission to use camera

A different message displays if you do not have a camera connected to your PC, as shown in Figure 6-14.

FIGURE 6-14 Message displayed when no camera is connected

Listing 6-15 shows an example of *CaptureFileAsync* usage. Because you do not need to check for permission in this case, the resulting code is simple.

LISTING 6-15 Using *CaptureFileAsync*

```
private async void TakePhoto_Click(object sender, RoutedEventArgs e)
{
    try
    {
        var camera = new CameraCaptureUI();
        var img = await camera.CaptureFileAsync(CameraCaptureUIMode.Photo);
        if (img != null)
        {
            var stream = await img.OpenAsync(FileAccessMode.Read);
            var bitmap = new BitmapImage();
            bitmap.SetSource(stream);
            ImageView.Source = bitmap;
```

```
            }
        }
        catch (Exception ex)
        {
            ErrorMessageText.Text = "Unable to access the webcam";
        }
    }
```

Although the *CameraCaptureUI.CaptureFileAsync* does not throw any exceptions when the permission is missing, you should still wrap the call to the API with a *try/catch* block. That's because, permissions aside, something else can go wrong. For example, Figure 6-15 shows a *System.Exception* raised due to an unpredictable malfunction of the webcam device.

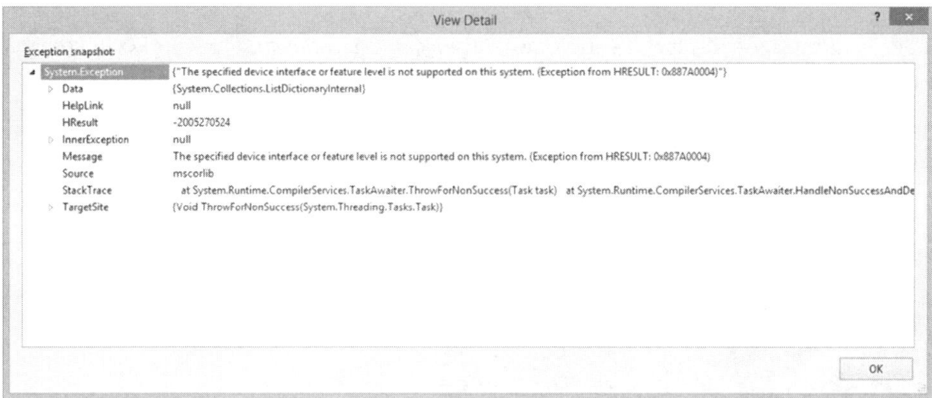

FIGURE 6-15 The View Detail window displaying information about system exceptions

When dealing with device capabilities, remember that the first call to a device capability should be done from the UI thread so that the permission dialog box can be shown to the user. Otherwise, the user cannot grant permission for access to the device capability. For this reason, you should never use a background task for the first use of the device. In apps using C# or C++, the first use of an object that accesses the device should typically be done in the page that actually needs to use the device, not the *App* class.

Finally, in case of device capabilities that do not represent the main feature of the app, the official Microsoft guidelines suggest displaying the error message only when the user attempts to use the feature. This means you should not display an error message for a device capability that has not yet been requested by the user. Besides, the user should be aware of the loss of functionality, so try to make the message clearly visible to the user.

Handling asynchronous errors

As you have learned so far, exceptions thrown in synchronous code keep propagating up the call stack, back through the sequence of method calls, until they are caught by a *try/catch* block or go unhandled and the application is terminated. In asynchronous code, however, things are more complicated because of the different threads involved in regular *Task* objects.

Fortunately, the new asynchronous pattern introduced by C# 5.0 (which ships with .NET Framework 4.5) simplifies exception handling in asynchronous calls. By using the *async/await* pattern, you can now place *try/catch* blocks around any asynchronous call in your code, and they will catch any exception raised during the asynchronous execution of that method in the same way as synchronous code. The following snippet shows an example:

```
public async Foo()
{
    try
    {
        // call to a method that raises an exception
        await this.DoSomethingAsync();
    }
    catch (Exception ex)
    {
        // exceptions raised during the execution of the awaited method
        // are caught here
    }
}

private Task DoSomethingAsync()
{
    // async operation
}
```

When an exception is raised during the execution of the asynchronous method (*DoSomethingAsync*, in this case), it is "stored" into the *Task* object returned by the method.

However, exceptions are thrown in correspondence of the *await* keyword. So, if you split the call to the asynchronous method and the *await* keyword, the asynchronous operation is not performed, and no exceptions are raised until the execution of the task, that is, when the task is awaited.

Consider the following code sample:

```
try
{
    var file = await ReadFileAsync();
    Task<string> processResult = ProcessFileAsync(file);
    DisplayInfo();
    string result = await processResult;
}
catch (Exception ex)
{
    // write exception handling code here
}
```

The *DisplayInfo* method is always called and completed regardless of whether an exception is thrown during the asynchronous execution of the *ProcessFileAsync* call. Thus, you must be careful when you split the *await* statement from the asynchronous call, save the task in a variable and then wait for the completion of the task. An exception thrown in the asynchronous method might be hidden by subsequent exceptions thrown in methods that are executed before the *await* keyword.

If you forget to *await* an asynchronous method returning a *Task* (perhaps because you are not interested in its returning value), and an exception is raised, the exception is stored in an anonymous *Task* instance and consequently ignored. This type of exception is referred to as an "unobserved exception." An unobserved exception can lead the application to an inconsistent state because it assumes that the asynchronous operation, such as sending an email or saving a customer via a remote service, has been successfully completed.

Something different happens when you invoke an async method that has a void return type (instead of returning a *Task*). Because this kind of method cannot be awaited, the caller cannot catch any exceptions thrown by the async method. In this case, the exception is not stored in an anonymous task; it will go unhandled, and your application will terminate. It is important to understand that async void methods exist only for being used as UI element event handlers, such as a button click's event handler. In any other case, your async method should always return a *Task* instance to avoid undesirable side effects.

> ***NOTE*** **ASYNCHRONOUS VOID METHODS**
>
> **The reason behind this different behavior is that an asynchronous void method is handled differently by the compiler. Async void methods are managed by the *AsyncVoidMethodBuilder* class, whereas async methods returning a *Task* are managed by the *AsyncTaskMethodBuilder* class.**

So far, this section has addressed asynchronous methods throwing single exceptions. However, when working with tasks and threads, there are many scenarios in which multiple exceptions might be raised concurrently. For example, concurrent multiple exceptions are raised when using the *Task.WhenAll* method to wait for a group of tasks to complete or when using parallel loops.

For these scenarios, the .NET Framework includes a particular type of exception called *System.AggregateException* that provides a way to handle multiple exceptions. The *Exception* class, from which *AggregateException* derives, already has the capability to wrap a single *Exception* instance and expose it through the *InnerException* property.

The *AggregateException* works in a similar way. The major difference is that it enables storing a collection of inner exceptions. The collection is then exposed through the read-only *InnerExceptions* property. Because the *AggregateException* derives from the *Exception* class, it also inherits the "traditional" *InnerException* property, together with all the other methods and properties.

> ***NOTE*** **MULTIPLE EXCEPTIONS**
>
> **When multiple exceptions are caught, the *InnerException* property contains the first exception in the collection.**

Listing 6-16 shows an example of its usage.

LISTING 6-16 Using *AggregateException*

```
private void DoSomething()
{
    Task task1 = new Task(() =>
    {
        // code omitted
    });

    Task task2 = new Task(() =>
    {
        // code omitted
    });

    Task task3 = new Task(() =>
    {

        // code omitted
     });

    task1.Start();
    task2.Start();
    task3.Start();

    try
    {
        Task.WaitAll(task1, task2, task3);
    }
    catch (AggregateException aex)
    {
        foreach (var inner in aex.InnerExceptions)
        {
            Debug.WriteLine("Exception type: {0}", inner.GetType());
            Debug.WriteLine("Message: {0}", inner.Message);
        }
    }
}
```

In some scenarios, an *AggregateException* instance might contain other *AggregateException* objects. In this case, you might want to simplify the hierarchy of exceptions by calling the *AggregateException.Flatten* method. This method returns a new *AggregateException* containing a flat list of inner exceptions. The following snippet shows an example:

```
catch (AggregateException aex)
{
    foreach (Exception ex in aex.Flatten().InnerExceptions)
        this._log.SaveException (ex);
}
```

When using the *AggregateException* class, you might want to discriminate between exceptions you were expecting (and that you can consequently handle) and unexpected exceptions that need to bubble up. The *AggregateException* class provides a *Handle* method that enables you to specify a predicate to be called for each exception in the collection. The predicate should return *true* if you want to propagate the exception, and *false* otherwise. The following code excerpt shows a possible usage of the *Handle* method that returns *true* when it comes across certain types of exceptions (*ArgumentNullException* and *InvalidOperationException*, in our sample) and *false* for all the other exceptions that it might encounter:

```
catch (AggregateException aex)
{
    aex.Handle((ex) =>
    {
        if (ex is ArgumentNullException)
        {
            //Log the exception
            return true;
        }
        if (ex is InvalidOperationException)
        {
            //Log the exception
            return true;
        }
        return false; // Unhandled exception
    });
}
```

The Task Parallel Library (TPL) provides an *UnobservedTaskException* event that represents a kind of last resort to catch unobserved asynchronous exceptions in a way that resembles the *UnhandledException* event discussed in the previous sections of this objective. If you forget to await a task-returning async method, any exception raised during the async operation will be stored in an anonymous task and consequently ignored. However, you can use the *UnobservedTaskException* event to handle these exceptions. The next code snippet shows an example of its usage:

```
public App()
{
    (code omitted)

    TaskScheduler.UnobservedTaskException += TaskScheduler_UnobservedTaskException;
 }

private void TaskScheduler_UnobservedTaskException(object sender,
    UnobservedTaskExceptionEventArgs e)
{
    foreach (Exception ex in e.Exception.Flatten().InnerExceptions)
    {
        // Log exception
    }
    e.SetObserved();
}
```

The *UnobservedTaskException* instance received by the event handler exposes an *Exception* property that, despite its name, is of type *AggregateException*. The *SetObserved* method can be used to mark the exception as observed, thus preventing it from triggering exception escalation policy that terminates the process by default.

Thought experiment

Exceptions and security

In this thought experiment, apply what you've learned about this objective. You can find answers to these questions in the "Answers" section at the end of this chapter.

You are developing a Windows Store app that handles sensitive user information, such as Social Security number, home banking account information, and other data that should remain confidential. This information can be exposed by incautious error-handling strategies, such as displaying the inner message or the stack trace of an exception on the screen.

What precaution could you adopt when implementing your error-handling strategy to ensure that your application does not leak sensitive information?

Objective summary

- Set up a *try/catch* block wherever you are trying to access a resource that might be unavailable or missing, or you are relying on types and functions over which you have no control. Use the *finally* block to release any unmanaged resource and perform any necessary cleaning up as soon as possible.
- The *UnhandledException* event handles exceptions that have not been handled by the application code. Set the *Handled* property of the *UnhandledExceptionEventArgs* to *true* to tell the framework not to process the exception any further. In this case, the app cannot be terminated.
- A user must grant permission before a Windows Store app can access a sensitive device capability for the first time. Because your app might not be able to access a sensitive device, you need to handle the errors that can occur when trying to access a disabled or missing device capability.
- When using the *async/await* pattern, you can place *try/catch* blocks around any asynchronous call in your code, and they will catch any exception raised during the asynchronous execution of that method.
- When you expect multiple exceptions to be raised during an asynchronous call, you can use the *AggregateException* class to handle them.
- Implement the *UnobservedTaskException* event handler as a safety net to handle unobserved exceptions.

Objective review

Answer the following questions to test your knowledge of the information in this objective. You can find the answers to these questions and explanations of why each answer choice is correct or incorrect in the "Answers" section at the end of this chapter.

1. When is the *UnhandledExceptionEvent* event raised by the XAML framework?
   - **A.** Every time an exception is caught in a *try/catch* block and then handled by the application code in the *finally* block
   - **B.** Every time an exception is thrown in a void-returning asynchronous method
   - **C.** When the *Handled* method is invoked on an exception
   - **D.** When there is no longer any possibility for the application code to catch an unhandled exception
2. What type of exception is usually raised when an app tries to invoke the *Windows.Media.Capture.MediaCapture.InitializeAsync* method without having the user's permission to use the device?
   - **A.** An *UnauthorizedAccessException*
   - **B.** An *InvalidOperationException*
   - **C.** A generic *System.Exception*
   - **D.** None
3. What happens when you forget to await a task-returning asynchronous method and an exception is raised during the async operation?
   - **A.** The exception is propagated to the caller as soon as the asynchronous operation is executed.
   - **B.** The exception is stored in an anonymous *Task* instance and then ignored (an unobserved exception).
   - **C.** The exception goes unhandled and eventually bubbles up, determining the process termination.
   - **D.** The exception is added to the *AggregateException.InnerExceptions* collection that is returned to the caller.

Objective 6.3: Design and implement a test strategy

In this objective, you learn some introductory principles for testing your Windows Store app. You find out how the test framework for Windows Store apps differs from the classic Microsoft unit test framework for .NET applications. Finally, you learn how to implement your first test library for Windows Store apps.

This objective covers how to:

- Recommend a functional test plan
- Implement a coded UI test
- Recommend a reliability test plan (performance testing, stress testing, scalability testing, duration testing)
- Implement unit testing in an app

Understanding functional testing vs. unit testing

Testing is a fundamental part of any software development process, including Windows Store apps. Testing is not just executing the code that you have written (whether it's just a small piece, one or more components, or the entire app) with the intent of finding bugs. It is also a process of verifying that your app meets all of the functional and nonfunctional requirements, and that it behaves as expected. One of the most commonly accepted distinctions between test methodologies is the one between functional testing and unit testing.

Functional testing

An application's functional requirements are the tasks the software is supposed to perform. Functional testing is a generic category that includes all tests that verify that the functional requirements of the software are working properly from a user's perspective. Functional testing requires prior identification of the functions (or tasks) that the software is supposed to perform and of the expected outcomes based on the functions' specifications.

For example, in a hotel booking application, a user asks to reserve a room for a specific night. A functional test might verify that the app actually sends the request to a remote service, the service processes the request and then sends a response back to the app, informing the user whether the booking operation has succeeded. The app should be able to handle the scenario successfully and any issues that could affect execution flow, such as when the Internet connection is not available, when someone else has reserved the same room, and so on.

> ***MORE INFO*** **NONFUNCTIONAL TESTING**
>
> **Nonfunctional testing includes all tests that are performed on nonfunctional requirements, that is, every requirement that depends on external properties of the system, such as its performance under stress, security, and scalability. Examples of nonfunctional testing are security testing, usability testing, stress testing, and load testing. For further information about nonfunctional testing, you can start from the Wikipedia definition at *http://en.wikipedia.org/wiki/Non-functional_testing*.**

There are three approaches to functional testing:

- **Bottom-up approach** The lower-level components are integrated and tested first. After all the lower-level modules have been tested and their outcome verified, it is the turn of the higher-level components. The process is repeated until the components at the top of the hierarchy have been tested.
- **Top-down approach** Follows the opposite direction, where the higher-level components are integrated and tested first and then each branch of the flow is systematically tested until all the lower-level components involved in the use case are also tested.
- **Combination** This approach combines top-down testing with bottom-up testing to leverage the advantages of both approaches.

INTEGRATION TESTING

A particular type of functional testing is represented by integration testing, whose purpose is to verify that the various components and resources of an application work together as expected. In this type of testing, software modules are coupled to form composite aggregates that can be tested to verify how the different parts integrate as a whole. Unlike unit testing, in which specific classes and methods are tested after they have been isolated and their dependencies replaced with stubs and mock objects, integration testing tests all the code between the method under test and the lower-lever components upon which the application was built. However, despite their differences, both unit and integration tests can usually be created using the same test framework. For example, in Visual Studio 2012 you can leverage the same Unit Test Library template for Windows Store apps to perform both unit and integration testing.

CODED UI TESTING

Another type of functional testing is UI testing, which enables you to test the application by driving it through the user interface. Conceptually, this is nothing different from manually testing the entire application by pressing F5 and then interacting with the elements of the user interface. Visual Studio 2012 enables you to automate this kind of test by recording the sequence of actions performed on the user interface and then generating the code to automatically repeat the same steps and verify the outcome (hence the name "coded UI testing," or CUIT). Unfortunately, Windows Store apps do not support this feature at the time of this writing. (You can refer to *http://msdn.microsoft.com/en-us/library/vstudio/dd380742.aspx* for further clarification.) The only way to test your application is through manual interaction with the user interface. To keep track of manual tests, you can use the Microsoft Test Manager to describe them and then associate the test results to the build in Visual Studio Team Foundation Server.

> ***MORE INFO*** **REMOTE DEBUGGING**
>
> **When manually testing the user interface of a Windows Store app, the Visual Studio remote debugger enables you to run, debug, and test the app remotely from a second computer running Visual Studio. Running on a remote device can be especially effective when the Visual Studio computer does not support functionality that is specific to Windows Store apps, such as touch, geolocation, and physical orientation. For further information about this topic, visit *http://msdn.microsoft.com/en-us/library/windows/apps/hh441469(v=vs.110).aspx.***

Unit testing

Functional testing, and especially integration testing, should not be confused with unit testing. In unit testing, you take the *smallest* piece of testable software in the application, *isolate* it from the rest of the code, and determine whether it behaves as you would expect by testing it as a *single unit*. Isolating the class or method under test requires you to remove any external dependency; that is, any object or component that the unit of code under test interacts with, but over which you have no control (such as file systems, databases, and remote services). To do that, you can replace external dependencies with stubs and mock objects.

Isolating a piece of software for unit testing involves adopting a design that encourages separation of concerns and coding against interfaces rather than concrete implementations. Isolation also means that unit tests should not depend on each other to succeed or fail, or require to be executed in a specific order.

Unit testing can also be used for regression testing. Any time you have to modify your code, you can run the existing unit tests against the modified code to verify whether the changes have affected the rest of the code. This way, you can modify your code more easily because when you add new features to your software, regression tests greatly reduce the risk of introducing new bugs.

> ***MORE INFO*** **UNIT TESTING AND SOFTWARE DEVELOPMENT METHODOLOGIES**
>
> **Discussing the philosophies behind the notion of unit testing and enumerating the differences with other test strategies, as well as the different methodologies of software development (such as test-driven and model-driven development) is beyond the scope of this book. If you are interested in design patterns, methodologies, and tools for testing, you can start by visiting *http://msdn.microsoft.com/en-us/library/bb969130.aspx.***

Implementing a test project for a Windows Store app

Windows Store apps do not use the classic Visual Studio Unit Testing Framework for .NET applications defined in the *Microsoft.VisualStudio.TestTools.UnitTesting* namespace. Instead, they use a framework specifically designed for Windows Store apps that reside in a different namespace: *Microsoft.VisualStudio.TestPlatform.UnitTestFramework*.

This new namespace contains types and methods that provide specific support for testing Windows Store apps and relies on the same WinRT engine of a Windows Store app. In fact, the test code executes in the same sandboxed environment of a Windows Store app. Therefore, not only can you call the WinRT APIs from the test code but a unit test project for Windows Store apps also includes a Package.appxmanifest file, the same kind of application manifest you would expect in a Windows Store app project. To test how your app interacts with certain resources or devices, such as user libraries, a webcam, or a microphone, you have to declare the corresponding capability in the application manifest of your unit test project as you would in any Windows Store project.

There are other differences between the traditional test framework for .NET applications and the one specific for a Windows Store app. For example, in the newer framework, the *ExpectedException* attribute is no longer supported. Instead, the framework introduces a new generic method in the *Assert* class named *ThrowsException<TException>*. This method explicitly states that raising an exception is the behavior you actually expect from the method under test. Another difference is the new *UITestMethodAttribute* attribute, which enables you to run unit tests on the main UI thread, without the need to use a *Dispatcher* for marshaling. Finally, the unit test framework for Windows Store apps provides basic support for data-driven testing, a particular form of functional testing in which test input and output values are separated from the code. These new features are further discussed in this section.

> ***NOTE*** **VISUAL STUDIO 2012 UPDATE 2**
>
> **Both the *ThrowsException* method and the *UITestMethodAttribute* attribute were introduced with Visual Studio 2012 Update 2. You can download the update from *http://www.microsoft.com/en-us/download/details.aspx?id=38188*.**

Finally, the test framework for Windows Store apps does not include the Microsoft Fake framework shipped with Visual Studio 2012. For this reason, if you want to isolate your code by using stubs and fake objects, you must write your own code or use third-party libraries.

The first thing to do to implement tests for your app is to add a new Unit Test Library project template to the solution that hosts your Windows Store app, as shown in Figure 6-16. You must also add a reference to the Windows Store project that you want to test.

NOTE **TEST CODE IN THE ASSEMBLY OF A DISTRIBUTED APP**

You should never implement tests of any sort in the same project of your app. Including the test code in the assembly that will be distributed via the Windows Store occupies valuable disk space, increases the download size of the app, and consumes bandwidth. It also makes future releases much harder to manage because it would inevitably lead to many different versions not only of your app but also of your test code, with inevitable impacts on any continuous integration strategies.

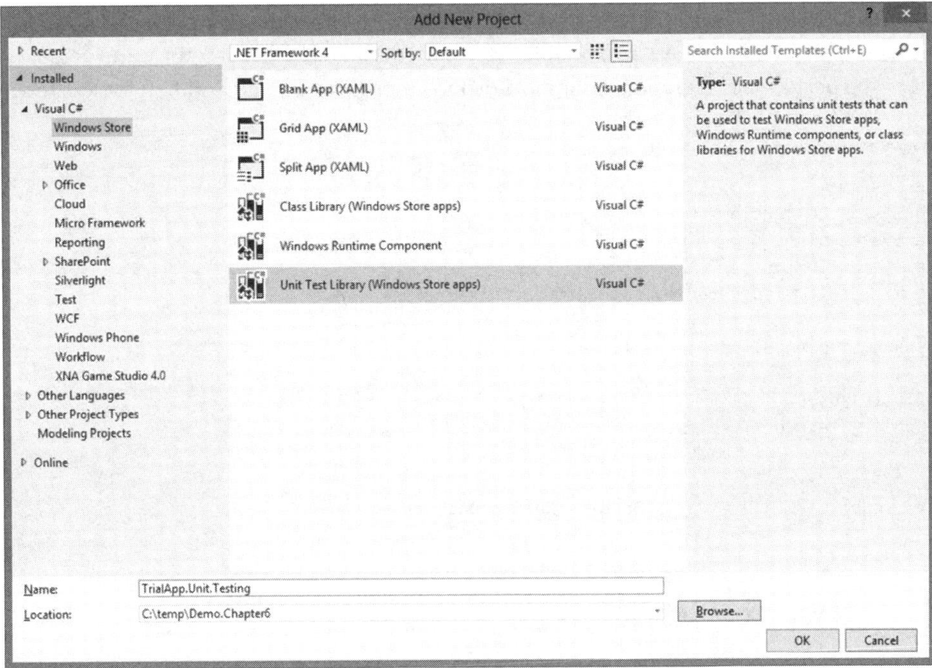

FIGURE 6-16 The Unit Test Library (Windows Store apps) template in Visual Studio 2012

Before you begin coding your first test, you must add a new class to test in your Windows Store project. The following code excerpt shows the complete definition of a sample *Utility* class that contains a trivial method that needs to be tested:

Sample of C# code

```
using System;
using System.Collections.Generic;
using System.Linq;
using System.Text;
using System.Threading.Tasks;
```

```
namespace SimpleApplication
{
    public class Utility
    {
        public Double Divide(Double a, Double b)
        {
            return a / b;
        }
    }
}
```

In this example, the *Utility* class contains a single method named *Divide* that takes two doubles as parameters and returns the result of a simple division operation. The first thing to be tested is that when you pass two doubles to the method under test, it returns the actual result of the performed operation. Listing 6-17 shows a possible implementation for this test.

LISTING 6-17 Unit testing the *Divide* method

```
using System;
using System.Collections.Generic;
using System.Linq;
using System.Text;
using Microsoft.VisualStudio.TestPlatform.UnitTestFramework;

namespace SimpleApplication.Unit.Test
{
    [TestClass]
    public class UtilityTest
    {
        [TestMethod]
        public void Divide_TwoDoubles_ReturnsDouble()
        {
            // Arrange
            var expected = 2.4; // expected result
            var utility = new Utility(); // set up fixture

            // Act
            var actual = utility.Divide(4.8, 2.0); // actual result

            // Assert
            Assert.AreEqual(expected, actual); // verify condition
        }
    }
}
```

NOTE **NAMING CONVENTIONS**

If you are familiar with unit testing, you might have noticed that Listing 6-17 uses the traditional naming convention according to which class names follow the *<ClassUnderTest>Test* pattern. (This sample tests a class named *Utility*, so all the tests that concern this class are grouped into a unit test file named UtilityTest.) The single tests are named based on the following pattern: *<MethodUnderTest>_<StateUnderTest>_<ExpectedBehavior>*. *StateUnderTest* indicates the conditions under which the method is being tested (for example, whether you are passing the right parameters or invalid values). *ExpectedBehavior* enables you to state what behavior you are expecting from the method under the provided conditions (for example, to return a certain value or throw an exception of some sort). No matter what naming convention you choose for your test project, remember to follow the same standard for all tests, and be clear about what each test state is and what behavior you expect.

As in the classic test framework for .NET apps, the *TestClass* attribute is used to identify the groups of unit tests to run, whereas the *TestMethod* attribute indicates each unit test that needs to be run. In the sample, the test verifies that, provided two doubles as parameters, the method under test returns the right result. The body of the method also illustrates the so-called Three A's rule: you set up the object to be tested (*arrange*), exercise the method under test (*act*), and then make claims about the object (*assert*).

The *Assert* class contains methods to verify conditions in unit tests using *true/false* propositions. For example, the *AreEqual* method used in Listing 6-17 verifies whether two values are equal through a call to the *Object.Equals* method under the hood. The sample asserts that, given the provided parameters, the method should return a specific value, which is represented by the *expected* variable. If it does, the assertion would be *true*, and the test would pass. (To verify whether two objects point to the same reference, you have to use one of the *AreSame* overload methods.)

If you run the unit test, the Test Explorer window indicates that your app passed the test, indicated by a green check mark. See Figure 6-17.

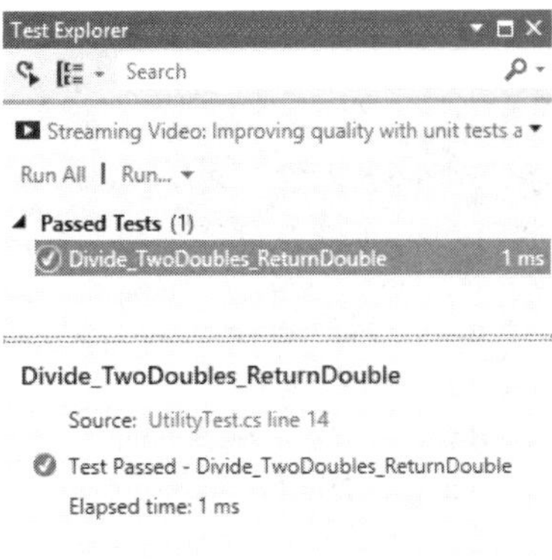

FIGURE 6-17 Unit test results

What happens if you pass different values to the method, let's say a zero as the second parameter? When you try to divide a double by zero, instead of the classic *DividedByZeroException*, you receive a particular value: *Infinity* (in two flavors: *PositiveInfinity* and *NegativeInfinity*). Therefore, in a second test, you can verify this behavior by calling the *IsInfinity* method of the *Double* class and check whether this method returns *true* by leveraging a different assert. The following code excerpt shows a possible unit test definition that uses the *Assert.IsTrue* method instead of the *Assert.AreEqual*:

```
[TestMethod]
public void Divide_ZeroAsSecondParameter_ReturnsInfinite()
{
    // Arrange
    var utility = new Utility();

    // Act
    var actual = utility.Divide(4.8, 0.0);

    // Assert
    Assert.IsTrue(Double.IsInfinity(actual));
}
```

Besides verifying that a method will behave correctly when supplied with the right parameters, you also have to test what happens when you provide the wrong parameters or when the state of the object under test is not what it should be. For example, suppose that you are expecting a certain method to throw an exception of type *ArgumentNullException* when supplied with a null value as a parameter. To test this behavior, you can use another type of assertion: the *ThrowsException<TException>* method, where *TException* indicates the type of exception expected. The following code shows an example of its usage:

```
[TestMethod]
public void GetCustomerName_EmptyId_ThrowsArgumentNullException()
{
    // Arrange
    var biz = new Biz();

    // Act & Assert
    Assert.ThrowsException<ArgumentNullException>(() => biz.GetCustomerName(""));
}
```

It is also possible to test asynchronous calls by using the classic *async/await* pattern, as shown in the following code excerpt:

```
[TestMethod]
public async Task GetCustomerNameAsync_ValidId_ReturnsCustomerName()
{
    // Arrange
    var biz = new Biz();
    var expectedName = "Expected Name";

    // Act
    var actualName = await biz.GetCustomerNameAsync("123");

    // Assert
    Assert.AreEqual(expectedName, actualName);
}
```

As mentioned previously, Visual Studio 2012 Update 2 introduced a new attribute to run code on the UI thread. When you create a unit test project for a Windows store app, tests marked with the *TestMethod* attribute do not run on the UI thread. Before the introduction of this new attribute, if you wanted to perform an action on the UI thread, you had to use a dispatcher. Now, all you have to do is to mark your test with the new *UITestMethod* attribute, as shown in the following code snippet:

```
[UITestMethod]
public void Some_UI_Test()
{
    //Some code to execute on UI Thread
}
```

EXAM TIP

Following the unit testing philosophy, each test needs to start in a well-known condition and clean up things at the end. This way, the test is not affected by other tests or external conditions.

You can centralize the code for setting up all the things that must be in place before running the tests (also known as a "test fixture," or just "fixture"), such as creating fake objects to supply to the methods under test or opening a connection to a database, by using the *ClassInitialize* and *TestInitialize* attributes. After the fixture has been used, it can be torn down by leveraging, respectively, the *ClassCleanup* and *TestCleanup* attributes.

The difference between these two kinds of attributes is that methods with the *ClassInitialize* and *ClassCleanup* attributes are called, respectively, before and after *all* the tests in a test battery are run. On the contrary, methods marked with the *TestInitialize* and *TestCleanup* attributes are called, respectively, before and after *each* unit test. Therefore, if you need to share a fixture among different unit tests, you can set up the fixture in a method marked with the *ClassInitialize* attribute, share it among different tests, and then tear down the fixture in the *ClassCleanup* method. On the contrary, if you want to re-create a fresh fixture for each single test, you can mark the method with the *TestInitialize* attribute, while the method responsible for tearing down the resource after each test will be marked with the *TestCleanup* attribute. Re-creating a fresh fixture for each single test represents the best-case scenario because it avoids test coupling.

NOTE ***ASSEMBLYINITIALIZE/ASSEMBLYCLEANUP*** **ATTRIBUTES**

You can also use the *AssemblyInitialize/AssemblyCleanup* attributes to identify the methods that contain code to be used before and after *all* tests included in the assembly have run.

The following code snippet shows an example of the *TestInitialize/TestCleanup* pattern, in which a simple object is created before each test and then destroyed:

```
[TestInitialize]
public void TestSetup()
{
    // Set up a fresh fixture that will be used by each unit test
}

[TestMethod]
public void Test_Using_Fresh_Fixture()
{
    // Use the fixture
}

[TestCleanup]
public void TestTearDown()
{
    // Tear down the fixture before moving to the next unit test
}
```

Finally, the unit test framework for Windows Store apps introduces a basic support for lightweight data-driven testing, a particular test strategy that enables executing the same test method with different input values. The following code excerpt shows an example of its usage:

```
[DataTestMethod]
[DataRow("25892e17-80f6-715f-9c65-7395632f0223", "Customer #1")]
[DataRow("a53e98e4-0197-3513-be6d-49836e406aaa", "Customer #2")]
[DataRow("f2s34824-3153-2524-523d-29386e4s6as1", "Customer #3")]
public void GetCustomerName_RightID_ReturnExpected(String id, String customerName)
{
    var biz = new Biz();

    var actualCustomer = biz.GetCustomerName(id);

    Assert.AreEqual(customerName, actualCustomer);
}
```

This particular test strategy is based on two new attributes: *DataTestMethod* (which takes the place of the standard *TestMethod* attribute) and *DataRow*. In addition, the signature of the test method is different; it now accepts two strings as parameters (in our sample). The *DataRow* attributes define the data set that will be passed to the test method as parameters. Then the test method, along with the associated setup and teardown methods, is executed several times, each time using the values provided by a different attribute. The first value, which is a string representing the customer ID in our sample, corresponds to the first parameter accepted by the test method and represents the value that will be supplied to the method under test (*GetCustomerName*). The second value passed to the test method represents the return value that we expect the method under test will return.

Thought experiment

Checking the user's permission

In this thought experiment, apply what you've learned about this objective. You can find answers to these questions in the "Answers" section at the end of this chapter.

You have the following method that needs to be tested:

```
public async Task<String> LoadDocumentSample(String fileName)
{
    try
    {
        var folder = KnownFolders.DocumentsLibrary;
        var file = await folder.GetFileAsync(fileName);
        var text = await Windows.Storage.FileIO.ReadTextAsync(file,
            Windows.Storage.Streams.UnicodeEncoding.Utf8);
        return text;
    }
    catch (UnauthorizedAccessException ex)
    {
        // handle exception
    }
    catch (Exception ex)
    {
        // handle exception
    }
}
```

As the first test, you want to be sure that if you provide the name of an existing text file in the user's Documents library, the method returns the actual content of the file (just "some content," in this example). The following code shows the implementation of your first integration test:

```
[TestMethod]
public void SaveDocumentSample_ExistingFileName_
    ReturnsExpectedText()
{
    var utility = new Utility();
    var t = utility.LoadDocumentSample("document.txt");
    Assert.IsTrue(t.Result == "some content");
}
```

You run the test, but it fails due to an *AggregateException* raised during the execution of the asynchronous operation. What is the first thing you should check in your test project to solve the problem?

Objective summary

- When developing a Windows Store app, consider adopting a functional test plan to verify that all the functional requirements of the software are working properly from the user's perspective.
- Adopt a unit test plan to verify whether the single units of software, isolated from any external dependency, behave as expected.
- The unit test framework for Windows Store apps resides in the *Microsoft.VisualStudio.TestPlatform.UnitTestFramework* namespace, which is different than the "classic" test framework for .NET applications. This new namespace contains types and methods that provide specific support for testing Windows Store apps and relies on the same WinRT engine of a Windows Store app.
- In the unit test framework for Windows Store app, the *ExpectedException* attribute is no longer supported. Use the *Assert.ThrowsException<TException>* method instead.
- Implement your data-driven test by using the *DataTestMethod* attribute.
- When implementing a unit test, remember to follow the "Three A's" rule: set up the object to be tested (arrange), exercise the method under test (act), and make claims about the object (assert).

Objective review

Answer the following questions to test your knowledge of the information in this objective. You can find the answers to these questions and explanations of why each answer choice is correct or incorrect in the "Answers" section at the end of this chapter.

1. Which of the following statements is incorrect when referring to unit testing?
   - **A.** Small units of software are tested after they have been isolated from external dependencies.
   - **B.** Tests should never depend on each other to succeed or fail, nor should they require to be executed in a specific order.
   - **C.** Unit testing encourages separation of concerns and coding against interfaces.
   - **D.** Different components and resources of an application are tested together to verify they work as expected.
2. When are the methods marked with the *TestInitialize* and *TestCleanup* attribute executed?
   - **A.** Before and after all tests in the assembly are executed
   - **B.** Before and after all tests belonging to the same class are executed
   - **C.** Before and after each test is executed
   - **D.** Before and after all the tests marked with the *DataTestMethod* attribute are executed

3. Which of the following features is not supported in the unit test framework for Windows Store apps?

    A. *Assert.ThrowsException<TException>* method

    B. *TestMethod* attribute

    C. *DataTestMethod* attribute

    D. *ExpectedException* attribute

Objective 6.4: Design a diagnostics and monitoring strategy

In this section, you learn how to profile your Windows Store app by using the analysis tools provided by Visual Studio 2012 to detect performance issues that could affect your app. You also learn how to use Event Tracing for Windows (ETW) to log the most significant events your app will encounter during its life cycle and how to implement different strategies for logging those events. Finally, you explore the Quality reports provided by the Windows Store, which identify the most common issues affecting your app.

This objective covers how to:

- Design profiling, tracing, performance counters, audit trails (events and information), and usage reporting
- Decide where to log events (local vs. centralized reporting)

Profiling a Windows Store app and collecting performance counters

A Windows Store app is a client app that executes in a sandboxed and highly responsive environment. In some scenarios, however, you (or, in the worst case, your customers) might find that your app is performing slowly. The reasons behind poor performance can vary: inefficient code that slows down your app, calls to third-party libraries or remote services that require too much time to complete, complex calculations that consume too much CPU, and so on.

EXAM TIP

Visual Studio 2012 profiling tools for Windows Store apps enable you to observe and record metrics about the behavior of your app by using a sampling method that collects information from the CPU call stack at regular intervals, navigating through the execution paths of your code and evaluating the cost of each function. It's also important to note that a Windows Store app does not support gathering performance counters programmatically, as you can do in a traditional .NET application. You have to rely on the provided profiling tools only.

Visual Studio 2012 provides a suite of tools for debugging, profiling, testing, and collecting information about Windows Store apps and the overall execution environment. The profiling tools enable you to observe and record performance counters about the behavior of your app by using a sampling method that collects information from the CPU call stack at regular intervals, navigating through the execution paths of your code and evaluating the cost of each function. In other terms, a sampling tool collects statistical data about the work performed by an application, taking snapshots of the system at regular intervals, without modifying any code.

Many profiling tools and options are not available in Visual Studio 2012 for Windows Store apps, however. The following list refers specifically to the unsupported features for Windows Store apps developed in C#, but most of these limitations are common to all the WinRT languages:

- **Instrumentation profiling** There are two main profiling techniques: sampling and instrumentation. Sampling is the only option available in a Windows Store app, although with some limitations (some sampling options, such as setting the sampling event and timing interval, or collecting additional performance counter data, are not supported for Windows Store apps). On the other hand, an instrumentation profiler follows a more invasive approach because it injects specific tracing code at the beginning and end of each function. This tracing code (also known as "tracing markers" or "probes") enables the profiling tool to record each time the execution flow enters and exits an instrumented function.
- **Concurrency profiling** This profiling method collects detailed information from the call stack each time competing threads are forced to wait for access to a shared resource (resource contention). It also provides useful information about how an application interacts with the overall environment, enabling you to identify performance bottlenecks, synchronization issues, and so on.
- **.NET memory profiling** This profiling method collects detailed information about memory allocation and garbage collection.
- **Tier interaction profiling (TIP)** This profiling method collects information about ADO.NET function calls to a SQL Server database. This profiling option does not exist for Windows Store apps because an app does not have access to the *System.Data** namespaces and has to rely on remote services (or the local storage) to consume data.

Now that you understand which features and options are not available for a Windows Store app, let's examine what you can use to identify possible performance issues.

> ***MORE INFO*** **WINDOWS PERFORMANCE TOOLKIT (WPT)**
>
> **If you want to collect broader information about your app's performance, you can use the Windows Performance Toolkit (WPT). This tool contains performance analysis tools that are useful to a broad audience, including general application developers, driver developers, hardware manufacturers, and system builders. These tools are designed for measuring and analyzing system and application performance on Windows 8. You can download the toolkit from *http://msdn.microsoft.com/en-us/performance/cc825801.aspx*. If you are experiencing memory related issues in a Windows Store app, you can also try other profiling tools such as the Microsoft NP .NET Profiler Tool available at the following address: *http://www.microsoft.com/en-us/download/details.aspx?id=35370*. A discussion about these tools, as well as about any other third-party tool for performance analysis, is beyond the scope of this book.**

To help you understand the profiling tools available in Visual Studio 2012, let's analyze a dummy application whose only purpose is to display a list of names. The method invoked to retrieve this list simulates a time-consuming call to a remote service by iterating through an empty loop.

The following snippet shows a basic default page with a *Button* control and a *ListView* control nested within a *StackPanel* control:

Sample of XAML code

```
<Page
    x:Class="PerformanceAnalysisSample.MainPage"
    xmlns="http://schemas.microsoft.com/winfx/2006/xaml/presentation"
    xmlns:x="http://schemas.microsoft.com/winfx/2006/xaml"
    xmlns:local="using:PerformanceAnalysisSample"
    xmlns:d="http://schemas.microsoft.com/expression/blend/2008"
    xmlns:mc="http://schemas.openxmlformats.org/markup-compatibility/2006"
    mc:Ignorable="d">

    <StackPanel Background="{StaticResource ApplicationPageBackgroundThemeBrush}">
        <Button Width="300" Height="50" Content="Customer list"
            Click="GetCustomerListButton_Click" Margin="20, 5"/>
        <ListView x:Name="CustomerListView" DisplayMemberPath="Name" Margin="20, 5" />
    </StackPanel>
</Page>
```

In the code-behind of the page, the button click's event handler retrieves the collection of customers by calling a fake business layer and binding it to the *ListView* control, as shown in the following code excerpt:

Sample of C# code

```
private void GetCustomerListButton_Click(object sender, RoutedEventArgs e)
{
    var biz = new FakeBiz();
    var customers = biz.GetCustomers();
    CustomerListView.ItemsSource = customers;
}
```

> ***NOTE* EXAMPLE CODE**
>
> **You would never use code like this in a real app. The code freezes the user interface until the customer's collection has been retrieved. Instead, you should use the *await/async* pattern. The only purpose of this code is to illustrate the usage of the profiling tools in Visual Studio 2012.**

The *FakeBiz* class contains only a public method, *GetCustomer*, which retrieves the collection of customers by simulating a call to a remote service, represented by the *SimulateRemoteServiceCall* method. Listing 6-18 shows the complete C# code for the *FakeBiz* class.

LISTING 6-18 Complete code for the *FakeBiz* class

```
using System;
using System.Collections.Generic;
using System.Linq;
using System.Text;
using System.Threading.Tasks;

namespace PerformanceAnalysisSample
{
    public class FakeBiz
    {
        public List<Person> GetCustomers()
        {
            return this.SimulateRemoteServiceCall();
        }

        private List<Person> SimulateRemoteServiceCall()
        {
            for (int i = 0; i < Int32.MaxValue; i++)
            {
                // code omitted
            }
            return new List<Person>()
            {
                new Person() { Name = "Roberto Brunetti" },
                new Person() { Name = "Vanni Boncinelli" },
```

```
                new Person() { Name = "Luca Regnicoli" },
                new Person() { Name = "Katia Egiziano" },
                new Person() { Name = "Paolo Pialorsi" },
                new Person() { Name = "Marco Russo" },
            };
        }
    }

    public class Person
    {
        public string Name { get; set; }
    }
}
```

To analyze the code in Visual Studio, click the Start Performance Analysis menu item in the Debug menu, highlighted in Figure 6-18.

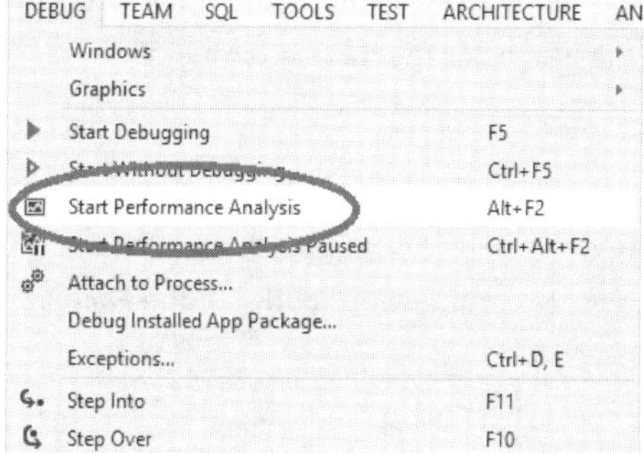

FIGURE 6-18 Selecting Start Performance Analysis in the Debug menu

Visual Studio starts the profiling tools and launches the application. In the app's default page, if you click the Get Customers button and wait until the collection of customers appears on the screen, the profiler records the operations the code performs under the hood. At the end of the process, you can go back to Visual Studio and click the Stop Profiling link shown in Figure 6-19.

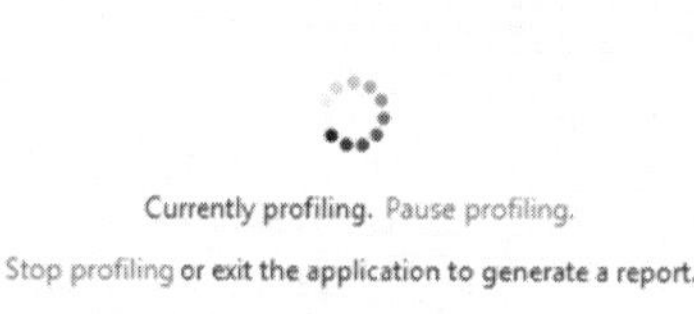

FIGURE 6-19 The Stop Profiling link

After you stop the profiling analysis, Visual Studio 2012 generates a report containing all the information collected during the sampling. Figure 6-20 shows the generated report.

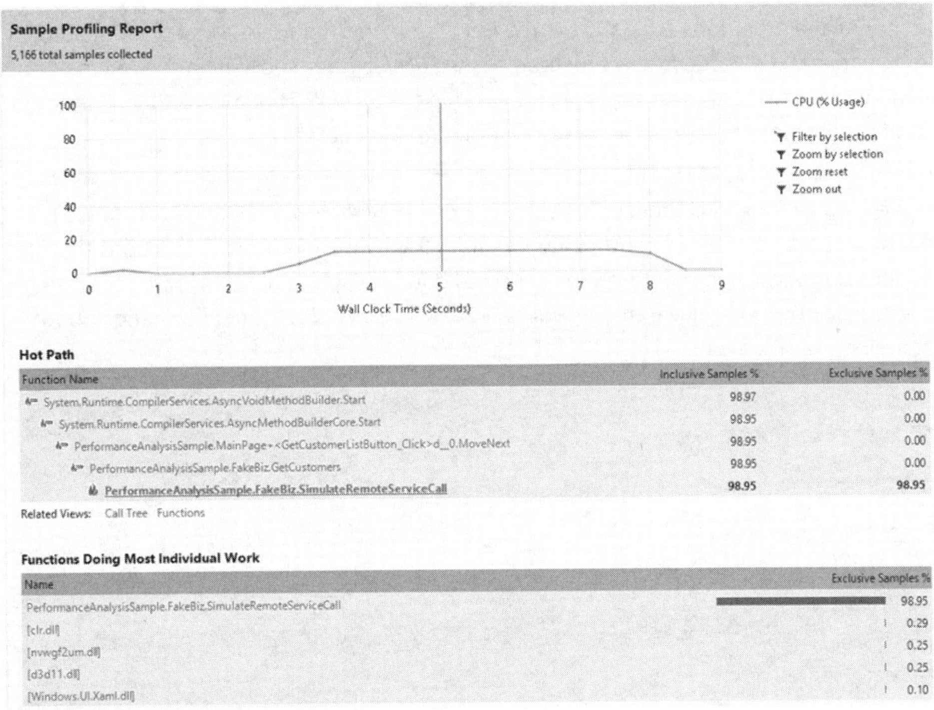

FIGURE 6-20 A profile analysis report

The report contains data collected during the execution of your app. The upper part of the screen is occupied by a chart showing the percentage of CPU usage during the execution of the app. You can select a specific area in the chart, for example a spike indicating a burst in the CPU usage, to zoom or filter the samples collected within a specific interval. Just below the CPU usage chart, the Hot Path section shows the most expensive call paths in terms of CPU usage. These hot paths are highlighted with a flame-shaped icon by the function name. Each function call included in the path has two indicators: inclusive samples and exclusive samples.

EXAM TIP

The inclusive sample percentage (or inclusive time) indicates the CPU time spent to complete a specific function, including the time spent waiting for any other function that it might call. The exclusive samples percentage (or exclusive time) does not take into account the time spent waiting for other functions called from the current one to complete; it indicates only the amount of time consumed by the inner work of a function.

In this sample, the *SimulateRemoteServiceCall* method shows an impressive 98.95 percent value in both indicators (inclusive and exclusive CPU usage), which means that almost all the CPU time consumed by the app has been used by this method. (Your values might be slightly different.) All the other functions, such as the *GetCustomerListButton_Click* of the default page code-behind and the *GetCustomers* method of the *FakeBiz* class, show an inclusive time of 98.95 percent and an exclusive time approximately close to zero. That means that all they did was wait for the *SimulateRemoteServiceCall* method to complete.

The Functions Doing Most Individual Work section shows which individual functions have consumed most of the CPU time. In this case, it shows only the exclusive time consumed by each function, that is, without considering the time spent waiting for other functions to complete. You can also navigate through the collected data by using other more specific views, such as the Call Tree view illustrated in Figure 6-21, which includes more information about the sampled execution paths.

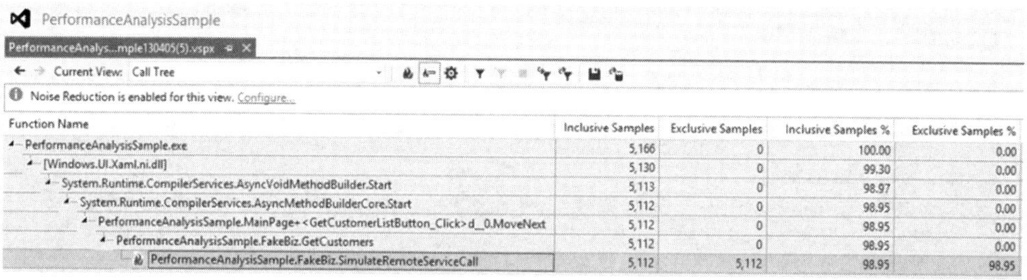

PerformanceAnalysisSample

PerformanceAnalys...mple130405(5).vspx

Current View: Call Tree

Noise Reduction is enabled for this view. Configure...

Function Name	Inclusive Samples	Exclusive Samples	Inclusive Samples %	Exclusive Samples %
PerformanceAnalysisSample.exe	5,166	0	100.00	0.00
[Windows.UI.Xaml.ni.dll]	5,130	0	99.30	0.00
System.Runtime.CompilerServices.AsyncVoidMethodBuilder.Start	5,113	0	98.97	0.00
System.Runtime.CompilerServices.AsyncMethodBuilderCore.Start	5,112	0	98.95	0.00
PerformanceAnalysisSample.MainPage+<GetCustomerListButton_Click>d__0.MoveNext	5,112	0	98.95	0.00
PerformanceAnalysisSample.FakeBiz.GetCustomers	5,112	0	98.95	0.00
PerformanceAnalysisSample.FakeBiz.SimulateRemoteServiceCall	5,112	5,112	98.95	98.95

FIGURE 6-21 Call Tree view

If you click a function name in one of the preceding views, you can get more details about that function. Figure 6-22 shows the Function Details view for the *FakeBiz.GetCustomer* method.

FIGURE 6-22 Function Details view

The upper part of the screen displays the inclusive time allocated along the path that includes the current function. The bars illustrate the relationships between the currently selected function (in this case, the *GetCustomers* method), the calling functions that executed the selected function (shown in the Calling functions bar), and any functions called by it (the *SimulateRemoteServiceCall* method, shown in the Called functions bar). The size of each bar indicates the relative amount of the total execution time that the corresponding function has consumed.

The Called functions bar indicates that 99.7 percent of the CPU time has been consumed by the *SimulateRemoteServiceCall* method invoked inside *GetCustomers*, while the body of the current method consumed less than 0.1 percent of the CPU time to accomplish its internal work.

The Function Code View pane in the lower part of the screen shows the lines of code that caused the bottleneck (highlighted). If you click the *SimulateRemoteServiceCall* method, the Function Code View pane displays even more details that can help you isolate the problem. In

Figure 6-23, the bottleneck represented by the *for* block is highlighted and indicates the CPU consumed by each line of code.

```
                private List<Person> SimulateRemoteServiceCall()
                {
87.0 %              for (int i = 0; i < Int32.MaxValue; i++)
12.7 %              {
                        // code omitted
                    }

                    return new List<Person>()
                    {
```

FIGURE 6-23 The *for* block

Another useful view, especially when your app is using a multitier architecture or third-party libraries, is the Modules view, which displays the details of the profiling data grouped by modules. Figure 6-24 shows the Modules view for the sample application.

PerformanceAnalysisSample

PerformanceAnalys...mple130405(5).vspx

Current View: Modules

Name	Inclusive Samples	Exclusive Samples	Inclusive Samples %	Exclusive Samples %
PerformanceAnalysisSample.exe	**5,132**	**5,112**	**99.34**	**98.95**
PerformanceAnalysisSample.FakeBiz.SimulateRemoteServiceCall	5,112	5,112	98.95	98.95
PerformanceAnalysisSample.App..ctor	1	0	0.02	0.00
PerformanceAnalysisSample.App.GetXamlType	4	0	0.08	0.00
PerformanceAnalysisSample.App.OnLaunched	12	0	0.23	0.00
PerformanceAnalysisSample.FakeBiz.GetCustomers	5,112	0	98.95	0.00
PerformanceAnalysisSample.MainPage..ctor	6	0	0.12	0.00
PerformanceAnalysisSample.MainPage.Connect	1	0	0.02	0.00
PerformanceAnalysisSample.MainPage.GetCustomerListButton_Click	1	0	0.02	0.00
PerformanceAnalysisSample.MainPage.InitializeComponent	4	0	0.08	0.00
PerformanceAnalysisSample.MainPage+<GetCustomerListButton_Click>d__0.MoveNext	5,112	0	98.95	0.00
PerformanceAnalysisSample.PerformanceAnalysisSample_XamlTypeInfo.XamlTypeInfoProvider.Activate_0_MainPage	6	0	0.12	0.00
PerformanceAnalysisSample.PerformanceAnalysisSample_XamlTypeInfo.XamlTypeInfoProvider.CreateXamlType	1	0	0.02	0.00
PerformanceAnalysisSample.PerformanceAnalysisSample_XamlTypeInfo.XamlTypeInfoProvider.GetXamlTypeByName	1	0	0.02	0.00
PerformanceAnalysisSample.PerformanceAnalysisSample_XamlTypeInfo.XamlTypeInfoProvider.GetXamlTypeByType	1	0	0.02	0.00
PerformanceAnalysisSample.PerformanceAnalysisSample_XamlTypeInfo.XamlUserType.ActivateInstance	6	0	0.12	0.00
PerformanceAnalysisSample.Program.<Main>b__0	1	0	0.02	0.00
PerformanceAnalysisSample.Program.Main	5	0	0.10	0.00
System.Runtime.CompilerServices.AsyncMethodBuilderCore.Start	5,112	0	98.95	0.00
System.Runtime.CompilerServices.AsyncVoidMethodBuilder.Start	5,113	0	98.97	0.00
clr.dll	**15**	**15**	**0.29**	**0.29**
d3d11.dll	**13**	**13**	**0.25**	**0.25**
nvwgf2um.dll	**31**	**13**	**0.60**	**0.25**
Windows.UI.Xaml.dll	**14**	**5**	**0.27**	**0.10**
ntdll.dll	**4**	**4**	**0.08**	**0.08**
mscorlib.ni.dll	**3**	**2**	**0.06**	**0.04**
kernel32.dll	**1**	**1**	**0.02**	**0.02**
System.ni.dll	**1**	**1**	**0.02**	**0.02**
Windows.UI.Xaml.ni.dll	**5,135**	**0**	**99.40**	**0.00**

FIGURE 6-24 Modules view

An additional option to profile your app is provided by the *DebugSettings* property of the *Application* class. The *DebugSettings* class incudes an *EnableFrameRateCounter* static method that displays the frames per second (FPS) counter in the upper-left corner of your app's window. The FPS counter enables you to watch the overall performance of your app's user interface, including memory utilization for textures and CPU utilization. The following code snippet shows how to activate the frame rate counter in your *App* class, followed by an image of the frame rate counter in action:

Sample of C# code

```
public App()
{
    this.InitializeComponent();
    this.Suspending += OnSuspending;

    DebugSettings.EnableFrameRateCounter = true;
}
```

045 027 040965 003 000 001

The digits displayed in the counter provide the following indicators (from left to right):

- ***Composition thread FPS*** The frames-per-second frame rate for the composition thread
- ***UI thread FPS*** The frames-per-second frame rate for the UI thread
- ***Memory*** Video memory utilization for textures
- ***Batch*** The count of surfaces that are sent to the video card to be drawn (GPU)
- ***Composition thread CPU*** Time in milliseconds spent on the composition thread's processor
- ***UI CPU*** Time in milliseconds spent on the UI thread's processor

Another useful function exposed by the *DebugSettings* class is the *IsOverdrawHeatMapEnabled* property. This property offers a debugging visual aid to detect areas of the user interface in which your app is drawing objects on top of one another. Figure 6-25 shows a sample application with *IsOverdrawHeatMapEnabled* set to *true*. Darker shades indicate higher amounts of overdraw.

FIGURE 6-25 A sample application heat map

The particular visualization enabled by this tool can be useful during the application development for detecting layout, animation, and other operations that are graphics processing–intensive. In these cases, you might consider setting the *CacheMode* property to *BitmapCache* on the *UIElement* that contains the entire conceptual element. Doing so enables the framework to render the element to a bitmap once and then use that bitmap instead of re-rendering the subobjects for every frame.

To activate this particular visualization, just set the *IsOverdrawHeatMapEnabled* property to *true*, as shown in the following code excerpt:

```
public App()
{
    this.InitializeComponent();
    this.Suspending += OnSuspending;

    DebugSettings.EnableFrameRateCounter = true;
    DebugSettings.IsOverdrawHeatMapEnabled = true;
}
```

Tracing and logging events for Windows Store apps

The *System.Diagnostics.Tracing* namespace provides types and members that enable you to create strongly-typed events for logging purposes, to be captured by ETW. (This practice is also known as creating an "audit trail" or "audit log.") However, Windows Runtime supports only a subset of the available types. For example, in a Windows Store app, the *TraceListener* class (and its derived types, such as the *DefaultTraceListener*, *TextWriterTraceListener*, and *EventLogTraceListener* types) are not supported by the Windows Runtime. In this section, you see how to create, trace and log events that can greatly enhance the overall quality of your software by keeping track of errors and other significant events encountered during your app life cycle.

The first thing you need to do is to provide your own *EventSource* implementation. The *EventSource* class provides the ability to create different event types that need to be traced. Listing 6-19 shows an example of its implementation.

LISTING 6-19 Implementing the *EventSource* class

```
using System;
using System.Collections.Generic;
using System.Diagnostics.Tracing;
using System.Linq;
using System.Text;
using System.Threading.Tasks;

namespace SimpleEventTracing
{
    public class MyCustomEventSource : EventSource
    {

        [Event(1, Level = EventLevel.LogAlways)]
        public void WriteDebug(string message)
```

```
        {
            this.WriteEvent(1, message);
        }

        [Event(2, Level = EventLevel.Informational)]
        public void WriteInfo(string message)
        {
            this.WriteEvent(2, message);
        }

        [Event(3, Level = EventLevel.Warning)]
        public void WriteWarning(string message)
        {
            this.WriteEvent(3, message);
        }

        [Event(4, Level = EventLevel.Error)]
        public void WriteError(string message)
        {
            this.WriteEvent(4, message);
        }

        [Event(5, Level = EventLevel.Critical)]
        public void WriteCritical(string message)
        {
            this.WriteEvent(5, message);
        }
    }
}
```

Each event is marked with an *EventAttribute* attribute that enables you to specify additional event information, which can be used by the event listener to filter the event to be traced. The information that can be specified for each event is as follows:

- ***EventId*** Represents the identifier for the event
- ***Keywords*** Specifies the keywords associated to an event as defined in the *EventKeywords* enum
- ***Level*** Indicates the level of the event; it can assume one of the following values (defined in the *EventLevel* enum):
  - ***LogAlways*** Is typically used by the listener to indicate that no filtering will be performed on the events
  - ***Critical*** Corresponds to a critical error, which has caused a major failure
  - ***Error*** Indicates a standard error
  - ***Warning*** Represents a warning event
  - ***Informational*** Provide additional information on events that are not considered errors (such as the progress state of an application)
  - ***Verbose*** Adds lengthy events or messages
- ***Message*** Specifies the message for the event

- ***Opcode*** Indicates the operation code for the event
- ***Task*** Specifies the task for the event
- ***TypeId*** When implemented in a derived class, represents a unique identifier for this attribute
- ***Version*** Indicates the version of the event

Because the same event source instance can be shared throughout the entire application, you might want to use a singleton to get a reference to the custom event source, as shown in Listing 6-20. Remember, however, that if you are planning to use multiple *EventSource* instances instead of sharing the same instance throughout the application, you should call the *Dispose* method when you no longer need to work with a specific instance.

LISTING 6-20 Using the singleton pattern to get a reference to the custom event source

```
using System;
using System.Collections.Generic;
using System.Diagnostics.Tracing;
using System.Linq;
using System.Text;
using System.Threading.Tasks;

namespace SimpleEventTracing
{
    public static class EventSourceFactory
    {
        private static MyCustomEventSource _eventSource;

        public static MyCustomEventSource EventSource
        {
            get
            {
                if (_eventSource == null)
                {
                    _eventSource = new MyCustomEventSource();
                }

                return _eventSource;
            }
        }
    }
}
```

After you decide what events to trace, you must implement an event listener. Because the *EventListener* class is marked as abstract, you must derive your custom listener and provide your own implementation of the *OnEventWritten* abstract method that will receive the callback for the traced events. You can also define multiple event listeners. Each listener is logically independent of the other listeners, which means you can use different listeners to trace different event types. For example, a listener might trace only the most severe errors that need to be immediately sent to the cloud or to a remote service for further analysis, whereas another listener might take care of the less-critical events that can be logged in the local storage and then collected at a later time. Listing 6-21 shows the skeleton of two implementations of the *EventListener* abstract class used to log different kinds of events.

LISTING 6-21 Two implementations of the *EventListener* abstract class

```
using System;
using System.Collections.Generic;
using System.Diagnostics.Tracing;
using System.Linq;
using System.Text;
using System.Threading.Tasks;

namespace SimpleEventTracing
{
    public class RemoteEventListener : EventListener
    {
        protected override void OnEventWritten(EventWrittenEventArgs eventData)
        {
            // log the event via a remote service or in the cloud
        }
    }

    public class LocalStorageEventListener : EventListener
    {
        protected override void OnEventWritten(EventWrittenEventArgs eventData)
        {
            // log the event in the local storage;
        }
    }
}
```

The *OnEventWritten* is called whenever the *WriteEvent* method of the associated *EventSource* has been invoked. The *OnEventWritten* method receives an instance of the *EventWrittenEventArgs* class as a unique parameter, which contains all the information concerning the event written by the event source. The following code snippet shows how an event listener can filter the set of events to trace based on the event attributes defined in the *EventSource* associated to the listener:

```
protected override void OnLaunched(LaunchActivatedEventArgs args)
{
    this.InitializeEventListener();

    (code omitted)
}

private void InitializeEventListener()
{
    EventListener remoteListener = new RemoteEventListener();
    remoteListener.EnableEvents(EventSourceFactory.EventSource,
        EventLevel.Error | EventLevel.Critical);
```

```
    EventListener storageListener = new LocalStorageEventListener();
    storageListener.EnableEvents(EventSourceFactory.EventSource,
        EventLevel.Informational | EventLevel.Verbose | EventLevel.Warning);
}
```

The first listener accepts only the most critical events that need to be addressed as soon as possible, whereas the second listener takes care of those events that do not represent an actual error, but nonetheless can offer important information that you might want to store for future actions.

You can log events by invoking the *Write** method that best suits your needs. The following code excerpt shows a revised version of a method used in Listing 6-5 to purchase the full version of an app that traces any exception encountered during the purchase process:

```
private async void BuyButton_Click(object sender, RoutedEventArgs e)
{
    try
    {
        await CurrentAppSimulator.RequestAppPurchaseAsync(false);
    }
    catch (Exception ex)
    {
        PurchaseErrorMessage.Text = String.Format("Unable to buy: {0}", ex.Message);
        PurchaseErrorMessage.Visibility = Windows.UI.Xaml.Visibility.Visible;

        EventSourceFactory.EventSource.WriteCritical(ex.Message);
    }
}
```

Using Windows Store reports to improve the quality of your app

After you publish your app in the Windows Store, the store provides you with two types of information:

- **Analytics** Refers to data collected from the Windows Store. Analytics data includes information such as app listing views, downloads, and customer ratings and reviews. This data provides you with a considerable amount of information that can help you improve app sales and revenues. Collecting analytics data cannot be disabled.
- **Telemetry** Refers to data collected when your app is running on a user's device and provides information such as how often it has been launched; how long it has been running; and whether it has experienced crashes, unresponsiveness (hangs), or JavaScript exceptions. From a developer's perspective, telemetry data represents a highly valuable source of information that can help you improve the reliability of your app. You can enable or disable telemetry data collection from your Profile section in the Windows Store Dashboard, as shown in Figure 6-26.

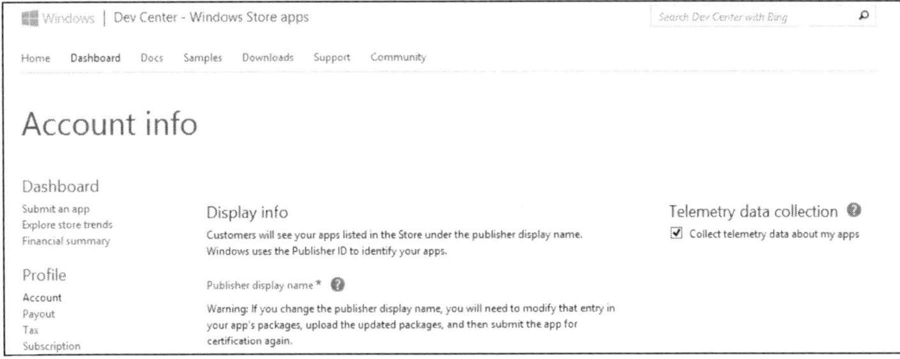

FIGURE 6-26 The Profile section of the Account info screen

Analytics information concerning your app are provided through Adoption reports, which include various analytics data that can help you understand the download trends for your app and review customer feedback. These reports also include useful information about the conversion rate of your app (from trial to full version) and in-app purchases. Figure 6-27 shows an example of a Downloads report that helps you track the download trends of your app and understand how you are performing with respect to your competitors.

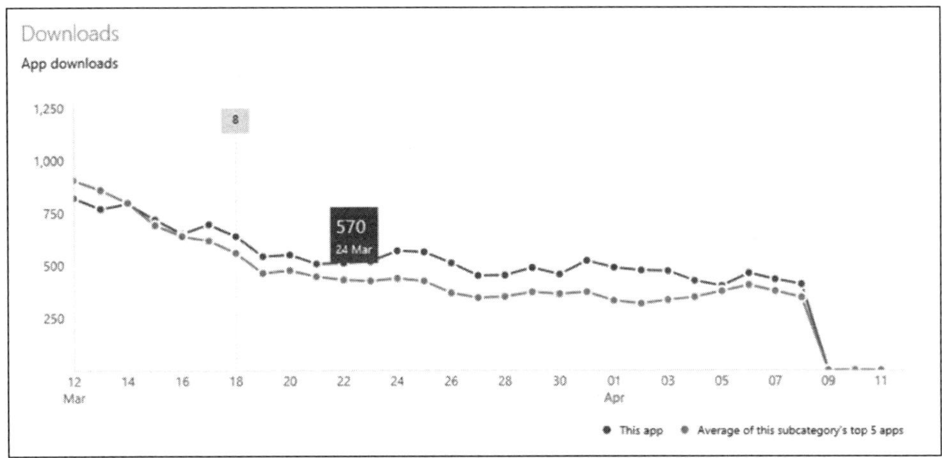

FIGURE 6-27 A Downloads report available from the Windows Store Dashboard (Source: *http://blogs.msdn.com/b/windowsstore/archive/2012/05/10/making-customer-focused-decisions-with-adoption-reports.aspx*)

Telemetry data, on the other hand, is collected and summarized though Quality reports, which measure your app's reliability. To access the Quality reports of your app, go to the app's summary page and, from that page, click the Quality link in the left pane.

EXAM TIP

Quality reports measure the failure rate of your app; that is, the number of unexpected errors experienced by your customers due to a crash, an unresponsive app, or an unhandled exception for apps written in JavaScript.

If you click the *Details* link, you will get detailed information about the different errors encountered by your app. Figure 6-28 shows the Quality report summary.

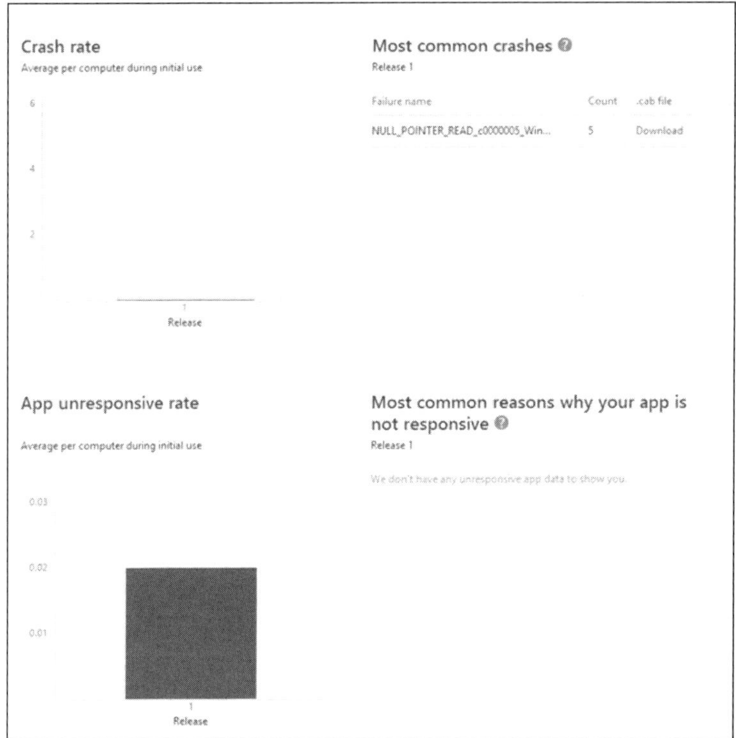

FIGURE 6-28 A Quality report summary

You can use this information to improve the quality of your app by identifying (and then fixing) the most common errors faced by your customers. You can also compare the quality of different versions of your app published to the Windows Store.

According to the Microsoft documentation, failure rates are computed for each failure type: crashes, unresponsiveness, or unhandled JavaScript exceptions (in the case of JavaScript apps). The data for calculating the failure rate is collected from a random sample of machines—called a quality panel—on which your app is used. Microsoft considers a quality panel of at least 500 machines to be an adequate sample size for calculating failure rates.

In the Most Common Crashes section, you can find the top five crashes that have affected your app. Each crash's name is uniquely identified by its name. Each name provides the following information: the problem that originated the crash, the error code, and the debug symbols.

Next to the error, you can find a link to the .cab file containing the process dump associated with that specific failure. A dump file represents a snapshot of an app that shows the process being executed and the modules that were loaded when the snapshot was taken. By analyzing the process dump, you can get the stack traces and other details regarding the error. You can open the dump file with Visual Studio 2012 or with an external tool such as the WinDbg.exe tool to analyze the collected data.

MORE INFO **DUMP FILES**

For further details on using dump files to debug app crashes and unresponsiveness in Visual Studio 2012, visit ***http://msdn.microsoft.com/en-us/library/vstudio/d5zhxt22.aspx.***

Thought experiment

Solving a performance issue

In this thought experiment, apply what you've learned about this objective. You can find answers to these questions in the "Answers" section at the end of this chapter.

Your app uses code similar to the one shown in Listing 6-18 (in the "Profiling a Windows Store app" section) to retrieve a list of customers by simulating a request to an external web service and display their names on the screen. When profiling your app, you notice that the *SimulateRemoteServiceCall* method represents a bottleneck in your code that takes 99 percent of the execution time and freezes the UI until the operation is completed.

How would you change the presented code to solve this performance issue without freezing the UI?

Objective summary

- Visual Studio 2012 profiling tools for Windows Store apps enable you to observe and record metrics about the behavior of your app by using a sampling method that collects information from the CPU call stack at regular intervals, navigating through the execution paths of your code, and evaluating the cost of each function. To activate this feature, in the Debug menu of Visual Studio 2012, click the Start Performance Analysis menu item.
- To trace strongly-typed events (ETW), use the *EventSource* class to create different event types that need to be traced. Use the *EventAttribute* attribute to specify additional event information that can be used by the listener to filter the event to be traced. Finally, provide a custom event listener by deriving it from the *EventListener* class and implement the *OnEventWritten* callback that will receive the traced events.
- Take advantage of the Quality reports provided by the Windows Store to discover the failure rate and the most common issues of your app.

Objective review

Answer the following questions to test your knowledge of the information in this objective. You can find the answers to these questions and explanations of why each answer choice is correct or incorrect in the "Answers" section at the end of this chapter.

1. Which of the following statements regarding the performance analysis tool in Visual Studio 2012 is incorrect?
   - **A.** The performance analysis tool takes snapshots of the system at regular intervals, keeping track of the calls being executed and evaluating their execution cost.
   - **B.** The inclusive sample percentage (or inclusive time) indicates the CPU time spent to complete a specific function, including the time spent waiting for any other function that it might call.
   - **C.** The exclusive samples percentage (or exclusive time) does not take into account the time spent waiting for other functions called from the current one to complete, but only indicates the amount of time consumed by the inner work of a function.
   - **D.** You can display a frame rate counter in the upper-left corner of the screen just by setting the *DebugSettings.IsOverdrawHeatMapEnabled* property to *true*.
2. Which class provides the ability to create the different types of events that need to be traced?
   - **A.** *EventSource* class
   - **B.** *EventListener* class
   - **C.** *EventWrittenEventArgs* class
   - **D.** *TraceListener* class
3. In the Quality reports provided by the Windows Store, how is the quality of your app measured?
   - **A.** By user reviews and ratings
   - **B.** By the number of downloads
   - **C.** By the number of hours that users have spent using the application
   - **D.** By the failure rate of the app, based on a random sample of machines on which your app is used

Chapter summary

- Choose the business model that best suits your needs. Use the *CurrentAppSimulator* to test your app's behavior locally in a simulated scenario before publishing the app in the Windows Store. Before publishing, remember to replace any instance of the *CurrentAppSimulator* class with *CurrentApp*.
- Set up a *try/catch/finally* block every time you are trying to access a resource that might be unavailable or missing, or when you are relying on types and functions over which you do not have any control.
- Use the *UnhandledException* event as a last resort to catch any exception that has not been handled by the application code, but keep in mind that some exceptions might not raise the event.
- The first time your Windows Store app needs to access a sensitive device, users are asked to grant their permission before the app can use the corresponding feature. Because your app might not be able to access a sensitive device, you need to handle the errors that can occur when trying to access a disabled device capability.
- In the *async/await* pattern, you can place your *try/catch* blocks around an asynchronous call as you would do in synchronous code. However, do not forget to await asynchronous calls, or any exception raised during the async operation will not be caught. Implement the *UnobservedTaskException* event handler as a safety net to handle unobserved exceptions.
- When developing a Windows Store app, consider adopting a functional test plan to verify that all the functional requirements of the software are working properly from a user's perspective, and a unit test plan to verify whether the single units of software, isolated from any external dependency, behave as expected.
- When implementing a unit test, remember to follow the Three A's rule: set up the object to be tested (arrange), exercise the method under test (act), and finally make claims about the object (assert).
- Use the Visual Studio 2012 profiling tools for Windows Store apps to record performance counter metrics about the behavior of your app, collect information from the CPU call stack, and evaluate the time required by each function to complete.
- To trace strongly-typed events (ETW), use the *EventSource* class to create different event types that need to be traced and provide a custom event listener by deriving it from the *EventListener* class.
- Take advantage of the Quality reports provided by the Windows Store to discover the failure rate and the most common issues affecting your app.

Answers

This section contains the solutions to the thought experiments and answers to the lesson review questions in this chapter.

Objective 6.1: Thought experiment

The app can be installed on up to five devices. After extra content has been purchased, you want to make sure the user can play the new levels on a different Windows 8 device. To do so, you can leverage one of the APIs exposed by Windows Runtime to retrieve the purchase's receipt (such as the *GetAppReceiptAsync* and the *GetProductReceiptAsync* methods) and use it to validate the user's purchase on a different machine.

In fact, when the user launches the app from a different device, you can ask the Windows Store for the receipt, validate it against your web server or service to make sure it has not been tampered with (using the digital signature information shipped with the receipt, as shown in Listing 6-12), and then enable the extra content purchased by the user on a different device. The complete flow to validate the purchase's receipt can be found at *http://msdn.microsoft.com/en-us/library/windows/apps/jj649137.aspx*.

Objective 6.1: Review

1. **Correct answer:** C
   - **A. Incorrect:** You can use the *CurrentApp* class only if your app has been published in the Windows Store.
   - **B. Incorrect:** You can use the *CurrentApp* class only if your app has been published in the Windows Store.
   - **C. Correct:** You can use the *CurrentAppSimulator* to test your app locally. Remember to replace any reference to this class with the *CurrentApp* class before publishing your app; otherwise, it does not pass the certification process.
   - **D. Incorrect:** You can use the *CurrentAppSimulator* to test your app locally. If your app has not been published in the Windows Store yet, the *CurrentAppSimulator* class is your only option.
2. **Correct answer:** B
   - **A. Incorrect:** There is no evaluation period in a feature-based trial. The user purchases the app to enable all the available features.
   - **B. Correct:** In a feature-based trial, the *IsActive* property returning *false* means that your app's license has been revoked or is missing.

C. **Incorrect:** When the user purchases the full version of the app, the *IsTrial* property should return *false*.

D. **Incorrect:** There is no evaluation period in a feature-based trial. The user can purchase the app at any time.

3. **Correct answer:** D

   A. **Incorrect:** Whether the purchase is real or simulated depends on the class you are using (*CurrentApp* or *CurrentAppSimulator*), not on the value provided to the *RequestAppPurchaseAsync* method.

   B. **Incorrect:** The price of the app and other features does not depend on the *RequestAppPurchaseAsync*.

   C. **Incorrect:** To buy extra features or products offered through an in-app purchase, you have to leverage the *RequestProductPurchaseAsync*.

   D. **Correct:** It indicates whether you want the method to return the receipt for the app purchase.

Objective 6.2: Thought experiment

A well-planned exception handling strategy represents an important part of your app design and implementation. It can reduce the risks of exposing error messages containing sensitive information.

For example, you should always catch any exception that could potentially contain sensitive information, such as connection strings, URLs, login information, passwords, and so on. Replace them with custom exceptions that no longer contain this information before logging or rethrowing them, or before displaying the error message to the user. (This strategy is also known as exception shielding.)

Objective 6.2: Review

1. **Correct answer:** D

   A. **Incorrect:** The event is raised only for unhandled exceptions that propagate back to the XAML framework.

   B. **Incorrect:** When an exception is thrown in a void-returning asynchronous method, it is stored in the *Task* instance and then ignored.

   C. **Incorrect:** The *Handled* method of the *UnhandledExceptionEventArgs* class can be invoked after the *UnhandledException* event has been raised to signal the framework, not to process the exception any further.

   D. **Correct:** The *UnhandledExceptionEvent* event is raised when there is no longer any possibility for the application code to catch an unhandled exception.

2. **Correct answer:** A

   A. **Correct:** When using the *Windows.Media.Capture.MediaCapture* class to preview or capture photos, video, or audio, and the user has not granted the app with the permission to access the device capability (or the permission has been revoked), the system will raise an *UnauthorizedAccessException*.

   B. **Incorrect:** The *InvalidOperationException* is a generic exception that is thrown when a method call is invalid for the object's current state.

   C. **Incorrect:** A generic *System.Exception* is raised when using the *Windows.Media.Capture.MediaCapture* class to preview or capture photos, video, or audio, and the device is not present on the system.

   D. **Incorrect:** Other APIs behave differently when trying to access a device for which the user has not granted permission. For example, if you are using the *CaptureCameraUI* class and the webcam capability is turned off, invoking the *CaptureFileAsync* method does not raise an error.

3. **Correct answer:** B

   A. **Incorrect:** When you forget to await a task-returning asynchronous method and an exception is raised during the async operation, the exception is stored in an anonymous *Task* instance and it does not propagate back to the caller.

   B. **Correct:** When you forget to await a task-returning asynchronous method and an exception is raised during the async operation, the exception is stored in an anonymous *Task* instance and then ignored (an unobserved exception).

   C. **Incorrect:** If an exception is thrown in a void-returning asynchronous method, the exception goes unhandled and will eventually bubble up, determining the process termination.

   D. **Incorrect:** The *AggregateException* is used when you expect multiple exceptions being raised during the execution of asynchronous operations.

Objective 6.3: Thought experiment

The reason why the method under test is more likely to fail is that it is trying to access the user's Documents library. Before your app can programmatically access any user libraries, you need to add the corresponding declaration in the Package.appxmanifest file that is included in your unit testing project.

Your test code is subject to the same rules that apply to your Windows Store app. Therefore, any time you try to access a resource for which your app has to declare the corresponding capability in the app manifest (such as user library or webcam, for example), you need to modify the Package.appxmanifest file of your Windows Store app (so that it can use those resources) and the app manifest located inside your Unit Test project for Windows Store apps.

In the thought experiment example, to make the test pass, you have to declare the Documents Library capability and add one or more file associations on the Declaration tab.

Objective 6.3: Review

1. **Correct answer:** D
   - **A. Incorrect:** The statement is correct.
   - **B. Incorrect:** The statement is correct.
   - **C. Incorrect:** The statement is correct.
   - **D. Correct:** The statement is incorrect. It refers to integration testing, in which different components and resources of an application are tested together to verify that they work as expected.
2. **Correct answer:** C
   - **A. Incorrect:** Methods marked with the *AssemblyInitialize/AssemblyCleanup* attributes are invoked before and after all tests in the assembly are run.
   - **B. Incorrect:** Methods marked with the *ClassInitialize/ClassCleanup* attributes are invoked before and after all tests of the same test battery are run.
   - **C. Correct:** Methods marked with the *TestInitialize/TestCleanup* attributes are invoked before and after the execution of each single unit test.
   - **D. Incorrect:** The *DataTestMethod* attribute is used for data-driven testing.
3. **Correct answer:** D
   - **A. Incorrect:** The *Assert.ThrowsException<TException>* method is used in the test framework for Windows Store apps when the expected behavior of the method under test is to throw an exception.
   - **B. Incorrect:** The *TestMethod* attribute works in both frameworks.
   - **C. Incorrect:** The *DataTestMehod* attribute is supported only by the unit test framework for Windows Store apps.
   - **D. Correct:** The *ExpectedException* attribute is not supported in the unit test framework for Windows Store apps. You need to use the *Assert.ThrowsException<TException>* method instead.

Objective 6.4: Thought experiment

The main issue of the code shown in Listing 6-17 is that it executes synchronously, freezing the UI until the operation has been completed. To solve this issue, you can transform the method into an asynchronous call, using the *await/async* pattern, as shown in the following snippet:

```
public async Task<List<Person>> GetCustomers()
{
    return await this.SimulateRemoteServiceCall();
}

private async Task<List<Person>> SimulateRemoteServiceCall()
{
    return await Task.Factory.StartNew<List<Person>>(() =>
    {
        for (int i = 0; i < Int32.MaxValue; i++)
            // code omitted

        var list = new List<Person>()
        {
           (code omitted)
        };
        return list;
    });
}
```

Doing so, your code will be executed asynchronously, without blocking the UI until the operation is completed. Remember also to modify the button click's event handler according to the new asynchronous pattern.

Objective 6.4: Review

1. **Correct answer:** D
    - **A. Incorrect:** The statement is correct.
    - **B. Incorrect:** The statement is correct.
    - **C. Incorrect:** The statement is correct.
    - **D. Correct:** The statement is incorrect. To visualize the frame rate counter, you have to set the *DebugSettings.EnableFrameRateCounter* to *true*. The *IsOverdrawHeatMapEnabled* property is used to visualize overdrawing.

2. **Correct answer:** A
   - **A. Correct:** The *EventSource* class provides the ability to create events for event tracing for Windows (through ETW).
   - **B. Incorrect:** The *EventListener* class provides methods for enabling and disabling events from event sources.
   - **C. Incorrect:** The *EventWrittenEventArgs* class provides data for the *EventListener.OnEventWritten* callback.
   - **D. Incorrect:** The *TraceListener* class is not supported in a Windows Store app.
3. **Correct answer:** D
   - **A. Incorrect:** User reviews and ratings are not included in Quality reports, which measure the failure rate of the app. User reviews and ratings are summarized in the Ratings reports.
   - **B. Incorrect:** The number of downloads is not taken into account by Quality reports, which measure the failure rate of the app. Download data are summarized in the Download reports.
   - **C. Incorrect:** The number of hours spent using the application is not taken into account by Quality reports, which measure the failure rate of the app. Data about time spent by users with your app are summarized in the Usage reports.
   - **D. Correct:** The Quality reports provided by the Windows Store measure the app's failure rate, based on a random sample of machines on which your app is used.

Index

A

AAC (Advanced Audio Codec) audio profile, 76
Aborted value (DeviceWatcherStatus enum), 121
AccelerationReading class, 85
AccelerationX property, 85
AccelerationY property, 85
AccelerationZ property, 85
Accelerometer class, 82
AccelerometerReadingChangedEventArgs instance, 85
accelerometer sensor, 82–87
  intializing, 83
  polling, 85–86
  ReadingChanged event, 84–85
accessing
  files, programmatically, 298–300
  sensors, 81–99
    accelerometer, 82–87
    compass, 90–92
    gyrometer, 87–90
    inclinometer, 95–97
    light, 98–99
    orientation, 92–96
AccessToken property, 180
activating file pickers, 293
Active Directory User Object, 323
AddCondition method, 4–5
Added event (DeviceWatcher class), 117
AddEffectAsync method, 71
adding custom controls to Windows Store apps, 239–242
Add New Item dialog box, 239
AddPage method, 147
AddPagesComplete method, 147
AddPages event, 145
Add Reference dialog box, 47
adoption reports, 403
Advanced Audio Codec (AAC) audio profile, 76
advanced functionalities, trials, 337
Advanced Query Syntax (AQS) string, 115
AggregateException, 370
AggregateException.Flatten method, 371
AllowCropping parameter, 65
Allow Remote Control Of My Player option, 159
All value (DeviceClass enum), 113
All value (KeyUsages property), 322
ambient light intensity, 98–99
analytics information, 402–403
angular velocity, measuring with gyrometer, 87–90
animations, 221–237
  applying animations from the animation library, 233–237
  dependent versus independent animations, 225–227
  discrete animations, 232
  easing functions, 232
  interpolation logic, 229–232
  key-frame animations, 228–230
  storyboarded animations, 222–225
  visual states, 246
APIs (application programming interfaces)
  caching application data, 277–284
    local storage, 277–279
    roaming storage, 280–283
    temporary storage, 283–284
  media capture, 57–79
    CameraCaptureUI, 58–68
    MediaCapture class, 68–79
AppBar button control template, 248–249
AppBar control, fade in/out animation, 235
Append method, 310
AppId attribute, 357
AppId property, 342
Application class, 361

application data, caching, 276–286
APIs, 277–284
ESE (Extensible Storage Engine), 285
HTML5 Web Storage, 285
IndexedDB technology, 284–285
WinJS. Application.local, 286
WinJS.Application.roaming, 286
WinJS.Application.sessionState, 285–286
ApplicationData class, 277
ApplicationDataCompositeValue instance, 280
ApplicationDataContainer.CreateContainer method, 278
ApplicationDataCreateDisposition enum, 278
ApplicationData.Current class, 283
application manifest, declaring background task usage, 5
Application Manifest Designer
Application UI tab, 255–256
application programming interfaces (APIs)
media capture, 57–79
CameraCaptureUI, 58–68
MediaCapture class, 68–79
Application UI tab (Application Manifest Designer), 255–256
App Manifest Designer (Visual Studio), 23, 61–62, 101
AppReceipt element (receipt fragment), 357
apps (applications)
accessing sensors, 81–99
accelerometer, 82–87
compass, 90–92
gyrometer, 87–90
inclinometer, 95–97
light, 98–99
orientation, 92–96
data management
data caching, 275–289
saving and retrieving files, 291–304
development
consuming background tasks, 9–36
creating and consuming WinMD components, 38–51
creating background tasks, 1–8
implementing printing, 131–153
adding user interface, 138–140
creating custom print template, 140–142
custom print options, 152–153
in-app printing, 153
paginating/previewing documents, 144–148
preview window options, 148–149
print option changes, 149–151
PrintTask events, 137–138
print task options, 142–144
registering app for Print contract, 132–137
Play To feature, 155–174
registering app as Play To receiver, 167–174
source application, 161–167
testing sample code, Windows Media Player, 159–161
understanding the contract, 156–158
security, 306–327
certificates, 319–325
DataProtectionProvider class, 325–328
digital signatures, 316–319
generating random numbers, 311–313
hash algorithms, 308–311
MAC algorithms, 313–316
Windows.Security.Cryptography namespaces, 307–308
solution deployment
diagnostic and monitoring strategies, 388–406
error handling, 359–373
test strategies, 374–384
trial functionality, 335–357
UI enhancements
animations and transitions, 221–237
custom controls, 239–250
globalization and localization, 252–267
responsiveness, 193–219
WNS (Windows Push Notification Service), 176–186
notification channels, 176–178
sending notifications to clients, 178–186
AQS (Advanced Query Syntax) string, 115
AreEqual method, 381
ArgumentNullException, 372
AssemblyCleanup attribute, 384
AssemblyInitialize attribute, 384
Assert class, 378, 381
Assert.IsTrue method, 382
AsTask method, 26, 210
asymmetric encryption, 316
AsymmetricKeyProvider class, 318
async/await pattern, 25

asynchronous calls
  cancelling operations, 210–211
  implementation, 208–209
  LongCalculationAsync, 207
  parallel execution, 217–219
  synchronizing multiple calls, 215–216
asynchronous errors, 368–372
asynchronous operations, 194–202
  cancelling, 209–210
  implementing asynchronous methods, 204–207
  .NET 2.0, 197
  tracking progress, 211–215
async keyword, 199
async/method pattern, 197
AsyncTaskMethodBuilder class, 370
AsyncVoidMethodBuilder class, 370
async void methods, 370
AttachAsync method, 27
attributes
  AssemblyCleanup, 384
  AssemblyInitialize, 384
  ClassCleanup, 383
  ClassInitialize, 383
  DataRow, 385
  DataTestMethod, 385
  EventAttribute, 399–400
  ExpectedException, 378
  TestClass, 381
  TestCleanup, 383
  TestInitialize, 383
  TestMethod, 381
  UITestMethod, 383
  UITestMethodAttribute, 378
audio
  capturing from microphone, 78–79
  capturing with MediaCapture class, 68–79
  recording, 67
AudioDeviceId property, 74
authenticating a cloud service, Windows Live Services, 183
Authenticating Your Service link, 182
authentication
  receipt validation, 357
authentication, cryptography and, 307
autogenerated code, unhandled exceptions, 362–363
AutoReverse property, 229
await keyword, 199
axis orientation (tablets and notebooks), 82

B

BackEase class, 230
BackgroundAccessStatus enum, 33
BackgroundDownloader class, 23, 25
BackgroundExecutionManager class, 32
Background property, 242
BackgroundTaskBuilder class, 2
  AddCondition method, 4–5
BackgroundTaskRegistration class, 7
BackgroundTaskRegistration instance, 11
background tasks
  consuming, 9–36
    cancelling tasks, 15–17
    debugging tasks, 19–21
    keeping communication channels open, 28–37
    progressing through tasks, 11–13
    task constraints, 14
    task triggers and conditions, 9–11
    task usage, 21–22
    transferring data in the background, 22–27
    updating tasks, 18–19
  creating, 1–8
    declaration of task usage, 5–7
    enumeration of registered tasks, 7
    using deferrals, 7
BackgroundTranferCostPolicy, 23
Background Transfer APIs, 23
BackgroundTransfer namespace, 22
BackgroundUpload class, 23
Badge Logo, 30
badge updates, 179
Batch indicator (FPS counters), 397
BCP-47 language tag, 257
Begin method, 225
BeginSave method, 196
BindingFailed event, 363
Bing Maps Geocode service, 104
BitmapImage object, 60
BorderBrush property, 242
BorderThickness property, 242
bottom-up approach, functional testing, 376
BounceEase class, 230
Bounces property, 231–232
Bounciness property, 231–232
built-in easing functions, 230
Bureau of Industry and Security, 307

business model selection, trial functionality, 336–338
Button class, 241
Button control, 390
Button control template, 246

C

CA (certification authority), 319
CachedFileManager class, 298
caching, data, 275–289
 application data, 276–286
  APIs, 277–284
  ESE (Extensible Storage Engine), 285
  HTML5 Web Storage, 285
  IndexedDB technology, 284–285
  WinJS. Application.local, 286
  WinJS.Application.roaming, 286
  WinJS.Application.sessionState, 285–286
 understanding app and user data, 275–276
 user data, 287–289
  external services, 289
  HTML5 Application Cache API, 289
  HTML5 File API, 288
  libraries, 288–289
  SkyDrive, 288
Calendar class, 264
calendars, localization, 264–265
Called functions bar (profile analysis report), 395
calls, asynchronous, 208–209
Call Tree view (profile analysis report), 394
CameraCaptureUI class, 42, 58–68
CameraCaptureUIMaxPhotoResolution enumeration, 65–66
CameraCaptureUIMode parameter, 60
CameraCaptureUIMode.Video parameter, 66–67
CameraCaptureUIPhotoFormat enumeration, 65–66
CameraCaptureUIVideoFormat property, 67
Camera Capture user interface, 366
camera, capturing media, 57–79
 CameraCaptureUI, 58–68
 MediaCapture class, 68–79
CameraOptionsUI class, 76
Canceled event handler, 16
CancellationToken class, 209
CancellationTokenSource class, 209
cancelling
 asynchronous operations, 209–210
 operations in asynchronous calls, 210–211
cancelling tasks, 15–17
Cancel method, 210
CaptureCameraUI class, 366
CaptureElement XAML control, 70
CaptureFileAsync method, 41, 60, 366–368
Capture Photo button, 60
CapturePhoto_Click event handler, 60
CapturePhotoToStreamAsync method, 72
capturing media, camera, 57–79
 CameraCaptureUI, 58–68
 MediaCapture class, 68–79
catching errors at app level, 361–363
CertificateEnrollmentManager class, 322, 324
Certificate Enrollment Requests, 324
CertificateId attribute, 357
CertificateRequestProperties object, 321
certificates, enrolling and requesting, 319–325
certification authority (CA), 319
certified devices, Play To feature, 156
channels, notification (WNS), 176–178
CharacterGroupings class, 262
charms
 Devices, 133, 149
 Settings, 365–366
checking for task cancellation, 15–17
CheckResult method, 12
ChooseFile_Click event handler, 293
ChooseFile_Click method, 200
CircleEase class, 231
CivicAddress property, 104
ClassCleanup attribute, 383
classes
 AccelerationReading, 85
 Accelerometer, 82
 Application, 361
 ApplicationData, 277
 ApplicationData.Current, 283
 Assert, 378, 381
 AsymmetricKeyProvider, 318
 AsyncTaskMethodBuilder, 370
 AsyncVoidMethodBuilder, 370
 BackEase, 230
 BackgroundDownloader, 23, 25
 BackgroundExecutionManager, 32
 BackgroundTaskBuilder, 2, 4–5

BackgroundTaskRegistration, 7
BackgroundUpload, 23
BounceEase, 230
Button, 241
CachedFileManager, 298
Calendar, 264
CameraCaptureUI, 42, 58–68
CameraOptionsUI, 76
CancellationToken, 209
CancellationTokenSource, 209
CaptureCameraUI, 366
CertificateEnrollmentManager, 322, 324
CharacterGroupings, 262
CircleEase, 231
Compass, 90
Compressor, 304
ContentThemeTransition, 235
Control, 241
ControlChannelTrigger, 29
ControlTemplate, 242
CryptographicBuffer, 309, 311
CryptographicEngine, 314
CryptographicHash, 310
CryptographicKey, 318
CubicEase, 231
CurrentApp, 339
CurrentAppSimulator, 339
DataProtectionProvider, 325–328
DataWriter, 300
DateTimeFormatter, 263
DebugSettings, 396
Decompressor, 304
DeflateStream, 304
DeviceInformation, 113
DeviceWatcher, 117–122
DiscreteObjectKeyFrame, 232
Double, 382
DoubleAnimation, 223
DoubleAnimationUsingKeyFrames, 228
DownloadOperation, 25, 26
ElasticEase, 231
EntranceThemeTransition, 234
EventListener, 400
EventSource, implementation, 398–399
EventWrittenEventArgs, 401
Exception base, 360
ExponentialEase, 231
FadeInThemeAnimation, 235
FadeOutThemeAnimation, 235
FakeBiz, 391–392
FileIO, 279
FileOpenPicker, 292
Geolocator, 102–104
Geoposition, 104
Gyrometer, 87
HashAlgorithmNames, 309
HashAlgorithmProvider, 308–309, 310
HttpClient, 27, 29, 179
HttpClientHandler, 29
IXMLHTTPRequest2, 29
LightSensorReading, 98
LinearColorKeyFrame, 229
LinearDoubleKeyFrame, 229
LinearPointKeyFrame, 229
MacAlgorithmNames, 314
MacAlgorithmProvider, 313
MaintenanceTrigger, 3, 10
MediaCapture, 68–79
MediaCaptureInitalizationSettings, 74
MediaElement, 174
MediaEncodingProfile, 76
MessageWebSocket, 29
OAuthToken, 180–181
ObjectAnimationUsingKeyFrames, 229, 232
OrientationSensor, 94–95
PasswordVault, 327
PlayToReceiver, 170
PlayToSourceRequestedEventArgs, 164
PnpObject, 122
PointerDownThemeAnimation, 236
PointerUpThemeAnimation, 236
PowerEase, 231
PrintDocument, 144–145
PrintManager, 132
PrintPageDescription, 145
PrintTask, 142–144
PrintTaskOptions, 143
Program, 363
Progress<T>, 211
QuadraticEase, 231
QuarticEase, 231
QuinticEase, 231
ResourceLoader, 260
SimpleOrientationSensor, 92–94
SineEase, 231
SplineColorKeyFrame, 230

SplineDoubleKeyFrame, 230
SplinePointKeyFrame, 230
StorageFile, 288
StorageFile WinRT, 60
Storyboard, 222
StreamSocket, 29
StreamSocketControl, 35
StreamWebSocket, 29
System.Progress<T>, 25
SystemTrigger, 3
Task, 198
TileUpdateManager, 14
TileUpdater, 178
TraceListener, 398
Utility, 379
VideoEffects, 71
VideosLibrary, 163
VisualState, 246
Windows.Media.Capture.MediaCapture, 365
ZipArchive, 304
ClassInitialize attribute, 383
ClearEffectsAsync method, 71
Clear method, 178
cloud storage, caching user data, 289
CLR (common language runtime) exception handling, 359
CLR Windows 8 app
Windows Runtime, 41
code
capturing photos/video, 58
page code-behind, 213–215
coded UI testing (CUIT), 376
Collapsed custom print option, 152
ColorAnimation storyboard, 223
combination approach, functional testing, 376
combining data, orientation sensor, 92–96
common language runtime (CLR) exception handling, 359
CommonStates visual state, 248
communication, consuming background tasks, 28–37
Compare method, 310
Compass class, 90
compass sensor
retrieving data, 90–92
sensitivity, 92
Completed event, 137
Complete method, 7, 135
Completion property, 138–139
components, creating and consuming WinMD components, 38–51
native WinMD libraries, 40–46
understanding Windows Runtime, 38–40
WinMD libraries, 46–50
Composition thread CPU indicator (FPS counters), 397
Composition thread FPS indicator (FPS counters), 397
compressing files, 304–305
Compressor class, 304
concurrency profiling, 389
conditions, consuming background tasks, 9–11
confidentiality, cryptography and, 307
connections, keeping client-server communications open, 28–37
Connectivity namespace, 23
ConsentOnly value (KeyProtectionLevel enum), 321
ConsentWithPassword value (KeyProtectionLevel enum), 321
constraints, tasks, 14
consuming
background tasks, 9–36
cancelling tasks, 15–17
debugging tasks, 19–21
keeping communication channels open, 28–37
progressing through tasks, 11–13
task constraints, 14
task triggers and conditions, 9–11
task usage, 21–22
transferring data in the background, 22–27
updating tasks, 18–19
WinMD components, 38–51
native WinMD libraries, 40–46
understanding Windows Runtime, 38–40
WinMD libraries, 46–50
ContainsKey method, 278
Content property, 261
content, resource files, 258–259
ContentThemeTransition class, 235
Content transition animations, 234
ContinueWith call, 199
contracts
Play To, 155–174
registering app as Play To receiver, 167–174
source application, 161–167
testing sample code, Windows Media Player, 159–161
understanding the contract, 156–158
Print, registering apps, 132–137

contrast qualifier, 262
Control base class, 241
ControlChannelReset trigger, 11
ControlChannelTrigger, 10, 29
  guaranteed resource quota, 15
ControlChannelTrigger class, 29
controls
  AppBar, fade in/out animation, 235
  Button, 390
  custom, 239–250
    adding to Windows Store apps, 239–242
    dependency properties, 243–246
    visual state, 246–250
  Ellipse, 223
  Grid, 145
  ListBox, 299
  ListView, 390
  ProgressBar, 204
  Rectangle, 222
  ScrollBar, fade in/out animation, 235
  StackPanel, 141, 390
  TextBlock, 200, 212
ControlTemplate class, 242
conventions, naming, 381
converting asynchronous operations to tasks, 198–202
ConvertStringToBinary method, 309
cookies, 289
Coordinate property, 104
cost policies, 23
CostPolicy property, 25
CPU resource constraint, 14
CPU usage (profile analysis report), 393
CreateDownload method, 25
Created value (DeviceWatcherStatus enum), 121
CreateFileAsync method, 25, 279
CreateFolderQuery method, 299
CreateHash method, 310
CreateItemListOption method, 152
CreateKey method, 314
CreateKeyPair method, 318
CreatePrintTask method, 133
CreatePushNotificationChannelForApplicationAsync method, 176
CreateTileUpdaterForApplication method, 14
CreateUploadAsync method, 27
CreateUploadFromStreamAsync method, 27
CreateWatcher static method, 117
creating
  animations and transitions, 221–237
    applying animations from the animation library, 233–237
    dependent versus independent animations, 225–227
    discrete animations, 232
    easing functions, 232
    interpolation logic, 229–232
    key-frame animations, 228–230
    storyboarded animations, 222–225
  background tasks, 1–8
    declaration of task usage, 5–7
    enumeration of registered tasks, 7
    using deferrals, 7
  certificate requests, 320–321
  custom controls, 239–250
    adding to Windows Store apps, 239–242
    dependency properties, 243–246
    visual state, 246–250
  custom print templates, 140–142
  WinMD components, 38–51
    consuming native WinMD libraries, 40–46
    understanding Windows Runtime, 38–40
    WinMD libraries, 46–50
CroppedAspectRatio property, 66
CroppedSizeInPixels property, 66
crossfade animation, 236
CryptographicBuffer class, 309, 311
CryptographicEngine class, 314
CryptographicEngine.Sign method, 318
CryptographicHash class, 310
CryptographicKey class, 318
cryptography, 307–308
  certificates, 319–325
  digital signatures, 316–319
  hash algorithms, 308–311
  MAC algorithms, 313–316
  random number generation, 311–313
CubicEase class, 231
CUIT (coded UI testing), 376
currencies, localization, 264
CurrencyFormatter formatter, 264
CurrentApp class, 339
CurrentAppSimulator class, 339
CurrentTimeChangeRequested event, 170

custom controls, 239–250
  adding to Windows Store apps, 239–242
  dependency properties, 243–246
  visual state, 246–250
customizing storyboarded animations, 222–225
custom license information, trial functionality, 344–345
custom print options, 152–153
custom print templates, creating, 140–142
custom video effects, 71
C++ Windows 8 app, Windows Runtime, 42

D

data
  background tasks, transferring, 22–27
  combining using orientation sensor, 92–96
  integrity, cryptography and, 307
  management
    data caching, 275–289
    saving/retrieving files from file system, 291–304
    securing app data, 306–327
  retrieval
    compass, 90–92
    inclinometer sensor, 95–97
    sensors, 80–106
data caching, 275–289
  application data, 276–286
    APIs, 277–284
    ESE (Extensible Storage Engine), 285
    HTML5 Web Storage, 285
    IndexedDB technology, 284–285
    WinJS. Application.local, 286
    WinJS.Application.roaming, 286
    WinJS.Application.sessionState, 285–286
  Microsoft rules for roaming profiles, 286–287
  understanding app and user data, 275–276
  user data, 287–289
    external services, 289
    HTML5 Application Cache API, 289
    HTML5 File API, 288
    libraries, 288–289
    SkyDrive, 288
DataChanged event, 283
data-driven testing, 378
DataProtectionProvider class, 325–328
DataRow attribute, 385
DataTestMethod attribute, 385
data types, 40
DataWriter class, 300
dates, localization, 263
DateTimeFormatter class, 263
Deadline property, 164
debugging
  remote, 377
  tasks, 19–21
Debug Location toolbar, 20
Debug menu, 392
DebugSettings class, 396
DebugSettings property, 396
DecimalFormatter formatter, 264
declarations, manifest, 163
declaring background task usage, 5–7
Decompressor class, 304
Decryption value (KeyUsages property), 322
default C# definition, new controls, 241
default constructor (DataProtectionProvider class), 325
default contents, WinMD folder, 42
DefaultStyleKey property, 241
DefaultTile element, 30
Default value (print task option), 143
deferrals, using with tasks, 7
DeflateStream class, 304
DeleteContainer method, 279
dependency properties
  custom controls, 243–246
  defined, 222
dependent animations, 225–227
design
  considerations for exception handling, 360–362
  data caching, 275–289
    application data, 276–286
    Microsoft rules for roaming profiles, 286–287
    understanding app and user data, 275–276
    user data, 287–289
  diagnostic and monitoring strategies, 388–406
    profiling Windows Store apps, 388–398
    tracing and logging events, 398–402
DesiredAccuracy property, 103
development
  Windows Store apps
    consuming background tasks, 9–36
    creating and consuming WinMD components, 38–51
    creating background tasks, 1–8

device capability errors, 364–368
DeviceContainer value (PnpObjectType enum), 122
DeviceInformation class, 113
DeviceInformationCollection object, 110
DeviceInterfaceClass value (PnpObjectType enum), 122
DeviceInterface value (PnpObjectType enum), 122
DeviceItem object, 110
devices
- capturing media with the camera, 57–79
  - CameraCaptureUI, 58–68
  - MediaCapture class, 68–79
- DeviceWatcher class, 117–122
- enumerating, 110–118
- PnP (Plug and Play), 122–123
- polling, 81
  - accelerometer, 85–86
  - gyrometer, 89–90
  - inclinometer sensor, 96–97
- sensors, 80–106
  - accessing, 81–99
  - determining user's location, 99–106

Devices charm, 133, 149
devices, compatible with Play To feature, 156
DeviceWatcher class, 117–122
DeviceWatcherStatus enum, 121
diagnostic strategies, 388–406
- profiling Windows Store apps, 388–398
- reports, 402–405
- tracing and logging events, 398–402

dialog boxes
- Add New Item, 239
- Add Reference, 47
- Set Location, 100

digest, 308
digital signatures, 316–319
Disabled value (LocationStatus property), 104
Disabled visual state, 248
discrete animations, 232
DiscreteObjectKeyFrame class, 232
Dispatcher object, 196
DisplayData method, 208
DisplayInfo method, 369
displaying
- licensing information of a feature, 352
- listing information, 342–343
- video stream from webcam, 68–69

displaying video, XAML, 161
DisplayLicenseInfo method, 340
Dispose method, 300
Divide method, 380
documents, paginating/previewing for printing, 144–148
DoSomeWorkAsync method, 213
DoubleAnimation class, 223
DoubleAnimationUsingKeyFrames class, 228
Double class, 382
DownloadOperation class, 25, 26
Duration property, Rectangle control, 222

E

easing functions, animations and, 230–231
ElasticEase class, 231
Ellipse control, 223
EnableDependentAnimation property, 226
enabled webcam, standard UI, 64–65
EnableFrameRateCounter static method, 396
enabling Multilingual App Toolkit, 266
encrypting messages, MAC algorithms, 313–316
enhancements, UI (user interface)
- animations and transitions, 221–237
  - applying animations from the animation library, 233–237
  - dependent versus independent animations, 225–227
  - discrete animations, 232
  - easing functions, 232
  - interpolation logic, 229–232
  - key-frame animations, 228–230
  - storyboarded animations, 222–225
- custom controls, 239–250
  - adding to Windows Store apps, 239–242
  - dependency properties, 243–246
  - visual state, 246–250
- globalization and localization, 252–267
  - localizing apps, 256–265
  - localizing manifest, 265
  - Multilingual App Toolkit, 265–266
- responsiveness, 193–219
  - cancelling asynchronous operations, 209–210
  - cancelling operations in asynchronous calls, 210–211
  - choosing the right SynchronizationContext, 218–219

implementing asynchronous calls, 208–209
implementing asynchronous methods, 204–207
.NET asynchronous patterns, 194–202
synchronizing multiple asynchronous calls, 215–216
tracking operation progress, 211–215
waiting for events asynchronously, 207–208
waiting for multiple asynchronous calls in parallel, 217–219
writing methods using async techniques, 202–204
enrolling certificates, 319–325
enterprise authentication capability, 325
Enterprise Trust store (certificates), 323
EntranceThemeTransition class, 234
enumerating
devices, 110–118
PnP (Plug and Play), 122–123
registered tasks, 7
EnumerationCompleted event (DeviceWatcher class), 117
EnumerationCompleted value (DeviceWatcherStatus enum), 121
enums (enumerations)
ApplicationDataCreateDisposition, 278
BackgroundAccessStatus, 33
CameraCaptureUIMaxPhotoResolution, 65–66
CameraCaptureUIPhotoFormat, 65–66
DeviceWatcherStatus, 121
KeyProtectionLevel, 321
PositionStatus, 103
SimpleOrientation, 92–93
SystemConditionType, 10
SystemTriggerType, 3
WinRT PushNotificationType, 185
Error event, 164
error handling, 349–350, 359–373
asynchronous errors, 368–372
catching errors at app level, 361–363
device capability errors, 364–368
exceptions, 359–361
ESE (Extensible Storage Engine), 285
EventAttribute attribute, 399–400
event handlers
Canceled, 16
CapturePhoto_Click, 60
ChooseFile_Click, 293
Paginate, 146–147
PrintTaskRequested, 135
progress, 13–14
SourceRequested, 164
EventListener class, 400
events
AddPages, 145
BindingFailed, 363
Completed, 137
CurrentTimeChangeRequested, 170
DataChanged, 283
Error, 164
Failed, 69
GetPreviewPage, 144, 147
LicenseChanged, 347
logging, 398–402
MediaFailed, 174
MuteChangeRequested, 170
OnCompleted, 11–12
OnProgress, 13–14
OptionChanged, 149
OrientationChanged, 94
Paginate, 144, 150
PauseRequested, 170
PlaybackRateChangeRequested, 170
PlayRequested, 170
PositionChanged, 105
Previewing, 137
PrintTask, 137–138
PrintTaskRequested, 132
Progressing, 137
ReadingChanged, 81
accelerometer sensor, 84–85
Gyrometer class, 87–88
RecordLimitationExceeded, 69
Shaken, detecting user movements, 86–87
SourceChangeRequested, 170
SourceRequested, 158
StateChanged, 165
StatusChanged, 103
StopRequested, 170
TimeUpdateRequested, 170
tracing, 398–402
Transferred, 165
UnhandledException, 361, 363
UnobservedTaskException, 372
VolumeChangeRequested, 170
waiting for asynchronously, 207–208

EventSource class, implementation, 398–399
EventWrittenEventArgs class, 401
Exception base class, 360
exception handling, completed events, 12
exceptions, 359–361
  InvalidOperationException, 171, 196
  malfunctioning devices, 67–68
  TaskCanceledException, 211
  UnauthorizedAccessException, 168
ExpectedException attribute, 378
ExpirationDate property, 339
ExponentialEase class, 231
Exportable property, 322
Export method, 318
ExportPublicKey method, 318
Extensible Application Markup Language (XAML) page, 140
Extensible Storage Engine (ESE), 285
extensions, files, 301–303
<Extensions> section, Application tag, 5
external services, caching user data, 289

F

Facedown value (SimpleOrientation enum), 92
Faceup value (SimpleOrientation enum), 92
fade in/out animations, 235
FadeInThemeAnimation class, 235
FadeOutThemeAnimation class, 235
Failed event, 69
FakeBiz class, 391–392
feature-based trials, 336
file extensions, 301–303
FileIO class, 279
FileIO.ReadTextAsync method, 201
FileOpenPicker class, 292
FileOpenPicker picker, 200
file pickers, 291–297
files
  ISAM (Indexed Sequential Access Method), 284
  Package.appxmanifest, 162, 167–168, 378
    declaring device capabilities, 68–69
  Package.appxmanifest XML, 62–63
  resource, 257
    content, 258–259
    schema definition, 257–258
  saving and retrieving, 291–304
    accessing files programmatically, 298–300
    compressing files to save space, 304–305
    file extensions and associations, 301–303
    file pickers, 291–297
    files, folders, and streams, 300–301
  StandardStyles.xaml
    ObjectAnimationUsingKeyFrames animations, 232
  WindowsStoreProxy.xml, 341
  XLF, 266
FileSavePicker instance, 297
FileTypeFilter collection, 295
Filled visual state, 249
finally block, 360
FindAllAsync method, 110–111
FindTask method, 19
fixture, 383
FlowDirection property, 263
FlushTransport method, 36
FocusStates visual state, 248
folders, 300–301
format templates, 263
FPS (frames per second) counters, 396
frames per second (FPS) counters, 396
freshnessTime parameter, 10, 11
FriendlyName property, 167
From property, 249–250
FullScreenLandscape visual state, 249
FullScreenPortrait visual state, 249
functionality, trials, 335–357
  business model selection, 336–338
  custom license information, 344–345
  error handling, 349–350
  in-app purchases, 350–355
  licensing state of app, 338–343
  purchasing apps, 345–348
  retrieving/validating purchase receipts, 356–358
functional requirements, 375
functional testing, 375–377
Function Code View pane (profile analysis report), 395–396
Function Details view (profile analysis report), 394–395
Functions Doing Most Individual Work section (profile analysis report), 394
functions, Task.WhenAll, 216

G

gamma, 95
GeneratedDuration property, 249
GenerateRandom method, 314
GenerateRandomNumber method, 311
generating random numbers, 311–313
geographic data, determining user's location using sensors, 102–105
Geolocator class, 102–104
Geoposition class, 104
GetAppReceiptAsync method, 356
GetCurrentDownloadAsync method, 26
GetCurrentReading method, 83
GetCustomer method, 391
GetDefault static method, 81
  Accelerometer class, 82
  Compass class, 90
  Gyrometer class, 87
GetDeferral method, 7, 135, 164
GetForCurrentView static method, 132, 163
GetFromPrintTaskOptions method, 152
GetFromPrintTaskOptions static method, 149
GetGeopositionAsync method, 104–105
GetGlyphThumbnailAsync method, 110
GetIids method, 44
GetOAuthToken method, 181
GetOutputStreamAt method, 300
GetPageDescription method, 145
GetPreviewPage event, 144, 147
GetProductReceiptAsync method, 356
GetRuntimeClassName method, 44
GetThumbnailAsync method, 110
GetTrustLevel method, 44
GetValueAndReset method, 311
GetValue method, 244
globalization, 252–256
GPS sensor, 99–106
Grid control, 145
Guid property, 25
Gyrometer class, 87
gyrometer sensor, measuring angular velocity, 87–90
  polling, 89–90
  sensitivity, 89
GZipStream class, 304

H

Handled property, 363
Handle method, 371
handling errors, 349–350, 359–373
  asynchronous errors, 368–372
  catching errors at app level, 361–363
  device capability errors, 364–368
  exceptions, 359–361
hardware slots, 29
HashAlgorithmNames static class, 309
HashAlgorithmProvider class, 308–310
HashAlgorithmProvider instance, 310
hash algorithms, securing data, 308–311
HashData method, 309
HomeGroup content, accessing, 298
Hot Path section (profile analysis report), 393
HResult attribute, 350
HSTRING data type, 40
HTML5 Application Cache API, caching user data, 289
HTML5 File API, caching user data, 288
HTML5 Web Storage, caching application data, 285
HttpClient class, 27, 29, 179
HttpClientHandler class, 29

I

IAsyncResult pattern, 197
IBackgroundTask interface, 2–3
IBackgroundTrigger interface
  MaintenanceTrigger class, 10
IBuffer object, 326
Id attribute, 357
Identifying Your App link, 182
IInputStream object, 327
IInspectable interface, 44
ILDASM (Intermediate Language Disassembler) tool, 43
ImageLabel property, 244
ImagePath property, 244
images, localization, 262–263
implementation
  asynchronous calls, 208–209
  asynchronous methods, 204–207
  data caching, 275–289
    application data, 276–286
    Microsoft rules for roaming profiles, 286–287
    understanding app and user data, 275–276
    user data, 287–289

Play To feature, 155–174
registering app as Play To receiver, 167–174
source application, 161–167
testing sample code, Windows Media Player, 159–161
understanding the contract, 156–158
printing, 131–153
adding user interface, 138–140
creating custom print template, 140–142
custom print options, 152–153
in-app printing, 153
paginating/previewing documents, 144–148
preview window options, 148–149
print option changes, 149–151
PrintTask events, 137–138
print task options, 142–144
registering app for Print contract, 132–137
test projects, 378–385
ImportKeyPair method, 318
ImportPfxDataAsync method, 324
ImportPublicKey method, 318
in-app printing, 153
in-app purchases, 337–338, 350–355
inclinometer sensor, data retrieval, 95–97
polling, 96–97
sensitivity, 97
independent animations, 225–227
IndexedDB technology, caching application data, 284–285
Indexed Sequential Access Method (ISAM) files, 284
indirect targeting, 224
InitializeAsync method, 70, 73, 365
initializing
accelerometer sensor, 83
media capture devices, 73–74
Initializing value (LocationStatus property), 103
InnerException property, 370
InputData call, 207
InstallCertificateAsync method, 322, 323
InstallOption instance, 323
instances
ApplicationDataCompositeValue, 280
FileSavePicker, 297
HashAlgorithmProvider, 310
InstallOption, 323
MediaCapture, 365
PrintManager, 132
PushNotificationChannel, 176
Windows.Media.PlayTo.PlayToManager, 158
instrumentation profiling, 389
integration testing, 376
integrity of data, cryptography and, 307
interfaces
IBackgroundTask, 2
IBackgroundTrigger, 10
IInspectable, 44
IPrintDocumentSource, 135, 136
IProgress<T>, 211
IPropertySet, 71
IRandomAccessStream, 60, 65
IXMLHTTPRequest2, 289
Intermediate Certification Authorities, 323
Intermediate Language Disassembler (ILDASM) tool, 43
Internet (Client) capability, App Manifest Designer, 23
Internet (Client & Server) capability, App Manifest Designer, 23
interpolation logic, 229–232
InvalidatePreview method, 150
InvalidOperationException, 171, 372
InvalidOperationException exception, 196
invoking synchronous version
web service methods, 195
IOutputStream object, 327
IPrintDocumentSource interface, 135, 136
IProgress<T> interface, 211
IPropertySet interface, 71
IRandomAccessStream interface, 60, 65
IReadOnlyCollection<T>, 296
IsActive property, 339, 348
ISAM (Indexed Sequential Access Method) files, 284
IsInfinity method, 382
IsMailAddress method, 48
IsOverdrawHeatMapEnabled property, 397
IsTrial property, 339, 348
IXMLHTTPRequest2 class, 29
IXMLHTTPRequest2 interface, 289

K

keep-alive messages, 28
keep-alive network triggers, 30
KeepAlive property, 35
KeyAgreement value (KeyUsages property), 322
KeyAlgorithmName property, 322
keyed hashing algorithms. *See* MAC algorithms
key-frame animations, 228–230

KeyProtectionLevel enum, 321
KeySize property, 322
key storage provider (KSP), 322
KeyStorageProviderName property, 322
KeyTime property, 232
KeyUsages property, 321
keywords
  async, 199
  await, 199
KnownFolders.VideosLibrary storage folder, 25
KSP (key storage provider), 322

L

language settings, Windows, 253–255
Language window, 253–254
libraries, caching user data, 288–289
LicenseChanged event, 347
LicenseInformation property, 339
LicenseType attribute, 357
licensing API, trial functionality, 338–343
light sensor, 98–99
  sensitivity, 99
LightSensorReading class, 98
LinearColorKeyFrame class, 229
LinearDoubleKeyFrame class, 229
linear interpolation, 229
LinearPointKeyFrame class, 229
Link property, 342
ListBox control, 299
listeners, events, 400–401
listing information, 342–343
ListView control, 390
Live Connect, REST APIs, 288
LoadDataException resource, 260
LoadListingInformationAsync_GetResult method, 350
LoadListingInformationAsync method, 342, 352
load testing, 375
LocalFolder property, 277
localization
  localizing apps, 256–265
    calendars, 264–265
    dates and times, 263
    images, 262–263
    numbers and currencies, 264
    string data, 257–262
  manifest, 265
  Multilingual App Toolkit, 265–266
localized description strings, 361
LocalSettings property, 277
local storage, app data, 277–279
location data, sensors, 81
Location Provider, 99
LocationStatus property, 103
lock screen, 10
  registering applications for, 30
LockScreenApplicationAdded event, 11
LockScreenApplicationRemoved event, 11
lock screen-capable applications, 28
LockScreen element, 30
logging events, 398–402
logging to files, local user storage, 279
logical stores (Microsoft certificate store), 323
log.txt files, 279
Lookup method, 262
lumen, 98
luminanceLux property, 98
lux, 98

M

MacAlgorithmNames static class, 314
MacAlgorithmProvider class, 313
MAC algorithms, encrypting messages, 313–316
MainPage.xaml file
  adding a basic UI (user interface), 138–139
  adding XAML controllers, 168–169
  adding XAML to capture photos, 58–60
MaintenanceTrigger class, 3, 10
maintenance triggers, 10–11
management, data and security
  data caching, 275–289
  saving/retrieving files from file system, 291–304
  securing app data, 306–327
manifest declarations, 163
MANIFEST file, 43
manifest localization, 265
manually testing, Windows Store app user interface, 377
matrices, 95
MaxResolution property, 67
measuring angular velocity, gyrometer, 87–90
media capture, camera, 57–79
  CameraCaptureUI, 58–68
  MediaCapture class, 68–79

MediaCapture class, 68–79
media capture errors, 365–366
MediaCaptureInitalizationSettings class, 74
MediaCapture instance, 365
MediaElement class, 174
MediaEncodingProfile class, 76
MediaEncodingProfile.CreateMp4 method, 76
MediaFailed event, 174
Memory indicator (FPS counters), 397
menus
  Debug, 392
  Start Performance Analysis, 392–393
message authentication code algorithms. *See* MAC algorithms
message digest, 308
MessageWebSocket class, 29
MethodName attribute, 350
methods
  AddCondition, 4–5
  AddEffectAsync, 71
  AddPage, 147
  AddPagesComplete, 147
  AggregateException.Flatten, 371
  Append, 310
  ApplicationDataContainer.CreateContainer, 278
  AreEqual, 381
  Assert.IsTrue, 382
  AsTask, 26, 210
  AttachAsync, 27
  Begin, 225
  BeginSave, 196
  Cancel, 210
  CaptureFileAsync, 41, 60, 366–368
  CapturePhotoToStreamAsync, 72
  CheckResult, 12
  ChooseFile_Click, 200
  Clear, 178
  ClearEffectsAsync, 71
  Compare, 310
  Complete, 7, 135
  ContainsKey, 278
  ConvertStringToBinary, 309
  CreateDownload, 25
  CreateFileAsync, 25, 279
  CreateFolderQuery, 299
  CreateHash, 310
  CreateItemListOption, 152
  CreateKey, 314
  CreateKeyPair, 318
  CreatePrintTask, 133
  CreatePushNotificationChannelForApplicationAsync, 176
  CreateTileUpdaterForApplication, 14
  CreateUploadAsync, 27
  CreateUploadFromStreamAsync, 27
  CreateWatcher, 117
  CryptographicEngine.Sign, 318
  DeleteContainer, 279
  DisplayData, 208
  DisplayInfo, 369
  DisplayLicenseInfo, 340
  Dispose, 300
  Divide, 380
  EnableFrameRateCounter, 396
  event methods, 204
  Export, 318
  ExportPublicKey, 318
  FileIO.ReadTextAsync, 201
  FindAllAsync, 110–111
  FindTask, 19
  FlushTransport, 36
  GenerateRandom, 314
  GenerateRandomNumber, 311
  GetAppReceiptAsync, 356
  GetCurrentDownloadAsync, 26
  GetCurrentReading, 83
  GetDefault, 81
    Accelerometer class, 82
    Compass class, 90
    Gyrometer class, 87
  GetDeferral, 7, 135, 164
  GetForCurrentView, 163
  GetForCurrentView static, 132
  GetFromPrintTaskOptions, 149, 152
  GetGeopositionAsync, 104, 105
  GetGlyphThumbnailAsync, 110
  GetIids, 44
  GetOAuthToken, 181
  GetOutputStreamAt, 300
  GetPageDescription, 145
  GetProductReceiptAsync, 356
  GetRuntimeClassName, 44
  GetThumbnailAsync, 110
  GetTrustLevel, 44
  GetValue, 244
  GetValueAndReset, 311

Handle, 371
HashData, 309
implementing asynchronous methods, 204–207
ImportKeyPair, 318
ImportPfxDataAsync, 324
ImportPublicKey, 318
InitializeAsync, 70, 73, 365
InstallCertificateAsync, 322, 323
InvalidatePreview, 150
IsInfinity, 382
IsMailAddress, 48
LoadListingInformationAsync, 342, 352
LoadListingInformationAsync_GetResult, 350
Lookup, 262
MediaEncodingProfile.CreateMp4, 76
Notify*, 172
Object.Equals, 381
OnCanceled, 16
OnEventWritten, 400
OnFileActivated, 304
OnNavigatedTo, 132
OpenAlgorithm, 309
OpenAsync, 60
OtherActivity, 218
Pause, 25
PickSaveFileAsync, 297
PickSingleFileAsync, 201, 203, 295
PlayToManager.GetForCurrentView, 158
PreparePrintContent, 142
ProtectAsync, 325
ReadBufferAsync, 301
Register, 244
ReloadSimulatorAsync, 344
RequestAccessAsync, 11, 32
RequestAppPurchaseAsync, 345
RequestAppPurchaseAsync_GetResult, 350
RequestProductPurchaseAsync_GetResult, 350
Resume, 25
Run, debugger, 21
SetObserved, 372
SetPreviewPageCount, 146
SetRequestHeader, 28
SetSource, 135
SetValue, 244
Show, 76
ShowPlayToUI, 167
ShowPrintUIAsync, 153
Sign, 314
StartAsync, 25, 70
Start_Click, 212
StartPreviewAsync, 70
StartPreviewToCustomSinkAsync, 70
StartRecordToStorageFileAsync, 75
StartRecordToStreamAsync, 75
StopRecordAsync, 76–77
SubmitCertificateRequestAndGetResponseAsync, 323
Task.Factory.StartNew, 207
Task.WhenAll, 370
TextAsync, 300
ThrowsException, 378
ThrowsException<TException>, 378, 382
UnprotectAsync, 326
UnprotectStreamAsync, 327
Unregister, 19
VerifySignature, 314
WaitForPushEnabled, 35
WhenAll_Click, 217
Windows.UI.Xaml.Application.Start, 363
WriteEvent, 401
WriteTextAsync, 279
writing using async techniques, 202–204
microphone
capturing audio from, 78–79
recording audio, 67
Microsoft certificate store, 323
Microsoft NP .NET Profiler Tool, 390
Microsoft rules, roaming profiles, 286–287
Microsoft Test Manager, 376
Microsoft.VisualStudio.TestPlatform.UnitTestFramework namespace, 378
Microsoft.VisualStudio.TestTools.UnitTesting namespace, 378
MinimumReportInterval property, 84
Modules view (profile analysis report), 396
monitoring strategies, 388–406
profiling Windows Store apps, 388–398
reports, 402–405
tracing and logging events, 398–402
Most Common Crashes section (Quality reports), 404
MovementThreshold property, 106
MP3 audio profile, 76
MP4 video, creating an encoding profile, 76
Multilingual App Toolkit, 265–266
multiple asynchronous calls, synchronizing, 215–216

multiple catch blocks, 360
multithreading programming, 208
MuteChangeRequested event, 170

N

namespaces
  BackgroundTransfer, 22
  Connectivity, 23
  Microsoft.VisualStudio.TestPlatform.UnitTestFramework, 378
  Microsoft.VisualStudio.TestTools.UnitTesting, 378
  System.Diagnostics.Tracing, 398
  System.Net.Sockets, 29
  System.Text.RegularExpressions, 47
  Windows.ApplicationModel.Background, 32
  Windows.Devices.Enumeration.PnP, 122
  Windows.Devices.Geolocation, 102
  Windows.Devices.Sensors, 81
  Windows.Graphics.Printing, 132
  Windows.Networking.PushNotification, 176
  Windows.Security.Credentials, 327
  Windows.Security.Cryptography, 307
  Windows.Security.Cryptography.Certificates, 320
  Windows.Security.Cryptography, securing data, 307–308
  Windows.Storage.Pickers, 294
  Windows.UI.Xaml.Printing, 132
naming conventions, 381
native WinMD libraries, consuming, 40–46
.NET 2.0, asynchronous operations, 197
.NET asynchronous patterns, 194–202
  converting operations to tasks, 198–202
  .NET 2.0, 197
.NET Framework exceptions, 359–361
.NET memory profiling, 389
network access constraints, 14
network keep-alive interval, 35
NoConsent value (KeyProtectionLevel enum), 321
NoData value (LocationStatus property), 103
None value (KeyUsages property), 322
nonfunctional testing, 375
nonrepudiation, cryptography and, 307
Normal visual state, 248
NotAvailable value (LocationStatus property), 104
NotAvailable value (print task option), 142
notebooks, axis orientation, 82
notification channels (WNS), 176–178
notifications (WNS), sending to clients, 178–186
NotificationType property, 185
Notify* methods, 172
NotInitialized value (LocationStatus property), 104
No Trial option (trial functionality), 336
NotRotated value (SimpleOrientation enum), 92
numbers, localization, 264

O

OAuthToken class, 180–181
ObjectAnimationUsingKeyFrames class, 232
Object.Equals method, 381
objects
  BitmapImage, 60
  ColorAnimationUsingKeyFrames, 228
  DeviceInformationCollection, 110
  DeviceItem, 110
  Dispatcher, 196
  MediaCapture, 76
  MediaCaptureInitializationSettings, 73
  MediaEncodingProfile, 75
  PnpDeviceWatcher, 123
  Task, 204
  VisualStateGroup, 248
OnCanceled method, 16
OnCompleted events, 11–12
oneShot parameter, 3, 10
OnEventWritten abstract method, 400
OnFileActivated method, 304
OnNavigatedTo method, 132
OnProgress event, 13–14
Opacity property, Rectangle control, 222
OpenAlgorithm method, 309
OpenAsync method, 60
OptionChanged event, 149
Options property, PrintTask class, 142–144
OrientationChanged event, 94
Orientation property, 151
OrientationSensor class, 94–95
orientation sensor, combining data, 92–96
OrientationSensorReadingChangedEventArgs instance, 95
OtherActivity method, 218
Other People logical store (certificates), 324
overloaded constructor (DataProtectionProvider class), 325

P

Package.appxmanifest file, 162, 167–168, 378
  declaring device capabilities, 68–69
Package.appxmanifest XML file, 62–63
page code-behind code, 213–215
PageNumber property, 147
PageSize setting, 277, 280
PageTask, 197
Page transition animations, 234–235
Paginate event, 144, 150
Paginate event handler, 146–147
paginating documents for printing, 144–148
parallel execution, asynchronous calls, 217–219
parameters
  AllowCropping, 65
  authenticating a cloud service, Windows Live Services, 183
  CameraCaptureUIMode, 60
  CameraCaptureUIMode.Video, 66–67
  freshnessTime, 10, 11
  oneShot, 3, 10
PasswordVault class, 327
Pause method, 25
PauseRequested event, 170
PercentFormatter formatter, 264
performance
  diagnostic and monitoring strategies, 388–406
    profiling an app, 388–398
    reports, 402–405
    tracing and logging events, 398–402
PermilleFormatter formatter, 264
permissions
  lock screen apps, 33
  requesting user permission, 63
  sensitive devices, 364–365
Permissions flyout, Privacy settings, 365–366
Personal Information Exchange (PFX) message, 324
personal logical store (certificates), 323
PFX (Personal Information Exchange) message, 324
PhotoCaptureSource property, 73
PhotoSettings properties, 66
pickers, FileOpenPicker, 200
PickSaveFileAsync method, 297
PickSingleFileAsync method, 201, 203, 295
pictures
  capturing with CameraCaptureUI, 58–68
  capturing with MediaCapture class, 68–79
pitch, 95
PKI (public key infrastructure), 319
PlatformKeyStorageProvider (KSP), 322
PlaybackRateChangeRequested event, 170
PlayRequested event, 170
Play To feature, 155–174
  disabling default behavior, 157
  registering app as Play To receiver, 167–174
  source application, 161–167
  testing sample code, Windows Media Player, 159–161
  understanding the contract, 156–158
PlayToManager.GetForCurrentView method, 158
PlayToReceiver class, 170
PlayToSourceRequestedEventArgs class, 164
Plug and Play (PnP) devices, 122–123
PnpDeviceWatcher object, 123
PnpObject class, 122
PnP (Plug and Play) devices, 122–123
PointerDownThemeAnimation class, 236
pointer up/down transition, 236
PointerUpThemeAnimation class, 236
PointOver visual state, 248
polling devices, 81
  accelerometer, 85–86
  gyrometer, 89–90
  inclinometer sensor, 96–97
PositionChanged event, 105
PositionChangedEventArgs instance, 103
PositionStatus enum, 103
PowerEase class, 231
PreparePrintContent method, 142
prerequisites, roaming profiles, 287
Pressed visual state, 248
preview, camera, 70
previewing documents for printing, 144–148
Previewing event, 137
preview window (printing) options, 148–149
Print contract, registering apps, 132–137
PrintCustom value (print task option), 142
PrintDocument class, 144–145
PrintDocument type, 136
printing implementation, 131–153
  adding user interface, 138–140
  creating custom print template, 140–142
  custom print options, 152–153
  in-app printing, 153
  paginating/previewing documents, 144–148

preview window options, 148–149
print option changes, 149–151
PrintTask events, 137–138
print task options, 142–144
registering app for Print contract, 132–137
PrintManager class, 132
PrintManager instance, 132
PrintPageDescription class, 145
PrintSettings composite setting, 277
PrintTask class, Options property, 142–144
PrintTask events, 137–138
PrintTaskOptionDetails object, 148
PrintTaskOptions class, 143
PrintTaskRequested event, 132
PrintTaskRequested event handler, 135
PrintTaskSourceRequestedHandler delegate, 133
Privacy settings (Permissions flyout), 365
Private Networks capability, App Manifest Designer, 23
Private Networks capability (Package.appmanifest file), 168
ProcessFileAsync call, 369
ProductId attribute, 357
ProductLicenses property, 339
ProductReceipt element (receipt fragment), 357
ProductType attribute, 357
profile analysis report, 393
profiling Windows Store apps, 388–398
Program class, 363
programmatically accessing files, 298–300
program user interaction
implementing printing, 131–153
adding user interface, 138–140
creating custom print template, 140–142
custom print options, 152–153
in-app printing, 153
paginating/previewing documents, 144–148
preview window options, 148–149
print option changes, 149–151
PrintTask events, 137–138
print task options, 142–144
registering app for Print contract, 132–137
Play To feature, 155–174
registering app as Play To receiver, 167–174
source application, 161–167
testing sample code, Windows Media Player, 159–161
understanding the contract, 156–158
WNS (Windows Push Notification Service), 176–186
notification channels, 176–178
sending notifications to clients, 178–186
ProgressBar control, 204
progress event handlers, 13–14
Progressing event, 137
ProgressSomework ProgressBar, 212
Progress<T> class, 211
properties
AccelerationX, 85
AccelerationY, 85
AccelerationZ, 85
AccessToken, 180
AppId, 342
AudioDeviceId, 74
AutoReverse, 229
Background, 242
BorderBrush, 242
BorderThickness, 242
Bounces, 231–232
Bounciness, 231–232
CameraCaptureUIVideoFormat, 67
CivicAddress, 104
Completion, 138–139
Content, 261
Coordinate, 104
CostPolicy, 25
CroppedAspectRatio, 66
CroppedSizeInPixels, 66
Deadline, 164
DebugSettings, 396
DefaultStyleKey, 241
dependency
custom controls, 243–246
defined, 222
DesiredAccuracy, 103
Duration, Rectangle control, 222
EnableDependentAnimation, 226
ExpirationDate, 339
Exportable, 322
FlowDirection, 263
FriendlyName, 167
From, 249–250
GeneratedDuration, 249
Guid, 25
Handled, 363
ImageLabel, 244
ImagePath, 244
InnerException, 370

IsActive, 339, 348
IsOverdrawHeatMapEnabled, 397
IsTrial, 339, 348
KeepAlive, 35
KeyAlgorithmName, 322
KeySize, 322
KeyStorageProviderName, 322
KeyTime, 232
KeyUsages, 321
LicenseInformation, 339
Link, 342
LocalFolder, 277
LocalSettings, 277
LocationStatus, 103
luminanceLux, 98
MaxResolution, 67
MinimumReportInterval, 84
MovementThreshold, 106
NotificationType, 185
Opacity, Rectangle control, 222
Options, PrintTask class, 142–144
Orientation, 151
PageNumber, 147
PhotoCaptureSource, 73
PhotoSettings, 66
ProductLicenses, 339
ProxyCredential, 28
Quaternion, 95
RepeatBehavior, 229
RepeatBehavior, Rectangle control, 222
ReportInterval, 83
    Compass class, 90–91
Request, 133
RequestedUri, 25
ResultFile, 25
RotationMatrix, 95
ServerCredential, 28
StreamingCaptureMode, 73
SuggestedStartLocation, 298
SuspendedCount, 15
TargetName, 223
TemporaryFolder, 283
Timestamp, 85
TriggerDetails, 36
Uri, 177
VideoDeviceId, 74
VideoSettings, 67
VideoStabilization, 71
property path syntax, 224
ProtectAsync method, 325
ProxyCredential property, 28
pseudolanguage, 266
public key infrastructure (PKI), 319
PurchaseDate attribute, 357
purchase receipts, retrieving/validating, 356–358
purchasing apps, trial functionality, 345–348
PushNotificationChannel instance, 176
push notification network triggers, 30
PushNotificationTrigger, 10
    guaranteed resource quota, 15

Q

QuadraticEase class, 231
quality panel, 404
Quality reports, 403–404
QuarticEase class, 231
Quaternion property, 95
quaternions, 95
QuinticEase class, 231

R

random number generation, 311–313
ReadBufferAsync method, 301
ReadingChanged event, 81
    accelerometer sensor, 84–85
    Gyrometer class, 87–88
ReadToEnd call, 198
Ready value (LocationStatus property), 103
ReceiptDate attribute, 357
ReceiptDeviceId attribute, 357
Receipt element (receipt fragment), 357
receipts (purchases), retrieving/validating, 356–358
recording
    audio, 67
    video
        standard UI, 66–67
        Video library, 75
RecordLimitationExceeded event, 69
reference content (app data), 276
registered tasks, enumerating, 7

registering
applications for the lock screen, 30
apps as Play To receivers, 167–174
apps, Print contract, 132–137
Register method, 244
ReloadSimulatorAsync static method, 344
remote debugging, 377
Removed event (DeviceWatcher class), 117
RepeatBehavior property, 229
Rectangle control, 222
report interval, acclerometer sensor, 83
ReportInterval property, 83
Compass class, 90–91
reports, 402–405
Representational State Transfer (REST) APIs, 288
RequestAccessAsync method, 11, 32
RequestAppPurchaseAsync_GetResult method, 350
RequestAppPurchaseAsync static method, 345
RequestedUri property, 25
requesting certificates, 319–325
RequestProductPurchaseAsync_GetResult method, 350
Request property, 133
REQUEST store, 324
requirements, WinRT types, 46
Resource editor, 258
resource files, 257
content, 258–259
schema definition, 257–258
ResourceLoader class, 260
response parameters, authenticating cloud service, 183
responsiveness, UI (user interface), 193–219
cancelling asynchronous operations, 209–210
cancelling operations in asynchronous calls, 210–211
choosing the right SynchronizationContext, 218–219
implementing asynchronous calls, 208–209
implementing asynchronous methods, 204–207
.NET asynchronous patterns, 194–202
converting operations to tasks, 198–202
.NET 2.0, 197
synchronizing multiple asynchronous calls, 215–216
tracking operation progress, 211–215
waiting for events asynchronously, 207–208
waiting for multiple asynchronous calls in parallel, 217–219
writing methods using async techniques, 202–204
REST (Representational State Transfer) APIs, 288
ResultFile property, 25
Resume method, 25
retrieving
data
compass, 90–92
inclinometer sensor, 95–97
sensors, 80–106
files, 291–304
accessing files programmatically, 298–300
compressing files to save space, 304–305
file extensions and associations, 301–303
file pickers, 291–297
files, folders, and streams, 300–301
purchase receipts, 356–358
simulated license state, 339–340
roaming profiles, Microsoft rules, 286–287
roaming settings, 280
roaming storage, app data, 280–283
roll, 95
Rotated90DegreesCounterclockwise value (SimpleOrientation enum), 92
Rotated180DegreesCounterclockwise value (SimpleOrientation enum), 92
Rotated270DegreesCounterclockwise value (SimpleOrientation enum), 92
RotationMatrix property, 95
rules, roaming profiles, 286–287
Run method
debugger, 21
Runtime Broker, 41
runtime state (app data), 276

S

sampling tools, 389
saving files, 291–304
accessing files programmatically, 298–300
compressing files to save space, 304–305
file extensions and associations, 301–303
file pickers, 291–297
files, folders, and streams, 300–301
scale factor qualifier, 262
schema definition, resource files, 257–258
ScrollBar control, fade in/out animation, 235

SDDL (security descriptor definition language) strings, 325
SDK (Software Development Kit), 239
secret keys, MAC algorithms, 313–316
secrets, 180
security, app data, 306–327
  certificates, 319–325
  DataProtectionProvider class, 325–328
  digital signatures, 316–319
  generating random numbers, 311–313
  hash algorithms, 308–311
  MAC algorithms, 313–316
  Windows.Security.Cryptography namespaces, 307–308
security descriptor definition language (SDDL) strings, 325
security identifiers (SIDs), 180
security testing, 375
Selling Details section (Windows Store Dashboard), 336
sending notifications to clients (WNS), 178–186
sensitive devices, 364–365
sensitivity
  accelerometer sensor, 84
  compass sensor, 92
  gyrometer sensor, 89
  inclinometer sensor, 97
  light sensor, 99
Sensor platform
  accelerometer sensor sensitivity, 84
  compass sensor sensitivity, 92
  gyrometer sensor sensitivity, 89
  inclinometer sensor sensitivity, 97
  light sensor sensitivity, 99
sensors, 80–106
  accessing, 81–99
    accelerometer, 82–87
    compass, 90–92
    gyrometer, 87–90
    inclinometer, 95–97
    light, 98–99
    orientation, 92–96
  determining user's location, 99–106
    geographic data, 102–105
    tracking movements, 105–107
  location data, 81
server applications, caching user data, 289
ServerCredential property, 28
server keep-alive interval, 35
ServicingComplete task, 19
ServicingComplete trigger, 18
SessionConnected trigger, 11
Set Location dialog box, 100
SetObserved method, 372
SetPreviewPageCount method, 146
SetRequestHeader method, 28
SetSource method, 135
settings, camera, 76
Settings charm, 365–366
SetValue method, 244
Shaken event, detecting user movements, 86–87
Shared User Certificates capability, 324
Sharing option, 156
Show method, 76
ShowPlayToUI method, 167
ShowPlayToUI static method, 167
ShowPrintUIAsync method, 153
SIDs (security identifiers), 180
Signature element (receipt fragment), 357
signing messages, digitally, 316–318
Signing value (KeyUsages property), 322
Sign method, 314
Silverlight, 197
SimpleOrientation enumeration, 92–93
SimpleOrientationSensor class, 92–94
simulated license state, retrieving, 339–340
SimulateRemoteServiceCall method, 391
SimulationMode attribute, 350
Simulator, 100
SineEase class, 231
singleton pattern, custom event sources, 400
SkyDrive, caching user data, 288
SmartcardKeyStorageProvider (KSP), 322
Smart Card Trusted Roots store, 324
smooth animations, 226
Snapped visual state, 249
Software development kit (SDK), 239
software development methodologies, unit testing, 377
SoftwareKeyStorageProvider (KSP), 322
software slots, 29
solution deployment
  diagnostic and monitoring strategies, 388–406
    profiling Windows Store apps, 388–398
    reports, 402–405
    tracing and logging events, 398–402

error handling, 359–373
asynchronous errors, 368–372
catching errors at app level, 361–363
device capability errors, 364–368
exceptions, 359–361
test strategies, 374–384
functional versus unit testing, 375–377
implementing a test project, 378–385
trial functionality, 335–357
business model selection, 336–338
custom license information, 344–345
error handling, 349–350
in-app purchases, 350–355
licensing state of app, 338–343
purchasing apps, 345–348
retrieving/validating purchase receipts, 356–358
source application, Play To feature, 161–167
SourceChangeRequested event, 170
SourceRequested event, 158
SourceRequested event handler, 164
SplineColorKeyFrame class, 230
SplineDoubleKeyFrame class, 230
spline interpolation, 230–231
SplinePointKeyFrame class, 230
StackPanel control, 390
StackPanel controls, 141
StandardStyles.xaml file, ObjectAnimationUsingKeyFrames animations, 232
standard UI (user interface)
capturing media, 57–79
CaptureMediaUI class, 58–68
MediaCapture class, 68–79
enabling webcam, 64–65
StartAsync method, 25, 70
Start_Click method, 212
StartDevice_Click method, 69
Started value (DeviceWatcherStatus enum), 121
Start Performance Analysis menu, 392–393
StartPreviewAsync method, 70
StartPreviewToCustomSinkAsync method, 70
StartRecordToStorageFileAsync method, 75
StartRecordToStreamAsync method, 75
StateChanged event, 165
StatusChanged event, 103
Stopped event (DeviceWatcher class), 117
Stopped value (DeviceWatcherStatus enum), 121
Stopping value (DeviceWatcherStatus enum), 121
StopRecordAsync method, 76–77
StopRequested event, 170
StorageFile class, 288
StorageFile objects, 344
StorageFile WinRT class, 60
storing data
data caching, 275–289
file system, 291–304
Storyboard class, 222
storyboarded animations, 222–225
StreamingCaptureMode property, 73
streams, 300–301
writing text to files, 300–301
StreamSocket class, 29
StreamSocketControl class, 35
StreamWebSocket class, 29
stress testing, 375
string data, localization, 257–262
strings, localized description, 361
SubmitCertificateRequestAndGetResponseAsync method, 323
SuggestedStartLocation property, 298
SuspendedCount property, 15
symmetric encryption, 313
symmetric-key algorithms, 313
SynchronizationContext, 218–219
synchronizing multiple asynchronous calls, 215–216
System.AggregateException, 370
SystemConditionType enum, 10
System.Diagnostics.Tracing namespace, 398
System.Net.Sockets namespace, 29
System.Progress<T> class, 25
System.Text.RegularExpressions namespace, 47
SystemTrigger class, 3
SystemTriggerType enum, 3

T

tablets, axis orientation, 82
TAP (Task-based Asynchronous Pattern), 209
TargetName property, 223
Task-based Asynchronous Pattern (TAP), 209
TaskCanceledException exception, 211
Task class, 198
Task.Factory.StartNew method, 207
Task objects, 204
Task Parallel Library (TPL), 198, 372

tasks, background
- consuming, 9–36
  - cancelling tasks, 15–17
  - debugging tasks, 19–21
  - keeping communication channels open, 28–37
  - progressing through tasks, 11–13
  - task constraints, 14
  - task triggers and conditions, 9–11
  - task usage, 21–22
  - transferring data in the background, 22–27
  - updating tasks, 18–19
- creating, 1–8
  - declaration of task usage, 5–7
  - enumeration of registered tasks, 7
  - using deferrals, 7

tasks, converting asynchronous operations to, 198–202
Task.WhenAll function, 216
Task.WhenAll method, 370
TCP keep-alive interval, 35
Team Foundation Server (Visual Studio), 376
telemetry information, 402–403
Templated Control item template (Add New Item dialog box), 239
templates
- custom print templates, 140–142
- Unit Test Library project, 378

TemporaryFolder property, 283
temporary storage, app data, 283–284
TestClass attribute, 381
TestCleanup attribute, 383
Test Explorer window, 381–382
test fixture, 383
testing
- inclinometer, 97–98
- sample code, Play To feature, 159–161

testing strategies, 374–384
- functional versus unit testing, 375–377
- implementing a test project, 378–385

TestInitialize attribute, 383
Test Manager (Microsoft), 376
TestMethod attribute, 381
third-party databases, caching user data, 289
Third-Party Root Certification Authorities store, 323
ThrowsException<TException> method, 378, 382
tier interaction profiling (TIP), 389
TileNotification, 14
TileUpdateManager class, 14
TileUpdater class, 178
tile updates, 179
timed trials, 336
times, localization, 263
Timestamp property, 85
time triggers, 11–12
TimeUpdateRequested event, 170
TIP (tier interaction profiling), 389
toasts, 179
toolbars, Debug Location, 20
top-down approach, functional testing, 376
TPL (Task Parallel Library), 198, 372
TraceListener class, 398
tracing events, 398–402
tracking progress, asynchronous operations, 211–215
tracking user position, 105–107
Transferred event, 165
transferring task background data, 22–27
transitions, 221–237
- dependent versus independent animations, 225–227
- discrete animations, 232
- easing functions, 232
- interpolation logic, 229–232
- key-frame animations, 228–230
- storyboarded animations, 222–225

trial functionality, 335–357
- business model selection, 336–338
- custom license information, 344–345
- error handling, 349–350
- in-app purchases, 350–355
- licensing state of app, 338–343
- purchasing apps, 345–348
- retrieving/validating purchase receipts, 356–358

Trial Never Expires option (trial functionality), 336
TriggerDetails property, 36
triggers, 3
- consuming background tasks, 9–11
- keep-alive network, 30
- push notification network, 30

Trusted People store (certificates), 323
Trusted Publishers store (certificates), 323
Trusted Root Certification Authorities store, 323
Try button, feature-based games, 337
try/catch blocks, 176, 360
- asynchronous code, 369–370

types
- PrintDocument, 136
- X-WNS-Type, 181

U

UI CPU indicator (FPS counters), 397
UI testing, 376
UITestMethod attribute, 383
UITestMethodAttribute attribute, 378
UI thread FPS indicator (FPS counters), 397
UI (user interface)
  enhancements
    animations and transitions, 221–237
    custom controls, 239–250
    globalization and localization, 252–267
    responsiveness, 193–219
  implementing printing, 138–140
UnauthorizedAccessException, 168
UnhandledException event, 361, 363
UnhandledExceptionEventArgs, 363
unit testing, 375–377
Unit Test Library template, 376, 378
Unknown value (PnpObjectType enum), 122
unobserved exceptions, 370
UnobservedTaskException event, 372
UnprotectAsync method, 326
UnprotectStreamAsync method, 327
Unregister method, 19
Untrusted Certificates store, 323
Updated event (DeviceWatcher class), 117
updating background tasks, 18–19
Uri property, 177
usability testing, 375
usage, tasks, 21–22
UserAway trigger, 11
user data, caching, 287–289
  external services, 289
  HTML5 Application Cache API, 289
  HTML5 File API, 288
  libraries, 288–289
  SkyDrive, 288
user interaction
  implementing printing, 131–153
    adding user interface, 138–140
    creating custom print template, 140–142
    custom print options, 152–153
    in-app printing, 153
    paginating/previewing documents, 144–148
    preview window options, 148–149
    print option changes, 149–151
    PrintTask events, 137–138
    print task options, 142–144
    registering app for Print contract, 132–137
  Play To feature, 155–174
    registering app as Play To receiver, 167–174
    source application, 161–167
    testing sample code, Windows Media Player, 159–161
    understanding the contract, 156–158
  WNS (Windows Push Notification Service), 176–186
    notification channels, 176–178
    sending notifications to clients, 178–186
user interface. *See* UI (user interface)
user preferences (app data), 276
UserPresent trigger, 11
users
  determining location using sensors, 99–106
    geographic data, 102–105
    tracking movements, 105–107
  permissions, 63
Utility class, 379

V

validating receipts, 356–358
values, print task options, 143
verifying authentication, MAC algorithm secret keys, 314
VerifySignature method, 314
versioning-compliance, Windows Runtime architecture, 45
video
  capturing with CameraCaptureUI, 58–68
  capturing with MediaCapture class, 68–79
  displaying from webcam, 68–69
  recording
    standard UI, 66–67
    Video library, 75
VideoDeviceId property, 74
video, displaying using XAML, 161
VideoEffects class, 71
Video library, recording a video, 75
VideoSettings property, 67
VideosLibrary class, 163
VideoStabilization property, 71
Visible custom print option, 152
VisualState class, 246
VisualStateGroup objects, 248

visual states
animations, 246
custom controls, 246–250
Visual Studio
App Manifest Designer, 61–62
remote debugger, 377
Team Foundation Server, 376
Visual Studio App Manifest Designer, 6–7
VolumeChangeRequested event, 170

W

WaitForPushEnabled method, 35
WCF (Windows Communication Foundation) service, 289
webcam
displaying video stream, 68–69
enabling in standard UI, 64–65
web service methods
async/method pattern, 197
invoking synchronous version, 195
WhenAll_Click method, 217
Wide Logo, 30
Wi-Fi triangulation, 100
WinDbg.exe tool, 405
windows
Language, 253–254
Test Explorer, 381–382
Windows
language settings, 253–255
Phone, 197
Windows 8 Simulator, 100
Windows.ApplicationModel.Background namespace, 32
Windows Communication Foundation (WCF) service, 289
Windows.Devices.Enumeration.PnP namespace, 122
Windows.Devices.Geolocation namespace, 102
Windows.Devices.Sensors namespace, 81
Windows.Graphics.Printing namespace, 132
Windows Live service, 180, 183
Windows Location Provider, 99
Windows Media Audio (WMA) profi;e, 76
Windows.Media.Capture.MediaCapture class, 365
Windows Media Player, testing sample code, 159–161
Windows.Media.PlayTo.PlayToManager instance, 158
Windows Media Video (WMV) profile, 76
Windows Metadata (WinMD), 40
Windows.Networking.PushNotification namespace, 176
Windows Performance Toolkit (WPT), 390
Windows Push Notification Service (WNS), 176–186
defined, 29
notification channels, 176–178
sending notifications to clients, 178–186
Windows Runtime
CLR Windows 8 app, 41
creating and consuming Windows Runtime (WinMD) components, 38–51
architecture, 38–40
native WinMD libraries, 40–46
WinMD libraries, 46–50
C++ Windows 8 app, 42
Windows Runtime (WinRT)
app data storage, 276–286
APIs, 277–285
Windows.Security.Credentials namespace, 327
Windows.Security.Cryptography.Certificates namespace, 320
Windows.Security.Cryptography namespaces, 307–308
Windows Sensor and Location platform, 81
Windows.Storage.Pickers namespace, 294
Windows Store apps
accessing sensors, 81–99
accelerometer, 82–87
compass, 90–92
gyrometer, 87–90
inclinometer, 95–97
light, 98–99
orientation, 92–96
data management
data caching, 275–289
saving and retrieving files, 291–304
development
consuming background tasks, 9–36
creating and consuming WinMD components, 38–51
creating background tasks, 1–8
implementing printing, 131–153
adding user interface, 138–140
creating custom print template, 140–142
custom print options, 152–153
in-app printing, 153
paginating/previewing documents, 144–148

preview window options, 148–149
print option changes, 149–151
PrintTask events, 137–138
print task options, 142–144
registering app for Print contract, 132–137
language declaration, 255–256
Play To feature, 155–174
registering app as Play To receiver, 167–174
source application, 161–167
testing sample code, Windows Media Player, 159–161
understanding the contract, 156–158
security, 306–327
certificates, 319–325
DataProtectionProvider class, 325–328
digital signatures, 316–319
generating random numbers, 311–313
hash algorithms, 308–311
MAC algorithms, 313–316
Windows.Security.Cryptography namespaces, 307–308
solution deployment
diagnostic and monitoring strategies, 388–406
error handling, 359–373
test strategies, 374–384
trial functionality, 335–357
UI enhancements
animations and transitions, 221–237
custom controls, 239–250
globalization and localization, 252–267
responsiveness, 193–219
WNS (Windows Push Notification Service), 176–186
notification channels, 176–178
sending notifications to clients, 178–186
Windows Store Dashboard, Selling Details section, 336
WindowsStoreProxy.xml files, 341
Windows.UI.Xaml.Application.Start method, 363
Windows.UI.Xaml.Printing namespace, 132
WinJS. Application.local, caching application data, 286
WinJS.Application.roaming, caching application data, 286
WinJS.Application.sessionState, caching application data, 285–286
WinMD components, creating and consuming, 38–51
native WinMD libraries, 40–46
understanding Windows Runtime, 38–40
WinMD libraries, 46–50
WinMD folder, default contents, 42
WinMD (Windows Metadata), 40
WinRT
media capture, 57–79
CameraCaptureUI, 58–68
MediaCapture class, 68–79
Windows Sensor and Location platform, 81
WinRT Camera APIs, 42
WinRT core engine, 40
WinRT PushNotificationType enum, 185
WinRT (Windows Runtime), app data storage, 276–286
WMA (Windows Media Audio) profile, 76
WMV (Windows Media Video) profile, 76
WNS (Windows Push Notification Service), 176–186
defined, 29
notification channels, 176–178
sending notifications to clients, 178–186
WPT (Windows Performance Toolkit), 390
WriteEvent method, 401
WriteTextAsync method, 279
writing methods using async techniques, 202–204
Wsdl.exe command-line utility, 195

X

XAML (Extensible Application Markup Language) page, 140
XLF files, 266
X-WNS-Type, 181

Y

yaw, 95

Z

zero-duration animations, 227
ZipArchive class, 304

About the authors

ROBERTO BRUNETTI is a consultant, trainer, and author with experience in enterprise applications since 1997. Together with Paolo Pialorsi, Marco Russo, and Luca Regnicoli, Roberto is a founder of DevLeap, a company focused on providing high-value content and consulting services to professional developers. He is the author of a few books about ASP.NET and Windows Azure, plus two books on Microsoft Windows 8, all for Microsoft Press. Since 1996, Roberto has been a regular speaker at major conferences.

VANNI BONCINELLI is a consultant and author on .NET technologies. Since 2010, he has been working with the DevLeap team, developing several enterprise applications based on Microsoft technologies. Vanni has authored many articles for Italian editors on XNA and game development, Windows Phone, and, since the first beta version in 2011, Windows 8. He also worked on *Build Windows 8 Apps with Microsoft Visual C# and Visual Basic Step by Step* (Microsoft Press, 2013).